THE WAR FOR
UKRAINE

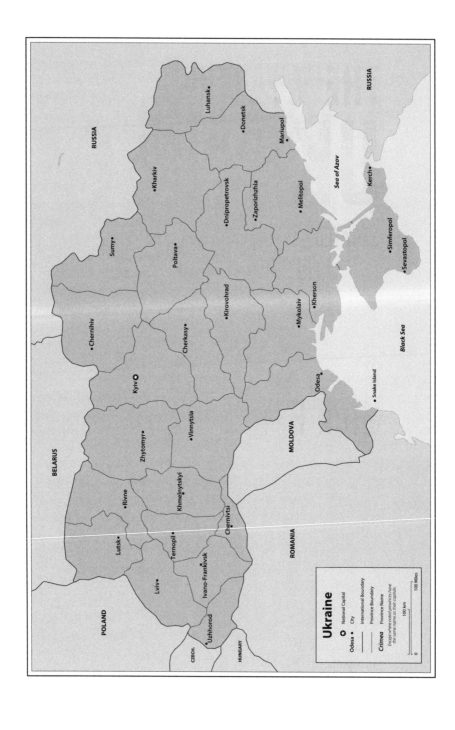

THE WAR FOR UKRAINE

STRATEGY and ADAPTATION
UNDER FIRE

Mick Ryan

Naval Institute Press
Annapolis, Maryland

Naval Institute Press
291 Wood Road
Annapolis, MD 21402

Library of Congress Cataloging-in-Publication Data

Names: Ryan, Mick, author.
Title: The war for Ukraine : strategy and adaptation under fire / Mick Ryan.
Description: Annapolis, Maryland : Naval Institute Press, [2024] | Includes bibliographical references and index.
Identifiers: LCCN 2024007848 (print) | LCCN 2024007849 (ebook) | ISBN 9781682479520 (hardcover) | ISBN 9781682479537 (ebook)
Subjects: LCSH: Russian Invasion of Ukraine, 2022. | Russo-Ukrainian War, 2014– | Strategy. | Ukraine—Strategic aspects. | Strategic culture—Russia (Federation) | Strategic culture—Ukraine. | Security, International—21st century.
Classification: LCC DK5467 .R93 2024 (print) | LCC DK5467 (ebook) | DDC 947.7086—dc23/eng/20230630
LC record available at https://lccn.loc.gov/2024007848
LC ebook record available at https://lccn.loc.gov/2024007849

♾ Print editions meet the requirements of ANSI/NISO z39.48-1992 (Permanence of Paper).
Printed in the United States of America.

32 31 30 29 28 27 26 25 24   9 8 7 6 5 4 3 2 1
First printing

За народ і воїнів України

(For the people and soldiers of Ukraine)

◼ CONTENTS

■ CHRONOLOGY
FEBRUARY 2022–JULY 2023

MAY 2022

13   Ukrainian forces push Russian forces attempting to encircle Kharkiv back to Russian border, ending the Battle of Kharkiv.

15   Sweden and Finland announce plans to join NATO.

20   Russian captures Mariupol, ending a three-month siege.

JUNE 2022

2   U.S. Cyber Command confirms it was conducting cyber operations on behalf of Ukraine.

10   Ukraine admits it has exhausted its artillery ammunition and is now reliant on the West for these supplies.

24   HIMARS first used in Ukraine.

30   Ukraine recaptures Snake Island.

JULY 2022

2   Fall of Severodonetsk and Lysychansk.

4–16   Russian "operational pause."

AUGUST 2022

1   Russian forces commence attacks on the eastern town of Bakhmut.

29   Ukraine launches counteroffensive on Kherson front.

SEPTEMBER 2022

6   Ukraine commences surprise offensive in Kharkiv, capturing large amounts of territory.

21   President Vladimir Putin of Russia announces partial mobilization.

23   Russian-occupied regions of Ukraine hold referendums to join Russia.

23   Recovery of mass grave of Ukrainians completed in Izium.

30   President Putin announces annexation of four Ukrainian regions.

OCTOBER 2022

1   Ukraine recaptures the city of Lyman in eastern Ukraine.

2–4   Ukrainian forces recapture multiple settlements in western Kherson.

8   Kerch bridge attacked for first time.

8   General Sergei Surovikin announced as overall commander of Russian forces in Ukraine. He immediately commences a concentrated series of missile and drone attacks on Ukrainian cities and infrastructure.

29 Russian base at Sevastopol attacked with Ukrainian uncrewed naval vessels and drones.

NOVEMBER 2022

1 Russia announces completion of partial mobilization.

9 Russia announces withdrawal of troops from Kherson.

11 Ukrainian forces liberate city of Kherson.

15 Large-scale Russian drone and missile attacks across Ukraine.

29 During speech in Bucharest, NATO secretary-general Jens Stoltenberg commits to alliance support to Ukraine for as long as required.

DECEMBER 2022

5 Explosions at two Russian airbases deep inside Russia as a result of Ukraine's use of converted Tu-141 drones.

7 President Putin acknowledges that his special military operation is taking longer than anticipated and refers to expansion of the Russian Empire.

21 President Zelenskyy visits the United States and addresses a joint session of Congress.

JANUARY 2023

11 Russian General Valery Gerasimov appointed as overall commander in Ukraine.

16 Russian forces capture Soledar.

17 Russia announces a reorganization and expansion of Russian military forces. Date unconfirmed. Russian 2023 offensive begins with attacks at multiple locations in eastern Ukraine.

24 Germany agrees to provide Leopard 2 tanks to Ukraine.

FEBRUARY 2023

8–23 Battle of Vuhledar sees two Russian brigades decimated by defending Ukrainians.

20 U.S. president Joe Biden visits Kyiv.

27 Russia announces creation of Bohdan Khmelnytsky Battalion, composed of Ukrainian prisoners of war.

MARCH 2023

7 President Zelenskyy announces that Bakhmut will continue to be defended.

9   Russian missile attack on multiple Ukrainian targets using hypersonic missiles.

16   Poland announced transfer of MiG-29 fighters to Ukraine. Slovakia announced transfer of thirteen MiG-29s the next day.

18–19   Putin visits Mariupol and Crimea, his first visit to occupied Ukraine in the war.

25   Putin announces deployment of nuclear weapons to Belarus.

APRIL 2023

6   Classified U.S. documents about the war leaked on social media sites.

9   Ukraine recommences energy exports for the first time since the war began.

12   Video released showing Russian soldiers beheading Ukrainian POWs.

19   Republic of Korea announces aid to Ukraine.

21   Jens Stoltenberg, secretary-general of NATO, states, "All NATO allies have agreed that Ukraine will become a member"—but only once the war with Russia is over.

MAY 2023

3   Drone attack on Kremlin.

19   President Biden announces at G7 that the United States will support transfer of F-16s to Ukraine.

10–11   Ukraine launches counterattacks on the northern and southern flanks of Bakhmut.

23   Russian forces (Wagner Group) secure the city of Bakhmut.

24–25   Raid into the Belgorod region of Russia by all-Russian pro-Ukrainian Russian Volunteer Corps (RDK) and the Freedom of Russia Legion (LSR).

JUNE 2023

4   Ukrainian 2023 offensive begins with attacks in eastern and southern Ukraine.

11   President Zelenskyy confirms that the 2023 Ukrainian offensive is under way.

23   Wagner head Yevgeny Prigozhin threatens armed rebellion to stop the Russian defense leadership's "evil."

24   Wagner march on Moscow. Prigozhin ends his mutiny late in the evening.

JULY 2023

11–12   NATO Summit in Vilnius.

INTRODUCTION

Unlike tsunamis, wars do not appear suddenly on calm waters.
Wars follow peace, but rarely are they preceded by peacefulness.
—James Sherr and Igor Gretskiy, *Why Russia Went to War*

THIS IS THE STORY of part of a war.

It is only part of a war because, at least when this manuscript was completed, the war in Ukraine that was the result of Russia's invasion of February 2022 remained an active conflict.

It is part of a war because, as with all wars, there are many things about it, even in this age of social media and greater battlefield transparency, that are yet to be revealed. Some of these unknown elements include secret intelligence activities and special operations missions undertaken by both sides, as well as the fears and motives of many key actors.

And it is a partial story of a war because it would be impossible to cover every aspect of this war in a single volume. The study of war is unbelievably vast. This is partly because of war's multiple levels, from tactical to political, but also because war involves many human, technological, conceptual, societal, and organizational aspects. A particular conflict might be studied from many angles, as evidenced by the tens of thousands of books on the U.S. Civil War alone, and similarly about World Wars I and II. This book, like any other to be written about the Russo-Ukraine War, can only ever tell part of its overall story.

But even at this point in history, there are sufficient stories to tell, and ample observations, that might inform other government and military institutions to evolve and improve their future effectiveness. As such, this book tells the story and makes observations about the period from the beginning of the Russian invasion in February 2022 through to 2023 NATO Summit in Vilnius, during which the initial phase of the Ukrainian 2023 counteroffensive was being executed.

On 11 June 2023, President Volodymyr Zelenskyy of Ukraine confirmed that a series of Ukrainian offensives were under way in the country's eastern and southern regions. While providing few details about progress or the forces involved, Zelenskyy noted, "Counteroffensive and defensive actions are taking place in Ukraine, but I will not say in detail what stage they are at. . . . They are all in a positive mood."[1]

This start of the ultimately unsuccessful 2023 campaign by the Ukrainian armed forces to recapture territory occupied by the Russians and liberate their citizens was the culmination of sixteen months of effort by the Ukrainians and their international supporters. Over that time, the Ukrainians lost tens of thousands of soldiers defending their nation and lost approximately 20 percent of their territory. Multiple cities and towns were destroyed, and Ukrainian citizens had been tortured, raped, killed, maimed, and terrorized by the invading Russian military forces.

Concurrently, Western nations—led by the United States of America—provided mountains of assistance to the government of Ukraine. Tens of billions of dollars in military equipment and munitions had been provided, as had training assistance by multiple nations. Economic assistance, humanitarian aid, and intelligence support rounded out the unique international coalition of nations that were helping Ukraine to defend itself and retain its sovereignty.

The antecedents of this war can be traced back months, years, decades, or even centuries. Eminent historian of Ukraine Serhii Plokhy has written, "Russia's aggression against Ukraine produced a nineteenth century war fought with twentieth-century tactics and twenty-first century weapons. Its ideological underpinnings come from visions of territorial expansion that characterized the Russian imperial era."[2] The immediate cause of the war, however, was Russia's invasion.

On the morning of 24 February 2022, a live video feed from the southern Ukrainian Kalanchack border outpost showed Ukrainian policemen chatting with border guards at this frontier crossing from Crimea into Ukraine. Shortly afterward, soldiers and civilians flee across the screen. Russian vehicles are then seen moving through the crossing, and not long afterward the video feed is severed.[3]

These images, which were shared on Twitter within minutes of the event, are the first known pictures of the Russian military invasion of Ukraine that commenced that day.[4] It is a very modern way for a war to announce itself in the consciousness of people in Ukraine and beyond. And while news of the beginning of the war may have been transmitted in a very twenty-first-century manner, much of the war that has followed has hewed more closely to twentieth- and even nineteenth-century ideas and tactics.

The war has featured large-scale battles with armored vehicles and human waves of infantry. Artillery, often described as the King of Battle, has reasserted its place in the contemporary battlefield as the most prolific killer of all weapons used. Industrial-scale warfare with massive use of autonomous systems and munitions has become the norm.

At the same time, old ideas of city destruction and the deliberate and systemic terrorizing of civilians have been widely practiced by the Russian military. Places such as Bucha, Irpin, and others have been seared into the psyche of Ukrainians and many around the world because of the brutal and systemic torture, rape, and murder that were inflicted on innocent Ukrainian civilians in those places. In every town and city occupied by the Russians, they have established facilities for the detention, processing, and interrogation of Ukrainian civilians. These facilities had layouts that were almost exactly the same across occupied Ukraine, including the similar electrocution machines and torture chambers.[5]

Beyond these tactics of systemic terrorism, the injection of new technologies has also played a role. Autonomous systems in the air, at sea, and on the ground have improved reconnaissance, lengthened the reach of military forces, and closed the time between the detection and destruction of military units, establishments, and individuals. Digitized battlefield command support networks have shared awareness and permitted improved command and control of troops on the ground as well as the enhanced integration of air and missile defense systems. Similar information technologies have also assisted the targeting of regional and global information operations to influence the perceptions of Ukraine's, and Russia's, allies and friends.

In *Conduct of War in the 21st Century*, Rob Johnson, Tim Sweijs, and Martijn Kitzen describe twenty-first-century warfare as kinetic, connected, and synthetic. Written and published a year before the Russian invasion of Ukraine, this is an apt description of the brutal war that has ravaged Ukraine. But the authors also propose one important further element of future war that has played out during operations in Ukraine: despite the many new technologies starting to have an impact on war, it "is the human dimension that will surely assert itself in war in the near future just as it does in the present."[6] The speeches and influence of President Zelenskyy, the organic Ukrainian resistance that has played a part throughout the war, and the many instances of poor Russian strategic and battlefield leadership are exemplars of this fact.

War in central Europe is not an unusual thing if we take a longer-term view. Humans have fought over land, titles, treasure, and ideas throughout the modern history of Europe. Most recently, in the 1990s, Europe was convulsed over the conflict in the former republic of Yugoslavia. The many different elements of this conflict reintroduced Europe to concepts such as ethnic cleansing, land warfare, and air campaigns, notions that been thought to have been now just a part of history, and not an element in Europe's future.

Since then, Europe has been largely peaceful (with the exception of Russia's invasions of Georgia and Ukraine in 2014). It dispatched troops to faraway lands such as Sudan, Iraq, and Afghanistan for stabilization, peacekeeping, and counterinsurgency missions. But until 2021, when Russia's President Putin began a military buildup on the borders of Ukraine, the prospect of war in Europe itself was a distant one. Even the buildup of Russian ground and air power, obvious through openly available satellite imagery, did not convince many people in Europe that a large-scale war might be a possibility in the near future. Almost up to the moment that Russian soldiers crossed the Ukrainian frontiers, there were hopes that war could be avoided.

It is natural that most people might think this way. As Victor Davis Hanson writes in *The Father of Us All*, "By ignoring military history, those today are naturally liable to interpret war because of the failure of communication, of diplomacy—as if aggressors do not know exactly what they are doing. Who, after all, would knowingly start a violent, unnecessary war?"[7] Unfortunately for Ukraine and Europe, Putin had long harbored resentments to those former members of the Soviet Union who had left during the dissolution of the Russian Empire after the Cold War. He had also been telegraphing his future intentions in speeches and other media.

In July 2021 Putin published an article titled "On the Historical Unity of Russians and Ukrainians."[8] In it he described Russians and Ukrainians as "one people—a single whole." Reaching back to the ancient state of Rus, Putin justified his position by describing Russians and Ukrainians as the descendants of this common ancestor. After a long description of his view of the history of Ukraine and Russia, Putin then described the situation in 2021 thus: "We are facing the creation of a climate of fear in Ukrainian society, aggressive rhetoric, indulging neo-Nazis and militarising the country. Along with that we are witnessing not just complete dependence but direct external control, including the supervision of the Ukrainian authorities, security services and armed forces by foreign advisers, military 'development' of the territory of Ukraine and deployment of NATO infrastructure."[9] Here Putin lays the groundwork of his strategic narrative to justify his invasion of Ukraine just seven months later. NATO expansion, neo-Nazis, and anti-Russia hatreds all feature in Putin's publicly expressed rationale for invading Ukraine in his speech to the Russian people on the eve of the 24 February 2022 invasion. In this discourse, he describes how "the leading NATO countries are supporting the far-right nationalists and neo-Nazis in Ukraine" and declares that Russian forces will "demilitarise and denazify Ukraine."[10]

Russian forces crossed the Ukrainian border at multiple locations on 24 February 2022. While large ground formations made their way toward Kyiv, Kharkiv, Kherson, and other strategic objectives, Russian air force aircraft and missiles conducted a series of strikes against Ukrainian air defense radars, airfields, headquarters, and other critical military and government targets.

Envisioned as a ten-day campaign in which Russian soldiers rapidly advanced on the Ukrainian capital of Kyiv and were welcomed as liberators, the Ukrainian government fled, and the West did not assist Ukraine, the invasion went wrong almost from the very beginning.[11]

The strategic planning for their invasion was undertaken by a very small number of personnel, and operational security was very tight. This operational security, and the resulting deception, did allow the Russians to achieve some measure of tactical surprise in the early hours of the invasion. But it also meant that most commanders, until just hours before D-Day, remained under the impression that their presence along Ukraine's borders was an exercise. Units therefore were neither logistically prepared nor morally resilient enough for Ukrainian resistance or for the hard combat that would take place north of Kyiv.

The Russians had a laundry list of strategic objectives for their invasion. As one report on the invasion from Britain's Royal United Services Institute notes, "The goals of the Russian invasion were not only 'denazification,' the destruction of national sovereignty and the banning of Ukrainian identity and 'demilitarization,' the destruction and banning of the UAF and the export to Russia of enterprises of the defense industrial complex of Ukraine, but also 'denuclearization,' the capture of nuclear power plants and their transfer to the direct management of Rosatom."[12] To achieve these objectives, the Russians assembled a large invasion force, around 180,000–190,000 troops, which comprised approximately two-thirds of its existing strength of its ground forces. This figure does not include the many thousands of air force and other military personnel who played a supporting role away from the front lines. Unfortunately, this was not a big enough force if the Ukrainian military, numbering around 200,000 troops, put up any form of resistance.

This is where the Russian strategy began to break down. Their invasion force was too small for the tasks assigned to it in the seizure of a nation the size of Ukraine. The Ukrainians further confounded Russian planning by not conforming to any of the Russian leadership's assumptions about the conduct of the war. The Russian invasion, while taking nearly 22 percent of Ukrainian territory in the coming weeks, foundered on poor strategic assumptions, good Ukrainian leadership (particularly the inspiration of President Zelenskyy but also effective battlefield leaders), a lack of unity of command between different Russian commands, and bad Russian tactical leadership.

▬

While this book covers many aspects of the war, its focus is on observations about what can be learned by government and military institutions in Ukraine, Europe, and beyond.

An important function of senior leaders in the military and other national security institutions is providing incentives for learning and innovation during peacetime, so that the good ideas, the right organizational constructs, and cutting-edge technology can be combined to provide an advantage in conflicts. This, in turn, requires a cultural predisposition to learning and sharing lessons widely, the acceptance of failure as an opportunity to learn, and a well-honed understanding of risk.

War, the most destructive human endeavor yet devised, is also a learning opportunity for military institutions. But the study of learning in war is not as simple as drawing a direct line from learning to battlefield prowess. The large-scale collection, assessment, sharing, and absorption of lessons is complex, especially when considering all the other challenges and demands placed on military institutions that are concurrently amid fighting, planning for the next fight, and bringing in new members while steadily losing others to death, wounds, and sickness. But as hard as it is, it is harder to win if an institution has a suboptimal learning culture or lacks one altogether.

The process of how each side has learned during this war will absorb academics and military institutions for some time into the future. However, in this book, I propose that there are six guidelines that might be useful in a professional, strategic approach to learning and adaptation.

A foundational issue is that of purpose. Why should military organizations look at lessons from war in general, and this one in particular? The answer is that the world is constantly changing, and a clever institution will learn from the mistakes of others rather than constantly making its own mistakes in adapting to change. As David Barno and Nora Bensahel argue in *Adaptation under Fire*, this process of learning is easier to talk about in principle than to achieve in practice. Bureaucratic resistance, battlefield friction, and the enemy's adaptations all make it harder. But it is possible to learn and change, as historically successful military forces show.[13]

A second consideration in learning is to distinguish between lessons that are specific to this war and those that are broader and more widely applicable. This is hard because only in retrospect can such a judgment generally be made. Consequently, at this point in the war (and given our limited insights into Ukrainian military strategy and force generation), almost all our observations appear to have wider—or general—utility. These include leadership, combined arms, air-land integration, information warfare, air defense, alliances, and logistics.

A third consideration for exploring military learning from the war in Ukraine is the level at which this occurs. In their 1988 exploration of learning, innovation, and military effectiveness, Williamson Murray and Alan Millett propose a four-layered approach—political, strategic, operational, and tactical. In making the most of the opportunity to learn from the Russo-Ukrainian War, military institutions, operational analysts, and academics must invest in each of these four levels to gain a full view of the war and understand how each level interacts with (and changed) activities in the other layers.

A fourth issue in learning from Ukraine is that it provides the opportunity to identify both solutions (from either side) as well as future challenges for which there no current solutions. A strategic learning and lessons process that examines the Russian invasion and subsequent war must not only be about copying what the eventual victor did. Military institutions and strategists must dig deeper for other challenges that are not obvious or that neither side may have produced a robust solution for.

A fifth consideration in collecting, analyzing, disseminating, and absorbing the lessons from this war is understanding the difference between "lessons" and "lessons learned." It is one matter to make observations. It is quite another to effect change in a military (or other government) institution based on those lessons. The U.S. Army has useful definitions for both. A lesson is "knowledge or understanding gained by experience. Successes and failures are both considered sources of lessons." A lesson learned is "when you can measure a change in behavior." This is a useful distinction. For the purposes of this book, I would describe my observations and analysis as *lessons* rather than *lessons learned*.[14]

Finally, in observing the war and analyzing its many lessons, Western military institutions will also have to assess what other potential adversaries might learn from it. China has previously demonstrated a deep capacity for learning and change, given the right political and strategic impetus. The 1991 Gulf War shocked the Chinese military into a decade's long recapitalization of its military, which has included advanced ships, aircraft, ground combat vehicles, and satellites. It has also resulted in reforms to strategic and operational command and control, including better joint integration. Chinese lessons from the 1991 Gulf War—as well as the wars spawned by 9/11—have included a reformation in their operational doctrine and has resulted in concepts such as "intelligentization" and "systems destruction warfare." As with previous Western conflicts, it is highly likely that Chinese analysts will explore the war in Ukraine for its many relevant lessons.[15]

The Ukrainians, throughout this war, have arguably displayed a superior learning culture compared to the Russians. Margarita Konaev and Owen Daniels have written that "over and over, Ukraine has nimbly responded to changing battle. . . . By contrast, Russian forces have shown limited openness to new tactics or new technologies."[16] This learning culture, willingness to take risk and innovate, and capacity to rapidly absorb new technologies (such as HIMARS, Western main battle tanks, or HARM missiles) and integrate them into their operations clearly did not emerge on 24 February 2022. The Ukrainians learned from Russian operations in 2014, and their military operations in eastern Ukraine since. They have also benefited from their training and education interventions provided at NATO schools in Europe and their interaction with U.S. and European military forces. This provided a foundational capacity for learning and adaptation on which Ukrainian armed forces innovation and improvements in military effectiveness have been based since February 2022.

But as the early stages of the 2023 Ukrainian counteroffensive also demonstrated, there are limits to how much and how fast any institution can change. These "adaptation pains" show that while Ukraine has adapted at the tactical, operational, and strategic levels since February 2022, these have not driven major improvements in their ability to expand the level at which they can conduct effective combined-arms maneuver. The initial problems with Ukrainian attacks in southern Ukraine demonstrate that even good learning cultures can and do experience shortfalls in performance on the battlefield.[17]

When the Russians invaded Ukraine again in 2022, they brought with them a legacy learning culture, but it appears to often (though not always) be inferior to the Ukrainian model. This issue was covered in the recent report from the Royal United Services Institute, which notes that "those who fail are usually replaced or threatened with punishment. Far from incentivizing success, this often leads to dishonest reporting in which the blame for failure is transferred onto others. This . . . obscures the actual operational problems that must be solved. These only become apparent when they can no longer be concealed, slowing the learning of lessons."[18]

The Russians, however, clearly did learn from their operations in places such as Chechnya and Syria. Journal articles and speeches from senior Russian military officers frequently referred to these conflicts. Whether these were the right lessons, however, might be questioned.

The Russians also appear to have assumed they would be fighting the same Ukrainian army that existed in 2014. Multiple reports from human intelligence sources before the war led the Russians to believe that the Ukrainians—much like in Crimea in 2014—were unlikely to put up a sustained fight in resistance to the Russian forces entering the country from the north, east, and south. A 2017 RAND report on the 2014 Crimean annexation notes that "Ukraine's overall superior forces on the peninsula offered no resistance."[19] The Russian army and the Russian leadership assumed something similar would occur in February 2022. The Russian army's learning culture therefore entered the war with flaws. As a result, they possessed a suboptimal foundation for learning and adapting once fighting began.

With the war in its second year, there is a competitive learning environment in the Ukraine war. Both sides, in different ways, are continually reaching for tactical, operational, and strategic advantages. It is an ongoing adaptation battle and is likely to be one of the key factors in which side eventually wins this war. Many nations are watching this war closely with an eye to their own success in future warfare. In learning from this war, Western military institutions will need to invest in—and apply—collection, analysis, dissemination, and adaptation processes. Importantly, as Don Starry described in "To Change an Army," this will require leadership from the top.[20]

But it is a systemic undertaking, and must have leadership, incentives, and the rapid collection and processing of observations into lessons and then lessons learned. It must be deeply embedded in the culture of an organization. As Aimée Fox-Godden writes in *Learning to Fight*, "Culture determines how an organization responds to change. For the Army of the First World War, it determined how it identified lessons, how it innovated, and ultimately, how it learned to fight."[21]

The central hypothesis of this book is that while many factors have had an impact on the course of this war, there are two that have been of overriding importance. These two factors, around which the contents of this book are framed, are strategy and adaptation. It is these two areas where the differences between the approach of the Ukrainians and Russians in this war have been most stark. And arguably, it is these two areas where Ukraine has developed an asymmetric advantage over Russia.

The word "strategy" entered the modern European lexicon in 1771. The source was the publication of a translation of the Byzantine emperor Leo VI's *Taktiká*, by French officer Paul Gédéon Joly de Maizeroy. The translated work included descriptions of *strategía*. This word was translated as *stratégie*, and by the early 1800s, European military theorists were using the word "strategy."[22] Used to describe the higher arts of military planning in early nineteenth-century Europe, strategy has since then transformed in both theory and practice.

Over the last century, the application and meaning of strategy has evolved. Originally applied to the preparation of military organizations for war, it is a term that has come to be associated with larger national pursuits, particularly in the wake of the total wars of the twentieth century. And it used across other endeavors not related to national security. Most businesses now have corporate strategies, and it is a word that is used very widely across many human endeavors.

Sir Lawrence Freedman is an eminent scholar who literally wrote the book on strategy. In *Strategy: A History* (2013) he observes that "it only really comes into play when elements of conflict are present."[23] Conflict was present in the lead-up to the war and in the latest Russian invasion of Ukraine in February 2022. And it has existed throughout the conduct of the war thus far.

There is an important reason that the first part of this book is about strategy. The war in Ukraine offers academics, politicians, military leaders, and civil servants an abundance of observations on the development and execution of strategy from the perspectives of the Ukrainians, Russians, Americans, and others. There are many examples of effective strategy development and its implementation from the war. There are also examples of poor strategy, and even worse execution of it.

Russian strategy has been explored by a multitude of government analysts as well as experts in academia and think tanks throughout the Cold War, into the post–Cold War era, and now in what some have described as the post-post–Cold War era.[24] There is a significant body of literature that explores Soviet and Russian strategy over the past seven decades, including nuclear strategy, conventional warfare, and its strategy for confrontation with the West.

Ukrainian strategy in this war has much shallower roots. While it possesses a culture and history that extends back centuries, it has been a sovereign nation only since 1991. It has only had three decades to develop its contemporary strategy culture and approach to strategy. Despite this, Ukraine has demonstrated an adroit capacity for strategic thinking and action since the Russian 2022 invasion.

The aim of part I of the book is to explore the Russian and Ukrainian strategy as it has been used since February 2022. Across seven chapters, the Ukrainian and Russian development of strategy, and how their strategies have evolved, will be explored.

Part of this exploration of strategy is the role of leadership. Strategy and leadership are closely connected. Indeed, it is difficult to conceive of one without the other in modern war. Therefore, a chapter in part I is dedicated to the examination of strategic leadership in the war so far.

The final chapter in part I provides observations for contemporary strategists. While not a checklist in the strictest sense, it provides a list of issues that will be of import to current and future strategists. The issues raised in this chapter also provide the starting point for further examination of the strategic elements of this war, and how they might apply to future warfare.

Part II of the book examines the concept and practice of adaptation as it has occurred throughout the war since February 2022.

No government, military organization, or business institution is able to predict the future with any certainty. While trends can be utilized to prepare for "most likely" and "most dangerous" future scenarios, every human organization is surprised to some degree about how future events play out. This has unquestionably been the case for this war as well. Indeed, surprise is an important continuity in all wars, and this war has been no different. The Russians were surprised by the level of Ukrainian resistance and Western support for Ukraine. This necessitated Russian adaptation to their military campaign, where and how their forces fought, and their global narratives about the war.

Many have been surprised by the viciousness of the Russian onslaught—its destructiveness as well as the more recent Russian human wave tactics and the wide-scale use of Iranian drones against critical infrastructure. But the Ukrainians, facing an existential threat, have demonstrated a learning culture at different levels that not only blunted the Russian invasion in the early days of the war but has also seen them constantly adapt at the tactical, operational, and strategic levels over the course of the war.

This second part of the book is an exploration of how Ukrainian and Russian military reforms before the war provided a foundation for their respective adaptive stances during the war. Both nations had undertaken institutional-level reforms of their military and national security enterprises in the decade leading up to this war. But because the emergent behavior of military forces after fighting begins cannot be fully predicted, these prewar reforms only form a start point for adaptation during the war. Therefore, most of the chapters in this part of the book are dedicated to exploring tactical, operational, and strategic Ukrainian and Russian adaptation.

All wars are ultimately human endeavors. While machines and information are vital elements in human competition and war, it is humans who decide how these are used, where, when, and in what organizational constructs that ultimately decide victory and defeat. And even if humans now might have their decisions informed and improved by big data and artificial intelligence, humans remain the heart and soul of every government and military system. They drive how institutions learn and adapt.

As with part I, the final chapter in part II will provide insights and lessons for military and other organizations on institutional learning and adaptation. Importantly, these are linked to how they inform future war, and how military institutions might prepare for such conflicts.

Rarely do military personnel get to practice their profession at the scale being witnessed in Ukraine. For the vast majority of military personnel, their careers are spent in training, exchanges between nations, unit exercises, and staff appointments. As Sir Michael Howard has noted, the military profession is one where its practitioners may "have to exercise it only once in a lifetime, if indeed that often."[25] While this is a justification for studying military history, it is also a compelling argument for studying wars of the present.

The war in Ukraine, which began in 2014 and was massively escalated by Russia in February 2022, provides military personnel, strategists, and government leaders with a variety of observations on contemporary strategy, leadership, and the imperative to constantly evolve and improve. I hope this book provides a useful foundation to prepare our military and national security leaders for the inevitable crises and security challenges to come.

Part I
STRATEGY

I

A NEW STATE NATIONAL SECURITY POLICY

Russia's Strategic Foundations for Ukraine

RUSSIAN STRATEGY for overpowering Ukraine rests within a larger context of Russian grand strategy. For some, the notion of grand strategy is difficult to grasp because of the enormous number of permutations and interactions that are part of strategy making and execution. But it can be a useful tool for states that wish to improve their relations with a particular state or group of states, or occasionally attempt to change aspects of the entire international system.[1] And while the definitions of "grand strategy" can vary as much as those of "strategy" do, it does provide what Hal Brands describes as "a purposeful and coherent set of ideas about what a nation seeks to accomplish in the world, and how it should go about doing so."[2] Or, as a RAND report notes, "a grand strategy describes a state's most important and enduring interests and a theory for how the state will use its resources to defend or advance those interests given domestic and international constraints."[3]

Books such as Edward Luttwak's *The Grand Strategy of the Soviet Union* and John Gaddis' *The Cold War* provide a good foundation for the study of modern Russian strategy. Luttwak explains, "We must recognise in today's Soviet Union the old empire of the Russians."[4] In the same vein, modern Russian strategy is built on the remains of Soviet strategy. Since the downfall of the Soviet Union, Russian strategy has been studied for insights into how Russian governments are responding to their changed status and resources. The stature of Russia as a nuclear armed state, with large conventional forces, also means that there is great interest in the study of Russian grand strategy, and its subordinate plans including military strategy.

A variety of books provide some understanding into the thinking and strategic culture of contemporary Russian government leaders and strategists. These include Glenn Diesen's *Russia's Geoeconomic Strategy for a Greater Eurasia*, Ofer Fridman's *Strategiya: The Foundations of the Russian Art of Strategy*, Oscar Jonsson's *The Russian Understanding of War: Blurring the Lines between War and Peace*, Glen Howard's *Russia's Military Strategy and Doctrine*, Andrew Monaghan's *Russian Grand Strategy in the Era of Global Power Competition*, the Routledge *Handbook of Russian Security*, and Lawrence Freedman's *Ukraine and the Art of Strategy*.[5]

Reports and publications from Western think tanks and journals also permit an improved comprehension of Russian strategy. Among the better reports are a 2021 RAND Corporation report, *Russian Grand Strategy: Rhetoric and Reality*; the 2021 report from the Center for Naval Analyses' *Russian Military Strategy: Core Tenets and Operational Concepts*; Michael Kofman's *Drivers of Russian Grand Strategy*; and Ian Morris' *The Russian Grand Strategy Guiding the Invasion of Ukraine*.[6]

A central theme in this Western literature, which admittedly includes research from many Russian sources, is the role of the concept of vulnerability in Russian strategy. As Michael Kofman wrote in a report for Sweden's Frivarld Institute, "Moscow's strategic outlook has always been shaped as much by perceptions of vulnerability, threats foreign and domestic, as much as ambition and a drive for recognition."[7] Or, as Robert Pearson has described it, "the foundations of Russia's grand strategy can be found in the more universal, if mundane, condition of geo-political insecurity that informs the realist school of thought. Russia's worldview and grand strategic objectives are the product of a deep and enduring sense of geopolitical insecurity that has conditioned its relationship to the outside world for centuries."[8]

In a 2013 article, Andrew Monaghan sketched out four key themes in the exploration of Russian grand strategy. The first theme centers on Moscow's geostrategic interests and views Russia as "a 'heartland' state, a bridge between emerging markets; and that its specific conditions determine a specific kind of politics, its vast, underpopulated territory and permanent threat of invasion generating the need for a strong central authority." The second theme, employing strategic culture as a framework, emphasizes that "historical experiences shape a political culture that in turn determines strategic choices, and ties national decision-making to a state's traditions and perceptions of itself in history."[9]

A third theme identified by Monaghan involves the development of plans and their execution. This theme, however, is bounded more by a limited focus, something

Monaghan describes as "a Clausewitzian understanding of strategy: the military art that determines the principles of and preparation for war and its conduct." A final theme in Russian grand strategy has been the expansion of Russian strategic thinking to embrace many issues beyond military affairs. Not only is this evident in the more recent national security strategies issued by the Russian Federation; it is also closer in conception to what is understood in Western nations as grand strategy.[10]

In 2021, a team of researchers from RAND Corporation undertook a detailed exploration of Russian grand strategy. To do this, they employed an analytical method that complied open-source data into four strands: "a set of beliefs about how the international system works, a prioritized set of interests, an assessment of the threats and opportunities the country faces in the international system, and a logical approach for how to use all tools of national power to achieve its goals."[11]

In a report released less than a year before Russians crossed the border into Ukraine, the RAND Corporation released a detailed expose of Russian strategy titled *Russian Grand Strategy: Rhetoric and Reality*. This report, and the many studies of Russian strategy before the 2022 invasion, provide a useful baseline for exploring Russian strategy since February 2022. The RAND team identified six core elements of contemporary Russian grand strategy:

1. Internal and external threats are increasingly integrated.
2. Russia will pursue a benign leadership approach in its neighborhood.
3. Russia should prepare for noncontact warfare and small conflicts along its border.
4. Regional power projection is a greater priority than global expeditionary military capability.
5. The objective is to cooperate selectively while limiting Western ambitions, not to weaken the West.
6. Russia will pivot away from the West to "new centers of power."[12]

There is one final component of Russian strategy that could be included. In her chapter about Soviet strategy in the 1986 edition of *Makers of Modern Strategy*, Condoleezza Rice describes another strand of strategic thought that is a legacy of the Soviet system: "The greatest legacy bequeathed to modern Soviet strategists, though, is the concept of the preparation of the whole society for continuous struggle."[13] This idea, which may have lain dormant in recent official Russian documents on strategy, has reemerged in the speeches of Vladimir Putin since 2022.

There are also many documents from the government of the Russian Federation that can inform outsiders about Russian grand strategy. Their regularly updated national security strategy, Foreign Policy Concept, Military Doctrine, and presidential decrees all provide good insights into the framework and execution for modern

Russian grand strategy. Added to this mix are speeches and statements from senior Russian ministers and military personnel, as well as a myriad of policies and laws that are linked to, or guide, grand strategy.

One way Russia communicates its strategy has been regular development and issuing of national security strategies. The 2016 Russian national security strategy featured significant continuity from its 2009 predecessor, although it did take a more aggressive approach to the West. Like its predecessor, the 2016 Russian national security strategy featured a broad definition of security that incorporated health, social issues, and economic stability. As Mark Galeotti has written, "This is because the Kremlin understands full well that these issues have security dimensions: Bad health undermines the conscript pool, cultural security means keeping out challenges to state propaganda, economic instability drains defense budgets and generates public unrest, and so on."[14]

In July 2021, a new Russian national security strategy was released. Prepared by the Security Council of the Russian Federation, the 2021 iteration of the strategy, nine national security priority areas were described: (1) preservation of the Russian people and development of human capital; (2) national defense; (3) state and public security; (4) information security; (5) economic security; (6) scientific and technological development; (7) environmental security; (8) protection of traditional values, culture, and historical memory; and (9) strategic stability and mutually beneficial cooperation.[15]

One of the key distinctions of the 2021 strategy, as compared to its predecessors, is the larger place of "traditional Russian spiritual-moral values as the foundation of Russian society." The 2021 document discusses this subject over the course of four pages. The narrative of this aspect of the strategy aligns with the many speeches by President Putin before the war, and since its commencement, about protection of Russian values and heritage.

The 2021 Russian national security strategy also provides one of the intellectual foundations for the 2022 invasion. It outlines a series of grievances against the West and its neighbors. As Julian Cooper has written, "It reads like a defiant manifesto from the occupants of a besieged fortress. The publication of the NSS with its horizon of five years suggests that this defiance looks set to remain for the rest of Putin's presidential term."[16] Not only has it shaped or informed broader Russian security issues since 2021; it has also provided insights into the Russian politics and policy that govern its approach to the invasion of Ukraine and many tactical and strategic activities it has conducted as part of this military operation.

Political considerations have a significant impact on the planning and conduct of military operations. So too it was with Russian policy exerting itself on Russian military planning before the war. Because Putin and his small circle of advisers assumed that the Ukrainians would be unlikely to fight for a long period and that the key political leaders would flee, they developed a military concept of operations that focused on speed (hard fighting for advancing troops was assumed away in planning) and a rapid takeover of Ukraine. The Russians had little confidence that Ukraine would resist for more than several days. CIA director William Burns recalled a discussion with Putin in the lead-up to the invasion thus: "Putin 'was very matter of fact,' Burns said. He didn't deny the intelligence that pointed toward a Russian invasion of Ukraine. He was very dismissive of President Zelensky as a political leader."[17]

In reconciling these elements of modern Russian grand strategy, key aspects such as perceived and real threats, historical narratives, and securing its near region (against NATO threats) stand out. These themes have also influenced Russian thinking about the planning and execution of the special military operation in Ukraine, as well as the conduct of Russia's information, economic, and diplomatic activities that support its invasion of Ukraine.

▓ FOUNDATIONS OF RUSSIA'S UKRAINE STRATEGY

Russian strategy has been intensively studied and critiqued in the wake of the 24 February 2022 invasion of Ukraine. One of the key objectives of strategy is that military actions should align with desired political or national outcomes. This shapes how military strategies are developed, executed, and adapted. It is a very important concept for the development, testing, and execution of strategy. In this environment, the development of strategy is interactive; military and political leaders must frequently discuss desired outcomes, and how they might be achieved, in building national strategy.

On 21 and 24 February 2022, Russian president Vladmir Putin gave two important speeches that focused on the situation in Ukraine. In these speeches, Putin developed his "theory of the case" for Russian intervention. He provided a strategic narrative of the threat to Russia posed by the breakdown of the Soviet Union and, thereafter, the independent status of Ukraine. It was a narrative of historic grievance and designed to build a sense of outrage in the Russian domestic audience.

Putin then constructed a story that Ukraine was not a real state and did not deserve its status as a sovereign nation. Putin stated, "Ukraine actually never had stable traditions of real statehood. And, therefore, in 1991 it opted for mindlessly emulating foreign models, which have no relation to history or Ukrainian realities." He outlined "evidence" for corruption in Ukraine and the disastrous economic circumstances faced by the Ukrainian people because of poor government management, noting, "Their country has turned not even into a political or economic protectorate but has been reduced to a colony with a puppet regime."[18]

This description of Ukraine as "not a real state" has remained a central pillar in Putin's narrative to justify Russia's aggression. But it is part of a broader story that Putin was telling his own people, related to his aspirations for an imperial Russia.

It was not the first time that Putin had used this particular construct for the relationship between Russia and Ukraine. In a 2008 discussion with then-president George W. Bush, Putin allegedly told the American president, "You have to understand, George. Ukraine is not even a country."[19] And it was a theme in Putin's 2021 essay "On the Historical Unity of Russians and Ukrainians," published seven months before the 2022 invasion of Ukraine. It is an article that reaches back into history (or at least Putin's version), including Ancient Rus, the throne of Kiev, and Batu Khan's invasion as well as historical events in the seventeenth, eighteenth, and nineteenth centuries. In this essay Putin also writes, "The incorporation of the western Russian lands into the single state was not merely the result of political and diplomatic decisions. It was underlain by the common faith, shared cultural traditions, and—I would like to emphasize it once again—language similarity. . . . Ukraine and Russia have developed as a single economic system over decades and centuries."[20]

Putin's speeches often refer to Russia and Ukraine as a single entity. James Sherr and Igor Gretzkiy have described this as the "civilizational factor." For Putin, Russian civilization transcends the modern borders of Russia. As they describe in a January 2023 report for the International Centre for Defence and Security in Estonia, "The determination to write history and rewrite it, to reshape and deny memories, therefore plays a central role in policy. The struggle to control history is a struggle to control others. There is nothing new in this. The Soviet Union was described as the only country in the world whose past was unpredictable."[21]

Another pillar of Putin's narrative has been the threat from NATO. In his February 2022 and later speeches, Putin has consistently portrayed NATO and the West as aggressors toward Russia. He argues that "military contingents of NATO countries have been almost constantly present on Ukrainian territory under the pretext of exercises. The Ukrainian troop control system has already been integrated into NATO."[22] This strand of Putin's narrative about the war in Ukraine is foundational.

Putin has also used this narrative beyond Russia's shores to seek foreign support, or at least prevent nations joining the international sanctions regime established by the United States and the European Union. It has been successful to a degree. Nations such as China have continued buying Russian energy throughout the war, sustaining Putin's treasury and allowing him to continue fighting.[23] President Xi Jinping has refused to criticize Russia's actions. Other nations, such as India, have maintained largely neutral stances.[24] They may not be assisting Russia, but they are not helping the Ukrainian war effort either.

Another strand in Putin's strategic narrative has been the notion that Ukraine is run by Nazis and that it is conducting genocide against Russian citizens, Russian speakers, and others loyal to Russia within Ukraine's borders. He said on 24 February, "We will seek to demilitarise and denazify Ukraine, as well as bring to trial those who perpetrated numerous bloody crimes against civilians, including against citizens of the Russian Federation."[25] The use of the term "Nazis" evokes powerful images in the Russian domestic audience but also in many citizens in Ukraine and Europe. Like the theme that focuses on the threat from NATO, it has remained a central part of Putin's messaging and his justification for the actions of the Russian military in Ukraine.

Russia's desired political outcomes, based on Putin's narratives and poor assumptions, have had a catastrophic impact on their military strategy and its implementation of its invasion of Ukraine. The "delusional strategy" of Putin, described eloquently by Sir Lawrence Freedman in a 2022 article, has proved an abysmal guide for military and information operations in Ukraine. The Russian strategic assumptions—that Ukraine was a nonstate, that Ukraine would rapidly surrender, and that the West would not intervene—were all proven wrong in first month of the war.

▓ PUTIN'S STRATEGIC ASSUMPTIONS

Assumptions matter in strategy, and the Russians—most of all Vladmir Putin—failed in their assumptions that led to the 2022 invasion. These failures in strategy and the assumptions that underpinned them have had catastrophic consequences for both Russians and Ukrainians. This has led to a long and brutal conflict that has continued well beyond the two-week conflict envisioned by Russian strategic planners.

Putin, based on the advice of his most senior military commander, General Gerasimov, assumed his ground forces were more than capable of this task.[26] As Gerasimov allegedly informed some foreign interlocutors as the invasion commenced, "I command the second most powerful Army in the world." The shared assumption in Putin's small circle of advisers was that the Russian army, if it had to fight, would quickly defeat the Ukrainian military on the battlefield.[27]

With the forward-deployed Russian forces visible to ground, aerial, and space-based sensors, Putin hoped that there could be no mistake about Russian will to invade Ukraine if his political demands were not met. Russian combat units were arrayed in such a way as to allow them to rapidly cross the international frontier and drive on formed roads directly to key strategic objectives such as Kyiv and Kharkiv.[28]

However, because of the Russian emphasis on deploying combat units during the buildup phase before the February 2022 invasion, tactical and operational logistic systems were not deployed in sufficient quantities to provide anything other than the most basic life support for units in temporary field garrisons.

Complicating matters further, war plans were not being widely disseminated to battlefield commanders.[29] This was one reason that many in the Ukrainian government and military initially believed that a Russian invasion was unlikely: key indicators such as logistic units were not present. Given the old Soviet doctrinal templates for what an invasion force should look like, many in Ukraine were convinced that the lack of support forces meant that a Russian invasion was less likely.[30]

But Russia's own military doctrine also played a role in its logistics shortfalls. The Russian armed forces' operational concept was updated during transformation activities in 2009. Concurrently, the Russians had replaced the obsolete Soviet logistics system with a much leaner approach. This involved downsizing logistics support organizations as well as the outsourcing of some elements of logistics and sustainment. These successor systems to the Soviet approach, on 24 February 2022, remained largely untested in large-scale combat operations.[31]

Once offensive operations began, consumption of fuel, ammunition, precision munitions, food, cold weather equipment, and other resources accelerated rapidly. The Russian military logistic system was placed under significant strain because its initial plan, to seize the Hostomel airfield and conduct a coup de main, failed. At the same time, the Ukrainians had identified this as a targetable, critical vulnerability of the Russian invading force, so they attacked it mercilessly. This also had an impact on the eventual outcome of the Russian northern campaign in the early weeks of their invasion. The initial Russian plan would not have required a massive logistics footprint because the operation was supposed to be of a short duration. One report from the Royal United Services Institute notes that the entire Ukraine operation was to be completed in three to ten days: "After D+10, the role of Russia's conventional forces was to transition to a supporting function to Russia's special services, responsible for establishing occupation administrations on the territories."[32] The Russian logistics system failed because it was not supposed to be used for anything other than a very short period.

Because its strategy relied on quick Ukrainian capitulation, Russia also committed too small a force if it had to fight. This, as it turned out, was a massive tactical as well as strategic risk. While the invasion force of approximately 190,000 troops was a large proportion of the Russian army (which had a strength of around 350,000 at the start of the war), it was large enough only if the Ukrainians either did not fight or only offered desultory resistance. The Ukrainians, with a standing army of over 200,000 soldiers, outnumbered their attackers. This was a critical shortfall in Russian planning.

Attacks on the ground, over the past several centuries, have relied on a ratio of 3:1 in favor of the attacker to give the best chances of success. In his classic book *Understanding War*, American soldier and military theorist Trevor Dupuy described this as the "Three to One Theory of Combat": "As a gross measure for campaign planning the three-to-one rule is undoubtedly useful and stands up fairly well under historical scrutiny."[33] The Russian army entirely ignored this "rule" for their planning. Ukrainian resistance in the East and North, which resulted in large Russian losses, slowed down the Russian advance and slowly reduced the overall strength of the Russian invasion force.

The assumption of a quick capitulation by the Russians also meant that they did not put in place an operational mechanism to coordinate the forces that had deployed to Ukraine's northern, eastern, and southern borders during the buildup. Separate invasion axes of advance were controlled by different military regions in Russia, with minimal apparent coordination between them.

The consequence of these military planning mistakes, founded on poor strategic assumptions, was the defeat and withdrawal of Russian forces around Kyiv and Kharkiv. It also ensured that large proportions of Russian combat and logistic units were attrited and exhausted in the lead-up to subsequent phases of the war. It is highly likely that the initial strategic decisions in Moscow, and the battlefield performance of the Russians and their significant losses of infantry and equipment, compromised any hope of them being successful in their invasion of Ukraine—at least in the short term.

Even good wartime strategy is unlikely to be successful if military forces cannot win key battles. As the Russians have rediscovered in Ukraine, getting strategy (and its underpinning assumptions) right is critical to effective military operations. Effective strategic thinking is more important than tactical excellence. Alan Millett and Williamson Murray have noted, "It is more important to make correct decisions at the political and strategic level than it is at the operational or tactical level. Mistakes in operations and tactics can be corrected, but strategic mistakes live forever."[34]

As the war has progressed, Putin has shown no willingness to adapt his political objectives. From the beginning of the war in Ukraine in 2022, Russia has largely maintained dual-track aims. The first objective sought by Russian president Putin has been the subjugation of the Ukrainian people and the extinguishing of their sovereignty. This objective was described in Putin's speech on the eve of the invasion and has also appeared in his 9 May Victory Day speech and others, including the September mobilization and annexation declarations.

His second objective remains a unification of his domestic audience through the projection of the war as a defense of Russia against NATO, and the rebuilding of the greater Russian Federation. He noted in his 2023 New Year's speech, "The West lied to us about peace while preparing for aggression, and today, they no longer hesitate to openly admit it and to cynically use Ukraine and its people as a means to weaken and divide Russia. We have never allowed anyone to do this and we will not allow it now."[35]

Putin has sometimes slipped off message, however. At an event in June 2022, reclining casually in an armchair on stage before a large audience, Putin confirmed that in Ukraine, his nation is engaged in a war of imperialist conquest. Russia was not, as he had declared on 9 May 2022, defending itself against NATO aggression and encirclement. He described how, like the conquests of Peter the Great, it was Russia's "lot to return and strengthen."[36]

These objectives have resulted in the Russians not only seizing Ukrainian territory through military conquest. They have also begun to "Russianize" occupied lands in Ukraine. They have implemented measures in the Luhansk, Kherson, and Zaporizhzhia regions, such as the introduction of the Russian ruble and the appointment of Russian administrators.

British scholar Sir Lawrence Freedman wrote in late March 2022 that from Putin's perspective, "Ukraine must be seen to be defeated, no matter what the costs. Perhaps because he is aware of this, Putin shows no sign of relenting on any of his core demands. He dare not confirm the weakness in his position."[37]

What has evolved since 24 February 2022, however, has been the ways and means Putin has applied to achieve his political objectives.[38] Despite their many problems, the Russians have learned and adapted their strategy throughout the war. It has resulted in an evolved strategy for their war in Ukraine, which is the focus of the next chapter.

2

BUMBLING ALONG

Russia's Evolving Strategy for Ukraine

UKRAINIAN RESISTANCE since the first day of the invasion in February 2022 has forced the Russian military to continually adapt to conditions and reassess its strategy. While political objectives shape how war is conducted and what battles are fought, so too do battles reshape political objectives. There is an intense interaction between the two. American strategist Eliot Cohen has described this dynamic, writing that "retaining a sense of direction in war is a constant struggle for political and military leaders at the top, and so the staff officers (and the commentary journalists) are doomed to frustration."[1]

Putin's primary plan was a lightning military operation conducted on multiple fronts to shock the Ukrainian military and government into submission. This would facilitate the removal (possibly the murder) of the democratically elected government and the installation of a regime that would do the bidding of Putin and his oligarchs.[2] Documents recovered by Ukrainian forces late in 2022 confirmed this strategy. Indeed, Russia had planned on a ten-day conquest and minimal fighting. The battlefield performance of the Ukrainians, the unity of the Ukrainian people, and the strategic leadership of President Zelenskyy quickly showed the weakness of this Russian plan.[3]

The original Russian aim was to seize Kyiv, Kharkiv, and other key points; capture government leaders; and force a political accommodation from Ukraine. This plan, predicated on a rapid political collapse by the Ukrainians, adopted a risky multiaxis advance on Kyiv as well as other key Ukrainian cities in the northern, eastern, and southern regions.

By late March 2022, it was becoming clear that this initial Russian strategy had failed. Russian forces in the South had made significant gains in Kherson and Zaporizhzhia, but the northern assaults of Kyiv and Kharkiv bogged down into endless ambushes on Russian convoys and forward units running short of ammunition and supplies.

A revised Plan A for the Russians saw their multiaxis attacks in southern, eastern, northeastern, and northern Ukraine and in the skies above the country placed on a slower timetable. This Russian strategy, too, failed.

Five weeks after their invasion commenced, Major General Igor Konashenkov from the Russian Ministry of Defense reported that a planned regrouping of troops was under way around Kyiv and Chernihiv. This came after Russian negotiators said Russian forces would deescalate operations around those two cities. Russian General Rudskoy also stated during a public briefing that "the combat potential of the armed forces of Ukraine has been significantly reduced, allowing us, to focus the main efforts on achieving the main goal—the liberation of Donbas."[4]

Despite these battlefield setbacks in northern and northeastern Ukraine, Putin and his defense and intelligence chiefs apparently decided on an alternative strategy for their invasion and attempted takeover of Ukraine.[5]

First, the Russians began to prioritize their military operations, avoiding concurrent, multifront offensives. Deciding Kyiv and Kharkiv were too difficult, they began from April 2022 to instead focus on eastern offensive and southern defensive campaigns. This permitted the Russians to husband their remaining military forces for operations in the Donbas while building follow-on echelons for operations in the coming months.

The Russians were able for a time able to draw the Ukrainians into a war of attrition in eastern Ukraine. This was an important element of the revised Russian strategy: destroy the Ukrainian army faster than it can be rebuilt.[6] A principal method the Russian army used to do this was their artillery. Short on infantry from the start of the war, and demonstrably unable to effectively conduct combined-arms or air-land operations, the Russians turned to their traditional battlefield strength.

It was a significant asymmetry between the Russians and Ukrainians. In this second phase of the war, the Russians used the disparity in quantities of artillery systems to maximum effect. This should not have been a surprise. In the eight years of war since the original 2014 Russian invasion, artillery had caused nearly 90 percent of Ukraine's casualties.[7] But as the focus of the war moved to the Donbas in early April 2022, the Russian superiority in artillery became starker. One contemporary report noted that "during the offensive against Donbas, Russian artillery were firing around 20,000 rounds per day, with their peak fire rate surpassing 32,000 rounds on some days. Ukrainian fires rarely exceeded 6,000 rounds a day, reflecting a shortage of both barrels and ammunition."[8]

For the three months from April 2022, Russian forces held the initiative in Ukraine due to this massive overmatch in firepower. This resulted in large numbers of battlefield casualties for the Ukrainians and forced Ukraine to cede parts of its eastern territory to the Russians. This firepower-led Russian strategy was degraded only when the Ukrainians were provided with the U.S. High Mobility Artillery Rocket Systems (HIMARS). The long-range strike capabilities of HIMARS, superior to those held previously by Ukraine, permitted them to attack Russian artillery batteries and supply locations at a longer range and with greater precision than previously possible.

A second part of Russian strategy after their failures to capture Kyiv and Kharkiv was continuing to occupy and defend Ukraine's South, which includes Ukraine's only seaports. Ukraine's southern regions are a productive agricultural region. It is also the location of mines and heavy industry including steelmaking and shipbuilding. And while a growing Ukrainian resistance movement attempted to corrode Russian morale in the South, and Ukrainian counterattacks began in Kherson, holding the South was the second key element of Putin's evolved strategy because it offered the opportunity to strangle Ukraine economically. Wars are very hard to fight without money, and in holding the South, Putin sought to remove Ukraine's capacity to fund itself as a sovereign state and continue fighting for its defense.[9]

In September and October 2022, a series of Ukrainian attacks again forced the Russians to reconsider and adapt their strategy. The lightning Ukrainian offensive in the Kharkiv regions, the slow strangulation of the Russian force on the western bank of the Dnipro River and the first attack on the Kerch Bridge forced another reset in Russian strategy.

Despite the need to revise Russia's strategy, Putin retained his maximalist political objective to subjugate Ukraine. By October 2022, the contours of a new Russian strategy for its Ukrainian "special military operation" emerged.

ADAPTING STRATEGY IN 2022

The first aspect of this adaptation in late 2022 to Russia's strategy was the appointment of a unified commander for all of Russia's Ukraine operations.[10] General Sergei Surovikin, who had previously commanded Russian forces in southern Ukraine and in Syria, immediately made a mark. General Surovikin had a reputation for brutality in Syria and has been convicted of civil crimes and even jailed in the past.

Despite this, he apparently caught the eye of Putin as someone who could turn around the situation in Ukraine. His immediate focus became the destruction of the will of the Ukrainian people. Surovikin, who assumed command of a Russian army that was on the back foot and being consistently beaten on the battlefield by the Ukrainian army in the field, turned to an old doctrine to terrorize the Ukrainian people.

Thus, a second element of the evolved Russian strategy was systemic attacks on Ukrainian critical infrastructure. The new Russian commander launched a series of concentrated missile and drone attacks against civilian infrastructure across Ukraine. By targeting power and water infrastructure, Surovikin focused on breaking the will of Ukrainian people by freezing them in the winter of 2022–23.[11]

These attacks employed concentrated pulses of Iranian drones, primarily the lethal Shahed-136 unmanned aerial vehicle.[12] The Shahed is a small and relatively unsophisticated drone. Nonetheless, its low cost, range of up to 2,500 kilometers, and 50-kilogram warhead make it a useful tool for massed drone attacks against poorly defended targets.[13]

While many of the Russian missiles and Iranian drones used in this campaign were intercepted by an increasingly capable Ukrainian air and missile defense system, enough were able to penetrate the Ukrainian defenses. It resulted in rolling blackouts in major Ukrainian cities as well as issues with heating and water supply.

This strategy also targeted the confidence of foreign entities who might wish to invest in Ukraine. As hardy as the Ukrainian defense has been, their nation still requires masses of foreign capital to rebuild homes, businesses, and infrastructure and to keep their government functioning. The Russians, wanting to economically strangle Ukraine, used these late 2022 attacks to hopefully scare away foreign investors.[14]

Finally, these attacks provided useful propaganda for Russia to feed its domestic audience. Support for the war—or "special military operation," as it is known in Russia—has remained consistently high among Putin's domestic constituency. But with the battlefield reverses that could not be hidden from his people, Putin needed some form of military activity to project a sense of battlefield success. These strategic attacks on Ukraine's cities and infrastructure were used for that purpose and to buy time for the reinforcement and buildup of Russian forces in Ukraine from mobilized troops.

By late 2022, however, it became apparent that Putin was getting impatient for more offensively minded action. While Surovikin used mobilized troops to provide a "stabilizing" influence in the Russian army's scheme of defense in southern and eastern Ukraine, Putin clearly wanted a resumption of offensive operations to secure his annexed Ukrainian provinces.

On 11 January 2023, Russian changed its overall commander in Ukraine yet again.[15] The Russian Defense Ministry announced that General Valery Gerasimov had been appointed commander of the combined forces group for the special military operation in Ukraine.[16] Gerasimov, the Chief of the General Staff of the Russian armed forces since his appointment by President Putin in November 2012, would now be responsible for the campaign that he endorsed to the president before its commencement in February 2022.

RUSSIAN STRATEGY EVOLVES FOR 2023

Mark Galeotti is a British-born political scientist who has intensively studied Russian security affairs for decades. Author of books such as *Armies of Russia's War in Ukraine, We Need to Talk about Putin*, and *Russian Political Warfare: Moving beyond the Hybrid*, he has an informed and sophisticated understanding of Russian strategy. He has been an active commentator on many aspects of the war in Ukraine since the Russian invasion in February 2022. He has described how Putin's desired outcomes for the war have remained consistent: "President Putin's war aims have remained constant and continue to center on the destruction of Ukraine as an independent state capable of joining the EU or NATO, the breaking of the will of its people to resist and the will of the West to support it."[17]

While retaining a consistent political objective, the Russian strategy for the subjugation of Ukraine that evolved in first eighteen months of the war has six components: information warfare, nuclear threats, military campaigns, diplomacy, national mobilization, and economic warfare.

1. Narratives and information warfare. Russian narratives, including information operations to unify domestic support for the war and influence foreign populations, have been part of Putin's strategy from before the war. He has used historical narratives as a central part of his messaging. This approach can be traced back to Putin's statements after the Maidan Revolution in Kyiv in 2013–14, when Putin described the protests as "western-backed fascists trying to tear Ukraine from its historical roots."[18] At least in Putin's mind, any division between Russia and Ukraine is the work of the Western powers.

There are other elements of the narrative he has developed over many years about Ukraine. One is the notion that Ukraine is a neo-Nazi state—but this is belied by the fact that President Zelenskyy is Jewish. And in the parliamentary elections in 2019, the Ukrainian far-right party, Svoboda, won less than 3 percent of the vote.[19] This has not stopped Putin, though. In his September 2022 address to the nation that announced partial mobilization, Putin talked about "the majority of people living in the territories liberated from the neo-Nazis" and declared, "We cannot, we have no moral right to let our kin and kith be torn to pieces by butchers."[20]

Putin's speeches before the Russian invasion of Ukraine, and during the war so far, have contained a combination of pseudohistory and a longed-for vision of

Russian greatness from a distant past. Timothy Snyder, an American historian who specializes in the history of central Europe and speaks Ukrainian fluently, has debunked many of Putin's narratives on the history of Russia. Snyder has described Putin's historical views as "an imagined past enforcing a deadened future."[21] Nonetheless, these narratives have influenced formal Russian military information operations in Ukraine as well as its strategic influence operations in China, the subcontinent, and beyond.

The Russians have also undertaken a campaign to ensure that Russian, and not Ukrainian, narratives prevail in countries such as China and India and across large parts of South Asia, Africa, and South America. One example of these Russian operations is the Russosphere network in Africa. An investigation by the BBC's Global Disinformation Team unearthed a Russian influence campaign that was praising Russian and Wagner Group soldiers, describing Ukrainian army personnel as Nazis, and amplifying other Russian narratives.[22]

The aim to influence public opinion in Africa and shape the actions of African nations in their support for Russia's Ukraine invasion is having some success, particularly in multilateral institutions such as the United Nations (UN). At the one-year mark of this war, the resolution put before the UN General Assembly demanding that Russia leave Ukraine saw many African nations abstain from voting, and some, such as Mali and Eritrea, voted against the resolution.[23]

While Ukraine has dominated the information space (at least in the West) for much of the war, Russia is not absent. As Igor Gretskiy notes, "Vladimir Putin spent years preparing his invasion of Ukraine. Propaganda and disinformation were key elements of his plans."[24] British researcher Carl Miller has also challenged the widespread view in the West that Ukrainian influence campaigns and strategic information operations are dominant in this war. He has written, "A mistake we in the West too often make is to suppose that our information spaces are far more universal than they are. . . . We're in danger of making that same mistake over Russia's invasion of Ukraine. The fact that we don't see information warfare doesn't mean it isn't happening, and it doesn't mean we've won."[25]

Miller offers a caution in assuming this battle for influence has been won by Ukraine. The Russians have been undertaking information operations against Ukraine and its supporters for years. In the wake of the 2014 Ukrainian Revolution of Dignity, Russia stepped up its pressure on its neighbor. This included narratives in state-controlled media about Ukraine's new leaders, including neo-Nazi and Russian imperial narratives that have been utilized by Putin more recently.[26]

After the Ukrainian government blocked Russian social media networks Vkontakte and Odnoklassniki in 2017, Russian television and other official media channels became more aggressive toward Ukraine. Putin's speeches about Ukraine began to incorporate the idea that Ukraine was not a true nation and that it was rightly part of Russia proper.[27]

From late 2022, and in 2023, Russian officials began to frame the war as an existential one for Russia. Putin notes in a 26 February 2023 speech on Russian television that he does not know whether "such an ethnic group as the Russian people can survive in the form in which it exists today" if the West succeeds in "destroying the Russian Federation and establishing control over its fragments."[28] Statements such as this, aimed at the domestic audience in Russia, are designed to reinforce support for the war in Ukraine and minimize opposition to Putin's rule. It is also a theme that Russian influence operations will continue to amplify in both domestic and international operations.[29]

2. Nuclear threats. Modern Russian thinking on the use of nuclear weapons dates to the 1960s, when the Soviets envisaged the use of tactical nuclear weapons on the battlefield to achieve localized tactical or operational outcomes. And while the development of precision weapons in the past several decades has seen the requirement for tactical nuclear weapons recede, Russian doctrine still proscribes their use in certain situations.[30]

The Russian approach to the use of tactical nuclear weapons is described by Michael Kofman and others in their 2021 exploration of Russian military strategy: "Nonstrategic nuclear weapons are reserved for escalation management in the context of a regional war, after conventional means have proven ineffective, and for nuclear warfighting in the context of a large-scale war. They too can be used for demonstration, or in single or grouped strikes as part of an escalation management strategy."[31]

At multiple points in this war, the Russian president has referred to the use of nuclear weapons. However, his threats have been inconsistent. In September 2022, he implied the use nuclear weapons when he noted that "our country has different types of weapons as well, and some of them are more modern than the weapons NATO countries have. In the event of a threat to the territorial integrity of our country and to defend Russia and our people, we will certainly make use of all weapon systems available to us. This is not a bluff."[32] But on 27 October 2022, Putin denied having any intentions to use the weapons. Speaking at the plenary session of an international colloquium, Putin responded to a question from a participant about nuclear weapons by stating, "We have no need to do so; there is no sense in it for us, neither political nor military."[33] He later made another U-turn: during a speech in February 2023 he again referred to their use.[34]

Despite these contradictions in Putin's statements, Russia's possession of tactical nuclear weapons has had an undeniable impact on the conflict. It has shaped the support provided by the United States and Europe to short-range, tactical weapons because Western governments have been cautious not to provide systems that might escalate the conflict. Proposals early in the war for a "no-fly zone" were rejected on similar grounds, and NATO has refused to provide any personnel to serve in Ukraine itself. This has been described as "the most significant attempt at prolonged, consistent, and conscious nuclear coercion against NATO and its partners in almost forty years."[35]

And while Putin's statements on nuclear capacity have had an impact, the nuclear arsenals of the United States and NATO have also had a mollifying impact on Putin's aspirations. This will be explored further in chapter 5.

3. Military campaigns. The deployment of tens of thousands of mobilized soldiers, as well as the recruitment of thousands of convicts to serve in the Wagner Group, stabilized the Russian position in Ukraine over the winter of 2022–23. This also began to redress one of Russia's fundamental shortfalls at the start of its invasion of Ukraine: a shortfall in the quantity of troops, especially infantry. Owen Matthews, in his book *Overreach*, wrote of the initial invasion force, "The estimated 120 BTGs [Battalion Tactical Groups] that attacked Ukraine all went in with their full complement of armor and support arms, but far from their full combat strength of men. And that shortfall made all the difference. With no dismountable men you've got a motorized infantry unit that doesn't have infantry."[36]

Even with additional troops provided by mobilization, Russia has yet to deploy sufficient troops to achieve the maximalist goals of Putin. Attacks on the ground, over the past several centuries, have generally relied on a ratio of 3:1 in favor of the attacker to give the best chances of success. In his discussion of this "Three to One Theory of Combat" (which we explored in the previous chapter), Trevor Dupuy acknowledged that as a rule of thumb it is generally useful but also stated, "As a basis for forecasting battle outcomes, however, it is less reliable."[37]

While Russia might be able to generate force ratios like this for short periods in key areas, it does not have a large surplus of military personnel to build an overwhelming advantage in manpower against the Ukrainians—or to effectively occupy captured territory. It also faces the additional difficulty of when it does concentrate forces before any offensive activity, as they are likely to be detected by the Ukrainians and attacked with long-range strike weapons such as HIMARS.

At the same time, it is becoming apparent that Russia has accepted it has an issue with its army and needs to fix it. As such, according to some reports, the Russian Ministry in 2023 is attempting to "improve the professionalism of its conventional forces and to test the effectiveness of its chains of command."[38] Also, early in 2023 the Russian announced a plan to restructure and expand the size of the Russian military. This will, in the medium term, increase the size of the Russian military by about 30 percent, to 1.5 million troops. Theoretically this could have an impact on the campaign in Ukraine in the medium term. But Russia faces many challenges in sustaining its current size, let alone expanding.[39]

Despite these institutional efforts, military manpower initiatives alone will not win this war for Russia; offensive action is a key part of Russia's strategy.

The capture and occupation of Luhansk and Donetsk oblasts appear to be the absolute minimum that Putin would accept from this war, notwithstanding his annexation of the two oblasts of Kherson and Zaporizhzhia. It will demand further offensive campaigns from the Russian military in Ukraine. And it will require Russian ground forces to improve their logistics while launching offensive campaigns in the East and South. The lack of success of the 2023 Russian offensives in eastern Ukraine demonstrates that the Russians have a ways to go in improving their overall military effectiveness. But as General Valerii Zaluzhnyi acknowledged in his November 2023 paper on positional warfare, the conditions of modern war have evolved. Both Russia and Ukraine continue to search for evolved tactics and operational approaches to achieve breakthroughs against modern defenses that include electronic warfare, meshed sensor networks, mines, drones, and multiple echelons of well-constructed physical defenses.[40]

4. Diplomacy. The diplomatic efforts of the Russian Foreign Ministry, including Foreign Minister Sergey Lavrov, have been central to Russian strategy for this war. Lavrov has undertaken frequent overseas visits as part of his diplomacy to shape the perceptions of governments in south Asia, Africa, and Asia. This diplomatic strategy has included two tours of Africa; one was a long trip in 2022 that included visits to Ethiopia, Myanmar, Uganda, Republic of Congo, and Egypt. He also began 2023 with a round of official visits to nations in Africa.[41]

The efforts of Lavrov, and those of his fellow diplomats, have not been entirely unsuccessful. Despite the efforts of President Biden and leaders in Europe to rally nations to support Ukraine, many nations have declined to join sanctions against Russia. Countries such as China, India, Indonesia, and others have condemned the invasion (to a degree) but continued to trade with Russia and import energy from it. This is vital for Russia to generate income from weapons sales and its energy exports.

Russia's neighbor Belarus will be a continuing focal point for Russian diplomacy. It was from this former Soviet republic that the Russian army launched a large northern campaign against Kyiv in February 2022. President Putin visited Belarus in late December 2022 for discussions with President Lukashenko. Russia has drawn on ammunition and equipment reserves held by Belarus, and it has conducted joint training with the military forces of Belarus in 2022 and 2023. Russia also bases military aircraft at Belarus airfields and uses its airspace to fire missiles into Ukraine. In 2023, Russia also deployed tactical nuclear weapons to Belarus.[42] An integration framework, guided by a new joint military doctrine of the Union State of

Belarus and Russia, is progressing slowly.[43] But the president of Belarus, Alexander Lukashenko, has remained wary of becoming a belligerent in the war. The main strategic utility of Belarus will probably be as an "economy of force" threat that makes Ukraine keep its troops in the North.[44]

Countries such as India and China also remain vital for Russia and will be a continuing focus for Putin's diplomatic efforts. As one analyst has written, "Having chosen confrontation with the West, Putin can ill afford to have bad relations with China. Putin's embrace of China helps him achieve his strategic goals. It frees him to concentrate Russia's resources on the European theater . . . and it increases his ability to ignore Western demands to change Russia's domestic political arrangements in ways that threaten the regime he has built."[45]

India remains another important target of Russian diplomacy.[46] While the India-Russia relationship has historically been based on a geopolitical alignment against the United States, Pakistan, and China, as well as heavy Soviet aid and Soviet arms sales, it currently rests on the supply of oil and weapons to India. In a 2022 report for the Carnegie Endowment, Rajan Menon and Eugene Rumer describe the India-Russia relationship thus: "India and Russia have important sunk costs in a relationship that has endured for over two generations and has served them well, including in difficult times. India has no reason to forsake the multiple benefits it has received from a decades-long relationship with Russia, and it would be a mistake to expect that it will do so, no matter the growing tensions between Russia and the West."[47] Russia's diplomatic efforts are likely to continue, ensuring that as many nations as possible refrain from supporting Ukraine (and NATO), and at a minimum, remain on the sidelines of the conflict.

5. National mobilization. Another part of Russia's strategy is the mobilization of the Russian people and industry. The mobilization declaration by Putin on 21 September 2022 was the first time that Putin reached beyond standing military forces to fight his war in Ukraine. Described as "necessary, imperative measures to protect the sovereignty, security and territorial integrity of Russia," it has seen at least 300,000 Russians inducted into the Russian military.[48]

While at times chaotic and disorganized, the Russian mobilization of personnel for military service gradually smoothed out its problems and has continued since late 2022 to induct and provide very rudimentary training to tens of thousands of Russians to serve in Ukraine.[49] For a short period, the Wagner Group was also permitted to recruit prisoners from Russian penal establishments to serve in the war. These convicts were provided pardons to serve in Ukraine, but also suffered a very high casualty rate. The scheme was terminated by the Russian government in February 2023.[50]

As Russia was mobilizing people, it also began to mobilize its defense and wider industry to increase production for the war. With a massive consumption of munitions and the destruction of thousands of armored vehicles and dozens of aircraft, the Russian military has struggled to equip its forces with cutting-edge equipment. One example is ancient tanks such as the T-54/55 tank. Developed in the late 1940s, produced in massive quantities and stored since the 1970s, they have been deployed to Ukraine by the Russian army.[51] The war has become one founded on a competition between industrial systems in Russia on one side, and in Ukraine and its supporters in the West on the other.[52]

On 21 October 2022, Putin established a new military council to coordinate "the activities of federal executive authorities and executive authorities of the subjects of the Russian Federation during a special military operation." It provides for military production to be controlled at a higher level, including the finances for war production.[53]

Russia will continue to hone its mobilization of personnel and industry. But there are significant challenges. As Elisabeth Braw has explained, "Both the mobilization and the flight of so many men, at least as numerous as those being drafted, will create another problem—the absence of qualified workers in every sector. And the country has no set system for the continuity of its society during wartime."[54]

While Russia may face other challenges as it mobilizes to support Ukraine operations, its ability to fight an industrial-scale war is an essential foundation for Russian strategy in this war.

6. Economic warfare. The economic strangulation of Ukraine is a deliberate part of Russia's strategy to constrain the ability of its former Soviet republic to generate revenue, while imposing costs through civilian deaths and destruction of infrastructure. The objective for Russia is to ensure that Ukraine has limited capacity to underpin its sovereignty with sources of income. The undermining of an adversary's economy has deep roots in Russian military strategy, as Michael Kofman wrote in 2021: "The overall task for Russian military strategy is to prevent an opponent from achieving a decisive outcome during the IPW, force them into a conflict of attrition, and inflict costs on their military and economic infrastructure so that they will seek war termination on acceptable terms."[55]

The Russian military campaign in southern Ukraine provides a buffer for its continued occupation of Crimea, as well as a land bridge between Russia and Crimea. But it has another important purpose too. Southern Ukraine is an important source of production that underpins the Ukrainian GDP. It is the location of power plants, mines, agricultural areas, and the ports through which goods are dispatched that represent over half of Ukraine's export earnings. Ninety percent of Ukraine's coal is located in the far eastern part of the country. Ukraine's largest privately owned company that generates the highest revenue, Metinvest, was based in the Russian-occupied Mariupol.[56] The Russian capture and occupation of the South has reduced Ukraine's capacity to generate revenue through exports.

Russian drone and missile attacks on civil infrastructure is another component of the economic attack on Ukraine. These have reduced the production capacity and the productive hours of Ukrainian industry. One report from the Centre for Economic Policy Research has estimated that Ukrainian productive capacity has decreased by 7.5 percent over the course of 2022.[57] Further, these Russian attacks have targeted the confidence of foreign entities who might wish to invest in Ukraine. The Russians, who aim to economically strangle Ukraine, use missile and massed drone attacks on infrastructure to scare away foreign investors.

At the same time, Russia is evolving its own economy for what is likely to be a longer war than anticipated. While Russian exports plunged by over 40 percent in the wake of their invasion in February 2022, exports rebounded to pre-February 2022 norms in September 2022. China and Hong Kong have been filling shortfalls in goods needed by Russia such as integrated circuits requirements, and the Russian supply chain for consumer goods, smartphones, and motor vehicles has been rebuilt.[58]

Russia wants to sustain its own economy while it gradually strangles the economy of Ukraine. This is a critical element of the Russian strategy for Ukraine. According to the World Bank, the Russian invasion resulted in a 29 percent contraction in Ukraine's economy in 2022. However, the World Bank also forecast a 3.5 percent growth of the Ukrainian economy in 2023 and a 4 percent growth in 2024. The Ukrainian economy, after initial shocks, has begun to demonstrate resilience against Russia's plans to economically strangle it.[59]

A RUSSIAN THEORY OF VICTORY

To win a war, a nation must be guided by a theory of victory. This should comprise a plausible set of principles for overcoming an adversary, as well as a unifying idea.[60] The 2017 U.K. publication *Getting Strategy Right (Enough)* notes that "a strategy which has no unifying idea is not a strategy. . . . The innovative and compelling 'big idea' is often the basis of a new strategy. It must not only bind the ends, ways and means but also inspire others to support it."[61]

A theory of victory does not include all aspects of strategy making, but as Frank Hoffman notes, "it is central to strategic success." Further, Hoffman describes how "a theory of success is captured in a single concept like containment or . . . an orchestrated series of strategic activities akin to a campaign plan."[62]

Anthony Cordesman and Hy Rothstein have examined victory in a chapter of *Assessing War: The Challenges of Measuring Success and Failure*. The question of how war serves the highest political objectives is something that must be a core part of military planning. They note that "implicit to any strategy is the theory of victory, or underpinning logic. . . . This theory is a declaration of how you believe the things you are planning to do will lead to the goals you seek."[63]

This has also been described as a "theory of war." Colin Gray explored the concept in his 1990 book *War, Peace and Victory: Strategy and Statecraft for the Next Century*, where he defines a theory of war as something that explains how a war can be won. He also further clarifies the matter by explaining what a theory of war is not: it does not describe how a war should be waged, nor what its aims are. Instead, a theory of war should explain "how a particular country or coalition can be beaten at a tolerable cost."[64]

What might a Russian theory of victory look like?

Victory for Russia is the subjugation of the Ukrainian state, through a combination of occupation and political accommodation. Russia has already achieved this strategic goal in Belarus, but the cost of attempting to do so in Ukraine has, so far, been extraordinarily high. Victory for Russia now would include extensive damage to the credibility of the NATO alliance and to the level of support it is able to provide to frontline states in eastern Europe.

To achieve this, Russia's strategic approach embraces actions up to and including nuclear threats that persuade Ukraine's neighbors and the NATO alliance to minimize their support for Ukraine. If they do support Ukraine, they do not commit military forces. Thus far, this has worked.

Second, the Russians have sought to persuade NATO, the United States, and Ukraine that it is able to outlast all of them in this conflict. Through public declarations, mobilization of its people and industry, and reallocation of resources in the Russian economy, Russia is at least generating the impression that it believes it can wage and win a long war because the public in Ukraine and the West are not willing to bear the same costs that Russia is.

One of Putin's assumptions going into the war was that the West was unlikely to assist Ukraine. While that assumption had been proven wrong, the evolved Russian strategy and Putin's theory of victory appear to embrace the idea that while assistance might be flowing for a short time, Western populations and politicians would eventually tire of the war. It is possible Putin believes that a lack of strategic patience within the populations of Europe and the United States—particularly in previous conflicts like Somalia, Iraq, and Afghanistan—will also occur with their support for the war in Ukraine. He will have also been heartened by statements from a minority of Republican members of the U.S. Congress who wish to reduce or even stop American assistance to Ukraine.[65] For Putin, this may be his only viable theory of victory for his special military operation.[66]

In early December 2022, Putin stated that he expects a long war in Ukraine when he described the Russian invasion as "a long process."[67] With Ukraine reliant on Western weapons, munitions, intelligence, and economic aid to continue the war, Putin is—at least on the surface—comfortable to wait out Ukraine and the West with his strategy.[68] Delays in approving additional military support for Ukraine by the U.S. Congress in late 2023, and the lack of a significant expansion in European defense industrial capacity since the beginning of the war, will have only encouraged Putin in this view.[69]

Even so, it might still be a long wait for Putin. The United States and its coalition partners entered Afghanistan in October 2021 and did not depart until nearly twenty years later. There is every reason to believe that, with no Europeans or Americans deployed to or dying in Ukraine, these governments could sustain their support to Ukraine for a long time to come. Indeed, as the first year turned into the second in this war, European nations increased their assistance to Ukraine.[70] NATO also reinforced its support for Ukraine by committing to long-term assistance, and entry into NATO, at the 2023 Vilnius Summit.[71] Such increases in support indicate that not only do the United States and Europe wish to see Ukraine to defend itself. They wish to see Russia defeated in Ukraine.

Consequently, Putin's theory that he will be able to outwait and outlast the West may be another of his strategic illusions about the launching and conduct of his war. It is a course of action that holds significant peril for Putin. Owen Matthews has written that Putin has "gained a fifth of Ukraine and increased the size of Russia by half a per cent. The price of his illusions was not only thousands of lost lives, but also a lost future for Russia. . . . The misbegotten war had opened a Pandora's box of alternative futures for Russia that were much scarier than Putin's regime had ever been."[72]

Regardless of Putin's assumptions about Ukrainian—or European—patience, strategy also remains an interactive undertaking. Russian strategy for this war is competing against that of its main opponent, Ukraine. Therefore, Ukrainian strategy is the focus of the next chapter.

3

INCREASE THE ENEMY'S SUFFERING
Ukraine's Strategic Response

WHEN EXAMINING the strategy of Ukraine in this war, it is worth recalling how the late Colin Gray described strategy as "the glue that holds together the purposeful activities of state" and how that "glue" has value only when it acts as the "bridge between purpose and action."[1] The Ukrainian strategy since February 2022 can be viewed in this context. It has acted as a mechanism to hold together many elements and actions of the nation in the service of a higher purpose. That purpose, while always founded on defending Ukrainian sovereignty, has evolved throughout the war. This should not be surprising. As Clausewitz describes it, the political aim "must adapt itself to its chosen means, a process which can radically change it."[2]

Just before the Russian invasion, Ukrainian president Zelenskyy spoke to the 2022 Munich Security Conference. His approach then was defensive. Yet his speech displayed the glimmerings of the larger "defense of Europe" theme that has appeared in Ukrainian strategic narratives during the war. He noted that "we will defend our land with or without the support of partners. . . . This is your contribution to the security of Europe and the world, where Ukraine has been a reliable shield for eight years."[3]

Five days later, after Russian forces had attacked his nation, Zelenskyy's speech to his people again demonstrated a defensive strategy. He declared that "no one will be able to convince or force us, Ukrainians, to give up our freedom, our independence, our sovereignty."[4] If this defense of freedom, independence, and sovereignty is the political objective, Zelenskyy's speech on 24 February also contains two other important elements of Ukraine's strategy.

First, it is a call to arms by the democracies of the world to assist Ukraine. Zelenskyy notes that "if you, dear European leaders, dear world leaders, leaders of the free world, do not help us today, then tomorrow the war will knock on your door." And second, it is his initial attempt at corroding Russian public opinion for the war: for example, he states, "We see that many Russians are shocked by what is happening. Some Russians are already calling on social media that they are against the war. . . . If you understand us, if you understand that you are attacking an independent country, please go out to the squares and address the President of your country." These two themes, internationalizing the war and operations to influence the Russian population, have remained critical elements of Ukrainian strategy.[5]

By late 2022, the Ukrainian government had further evolved its political objectives for the war. In the wake of the victory over Russia in September in the Battle of Kharkiv, and the subsequent Russian withdrawal from western Kherson, a more confident Ukrainian president was able to define his more expansive view of war termination. Speaking to the G20 Summit that was being held in Indonesia, President Zelenskyy outlined his vision for the termination of the war. In essence, his speech was a description of the political objectives—described as "proposals"—that he now sought.[6]

The G20 speech contained ten Ukrainian political objectives. These ranged from nuclear safety and food security to restoration of Ukraine's territorial integrity, war crimes trials, and a definitive end to the war. In subsequent addresses, Zelenskyy reinforced these national goals, including during his 22 December 2022 speech to the U.S. Congress, and his 2023 New Year's address, where he called for victory in the coming year.[7]

▨ ATTRITION, EXHAUSTION, AND CORROSION

In the late nineteenth and early twentieth centuries, German scholar Hans Delbrück described how all military strategy could be divided into two forms. The first type was *annihilation*, where the aim was to completely destroy an enemy's military forces in order to achieve victory. The second type of strategy was *exhaustion*. This was the application of multiple means, including battles, to achieve the political aim in a war.[8] Throughout history, weaker states in war have often chosen the later because, as Lawrence Freedman explains, "exhaustion is different, which is why this is a strategy favored by an underdog. With inferior resources, the underdog has no interest in regular battle."[9]

Much has changed, however, since Delbrück wrote about these two kinds of strategy. Superpowers have risen and fallen. Technologies have transformed trade, societies, and military institutions. The proximity of citizens to warfare has decreased through constant media reporting, crowdfunding weapons, or reporting enemy movements on smart devices. Might there now be other concepts of strategy more aligned with society and contemporary geopolitics?

Thomas Bruscino has written that "there is no good reason to think that there are only two forms of strategy, or that they are annihilation and exhaustion."[10] It is possible that neither model neatly fits the Ukrainian strategic response to the Russian invasion. To that end, I propose that the Ukrainians have adopted a third form of strategy: *corrosion*.

The word "corrosion" was not widely used in Delbrück's time. It is most commonly associated with the science of materials and defined as the "gradual deterioration of materials in reaction with their environment." However, it is a word that has also been used to describe nonmaterial situations. For example, "we are observing a corrosion of moral standards in our society."[11]

The reason the term "corrosion" may be a third approach to strategy is that the concept covers the *larger potential surface contact between societies* at war than when Delbrück produced his theoretical construct over a century ago. What does this mean?

Modern technologies allow citizens to view many elements of the war almost in real time. Social media and the work of journalists in traditional media organizations mean that citizens are exposed many aspects of war that in previous eras were only experienced by combatants. This can lead to vicarious trauma but also allows massively expanded citizen participation in war efforts. No longer restricted to raising war bonds or paying higher taxes to fund war, citizens can now directly raise funds to procure war material including socks, first aid kits, drones, and satellites.[12]

At the same time, citizens play an active role in the real-time reporting of threats. For example, Ukrainians can download an application on their smart devices for reporting enemy units, drones, or missiles, which can then be engaged by military forces. In doing so, the line between combatant and citizen is greatly narrowed.

New-era information warfare also permits governments to target enemy populations and subelements of those populations with more discrete and precise messaging than has been possible before. Big data, generative artificial intelligence, social media, smart devices, and new analytical capabilities are contributing to an unprecedented level of access to adversary citizens.

Finally, the reach of weapon systems—cyber activities, hypersonic missiles, or other long-range munitions—means that all citizens are potential targets of an enemy nation. While this has been the case since World War II, the array of weapons available and the cost of delivering these weapons—in financial terms and in the lives of military personnel delivering the weapons—has fundamentally changed the level of engagement between societies.

In Delbrück's construct, most of the attrition and exhaustion was suffered by military forces, with exhaustion of civil populations being a secondary effect. Now, the targeting of civilians and military elements of an enemy society is done concurrently, and with a vast array of physical and nonphysical, kinetic, cyber, informational, and economic means. And to make matters more complex, citizens using cyber operations, crowdfunding, and commercially available information are able to directly target citizens of their enemy.

The strategy of corrosion therefore is distinct from attrition and exhaustion because of the breadth of society that is now involved in warfare, and because of the unparalleled means that each society has to attack each other, not just through their representative military institutions but also directly.

Therefore, the government, military, and citizens—a Clausewitzian trinitarian construct—are able to participate in war in different ways simultaneously. This represents a vast expansion of the societal surface area that is attacking and is defending during any conflict. Therefore, the word "corrosion," and its application as a concept that involves degradation due to exposure to "the environment," is apt.

This is not an entirely new theoretical construct for strategy. War is an aggregation of many new ideas and some new ones. The strategy of corrosion incorporates older ideas like attrition and exhaustion but applies these and newer constructs of total societal interaction in conflict, as described earlier. In this combination can be found an evolved yet separate theoretical construct on strategy that is worthy of further examination and testing.

The Ukrainians have embraced a model that uses every element of their society—military, government, commercial, and civil—to degrade and destroy enemy forces on the battlefield, as well as to employ clever diplomacy and strategy influence campaigns to corrode the will of the Russians and exhaust their ability to wage war on Ukraine. While in some respects the strategy of exhaustion applies, it also uses multiple military campaigns as well as a global influence campaign, something that Delbrück probably could not have imagined in his day.

It is an approach that uses the combination of old and new ideas to make war more costly for the Russians in the physical, economic, information, and moral domains than for Ukraine. The idea of corrosion, making a war more expensive in lives and resources to the enemy, is described in Clausewitz's On War. He describes how a military force should "give priority to operations that increase the enemy's suffering."[13] However, this should be complemented with something Clausewitz describes as even more effective: "The most important method, judging from the frequency of its use, is to wear down the enemy."[14]

This strategy of corrosion has resulted in Ukraine generally attempting to attack the Russian military forces where they are weak.[15] British military historian and theorist Basil Liddell Hart described this as the indirect approach. In his classic book *Strategy*, he writes that "effective results in war have rarely been attained unless the approach has had such indirectness as to ensure the opponents unreadiness to meet it. This indirectness has usually been physical and *always psychological*."[16]

The Ukrainians have absorbed this advice from Liddell Hart over the course of the war and applied it to their strategy. In the Battle for Kyiv, the Ukrainians were able to fight the Russians to a standstill because they were able to penetrate Russian rear areas and destroy parts of their logistic support. They were able to do so largely because the Russian military biased toward a combat force in their advance on Kyiv, moving in administrative rather than tactical formations, with less than the usual array of logistic support units. As an in-depth report by the *Washington Post* explained in 2022, "What transpired in and around Kyiv in the ensuing 36 days would represent the biggest foreign blunder in the 22-year rule of Russian President Vladimir Putin. To the surprise of the world, the offensive against the Ukrainian capital would end in a humiliating retreat, which would expose deep systemic problems in a Russian military he had spent billions to rebuild."[17]

The Ukrainians were subsequently able to destroy many of the logistic and combat support elements of the Russian force, in addition to the frontline Russian combat elements. This hollowed out the ability of the Russians to resupply themselves and denied frontline troops ammunition, fuel, and other essential supplies. It had the effect of corroding the Russian's northern axis of advance from within. After several weeks of desperate fighting in the cold weather of February and March, Ukraine forced Russia to retreat back into Belarus.

CORRODING THE FIGHTING POWER OF RUSSIA

The components of any nation's capacity to fight have been described as "fighting power." Originally used by Martin van Creveld in his 1982 book, *Fighting Power: German and U.S. Army Performance 1939–1945*, the term has made its way into the doctrinal publications of military institutions. At least in the doctrinal application of the term, fighting power comprises physical, moral, and intellectual components.[18]

The Ukrainian strategy for this war has incorporated the corrosion of the Russian physical, moral, and intellectual capacity to fight and win in Ukraine. They have attempted this on the battlefield, and they have done it in the global information environment.

An important foundation of Ukraine's fighting power is that it possesses a different political construct with which it can develop, test, implement, and evolve its strategy. Ukraine appears to have been able to reconcile the civil and military aspects of its government in a manner similar to other Western democracies. Although the arrangement is not without the normal bureaucratic, historical, personal, and institutional tensions, it has helped President Zelenskyy to more effectively govern his nation and interact with foreign leaders and request their assistance.[19] And it has ensured that the Ukrainian military has a president, a defense minister, and a military commander in chief whose responsibilities are clearly delineated and who are able to collaborate to produce aligned national and military strategies.[20]

This is one of the key asymmetries between Ukraine and Russia in this war. Russia, with its authoritarian, aging president and centralized decision-making, does not possess this effective interplay of civil and military authorities. It is therefore denied robust debate and the consideration of a wide range of options for problem solving. It has led to unrealistic assumptions and political aspirations that are at odds with military capabilities. This is a challenge that Russia—with its territorial annexation—has yet to resolve in this war.

Ukraine has seen many changes since it regained its independence from the Soviet Union in the wake of the Cold War. But perhaps one of the most important has been growth of democratic institutions, including an effective civil-military relationship. This notion of civil primacy is described by Eliot Cohen, in his book *Supreme Command*, as the "unequal dialog." Cohen describes how "the issue of civil military relations is one of the oldest subjects of political science. Plato's *Republic* discusses the difficulties inherent in creating a guardian class who would at once be gentle to their own and cruel to their enemies, men who like noble dogs would serve as the ideal city's guardians."[21]

This demarcation of civil and military responsibilities, and the subordination of the military to democratically elected civilians, is an important component of strategy making and the building of effective warfighting capacity. By its nature an ongoing dialogue, it exposes military ideas and plans to wider scrutiny and the realism of politicians (and economic officials). But it also exposes political leaders to the realities of building, sustaining, and employing military force in all its forms. In a well-functioning civil-military relationship, a wider range of strategies and plans can be considered, and there is an effective competition among ideas. Additionally, this interplay of policy and military strategy aims to ensure a better alignment of the two. Political objectives in war are realistic only if they can be matched to commensurate military capacity. The Ukrainian strategy of corrosion has sought to better align the politics and the military outcomes of the war.

UKRAINE'S STRATEGY OF CORROSION

What is Ukraine's strategy of corrosion and its key components? I propose that there are seven elements: purpose, the global influence campaign, integrated civil-military actions, foreign support, national mobilization of people and resources, fighting a just war, and continuous learning and adaptation.

1. Purpose. Purpose is a fundamental aspect of strategy. For some, this is the "ends" in the "ends-ways-means" conception of strategy. For others, like Colin Gray, purpose is the near bank in a construct that sees strategy as a bridge between purpose and action.[22] American strategist and naval officer J. C. Wylie defines strategy as "a plan of action designed in order to achieve some end; a purpose together with a system of measures for its accomplishment."[23] As Clausewitz writes, "The political object—the original motive for the war—will thus determine both the military objective to be reached and the amount of effort it requires."[24]

The development and communication of clear, unambiguous purpose is a core responsibility for leaders; purpose, or the "why," is more important than the "what." The very best leaders, regardless of their level or industry, inspire others by giving them meaning. But this requires a deep understanding of the culture of the nation and organization that the leader serves. And it demands highly developed communication skills. As the leadership doctrine for the Australian Defence Force notes, "Your people must understand their purpose. Without it they will lack focus. They need to know what is to be done, why it is necessary, the standard to be achieved, and the time frames within which it is to be achieved."[25] Purpose for Ukraine is often delivered in President Zelenskyy's speeches. Zelenskyy's words "I need ammunition, not a ride" unified his people at a critical point of the war. It gained him global attention and influence, which has been essential for economic, humanitarian, diplomatic, intelligence, and military assistance.[26] His words also sent a message that although Ukraine needed assistance, it also had the resilience and courage to help itself.

In his speeches and video broadcasts, Zelenskyy has consistently described why Ukraine is worth defending and why Ukraine is worthy of foreign assistance. Of all the talents that Zelenskyy has applied in this effort, the most effective has been his use of the written and spoken word. He has leveraged language and modern communications to inspire the Ukrainian people, provide purpose for his military personnel and his government, share the tragedy experienced by his people, and celebrate their successes.

Whether he is speaking to a major global conference, in the Ukrainian Parliament, or with soldiers during a visit to the front lines, Zelenskyy wants the Ukrainian people, his enemies, and the rest of world to believe that defending Ukraine is important—and that his nation is capable of winning the war against Russia with the right support. He has adroitly used the written and spoken word to outline why defending democracy is important, and why the price of doing so is much less than not doing so.[27] Every speech, and all of his strategic communications activities, are about providing purpose. It is an indispensable part of Ukraine's strategy of corrosion.

2. *The global struggle for influence*. The war in Ukraine has seen a transformation in how soft power and hard power are blended to achieve strategic outcomes.

While both remain important in war, Ukraine has used its information narrative of a small democracy being systemically exterminated by a vicious authoritarian power to leverage military, diplomatic, economic, and intelligence support from Western nations. This combination of hard and soft power has been one important way Ukraine has been able to "level the battlefield" against its larger and more technologically sophisticated invader.[28]

Sustaining Western support means that Ukraine, its president, its citizen information warriors, and its diplomatic corps must constantly engage and influence the politicians and populations of the United States, Europe, and beyond.[29] This engagement has resulted in strong statements of support from multinational institutions such as the European Union and NATO and has also underpinned the range of economic sanctions that have been levied on Russia since the beginning of their invasion.

This influence campaign has relied on what some have called a "democratization of intelligence," with government, military, and open sources of information being meshed and used for targeting in the physical and information environments.[30] Before the war, the United States released classified intelligence in an effort to coerce the Russians into not invading Ukraine. Similar measures were used to preempt the Russian use of chemical weapons early in the war.[31]

The Ukrainians have also sought to degrade Russia's international standing with their global influence activities. Using government sources as well as volunteers, Ukraine has also discredited Russian narratives and crowded the information space to degrade the impact of Russian influence campaigns.[32] This self-organized and self-directed army of global volunteers has undertaken a variety of online functions from building websites to combat Russian misinformation campaigns to disabling Russian government websites. This campaign has also aimed to undermine Russian capabilities while also seeking to degrade Russian popular support for the war.[33] But there are risks in such an approach. As Elisabeth Braw has written, "People from all corners of the world have joined the digital fight. But while the efforts on the part of this volunteer army have been impressive, they could very well backfire, threatening to escalate and prolong the conflict rather than delivering a decisive victory for either side."[34]

Despite these risks, social media has played a crucial role in the influence battle for Ukraine.[35] The exploitation of various social media by Ukrainian government and private organizations as well as individuals and Ukrainian diaspora populations has been used to influence the perceptions of humans in a way that is historically unprecedented. Other wars have been covered by social media. Examples include the Israeli operations in Gaza as well as the application of social media by ISIS during their invasion of northern Iraq. But there has been a broader use of social media in this war than in previous conflicts.[36] This has included grassroots movements to support Ukraine's strategic influence operations, such as the #NAFO movement.[37]

The audience for this influence has a short attention span, however. And Western support is vital to the Ukrainian war effort, and for its counteroffensives, to regain those parts of the country seized by the Russian military. Sustaining this support means that Ukraine, its president, its citizen information warriors, and its diplomatic corps must constantly engage the politicians and populations of the United States, Europe, and beyond.[38]

In generating this influence, the Ukrainians have also sustained their national unity in opposing the Russian invasion. So far, there has been a remarkable level of cohesion in the Ukrainian government, citizens, and a global diaspora of Ukrainian communities. This is foundational to their national mobilization of resources to resist the Russian military and to elicit global sympathy and aid.

An important part of this strategic influence campaign is the Ukrainians attempting continuous transparency about where Western aid is being sent and how it is used. Because of this, President Zelenskyy, in his address to the U.S. Congress in December 2022, included the following passage: "Your money is not charity. It's an investment in the global security and democracy that we handle in the most responsible way."[39]

3. Integrated civil and military actions. Since the beginning of the twentieth century, an expansion has occurred in the domains where humans compete and fight. The challenges of global war in the twentieth century demanded a closer integration of ground, air, and land operations. The conduct of the wars spawned by 9/11 forced many nations undertaking counterinsurgency operations to better integrate military and other government activities. As I explored in *War Transformed*, military institutions must be able to integrate their activities in all domains concurrently.[40]

This integration of civil and military activities might appear at first glance to be an unusual combination for a nation's strategy to defend itself. However, Ukraine has discovered that while military endeavors are vital in war, so too are many other activities such as civil defense and the provision of emergency services such as firefighters and electricity workers. These military and civil actions are interrelated. Therefore, the integration of civil and military aspects of Ukrainian national power has been an important component of their strategy of corrosion, as it ultimately aims to achieve national resilience while corroding that of their enemy.

The Ukrainians have evolved their approach to civil defense since the Russian invasion of 2014. The Ukrainian approach detours from the "total defense" model of nations such as Sweden and Singapore. Instead, Ukraine has adopted a model in civil defense that is focused on the "resilience of society as a whole." It has incorporated state agencies as well as volunteer organizations that have become better coordinated as the war has progressed.

An important foundation for this approach to societal resilience was Ukraine's September 2021 National Resilience Concept. The Ukrainian concept adopted the 2016 NATO "commitment to enhance resilience"[41] and added two categories: resilience against information influence operations; and financial and economic resilience.[42]

The actions of government and volunteer organizations and the Territorial Defense Force have facilitated a much closer relationship and integration of civil and military organizations in achieving national resilience. This is important, as civilians, housing, and civil infrastructure have been targeted by the Russian military forces throughout their invasion. Capabilities such as air raid shelters, emergency services, battlefield clearance, ordnance removal and disposal, and the integration of air defenses remain critical to Ukraine's defense and its national resilience.

This resilience component of its larger strategy to defend itself and defeat the Russian invasion has continued to evolve. As a report from the International Centre for Defence and Security notes, "Ukraine's experience is a perfect example to demonstrate that although war-related damage to civilian infrastructure appears—and, in fact, is—horrendous, societies may prove resilient enough to persevere without collapsing."[43] Civil defense and resilience are critical to sustaining a sovereign Ukraine, keeping the economy operating, preserving human life, and supporting the overall war effort.

Another dimension of this civil-military integration is the meshing of civil and military sensors to provide strategic and battlefield intelligence. Ukraine uses a combination of commercially available imagery; citizen-provided information; and government, military, and foreign intelligence to generate and share its knowledge of Russian forces and to undertake targeting activities. This integration of civil and military sensors, and the associated analysis, has been a significant trend in this war and has underpinned Ukraine's battlefield activities.

Ultimately, the Ukrainians must win battles to win this war. Engaging in combat is the ultimate expression of will of the Ukrainians. They understand that theirs is an existential fight. The Ukrainians must fight and recapture their territories in the eastern and southern parts of the country—including Crimea—if they are to win this war.

From the beginning of the war, the military effectiveness of the Ukrainian armed forces has confounded the Russians and been underestimated by Western governments. In the opening hours of the war, much speculation focused on how long it would take for Ukraine to be defeated or how an effective insurgency might be established and supported by European and American supporters.[44] Early in the war, Western observers also questioned the Ukrainian capacity to conduct offensive operations. This was decisively proved in Kherson and Kharkiv in 2022.

In the wake of this war, there should be much reflection about analytical methods in Western organizations, and their understanding of what might be described as the "Ukrainian Way of War."

After successfully beating Russia in the North, the Ukrainians continued to apply and evolve its strategy of corrosion in the East. They attacked Russian logistics, as well as critical enabling capabilities such as engineers, surveillance drones, and senior Russian commanders. Once again, the Ukrainians were corroding from within the physical capacity of the Russians to fight.[45]

These actions in the physical world have had an impact on the moral and intellectual components of Russian fighting power. Russian morale is corroded because of its battlefield defeats, supply challenges, and withdrawals in the face of Ukrainian pressure at Kyiv and Kharkiv. Russian human wave tactics have also had an impact. The Yevgeny Prigozhin mutiny of June 2023 will also have had a significant bearing on Russian morale in Ukraine.

Ukrainian use of social media, showing off Russian deficiencies and inviting the desertion of newly mobilized Russian troops, has at times magnified this moral corrosion. The corrosion in morale has resulted in declining battlefield discipline, with Russian desertions, battlefield refusals, and war crimes. Bad morale and discipline, if not addressed, can become pervasive in a military force under battlefield pressure.[46]

The Ukrainians also forced on the Russians a type of intellectual corrosion. Under pressure to achieve some form of victory due to previous setbacks, the Russians have at times taken tactical and operational risks with their military operations. The disastrous Russian assault crossing over the Siverskyi Donets River, where at least a brigade from the Russian army was destroyed, was an early indication of the Russian army becoming less capable of assessing the risks of significant operational or tactical decisions.

The Battle of Severodonetsk in mid-2022, and those at Bakhmut and Vuhledar in 2022–23, are additional instances of Ukraine's strategy of corrosion. While costly to Ukraine, these battles have applied defensive and delaying tactics to corrode the size of the Russian force and degrade their morale through the numbers of casualties and delays in progress. Additionally, the Ukrainian actions have corroded the Russians intellectually by forcing them into increasing desperate and unsound tactics, such as human waves and piecemeal attacks, in order to advance.[47]

In their military endeavors over the first eighteen months of the war, the Ukrainian armed forces constantly surprised the Russians with their rapid absorption of equipment, and the adaptation of battlefield tactics to use it effectively.

4. Foreign support. Since the beginning of the Russian invasion, Western political, intelligence, military, and economic support has been a crucial element of Ukraine's defense. Modern wars since the beginning of the First Industrial Revolution, rapidly consume munitions, equipment, supplies, and humans.[48] While NATO has not committed military personnel to serve in Ukraine, support from Western nations is foundational to the flow of weapons into the nation. An international coalition is also overseeing a regime of economic and diplomatic sanctions on Russia and many of its citizens.

In the lead-up to the war, the donation of weapons such as Javelin antitank missiles enabled the Ukrainian armed forces to better equip themselves in the event of a Russian invasion.[49] But long before this, European, U.S., and Canadian military trainers spent years training a Ukrainian military that was slowly but surely diverging away from its Soviet-era roots.[50] This is not yet a complete task—many vestiges of the Soviet era still remain, including an inclination to rely on the firepower of artillery, and similar doctrinal approaches to combat operations.

However, the transformation of the Ukrainian armed forces since 2014 has proved to be an important foundation in Ukraine's response to the Russian invasion. The changes made by the Ukrainians in the years leading up to the war appear to have surprised the Russians and deceived them about the capability and will of Ukraine's military.

The Russian invasion has had a major impact on Ukraine's manufacturing, mining, and agricultural industries. It has also seen Ukrainian ports, through which a majority of Ukrainians export revenues are generated, captured by the Russians. Consequently, Ukraine has needed ongoing economic assistance, both from individual nations and from institutions such as the World Bank, to sustain the government and to cover the costs of the war.[51] Economic assistance from the West must continue if Ukraine is to sustain its defense and eject the Russians from its territory.[52]

Importantly, Ukraine has received intelligence from multiple countries and their national intelligence agencies from before the invasion through to the present. Often provided in real time and consisting of some of the most sensitive collection assets owned by the United States and other countries, this assistance supports the targeting of Russian high-value assets, as well as identifying Russian units and intentions and the longer-term planning of Ukrainian military operations. It also assisted in finding and targeting Russian generals commanding forces in Ukraine.[53]

This sharing of Western intelligence has also resulted in a closer relationship between Ukrainian and Western intelligence officials. As a *New York Times* report about this arrangement notes, "The Ukrainians were closely guarding their operational plans even as American intelligence was gathering precise details on what the Kremlin was ordering and Russian commanders were planning. But as Ukraine laid its plans to strike back against the Russians, senior leaders in Kyiv decided that sharing more information with the United States would help secure more assistance."[54]

This has been an important development not just for the Ukrainians but also for other U.S. allies. The sharing of intelligence is a very sensitive issue for most nations. The arrangements developed for the sharing of American intelligence with the Ukrainians will help to inform arrangements with other allies and security partners in the future.

Western equipment and munitions have bolstered Ukrainian stocks of Soviet-era weapons and have gradually begun to replace them. While the quantities of Soviet-era equipment possessed by the Ukrainian army, navy, and air force will take many years to replace, the provision of Western equipment and weapons such as Leopard 2 main battle tanks, Bradley infantry fighting vehicles, Stryker light armored vehicles, the High Mobility Artillery Rocket System (also known as HIMARS), towed and self-propelled artillery, Stinger antiaircraft missiles and other air defense systems, uncrewed autonomous aircraft, and a myriad of engineering and support vehicles have proven crucial in the expansion and increase in military effectiveness of the Ukrainian armed forces. [55]

The provision of such an extensive range of military assistance has allowed Western nations to avoid the deployment of military forces to Ukraine, thus dodging a direct confrontation with Russia. This is in line with Ukraine's requirements and expectations. It has sufficient personnel, having mobilized nearly 700,000 personnel for the war. But it lacks the capacity to clothe, arm, and equip them all.

At the one-year mark of the war, in late February 2023, assistance of all forms to Ukraine from forty-one donors had reached 143 billion euros, according to the Kiel Institute.[56] U.S. assistance, comprising financial, humanitarian, and military aid, stood at just over US$76 billion on the one-year anniversary of the Russian invasion.[57] This assistance has been vital in Ukraine's efforts to turn back the Russian invasion through battlefield victories, air and missile defense, and other military activities. Similarly, this foreign assistance has provided critical economic assistance at a time when Ukraine's GDP has decline precipitously because of the war.

The solicitation and absorption of foreign aid is an important part of Ukraine's strategy. It has been highly effective so far in allowing Ukraine to defend itself. The costs of such assistance are high and will continue to rise as Russia continues its aggression and destruction inside Ukraine's borders. But as American strategist Anthony Cordesman has written, "Ukraine certainly emerged as a highly effective force, and one that operated with exceptional skill and courage, but outside aid was critical to sustaining its operations, giving it a decisive edge in intelligence, target, and communications, and allowing it to operate without fear it would exhaust its supplies."[58] The Ukrainian government has worked extraordinarily hard to leverage its influence and relationships with members of the international community to provide aid as well as economic, military, and moral support. These have been vital to Ukraine's survival.[59]

5. National mobilization of resources. Ukraine has conducted a national mobilization to fight a total war against Russia since February 2022. The invading Russians have used every means at their disposal, short of nuclear weapons, to main, kill, rape, and torture Ukrainian civilians and destroy military formations and Ukrainian civil infrastructure. This has required the full mobilization of Ukrainian military, civil society, influence, economy, diplomacy, and industry resources for the war effort.

On 25 February 2022, Ukrainian president Zelenskyy signed a mobilization decree. This document prohibited Ukrainian males between the ages of eighteen and sixty from leaving the country and called up military reservists and conscripts to serve in the Ukrainian armed forces. The country subsequently raised a military of one million to defend against the Russian military.[60]

Ukrainian manufacturing industry has also been mobilized for the war effort. In the wake of the Cold War, Ukraine's once-robust defense industrial capabilities withered as the Ukrainian military procured little local equipment and the nation pursued neutrality. Companies folded and many well-educated engineers were lured to jobs in other industries or other countries. In 2022, the government of Ukraine also used a wartime law to take controlling stakes in businesses that were viewed as critical to the manufacture of war matériel. These businesses included engine-maker Motor Sich, two oil producers (Ukrnafta and Ukrtatnafta), truck producer AvtoKrAZ, and Zaporizhtransformator, which makes transformers.[61]

In early 2023, this mobilization of industry was given a boost through the introduction of new rules that exempted certain employees from mobilization. This is a core challenge in any nation that seeks to expand both its military and its sources of production for a national war effort. Personnel priorities must be established to ensure that *armies can fight and factories can produce* concurrently. The 27 February 2023 Ukrainian regulation, with the impossibly long title "Resolution No. 76: On Certain Issues of Implementing the Provisions of the Law of Ukraine on Mobilisation Preparation and Mobilisation regarding the Reservation of Persons Liable for Military Service for the Period of Mobilisation and Martial Law," aims to achieve a better balance between fighting and production for the Ukrainian government.[62]

Given supply constraints from other nations, and the need to repair and refit a range of different weapons, Ukraine's defense sector is rebuilding itself as part of the overall national effort to defeat the Russian invasion. Despite these measures, the neglect of Ukrainian defense industrial capacity before the 2014 invasion and its limited growth since then mean that Ukraine has a long way to go before it can regain a level of self-sufficiency in defense production and maintenance. Mobilization of national resources including people and industry is an important supporting component for Ukraine's strategy of corrosion, but it remains an incomplete journey.

6. *Fighting a just war.* The theory of "just war" has its origins in classical Greek and Roman philosophy. Just war theory seeks to reconcile several important aspects in warfare: first, taking human life is wrong; second, sovereign nations have a right and a duty to defend their citizens and to defend justice; and third, protecting innocent human life and defending important moral values sometimes require to use force and violence on behalf of a state. These principles have been incorporated into international law.[63]

International law—through various treaties and conventions—seeks to regulate the inception and application of force as well as the conduct of war and the protection of civilians, prisoners of war, and cultural sites. This is generally referred to as the Law of War and is often used interchangeably with the terms "international humanitarian law" and "the law of armed conflict." Two important concepts fall under the law of war. The first is *jus ad bellum*, the rules that govern when a country can use force. The second is *jus in bello*, the laws that govern the actual conduct of war and the application of force.

Throughout the war, Ukraine has fought the war within the bounds of these international laws, while at the same time proclaiming through various mechanisms where the Russians have transgressed. The Russians, who have often acted in shockingly brutal ways toward civilians and Ukrainian prisoners of war as well as important cultural sites, have not gone to similar lengths to comply with international law in the conduct of their special military operation in Ukraine.

The discovery of Russian atrocities not only shocked many people around the world; it was also seen as a statement of Russian intent against Ukraine by many Ukrainian citizens and political leaders. Owen Matthews has described the impact of the Bucha visit by Zelenskyy in his book *Overreach*: "On the day Zelensky visited Bucha 'something in him changed.' . . . For Zelensky personally, as well as his entourage, Western leaders, and millions of people around the world, Russia's invasion had been revealed as an act of savagery against civilians unprecedented in Europe since Bosnia—and before that, the Second World War. From that moment on, there could be no more compromise."[64]

As Zelenskyy himself noted after his visit to Bucha in early April 2022, "We see what's at stake in this war. We see what we are defending. There are standards of the Ukrainian army—moral and professional. And it is not our army that has to adjust now. There are many other armies that should learn from our military. And there are standards of the Ukrainian people. And there are standards of the Russian occupiers. This is good and evil."[65] In this speech, Zelenskyy is differentiating Russian military conduct from that of his army, while also communicating with the Ukrainian people that the war is an existential one. Ukraine has also reinforced in its strategic influence campaign that this war is about ensuring that Russia is not able to commit similar atrocities elsewhere in Europe.

Further differentiation between the Ukrainian and Russian approaches was provided by an independent report in mid 2022. In July 2022, the Organization for Security and Cooperation in Europe released a report that investigated allegations of multiple Russian atrocities in Ukraine. The report described how "some of the most serious violations encompass targeted killing of civilians, including journalists, human rights defenders, or local mayors; unlawful detentions, abductions and enforced disappearances of the same categories of persons; largescale deportations of Ukrainian civilians to Russia; various forms of mistreatment, including torture, inflicted on detained civilians and prisoners of war."[66]

In the aggregate, the findings of the report indicated a systemic approach to the brutalization of the Ukrainian people, the destruction of their cities and cultural sites, and a callous disregard for international law and the laws of war.[67] This report about the Russian invasion provided evidence for the Ukrainian leadership, and many others in the West, about Putin's mindset and his determination to erase the existence of the Ukraine state. It also provided additional impetus for foreign assistance and the imposition of additional sanctions against Russia.

In his book *Just and Unjust Wars*, Michael Walzer writes that "for as long as men and women have talked about war, they have talked about it in terms of right and wrong."[68] The war in Ukraine has provided nations in the West with the clearest example since the end of World War II of a conflict of good versus evil. The atrocious acts of the Russian army and its Wagner mercenaries in Ukraine have provided Ukrainians with additional cohesion in resisting the Russian invader and have provided many Western leaders with political justification for their support to Ukraine.

The approach to fighting a just war is one of the fundamental asymmetries between the Ukrainian and Russian strategies in this war. Russian uses nearly every means at its disposal—legal and illegal, moral and immoral. Ukraine does not.

This projection of legitimacy is an important component of Ukraine's strategy of corrosion. Not only does moral conduct in war ensure support from Europe and the United States; it also protects both soldiers and civilians from unnecessary physical and moral harm.

7. Learning and adaptation. It is impossible for any military leader or organization to foresee every potential eventuality in war. There are so many potential scenarios that accurately predicting the outbreak and conduct of wars is very difficult. Uncertainty and ambiguity are part of war's enduring nature. Because of this, a key virtue for military organizations in war must be the ability to absorb surprise and to adapt to unexpected events.

Both sides in the Ukraine War have adapted. For the Ukrainians, who face an existential threat to their nation, the old truism "adapt or die" is very literal in its application to their military forces and their country.[69] The Russians also brought with them a legacy learning culture. But adaptation and military effectiveness are two different things. An institution may adapt but those adaptations may not actually improve its battlefield effectiveness. Such as been the case with the Russians during this war. Therefore, the Russian model of military adaptation—at least at the tactical level—appears to be inferior to the Ukrainian model. This issue was covered in a 2022 from the Royal United Services Institution, which notes that one "fratricidal issue" is "the culture of reporting within the Russian military. Those who fail are usually replaced or threatened with punishment. Far from incentivising success, this often leads to dishonest reporting in which the blame for failure is transferred onto others."[70] This is hardly conducive to effective learning at the individual, unit, or institutional levels. That said, institutional learning in war is a substantial challenge. As Aimée Fox-Godden writes in *Learning to Fight*, her book exploring British army learning in World War I, "Organisations face a series of difficult tasks: they have to simultaneously acquire and assimilate new knowledge, whilst leveraging existing knowledge. They have to try and identify good ideas over bad ones. They also have to negotiate inherent frictions, such as trust, relevance, and motivation (or lack thereof)."[71]

The Ukrainians have demonstrated a better learning culture in this war, and it is an important asymmetry between the two sides. The Ukrainian learning culture, while imperfect, includes the willingness to take risk and innovate and the capacity to rapidly absorb new technologies (such as HIMARS or HARM missiles or Western tanks and armored vehicles) and integrate them into their operations. This culture did not emerge fully formed on 24 February 2022. The Ukrainians learned from the Russian invasion in 2014, and they have learned from their military operations against Russia throughout 2022 and 2023. The Ukrainian capacity to adapt has been an important element of Ukraine's strategy of corrosion to defeat Russia.

However, the Russians have increasingly demonstrated the ability to push down adaptation from the strategic level. Examples include the systemic deployment of enhanced electronic warfare, and protective cages for Russian military vehicles. The Russians may continue to improve their systemic adaptation processes throughout the war. Ukraine will need to ensure that while it preserves its edge in "bottom-up" tactical adaptation, it does not lose the advantage in "top down" systemic adaptation to the Russians.

A UKRAINIAN THEORY OF VICTORY

Like Russia, Ukrainian strategy for this war must be guided by a theory of victory. The concept of "theory of victory" was explored in the previous chapter. As Brad

Roberts has defined the concept, a theory of victory is "a set of propositions about how and why the behavior of one belligerent in war or conflict short of war will or might affect the behavior of another belligerent in a desired manner. It is a 'continuous thread' running through strategy with an 'internal logic' and 'causal links' among ends, ways, and means."[72] What is the underlying "big idea" that is integral to the various elements of Ukraine's strategy described in the preceding pages, and how will it affect Russia's behavior in a way Ukraine desires?

The fundamental element of a Ukrainian theory of victory is that it must undermine Russia's theory of victory. Therefore, there are two crucial elements of Ukraine's theory of victory over Russia. The first is will. Explored in detail by von Clausewitz and many others, Ukrainian strategy is founded on the belief that Ukraine's national will is stronger than Russia's. It seeks to project a more determined nation that is willing to do more to retain its sovereignty than Russia is to suppress it. It is undertaking actions to corrode Russian intellectual, moral, and physical fighting power as part of this demonstration of national will.

The second critical element of Ukraine's theory of victory is endurance. This is key to undercutting Russia's concept of being able to fight a longer war than Ukraine, Europe, or the United States is willing to tolerate. Not only does this include the mobilization of all national resources to defend Ukraine, and engaging in constant combat; it also encompasses the vast array of diplomatic, economic, and informational activities to solicit, sustain, and build the industrial, military, humanitarian, political, and economic support that Ukraine requires from its foreign supporters to outfight and outlast Russia.

▬

Founded on strategic planning, force development, and military operations conducted since 1991, the Ukrainians have developed and evolved a strategy and a theory of victory for defending their nation and gaining foreign support that proved effective in the first eighteen months of the war. It has incorporated clear purpose, as well as the near total mobilization of national resources to stop and repel the invading Russian forces.

This is not to suggest that it was either perfectly formed or implemented. Doubts among some of Ukraine's senior political leadership before the war about Russian intentions had an impact on Ukraine's initial response.[73] At the same time, the ongoing transition from Soviet doctrines to NATO approaches has at times hamstrung the Ukrainian military in its training and equipping and in the leadership of combat units. Western support, an important element of Ukraine's strategy, has not always flowed in the quantities, or at the times, desired by the Ukrainian leadership.

Despite these sources of friction, Ukraine has done a very commendable job of defending its territory and people against a much larger neighbor. Its military forces have consistently surprised Western observers—and the Russians. At the same time, Ukrainian strategic influence activities have set a new high bar for the conduct of global information operations, strategic communications, and public diplomacy.

But there is one final element that may be missing from all of this.

In many of his speeches, President Zelenskyy speaks of victory. It is important that he does so, because it provides an aiming mark for the military, and a light at the end of the tunnel for the Ukrainian people. He has provided broad definitions for what this might look like, including the ten-point plan for war termination that he offered during his G20 address in 2022.

I propose that this vision of national success in the war needs better definition. The reason for this is that even if Ukraine wins this war, it must still deal with a large, defeated, and nasty Russian polity that will pose an ongoing threat to Ukraine. A Ukrainian theory of victory must incorporate both winning the war and winning the peace. This concept of what a Ukrainian theory of victory might look like is the focus of the next chapter.[74]

4

A GRANDER VIEW

A Concept of Victory for Ukraine

IN PART 3 OF HIS PLAY *Henry the Fourth*, William Shakespeare wrote, "Sound trumpets! Let our bloody colours wave. And either victory, or else a grave."[1] Victory is a central concept in our understanding of war. It is an idea with ancient origins. Aristotle called it the telos, or the final natural form, of military science. Homer, in *The Iliad*, wrote about how "victory often changes her side."[2] In *The Art of War*, Sun Tzu described victory as the main object in war: "A skilled commander seeks victory from the situation, and does not demand it from his subordinates." Baron Antoine Jomini writes in *The Art of War* that "victory may with much certainty be expected by the party taking the offensive when the general in command possesses the talent of taking his troops into action in good order and boldly attacking the enemy."[3]

It is a term that has also been used in modern conflicts.

In a 1940 speech, British prime minister Winston Churchill asked, "What is our aim? Victory, victory at all costs, victory despite all terror; victory, however long and hard the road may be; for without victory, there is no survival."[4] General Dwight Eisenhower, in his postwar book *Crusade in Europe*, noted that "a normal part of every battle is maximum exploitation of victory."[5]

In the *Cambridge Dictionary*, "victory" is defined as "an occasion when you win a game, competition, election, war, etc. or the fact that you have won."[6] Cian O'Driscoll writes in *Victory: The Triumph and Tragedy of Just War* that "it can be hard to pin down exactly what victory means in practical terms. Although we know it stands for winning, what this means in practice is anyone's guess."[7] The word "victory" generally summons images of soldiers vanquishing their enemies on the battlefield. It is characterized as something that is emphatic and final. And most often, it represents a termination of hostilities.

The concept of victory is also one that some have tried to minimize in the modern discourse about war. In 2009, U.S. president Barack Obama informed the American ABC News channel that he was "always worried about using the word 'victory,' because, you know, it invokes this notion of Emperor Hirohito coming down and signing a surrender to MacArthur."[8] The word "victory" is absent from the NATO terminology database and does not appear in the latest edition of the U.S. Department of Defense dictionary.[9] As Beatrice Heuser has written, "For most Western liberals in the early twenty-first century, victory seems of little value as a thing in itself, as the price at which it might come seems disproportionate to the gains and it does not guarantee peace."[10]

Victory is also a concept that no longer incorporates only military notions of winning and losing on the battlefield. Basil Liddell Hart, writing in the *U.S. Naval War College Review* in 1952, described how "the object in war is a better state of peace—even if only from your own point of view. Hence, it is essential to conduct war with constant regard to the peace you desire."[11] Not only does this reflect a cynicism about major wars; it also reflects a world where connectivity between battle, populations, politics, and economics is growing ever more complex.

Beatrice Heuser, in *The Evolution of Strategy*, describes how military victory does not bring lasting achievement of one's war aims.[12] And writing in a 2013 edition of the *Joint Forces Quarterly*, Heuser describes how "the most important aim in any war must be 'to make a just and durable peace.' Victory is nothing if it does not lead to such a peace, and such justice must be seen as reasonable by both sides to make it durable."[13]

Gabriella Blum has also explored the increasing difficulty in defining victory in an article called "The Fog of Victory." Blum finds that changes both in the rules of war and in the targets of warfare, away from nation-states, have led to the concept of victory becoming more complex:

> Developments—in the goals of war, the rules of war, and the targets of war—are driven by a mix of strategic, political, moral, and legal forces, and it would be impossible to point at a clear trend of influence. . . . These developments, taken together, also mean that while the military, civilian, and political dimensions of war and victory were always inextricably intertwined, they have become even more so in contemporary wars. . . . War, in other words, can no longer be reduced into a military campaign.[14]

This doesn't preclude military victory being an objective in modern war. But it does mean that a concept of victory must embrace objectives beyond military activity. Now, notions of victory must include economic, diplomatic, and societal long-term needs as well as short- and medium-term military outcomes. As such, a theory of victory should include *winning the war* as well as *winning the peace*. The remainder of this chapter will explore what this might look like in the context of Ukraine and its struggle against Russia.

▨ VICTORY FOR UKRAINE

The concept of victory is an important one for Ukraine. To win a war, which is what the Ukrainians aim to do, a nation should be guided by a model of what victory might look like. This should comprise a plausible set of principles for overcoming an adversary and establishing a durable peace.[15] There are several reasons for this.

First, after two decades of inconclusive wars in the Middle East, Western polities seek more clear-cut ways to describe or consider conflict. This can inform the rationale behind and objectives of providing the array of military, intelligence, economic, and diplomatic support that they have since February 2022.

Second, the notion of victory provides a unifying influence for the Ukrainian people. Purpose is a fundamental component victory. As Clausewitz writes, "The political object—the original motive for the war—will thus determine both the military objective to be reached and the amount of effort it requires."[16]

Although Zelenskyy has described his ten principles for war termination, war termination and victory are not the same. Victory is a larger concept that looks beyond military success to ensure that the cost of such success is balanced by the improvements in the nation's prospects and future prosperity that were underpinned by the costs of war.

What might a larger concept of a Ukrainian victory look like? I propose that there are six components: (1) defeating Russia in Ukraine, (2) obtaining security guarantees for the future of Ukraine, (3) economic aid and prosperity, (4) reconstruction, (5) social reintegration, and (6) justice.

A final and separate aspect of an enduring peace must be that Russia eschews imperial or colonial strategic culture. It will take some time before Ukraine and its partners in the West can remove the sources of conflict with Russia. Therefore, while that is in progress, the Ukrainians will need to work toward the six components of victory. The remainder of this chapter is a short exploration of these six elements.

1. Defeating Russian forces in Ukraine. Since the defeat of Russians north of Kyiv, and the successful Kharkiv and Kherson offensives of 2022, Ukraine has taken back about a quarter of the territory that the Russians seized after 24 February 2022. There is little prospect for long-term stability if Russian retains these illegally seized territories.

As Zelenskyy described in his speech to the G20 meeting in 2022, "Article 2 of the UN Charter defines everything very clearly. . . . We must restore the validity of international law—and without any compromises with the aggressor. Because the UN Charter cannot be applied partially, selectively or 'at will.'"[17]

Therefore, as it has been doing since the beginning of the war, Ukraine must continue to fight to push all Russian forces from its territory. This includes Crimea and the Donbas. The Ukrainian 2023 offensives are part of this effort.

2. *Obtaining security guarantees.* Once the Ukrainians have been able to push all Russian military forces off Ukrainian soil, they must keep them off Ukrainian territory. Russia may use a period after any defeat to simply reequip itself, refill its treasury, and then attempt something similar in the future. Therefore, Ukraine will require a strong military in the wake of the war, as well as security guarantees of future assistance should Russian attempt more military coercion or aggression. The rearming of Ukraine along NATO structures and equipment commenced before the war as part of Ukrainian government policy. It has accelerated during the war with a mass influx of European and American arms, equipment, and munitions.

After the war, NATO standardization must continue. But it must be done in a way that consolidates the types of artillery, armor, and other systems into a fleet that is more efficient and manageable for training and logistic support. This will probably require the same type of assistance the United States has provided to Israel over many decades.

But beyond Ukraine's military capacity, the matter of security relationships and guarantees must be resolved. Russia has used potential Ukrainian NATO membership as a casus belli in this war. The 2023 NATO Summit in Vilnius went some way toward resolving this issue, with broad agreement that Ukraine would join NATO but that this would wait until the end of the war. As the summit communiqué notes, "We reaffirm the commitment we made at the 2008 Summit in Bucharest that Ukraine will become a member of NATO, and today we recognise that Ukraine's path to full Euro-Atlantic integration has moved beyond the need for the Membership Action Plan. . . . We will be in a position to extend an invitation to Ukraine to join the Alliance when Allies agree, and conditions are met."[18] Regardless of this NATO commitment about Ukraine's future participation in the alliance, this is likely to remain a difficult issue to resolve and may require bilateral alliances and security arrangements as an interim solution.

3. *Economic assistance and prosperity.* Throughout the war, Ukraine has received significant economic assistance to allow it to pay salaries and keep the government solvent. The International Monetary Fund, working with the Ukrainian Ministry of Finance, estimated in April 2022 that Ukraine required approximately $5 billion per month to sustain government expenditure needs.[19] The two largest donors of financial assistance in the first year of the war were European Union institutions (around 30 billion euros) and the United States (equaling around 25 billion euros). Multiple other nations have provided assistance.[20] Such assistance is likely to be required for some time to come.[21]

Assistance from multinational institutions has proved vital in sustaining Ukraine's economy and its ability to fund the war. Among these have been the European Union's Macro-Financial Assistance (MFA) program, an organization that supports non-EU countries facing a balance of payments challenge; the European Investment Bank (EIB); the International Monetary Fund; the World Bank; the European Bank for Reconstruction and Development (EBRD); and the United Nations.[22]

Before the Russian invasion of February 2022, Ukraine was on a positive economic path. Since 2014, the Ukrainian government had introduced new laws and policies to support more rigorous banking and financial systems. The nation's debt was sustainable, and the country had a clear path to long-term economic growth.[23] As a result of massive expenditures necessitated by the war, however, Ukraine will require long-term economic support.

At the same time, there is an opportunity to address some of the systemic challenges such as corruption that have been part of Ukraine's thirty-three years of independence. As Vladyslav Davydov has noted, "First and foremost, [this] must prepare a new institutional framework. Ukraine can draw on existing successes, particularly the country's rapid and effective digitisation. This has made bureaucracy more efficient and doing business easier. Digital solutions also greatly reduce corruption, which has always been seen as a major problem."[24]

And while reforming the Ukrainian economy and funding basic government expenditures of salaries and public services will be vital, a significant aspect of Ukraine's economy postwar is likely to be the massive task of rebuilding the nation.

4. Reconstruction. The physical reconstruction of Ukraine will be a significant undertaking. In March 2023, the World Bank updated its estimates of the cost of recovery and reconstruction for Ukraine and came up with a new figure of US$411 billion. It also described the need for a commitment of public and private funds over the first decade after the war.[25]

The damage and needs assessment undertaken by the World Bank at the one-year point of the war has provided a detailed examination of reconstruction needs. Sectors such as agriculture, commerce, energy, and transport as well as public housing, education, health, and culture have all been impacted by the war and will require a period of recovery and reconstruction.[26] And while there is much physical reconstruction to be undertaken, the more important need is to provide for the reconstruction of society, communities, and the basics of life for Ukraine's citizens.

Reconstruction will be required to address whole-of-nation impacts. As part of reconstruction, action will be required to ensure that Ukrainians are able to "return to some sort of 'normal' where people can live, go to school, and go to work."[27] The Ukraine Recovery Conference, held in Lugarno in July 2022, developed an outline for Ukraine's reconstruction and development and the necessary contributions from international partners.[28] Other institutions, such as London-based Centre for Economic Policy Research and the German Marshall Fund, have also offered plans and insights for Ukrainian reconstruction.[29] Preparing for programs such as this, as components of a wider program of Ukrainian reconstruction, is an essential part of "winning the peace" for Ukraine.

5. *Social reintegration.* While President Zelenskyy has worked hard to lead and unify the Ukrainian people, war causes unavoidable schisms in society that can only be resolved after the war has ended. Hundreds of thousands of mobilized soldiers, drawn from their civilian lives and jobs, will return to civil society. Not only will they bring different experiences and skills; they are also likely to return to normal society with different expectations of government and civilian leadership. This can be difficult for a society to reconcile with the added challenge of the psychological damage that many returning veterans must deal with, often for the remainder of their lives.

A prewar study of Donbas veterans found that reintegration measures in Ukraine were insufficient. Benefits were outdated and difficult for veterans to access. The study found three key challenges that needed to be addressed: a lack of ministerial capacity and intragovernmental cooperation, inadequately addressed risk of political marginalization and radicalization, and societal divisions leading to the alienation of veterans as a social group.[30] All of these may feature in a postwar Ukraine and will require solutions.

Returning refugees must also be reintegrated into a society that has been indelibly changed by war since their departure at its beginning. Over 9 million Ukrainians became displaced as a result of the war.[31] One report by the UN Office of the High Commissioner for Refugees (UNHCR) has found that over 75 percent of Ukrainian refugees wish to return home eventually.[32] In other words, there may be millions of refugees who wish to return their homeland, which is now very different, and to establish their lives in a changed society. A prosperous postwar Ukraine will need to plan for the reintegration of returning citizens into Ukrainian society.

Finally, the Ukrainian government and broader society must decide how to deal with those who collaborated with the Russians in occupied territories. There is a long, sad history of how societies have often dealt with collaborators, including post–World War II societies such as France, the Netherlands, and Russia.

While extrajudicial killings and assaults occurred, most European nations instituted legal measures to deal with those who collaborated with the Nazi occupiers.

In Norway, over 17,000 men and women were convicted of collaboration with the Nazis and handed prison sentences, and twenty-five death sentences were carried out. Over 100,000 Dutch citizens were similarly jailed for collaboration, although many of these were given amnesties shortly after being convicted. France, whose Vichy government was a collaborator with the Nazis, also jailed or executed many of its citizens after liberation.[33]

There are historical lessons from the experiences of returning refugees, the reintegration of soldiers back into society, and the legal approaches for dealing with collaborators. True Ukrainian victory must learn from these experiences and ensure effective postwar social reintegration.

6. Justice. Russia has overseen wide-ranging and systemic war crimes and abuses of human rights since the beginning of its invasion. Cities have been razed to the ground, critical civilian infrastructure has been destroyed, and civilians have been robbed, assaulted, raped, tortured, and murdered. Children have been abducted and sent to Russia from multiple areas of occupied Ukraine. On the battlefield, there have been multiple instances of abuse toward Ukrainian prisoners of war, including beheadings and castrations.

Organizations such as the UN, Human Rights Watch, and the Commission on Security and Cooperation in Europe have undertaken detailed investigations of alleged abuses and war crimes during the Russian invasion. According to a March 2023 report by the UN-backed Independent International Commission of Inquiry on Ukraine, "the body of evidence collected shows that Russian authorities have committed a wide range of violations of international human rights law and international humanitarian law in many regions of Ukraine and in the Russian Federation. Many of these amount to war crimes and include wilful killings."[34]

Just as Nazi perpetrators of crimes were brought to justice at the end of World War II, so too must accountability be established for those responsible for such abuses in Ukraine. It is a theme President Zelenskyy constantly emphasizes in his speeches.

▓ CLASHING THEORIES OF VICTORY

Ultimately, Ukrainian success is contingent on its theory of victory proving to be more compelling, realistic, and achievable than the Russian theory of victory. Ukrainian will and endurance must triumph over Russian brutality and patience.

The Ukrainian strategy of corrosion, which embraces a whole-of-society approach to war, and the associated physical, moral, and informational combat is a strategic construct that takes account of the many changes in technology, society, and military theories since Delbrück developed with binary attrition-exhaustion model for strategy at the end of the nineteenth century.

The strategy of corrosion, however, is far from elegant and is ripe for continued innovation and theoretical developments as this war, and other wars, progress in the twenty-first century. But alongside the Ukrainian will and endurance, it does offer the best hope for Ukraine eventually securing its sovereignty, all of its territory, and its people against the bleak and cruel Russian vision for the future of Ukraine.

Victory, a construct that incorporates "winning the war and winning the peace," provides for a more pragmatic and durable approach for the government of Ukraine. It will be very difficult, in a postwar environment where Russia still poses a military and economic threat, to base a vision of victory on just the ejection of Russian forces from Ukrainian territory. Postwar prosperity, reintegration, reconstruction, and justice will all be necessary elements of a more enduring "victory" for Ukraine.

In his 1966 book, *Arms and Influence*, Thomas Schelling examined the concept of victory. He noted that "even total victory over an enemy provides at best an opportunity for unopposed violence against an enemy population. How to use that opportunity in the national interest, or in some wider interest, can be just as important as the achievement of victory itself."[35]

Unfortunately, there is likely to be some ways to go before a Ukrainian victory is achieved. But the propositions in this chapter provide one pathway for achieving a Ukrainian victory that is durable and just. Vital to this victory will be the support of the United States and NATO. Their respective strategies for supporting Ukraine are explored in the following chapter.

5

STRATEGY FOR THE WEST

American and NATO Strategy

IN 1973, the Stanford Research Institute assembled a group of prominent intellectuals who represented the main national security research centers in the United States and Europe. They had assembled to discuss a reinvigoration of the U.S.-Europe relationship in the confrontation with the Soviet Union. With the SALT II talks ongoing between the United States and the USSR, negotiations being conducted about a reduction in conventional forces, and a sense that Soviet conventional capabilities were improving, the Stanford colloquium produced a variety of recommendations.

One of the principal recommendations was the need for a new grand strategy that would guide the Americans and Europeans in their military, economic, and political contest with the Soviet Union. The book *Strategy for the West*, which presented the conference's findings, noted, "If there was clearly a consensus on the nature of the Soviet challenge and the political dimension of the Soviet military threat, there was a similar expression on the need to evolve a broad overall strategy. Such a strategy should go beyond purely military considerations and harness the military as well as the political, economic and technological resources of the West."[1] This overall grand strategy to guide unified American and European action made sense during the Cold War. Something similar is needed to ensure the most effective use of Western resources to assist Ukraine to defend itself against Russia.[2]

Anthony Cordesman was an eminent strategist and author who for many years was the Arleigh Burke Chair in Strategy at the Center for Strategic and International Studies (CSIS) in Washington, DC. The author of over fifty books that focus on strategy and modern warfare, he was a keen observer of wars from the 1991 Gulf War through to the current war in Ukraine. Cordesman published an article on the first anniversary of Russia's 2022 invasion of Ukraine in which he proposed that the West—and the United States of America—still lacked a clear grand strategy for the war a year after it had begun. He wrote, "The only time Ukraine and the West will be able to seriously claim a true victory is when, and if, the fighting ends in an acceptable peace. This means the United States and its partners need to look beyond the current battlefield. They need to determine what grand strategy they should pursue to shape the longer-term course of the war and its lasting outcome."[3] This is a relevant observation for two important reasons. First, the Russian and Ukrainian strategies for this war, as important as they are, do not exist in a vacuum. The capabilities and actions of both nations are shaped by the strategic posture of the nations that are providing support. Consequently, it is also important to understand the strategies of the key nations that are influencing the conduct and outcomes in this war. Second, in Western nations' provision of support to Ukraine, there should be an overall theme guiding that support. But as Cordesman makes clear, there is no single overall plan. And many nations contribute assistance for a variety of reasons and do so in variable quantities and speeds.

Despite the lack of an overarching grand strategy for support to Ukraine, it is possible to examine the statements and actions of individual nations, or institutions such as NATO, to divine their implicit strategies. And in doing so, it is also possible to estimate the impact of their strategies since February 2022.

The two most important supporters for Ukraine are the United States and NATO. The aim of this chapter is to explore their approaches to the war. It will provide a more holistic view of how strategy guides and affects this war beyond the two belligerents.

THE U.S. STRATEGY FOR UKRAINE

The United States, as well as many European nations, possesses a range of strategic objectives for Ukraine. For all these nations, the initial strategic objective after Russia's invasion was the defense of the UN Charter as well as the defense of a fellow democratic nation.[4] Those objectives have shifted slightly over the course of the war. In April 2022, Secretary of Defense Lloyd Austin proposed that America "wanted to see Russia weakened to the degree that it can't do the kinds of things that it has done in invading Ukraine."[5] The October 2022 U.S. National Security Strategy clarified this goal: "America is helping make Russia's war on Ukraine a failure."[6]

American interests in both Europe and the Pacific are impacted by the war in Ukraine. The United States has had a vital national interest in a stable Europe that goes back to the end of World War II. If Ukraine were to fall to Russia, it would have a significant impact on the European security architecture and NATO. Many nations in Europe would need to further increase defense spending, particularly frontline states like Poland and the Baltic nations. Europe would be less stable and would undoubtedly require even more American investment in military assistance and U.S. forces stationed on the continent.

An additional impact of Russian success in Ukraine is that it would draw U.S. attention away from the Western Pacific in countering its principal competitor, China. The 2022 U.S. National Security Strategy states that "the PRC presents America's most consequential geopolitical challenge. Although the Indo-Pacific is where its outcomes will be most acutely shaped, there are significant global dimensions to this challenge."[7] Supporting an enhanced defensive posture in Europe would have an impact on U.S. and alliance activities in the Indo-Pacific region.

Finally, many countries are watching how America responds to Russia's invasion of Ukraine. If Putin's succeeds in subjugating the Ukrainians, this might encourage President Xi Jinping and the Chinese Communist Party to adopt a more aggressive posture in the Indo-Pacific, particularly with regard to Taiwan.[8] Therefore, it is in the direct national interests of the United States for Ukraine to remain sovereign and for Russia's special military operation to fail.

What strategic approach is the United States taking to effect this outcome?

Components of U.S. Strategy for Ukraine

There are multiple strands to U.S. strategy for Ukraine. The purpose of U.S. strategy, for Russia to fail, is explicit in American policy. It is described in the *2022 National Security Strategy* and in presidential speeches given in Kyiv and Poland in February 2023.[9] As President Biden notes in his May 2022 *New York Times* op-ed about Ukraine, "America's goal is straightforward: We want to see a democratic, independent, sovereign and prosperous Ukraine with the means to deter and defend itself against further aggression."[10]

The means to achieve this are various.

First, the United States has been active in rallying a coalition of over fifty nations to provide military, economic, humanitarian, and intelligence support to Ukraine. Some of these nations, such as Britain and Canada, have been active in their support for Ukraine since the 2014 Russian invasion of Crimea. Others have provided support since the February 2022 Russian invasion. This support is now synchronized through different organizations, with military assistance coordinated at regular meetings in Ramstein, Germany, and chaired by U.S. Secretary of Defense Austin. Known as the

Ukraine Defense Contact Group, all thirty members of NATO as well as twenty-four other nations are part of this group. Their regular meetings serve to oversee donations as well as prioritize deliveries of equipment and munitions to Ukraine.

A second element of U.S. strategy for Ukraine has been military assistance. The United States has been the leading provider of military assistance to Ukraine since the beginning of the war. Between 25 February 2022 and 5 October 2023, nearly fifty different military assistance packages from America were authorized. The longer the war has continued, the more sophisticated the assistance has been. Early equipment included antitank missiles, Stinger air defense missiles, and ammunition. More recent shipments have included HIMARS long-range artillery rockets, advanced air defense systems such as the National Advanced Surface-to-Air Missile Systems (NASAMS) and Patriot long-range systems, Advanced Tactical Missile Systems (ATACMS) infantry fighting vehicles, artillery, engineering equipment, and tanks. The administration of President Biden has also authorized third-party transfers of U.S. defense matériel and equipment from several EU and NATO countries to Ukraine.[11]

A third element has been avoiding a U.S.-Russia war, as well as shaping the strategic environment to prevent Russian escalation (including nuclear weapons) and the spillover of the war into other nations in Europe. Gen. Mark Milley, former chairman of the Joint Chiefs, described how he carried briefing cards with him in the early days of the war that outline how the United States must "underwrite and enforce the rules-based international order against a country with extraordinary nuclear capability, without going to World War III." There are four strategic outcomes: "No. 1: 'Don't have a kinetic conflict between the U.S. military and NATO with Russia.' No. 2: 'Contain war inside the geographical boundaries of Ukraine.' No. 3: 'Strengthen and maintain NATO unity.' No. 4: 'Empower Ukraine and give them the means to fight.'"[12] An important aspect of this is the avoidance of any escalation that could lead to the use of nuclear weapons. This has been a difficult balancing act for the United States given the importance of nuclear weapons in Russian doctrine, even for regional conflicts.

Michael Clarke and Matthew Sussex have written that "after the collapse of the Soviet Union, nuclear weapons came to occupy an increasingly important place in Russian strategic thinking. The primary reason for this, at least initially, was defensive and linked to the degradation of Russian relative conventional capabilities during the 1990s."[13] Throughout the war, Russian strategy for Ukraine has included nuclear saber-rattling by the Russian president. In response, President Biden noted his May 2022 *New York Times* op-ed that "any use of nuclear weapons in this conflict on any scale would be completely unacceptable to us as well as the rest of the world and would entail severe consequences."[14] In September 2022, U.S. national security adviser Jake Sullivan stated that there would be catastrophic consequences for Russia if it were to use nuclear weapons.[15] And the U.S. envoy to the United Nations, speaking in Ukraine in November 2022, stated, "We have messaged to them both privately and directly that should they take such a step, they will be held accountable. . . . Should they make that mistake, they can be assured that the entire world would turn on them."[16]

Concurrently, the United States has worked to ensure that it does not provide Russia with an excuse to escalate the war beyond the borders of Ukraine. These measures have included no U.S. military personnel being permitted into Ukraine, supporting NATO's enhanced forward deployments of military personnel, and limitations on the numbers of longer-range weapons such as ATACMS missiles.[17]

A fourth element of the U.S. strategy for Ukraine is economic sanctions. The United States and other nations have implemented a range of economic sanctions against the Russian state, financial institutions, military supply chains, the Russian technology and electronics sectors, its metals and mining sector, and arms dealers supporting Russia, as well as many individuals.[18] The United States and the EU have established a task force on sanctions enforcement to suspend preferential trade treatment for Russia under World Trade Organization rules and to implement a G7 price cap on the exports of Russian oil.[19]

Related to this has been the United States' warning to other nations about their support for Russia. The Biden administration has warned China repeatedly about providing any assistance to Russia. On 9 January 2023 State Department spokesperson Ned Price stated, "We've been very clear with the PRC, including in private . . . about any costs that would befall the PRC should they decide to assist Russia in a systematic effort to evade U.S. sanctions or in the provision of security assistance that would then be used against the Ukrainian people in Ukraine."[20]

▦ ▦ Results of the U.S. Strategy

There are several indications that this U.S. strategy is having an impact. First, U.S.-supplied weapons have made a measurable battlefield difference. U.S. air defense systems are contributing to a protective shield for Ukrainian cities and, to a lesser extent, armed forces in the field.[21] HIMARS and the small number of ATACMS missiles provided to Ukraine have proven effective against deep Russian targets, although the Russian army has adapted to reduce the effectiveness of these long-range strikes. On the economic front, the Ukrainian government has been able to stay liquid and pay its employees, although the impact of sanctions against Russia has had uneven results.

Perhaps most importantly, the war has not escalated beyond the borders of Ukraine and Russia. While Ukraine has undertaken limited strikes against Russian military infrastructure, along with power and industrial targets, there has been no spillover of fighting into neighboring countries. Nor has there been any use of nuclear weapons by Russia.

One failure of U.S. strategy so far has been its pace of execution. As Royal United Service Institute analyst Jack Watling has written of slow political decision-making about the war, "While the provision of Western support to Ukraine has seen some notable successes, the slow pace of decision-making has made it more difficult to capitalize on Russian weaknesses."[22]

While U.S. military assistance has been greatly appreciated by the Ukrainians, it is often slow in arriving. The debate over providing main battle tanks took months to resolve, and this delay ensured that the Ukrainians lacked these decisive armored vehicles when the Russians were at their most vulnerable at the end of 2022. The decision to finally allow F-16 fighter aircraft for Ukraine in 2023 was likewise too slow to help the Ukrainians achieve some measure of control of the air for their 2023 offensives.

While quantity of support is vital, getting it to the right people at the right place and time is also an important consideration for the future execution of American strategy in supporting Ukraine. As President Zelenskyy noted during his 2023 Munich Security Conference address, "We need speed. Speed of our agreements. Speed of delivery to strengthen our sling. Speed of decisions to limit Russian potential. There is no alternative to speed. Because it is the speed that life depends on. Delay has always been and still is a mistake."[23]

A second criticism that has been offered of the U.S. strategy for supporting Ukraine has been that it has engaged in self-deterrence. As the decisions on provision military assistance before the war and the slow deployment of HIMARS, tanks, and F-16s have shown, key decisions have been accompanied by handwringing by American (and European) leaders. During the war, "self-deterrence" by politicians, experts, and commentators, including well-placed leaks by unnamed officials that Western support might have limits or that crossing certain hypothetical Russian "red lines" should be avoided has frustrated the Ukrainians, compromised their ability to push back Russian offensive operations, and slowed the buildup of critical Ukrainian military capabilities.[24]

While caution is always warranted in dealing with an adversary armed with nuclear weapons and led by an unpredictable authoritarian like Putin, there has at times been excessive caution in U.S. assessments about the possible Russian reactions to U.S. arms shipments to Ukraine. Decisions on weapons such as longer-range air defense systems such as the Patriot, advanced armored fighting vehicles, and fighter jets have been influenced, in part, by Putin's nuclear saber-rattling. At the same time as its decision-making is influenced by Russian nuclear capabilities, the U.S. government has been issuing quiet warnings to the Russian government about the consequences of their use in Ukraine.[25] And while Putin's nuclear threats have proved hollow and been discredited, U.S. strategy has still led to some key weapons such as the ATACMs long-range strike missile being held back from Ukraine until late into the war. This practice of self-deterrence is one that needs to be studied and addressed in the wake of the war. It is certainly being watched closely by strategists in Beijing and Tehran.

▨ NATO STRATEGY

In November 2019, French president Emmanuel Macron told *The Economist* that "what we are currently experiencing is the brain death of NATO." These comments came after then–U.S. president Donald Trump's withdrawal of U.S. military forces from northeastern Syria in October 2019 without consulting the NATO alliance.[26]

Macron was hardly the first to question the relevance of NATO in the post–Cold War era. Just a few months before the French president's comments, the International Institute for Strategic Studies identified five important challenges for the alliance as it approached its seventieth birthday. These challenges were as follows: changing European defense budgets, transition back to territorial defense in the wake of Russia's 2014 Crimea invasion, greater strategic instability, the challenge of China, and the impact of President Trump.[27]

While these challenges have not all entirely disappeared from the security landscape, the Russian invasion of Ukraine in February 2022 has fundamentally shifted the focus of the alliance. It has reinvigorated NATO by giving it new purpose: supporting the defense of Ukraine and Eastern Europe. As one commentary from the RAND Corporation noted in March 2023, "For NATO in particular, history has not ended, but has become newly relevant. . . . Security issues have again become paramount among NATO members, making the alliance far more relevant."[28]

NATO has had relations with Ukraine since it gained its independence. Shortly after achieving its independence, Ukraine joined the North Atlantic Cooperation Council, and in 1994 it also became part of the NATO Partnership for Peace program.

At Warsaw in July 2016, a Comprehensive Assistance Package for Ukraine was endorsed that aimed to enhance NATO's assistance for Ukraine. This package included measures to build capacity in Ukraine's military and national security institutions, support Ukraine's modernization of its military command and control systems, better standardize Ukrainian military logistics along NATO lines, and collaborate in areas such as cybersecurity, countering improvised explosive devices, and other scientific endeavors.[29] In the wake of the February 2022 Russian invasion, the NATO Summit of 2022 in Madrid agreed to significantly strengthen this 2016 Comprehensive Assistance Package for Ukraine.

Two documents provide the intellectual foundations for NATO's strategy for supporting Ukraine in defending itself against Russia. The first is the July 1997 Charter on a Distinctive Partnership, which remains the foundation for relations between NATO and Ukraine.[30] This charter describes the rationale for the NATO-Ukraine collaboration, including the commitments to strengthen Ukrainian democratic institutions as well as its military capacity. It also commits NATO to supporting Ukraine's sovereignty in article 14 of the charter. This passage of the charter provides both the desired outcome of the relationship as well as its purpose: "NATO Allies will continue to support Ukrainian sovereignty and independence, territorial integrity, democratic development, economic prosperity and its status as a nonnuclear weapon state, and the principle of inviolability of frontiers, as key factors of stability and security in Central and Eastern Europe and in the continent as a whole."[31] The charter formed the foundation for NATO training and equipping assistance up to the beginning of Russia's invasion in 2022. It is also the framework for expanded support to Ukraine by NATO and its members since that time.

The second important document that guides NATO strategy for Ukraine support is the *2022 NATO Strategic Concept*, endorsed at the 2022 NATO Summit in Madrid. This concept has reasserted NATO principal function, which, as the document describes, is to provide "a world where sovereignty, territorial integrity, human rights and international law are respected and where each country can choose its own path, free from aggression, coercion or subversion."[32]

With regard to Russia, the document also outlines the threat posed by the Russian Federation as well as the strategic outcome desired by NATO and its constituent members: "The Russian Federation is the most significant and direct threat to Allies' security and to peace and stability in the Euro-Atlantic area. We will continue to respond to Russian threats and hostile actions in a united and responsible way. We will significantly strengthen deterrence and defense for all Allies, enhance our resilience against Russian coercion and support our partners to counter malign interference and aggression."[33]

One of the most fundamental aspects of NATO strategy for its support of Ukraine is to avoid any escalation of the conflict that would result in direct warfare between NATO and Russia. This is implied in its strategic concept but has also been made explicit by Secretary-General Stoltenberg. In a December 2022 interview he stated that "if things go wrong, they can go horribly wrong. . . . It is also a war that can become a full-fledged war that spreads into a major war between NATO and Russia. We are working on that every day to avoid that."[34]

While the avoidance of open conflict with Russia is an important objective, it must be balanced with support for Ukraine. NATO achieves this balancing act through four key measures: military support for Ukraine, enhanced conventional deterrence, cyber defense, and nuclear deterrence.

▓ ▓ Continued Military Support for Ukraine

NATO does not directly contribute arms and munitions to Ukraine. It does, however, play an important role in coordinating much (but not all) of the support provided to Ukraine by alliance members. The regular meetings of NATO and its partners at the Ramstein military base in Germany assist in prioritizing support as well as tracking its progress from donor to recipient.

Many NATO members provide training and education for Ukrainian troops, a program that predates the 2022 Russian large-scale invasion. Since February 2022, however, NATO members have undertaken technical, recruit, leadership, staff, and collective training in a variety of countries. For example, the U.S. Army trains Ukrainian soldiers in tactics and combined-arms operations in Germany. In the United Kingdom, Operational Interflex brings together military trainers from multiple NATO countries and has trained over 30,000 Ukrainians since June 2022.[35]

Military support has included provision of equipment and munitions from existing stockpiles of NATO members. Some members have also coordinated in funding new production of equipment or munitions. Examples of this include Canadian funding for a National Advanced Surface-to-Air Missile System to be delivered by the United States, and armored vehicles from Roshel; the procurement of reserve armored vehicles from Belgian arms supplier OIP; the collaborative project between Australia and France to produce artillery ammunition for Ukraine.[36]

Despite the imperative of Ukrainian munitions consumption, losses of equipment, and the need to replenish European stockpiles, European defense manufacturing has not expanded significantly since the beginning of the war. Without the impetus of large government contracts, the European defense industrial base remains largely in its post–Cold War paradigm.[37]

▓ ▓ Enhanced Conventional Defense and Deterrence

A range of measures have been announced by NATO since February 2022 to shore up European defenses and improve its ability to provide conventional deterrence to Russian aggression (nuclear deterrence is explored separately, below). The invasion of Ukraine has provided new focus to NATO and its territorial defense responsibilities. Well before the 2022 Russian invasion, NATO had forward-deployed four multinational battle groups as part of its Enhanced Forward Presence program. These deployments grew in the wake of the 2022 Russian invasion, and by the end of 2022, the Enhanced Forward Presence had grown to eight battle groups. In addition, the Madrid NATO summit agreed on a new NATO Force Model to expand the size of NATO forces to 200,000 personnel within thirty days.[38]

The United States has played a role in this process. After February 2022, additional U.S. troops have been deployed to Europe, bringing the total there to over 100,000 troops. This has included new deployments to Poland and Romania.[39]

The enhanced conventional defense and deterrence posture has also involved the expansion of NATO membership. Both Sweden and Finland applied to join NATO in 2022. This would add another country to the alliance with a shared border with Russia (Finland) and would also expand the military capacity of the alliance. While this expansion is important to NATO and to the two applicant nations, it does in some respects also play to Russian narratives about the threat from NATO. Despite this risk, the expansion of NATO—a direct result of Russia's 2022 invasion of Ukraine—will be a net gain for NATO enhanced conventional defense and deterrence posture.

Cyber Defense

Strengthened cyber defenses are another aspect of this program for improving defense and deterrence across NATO. It is not a new program; many preexisting projects aimed at cyber defense are being undertaken by NATO alliance members as well as by NATO itself. However, the NATO summit in 2022 reinforced the importance of cybersecurity to ensure assured communications, deny Russian and Chinese interference, and assist with confronting online misinformation campaigns.[40] As the 2022 Strategic Concept notes,

> We will expedite our digital transformation, adapt the NATO Command Structure for the information age and enhance our cyber defenses, networks and infrastructure. . . . Maintaining secure use of and unfettered access to space and cyberspace are key to effective deterrence and defence. We will enhance our ability to operate effectively in space and cyberspace to prevent, detect, counter and respond to the full spectrum of threats, using all available tools.[41]

Supporting Nuclear Deterrence

NATO has supported the United States in its posture to deter the Russian use of battlefield nuclear weapons in Ukraine. The 2022 NATO Strategic Concept reinforced the NATO stance on nuclear weapons and reiterated the importance of the U.S. security guarantee on nuclear weapons as well as the importance of the independent nuclear deterrents of Britain and France. The concept noted, "Any employment of nuclear weapons against NATO would fundamentally alter the nature of a conflict. The Alliance has the capabilities and resolve to impose costs on an adversary that would be unacceptable and far outweigh the benefits that any adversary could hope to achieve."[42]

The NATO secretary-general, Jens Stoltenberg, has spoken frequently about the Russian nuclear capability and its potential for use in Ukraine. In October 2022 he warned that Russia would be "crossing a very important line" if they were to use tactical nuclear weapons against the Ukrainians.[43] He has spoken on the topic on several other occasions during press conferences and prepared speeches, and his remarks have aligned with other official statements on deterring Russian use of nuclear weapons by NATO and the U.S. Biden administration.

▨ ▨ Impact on the War So Far

There is significant overlap between the U.S. and NATO strategies for Ukraine—a natural situation, given that the United States is the principal security contributor to the alliance. This has permitted close collaboration between all members throughout the war on their security and military assistance to Ukraine.

It has not been all smooth sailing, however. The German position has often been difficult for many other alliance members to reconcile with the threat posed to Ukraine, and overall European security and prosperity, by Russia. Although, in his 27 February 2022 *Zeitenwende* speech, German chancellor Olaf Scholz spoke about a significant change in the European security situation and the need for an altered stance,[44] his nation moved frustratingly slowly in the provision of assistance to Ukraine. This manifested itself in the long, drawn-out debate over the provision of main battle tanks to Ukraine as well as other lethal military aid to Ukraine. Speaking at the Munich Security Conference, Chancellor Scholz justified his nation's approach to Ukraine support by stating that "caution must take priority over hasty decisions, unity over solo actions."[45]

While exasperating to Ukraine, and many other members of the NATO alliance, the German approach is indicative of normal alliance relationships. Not all members move or decide at the same speed. All members have different national interests and imperatives.[46] That said, in strategic matters, sometimes speed matters—an issue that President Zelenskyy has highlighted throughout the war. And moving slowly with great deliberation does not remove or slow down the threat that such deliberations are seeking to address.

▨ STRATEGIZING IN AN ECOSYSTEM OF STRATEGIES

While the two belligerents in this war may be strategizing and constantly seeking advantage against each other, the reality is that their strategies are implemented within a larger ecosystem of other external strategies. Like planets in a solar system, these other plans exert a gravitational pull on those of the belligerents, influencing both their objectives and their execution of strategic plans.

While Ukraine has a strategic objective to recapture the territory seized by Russia and ensure its long-term security and sovereignty, how it does this is impacted by American and NATO strategy. For example, Ukraine has limits on striking targets in Russia for fear of killing Russian civilians and degrading the political support for Ukraine in Europe and beyond. As it demonstrated in 2023, its drone attacks on Moscow caused no deaths but had a significant political impact.[47]

At the same time, Ukraine has restraints on its battlefield operations because of limitations on munitions and precision weapons provided by its foreign supporters. This is the result of U.S. and NATO strategy over the past three decades that has not emphasized large stockholdings of such weapons or the possession of the means to produce them quickly and at scale.

Russia too is shaped by the strategies of the Americans and NATO as well as its Chinese "no limits" security partner.[48] All of these external entities have provided implicit and explicit guidance to Russia about the impact of their potential use of nuclear weapons. Additionally, the strategies of NATO and the United States to limit escalation in the war have meant that Russia has to fight only the Ukrainians on the ground, but have also meant a surge of Western weapons.

Therefore, any strategy in peace and war is influenced by the designs and stratagems of other nations, as well as large players like multinational institutions and corporations. It is something that clever strategists must always factor into their development, implementation, and evolution of strategy.

6

A COMEDIAN AND A LONG TABLE

Strategy and Leadership

LEADERSHIP IS a fundamental human skill that has many definitions. Bernard Montgomery called it a "battle for the hearts and minds of men." There have been many other definitions offered by individuals from government, commerce, the arts, and the military both before and since Montgomery wrote those words in *The Path to Leadership* (1961).[1] Leadership also provides another lens that can be used to understand this war and the strategies used by either side.

In every human endeavor, good leadership is essential. But no human undertaking possesses such high-stakes leadership as that of a nation in wartime. People who are elected or appointed to lead and command must have the presence to convince others to do most complex and difficult things in terrible and demanding circumstances. And while they are exercising their duties, leaders must also develop the ability to trust those they lead. As Martin Van Creveld writes in *Command in War*, "Historically speaking, those have been most successful which did not turn their troops into automatons, did not attempt to control everything from the top, and allowed subordinate commanders considerable latitude has been abundantly demonstrated."[2]

In *On War*, Clausewitz described the need for able intellects to lead. He described how complex activity, if it is to be carried out with any degree of virtuosity, requires leaders with intellect and the right temperament.[3] Their intellect is necessary so that "even in the darkest hour retains some glitterings of the inner light which leads to truth." And temperament is vital—leaders need "the courage to follow this faint light wherever it may lead."[4]

Good leadership is developed through experience, study, reflection, mentoring, and the mental capacity to embrace a variety of ideas. During this journey, most leaders learn that cooperation and collaboration are integral parts of good leadership.[5]

Providing the "why," or purpose, is also a central responsibility for leaders. Purpose is more vital than the tasks to be undertaken. Leaders inspire by giving their people meaning. But the authority granted to leaders has many limitations. Consequently, leading through influence is a critical skill. Clear purpose helps, but leaders must first invest in developing the logical and emotional appeal of tasks and missions and then communicate this using various media.

And because of the mass of information available and the expansion of the number of domains in which military operations must be conducted, the character of military leadership and command has evolved over the past century. As Lawrence Freedman notes in *Command*, "The challenges of command have moved beyond collecting information, organizing logistics, and planning and then executing campaigns, to synchronizing many disparate activities—while under pressure to make quick decisions and keep up with the pace of battle."[6]

This has been the case during the war in Ukraine.

The aim of this chapter is to explore the strategic leadership approaches of Zelenskyy and Putin in this war. Very different men by background and temperament, they have provided leadership of varying quality to their nations since February 2022.

Led by a young and charismatic former comedian from a small town in southern Ukraine, at least until the early 2024 civil-military crisis the Ukrainian government has so far demonstrated effective unity between the civilian and military arms of government. As a democracy, the primacy of civilians has been maintained in Ukraine throughout the war. Russia provides a contrasting model, with its authoritarian—almost monarchical—system, but there are also insights that can be drawn from the strategic leadership of Putin.

Thus, they have different approaches to the exercise of strategic leadership in war. In order to contrast the strategic leadership approaches of Putin and Zelenskyy, I have chosen five key elements that are important in contemporary leaders with which to assess them. These elements—the use of language, application of the media, battlefield visits, authenticity, and leading a leadership team—will be used to highlight the leadership that each man has applied to his provision of strategic purpose and direction of the war since February 2022.

ZELENSKYY

The three years leading up to the Russian invasion of February 2022 were hardly auspicious ones for the president of Ukraine. Elected with nearly three-quarters of the popular vote in April 2019, Volodymyr Zelenskyy was inaugurated on 20 May 2019.[7] His inaugural speech, which received a tepid reception in the Ukrainian Parliament,[8] nonetheless provides insights into Zelenskyy's style of communication:

> We have chosen a path to Europe, but Europe is not somewhere out there. Europe is here. And after it appears here, it will be everywhere, all over Ukraine. This is our common dream. But we also share a common pain. Each of us has died in the Donbas. . . . However, our first task is ceasefire in the Donbas. . . . I can assure you that I'm ready to pay any price to stop the deaths of our heroes. I'm definitely not afraid to make difficult decisions and I'm ready to lose my fame, my ratings, and if need be—without any hesitation, my position to bring peace, as long as we do not give up our territories.[9]

Zelenskyy had won the presidency by campaigning as a reformer. He primarily used social media and standup comedy routines instead of traditional political rallies. Despite his use of social media—a harbinger of Ukrainian strategic communications after the Russian invasion—in getting elected, it was of little assistance to Zelenskyy as he began his presidential term. His first major proposal, to amend the Ukrainian electoral system from a plurality voting system to proportional representation, was rejected by the Ukrainian Parliament. Several subsequent presidential proposals were also rejected by the Parliament.

Zelenskyy was also criticized for his bill that would create a public registry of Ukrainian oligarchs. Designed to curb the power of the oligarchs, Zelenskyy's critics claimed that it would remove power from Ukrainian oligarchs but centralize more power in the president.[10] Through all this, Zelenskyy's popularity steadily declined. By March 2021, his approval rating stood at just 48 percent.[11] By October 2021, this rating had dropped to just over 24 percent.[12] In a November 2021 article, Mykhailo Minakov described Zelenskyy's position at the midpoint of his five-year presidency as evolving "from a radical alternative to political cynicism he has turned into a 'just like all the others' politician whose popular support is waning."[13]

Mastery of Language

From the beginning of Russia's invasion of Ukraine, Zelenskyy has had to harness the full panoply of Ukrainian resources. Whether in mobilizing the Ukrainian people for military or civil defense purposes, conducting cyber operations, or engaging in a global influence campaign, Zelenskyy has been the leader that Ukrainians—and many others outside Ukraine—have come to look to.

Of all the means that Zelenskyy has applied to lead and support his military to push back the Russian assault on Ukraine, the most powerful has been his use of the written and spoken word. He has leveraged language to provide purpose for his soldiers and his government, to inspire Ukrainians, and to share the tragedy being experienced by his citizens with people around the world.

Zelenskyy's words were vital in the first twenty-four hours of the war.

On that first, shocking morning, as Russian forces poured over their shared border into Ukraine, Zelenskyy worked the phones. He spoke to President Biden, British prime minister Boris Johnson, and other leaders to request assistance. Shortly afterward, he sat down and self-recorded a video for the people of Ukraine. In the video, he said, "Today I ask you, each one of you, to remain calm. If it is possible, please stay home. We are working. The army is working. The entire security and defense sector of Ukraine is working. . . . We are ready for anything. We will defeat anyone. Glory to Ukraine!"[14]

The following day, the Associated Press reported that a U.S. intelligence officer had responded to U.S. offers of evacuation with the following: "The fight is here; I need ammunition, not a ride." While there is conjecture over whether Zelenskyy actually did utter these words, their impact was tremendous.[15] His words told the Ukrainian people that their government would be staying alongside them and would share their fate, whatever it was, as a multitude of Russian tanks bore down on Kyiv. And importantly, his words told political leaders and citizens in the West that the Ukrainians would fight on. This act of helping themselves before asking for assistance from others was critical in the decision-making of many Western leaders in their assistance for Ukraine in the coming days.

Zelenskyy's leadership on that day reinforced the two other elements that have been essential components of the strategic leadership of Zelenskyy: that the Ukrainian military would fight on; and that while it was prepared to fight alone, it would also seek outside assistance.

Zelenskyy has demonstrated, and continued to hone, his skill in this area. Few leaders have the capacity to consistently master the right language for a given moment, while also ensuring the right audiences are engaged, or inspired, by the key messages of a speech. During the war, Zelenskyy has often been compared with Britain's prime minister in World War II, Sir Winston Churchill. In a speech two decades after that war ended, President John F. Kennedy said of Churchill that "in the dark days and darker nights when Britain stood alone—and most men save Englishmen despaired of England's life—he mobilized the English language and sent it into battle. The incandescent quality of his words illuminated the courage of his countrymen."[16]

Since February 2022, Zelenskyy has mobilized language and sent it into battle. And not only has he mobilized language; his timing in the use of key speeches has also been vital. A little over a day after the Russian invasion commenced, he recorded a short speech, dressed in army green, outside a government building. He stated simply, "We are all here. Our soldiers are here. Civil society is here. We defend our independence. And this is how it will always be from now on."[17]

Zelenskyy used his speech to the U.S. Congress in late 2022 to again describe this as a war that all democracies have an interest in. He spoke about how Ukraine's fight is something that connects all free nations. As people in the United States—and beyond—were thinking about their forthcoming Christmas holidays, Zelenskyy asked that they keep Ukraine in their thoughts. And, as he has in many speeches, he tailored his message to the audience. He told his American listeners,

> In two days we will celebrate Christmas. Maybe candlelit. Not because it's more romantic, no, but because there will not be, there will be no electricity. Millions won't have neither heating nor running water. All of these will be the result of Russian missile and drone attacks on our energy infrastructure. . . . Standing here today, I recall the words of the president Franklin Delano Roosevelt, which are I think so good for this moment. "The American people, in their righteous might, will win through to absolute victory." The Ukrainian people will win, too, absolutely.[18]

His speech to Congress was just one of many examples of Zelenskyy's use of language and the opportunity to speak to large national or global audiences to influence opinion and gain support for his country. Whether he is speaking at the front lines with his soldiers, or in the legislature of the most powerful democracies, Zelenskyy wants his own people, his enemies, and the rest of world to believe that Ukraine can and will win this war. His speeches, and all of his strategic communications activities, aim to provide purpose. This where Zelenskyy's leadership and talent for strategic influence intersect. He is able to construct messages that describe the importance of the war in Ukraine for his citizens, his soldiers, and politicians in foreign countries. Zelenskyy adeptly employs the written and spoken word to explain why defending democracy is important, and why the price of doing so is much lower than that of not doing so.

The words and their timing electrified many in the West and resulted in additional commitments of support for Ukraine. Such is the influence demonstrated by only the finest wartime statesman. Speeches such as this have been a central part of Zelenskyy's strategic leadership in this war.

▦ ▦ Use of Media

The war in Ukraine has seen a massive expansion in the use of social media by the belligerents as well as those reporting on the war. No longer just a way to rapidly report newsworthy events, social media including Twitter and Telegram have been purloined by governments, corporate entities, humanitarian institutions, crowdfunders, and individuals to map the progress of the war, deliver rapid battle damage assessment for strikes against key targets, provide assessments about the war's progress, examine many different aspects of military institutions, and inspire foreign observers.

Zelenskyy and a supporting cast of clever strategic communications staff have overseen perhaps the most effective example of modern strategic communications and influence operations by a democratic country. The Ukrainians have mastered operational security while also showing off the many achievements of its soldiers.

The aggregated efforts of Ukrainian online activities, and their investment in a robust telecommunications infrastructure, has resulted in stories from the war being available globally and in near real time. It has allowed the world to see the abysmal behavior of Russian soldiers in places like Bucha, Lyman, and Kherson. It has permitted journalists to communicate with a massive global audience and has given analysts a way to share observations widely.

At the center of this social media maelstrom has been Zelenskyy. His daily speeches, images of visits, and talks to multilateral institutions, universities, and other groups, available in Ukrainian and English, are available for all in almost real time. It is an unprecedented capability for a strategic leader in wartime, and Zelenskyy, with his background in theater and performing, has been able to exploit it to the immense benefit of his nation.

Perhaps his approach is best explained by the words of Zelenskyy himself. In a prerecorded message for the 2022 Grammy Awards just six weeks after the Russian invasion, Zelenskyy exhorted his audience, "Fill the silence. Tell our story. Tell the truth about this war on your social networks, on TV. Support us in any way you can. Any—but not silence."[19]

■ ■ Battlefield Visits

Almost since the beginning of the war, Zelenskyy has regularly traveled around his country to visit his people. Perhaps the most important of these are his visits to the troops in the field. The battlefield visits conducted by Zelenskyy have many purposes. They allow him to gain a sense of the morale and capability of his military. While as president he would receive and read hundreds of reports each day, none of them are a substitute for walking the ground with leaders and soldiers who are fighting on the front line. Such visits also allow the president to engage with soldiers in the field, inspire them, recognize their sacrifice, and reiterate the purpose of their exertions.

This direct contact is vital for a leader during wartime. It allows a president or prime minister to ask questions, an important function of a national political leader in their interaction with military commanders. Not only does it provide ground truth, but even the best staff for a senior leader cannot anticipate all the questions their leaders might want answered. Eliot Cohen writes in *Supreme Command* that such questions were essential to Winston Churchill's leadership: "His art of leadership included a skill at questioning and challenging professional subordinates that few others have mastered."[20]

But these visits also serve another purpose for civilian leaders in wartime: to see the situation on the ground as it truly is. Eliot Cohen described this as follows: "In war to see things as they are, and not as one would like them to be, to persevere despite disappointments, to know of numerous opportunities lost and of perils still ahead, to lead knowing that one's subordinates and colleagues are in some case inadequate, in others hostile, is a courage of a rarer kind that a willingness to expose oneself to the unlucky bullet or shell."[21] It is this form of courage and leadership that Zelenskyy has demonstrated throughout the war. In doing so, he also demonstrates that he has trust in the Ukrainian armed forces by placing his life in the hands of the military. This is an important and strategic trust-building exercise between civilian politicians and the military leaders that are subordinate to them. Zelenskyy has set the strategic direction for his nation while allowing the high command to get on with the implementation of national defense. But battlefield visits, and their attendant briefings, provide a vital type of dynamic feedback in the Ukrainian civil-military relationship.

Authenticity

One of the most important principles of leadership, contained in almost every leadership publication one might choose, is authenticity. As Kirstin Ferguson has written in her book on leadership, "Having the humility and courage to be vulnerable means you can lead with greater authenticity."[22] And as the leadership doctrine for the Australian Defence Force notes, "Your character is who you really are; your reputation is only what others think you are. A leader of character in peace becomes a leader of courage in war. You cannot be selfish in peace and yet be unselfish in war. War magnifies the virtues of some, but it exposes the character of all."[23]

Part of Zelenskyy's authenticity is his sense of austerity that arose at the beginning of the war. Eschewing suits, he began to dress in simple military-like clothes, normally with a black or green jersey. This simplicity has become one of Zelenskyy's trademarks. Clothing choices by national leaders have long been regarded as another form of communication. For Zelenskyy, his choice to dress in T-shirts, hoodies, and simple sweaters and pants evokes a sense that he is sharing the pain of Ukraine as an equal with his citizens.

He also demonstrates an authentic form of leadership that is replete with both strength and empathy. During the frequent battlefield visits, and opportunities where he presents medals to soldiers or their families, Zelenskyy is clearly moved by such ceremonies and the interaction with his people. He frequently gets emotional when speaking, including when talking about his family at a press event on the first anniversary of the start of the war.[24]

Perhaps the defining moment of Zelenskyy's authenticity came during his visit to witness firsthand the appalling horrors inflicted on his citizens by Russian soldiers in April 2022. Appearing distressed and almost overwhelmed, he spoke to a gaggle of reporters in one of the main streets of Bucha, a town north of Kyiv, telling them, "It is difficult to talk. It is very difficult to negotiate when you see what they did here. Every day we find people in barrels, cellars and where else, some strangled, some clearly tortured. . . . We will not allow any pauses in finding these people."[25] This was Zelenskyy showing himself at his most vulnerable. Not only was he demonstrating empathy for the people of Ukraine; he was also steeling himself for the road ahead. Having viewed the carnage caused by the Russians in Bucha, he understood that there could be no backward steps in this war against Russia. It clearly had a profound impact on Zelenskyy. Owen Matthews writes, "On the day Zelenskyy visited Bucha 'something in him changed,' said the aide. And the war changed too. For Zelenskyy personally, as well as his entourage, Western leaders and millions of people around the world, Russia's invasion had been revealed as an act of savagery against civilians. . . . From that moment on, there could be no more compromise."[26]

Collaborative Leadership

One of the most important books on modern leadership is not one that was written solely about military leadership. To be sure, many fine works on the great captains of history have been published in this century and those preceding it. The ancient writings of Julius Caesar or Marcus Aurelius, or more recent works that explore leadership in the post-9/11 wars in Iraq and Afghanistan, are all valuable. The most valuable leadership book was also not one of the thousands of leadership books written by various captains of industry with insights on modern commerce and globalization.

Instead, a book exploring the interaction of statemen and military leaders in wartime, called *Supreme Command*, delivers the most relevant insights for modern wars. Exploring the function of civilian leaders in democracies, author Eliot Cohen offers the view that "politicians dealing with generals in wartime face exceptional difficulties. The stakes are so high, the gaps in mutual understanding so large, the differences in personality and background so stark, that the challenges exceed anything found in the civilian sector."[27]

A central theme of *Supreme Command* is that strategic leadership during war is not just a political or military endeavor. It is an integrated, interactive civil-military dialogue and a relationship that evolves as the conflict progresses. As Cohen describes it, "What occurred between president or prime minister and general was an unequal dialog—a dialog, in that both sides expressed their views bluntly, indeed, sometimes offensively, and not once but repeatedly—and unequal, in that the final authority of the civilian leader was unambiguous and unquestioned."[28] It is an interaction where the senior in the relationship, the civilian, is also providing a continuous audit of military judgment.[29] This form of strategic civil-military interaction has played out in both the Ukrainian and Russian governments before and during the war.

Around the time that Zelenskyy was struggling with a low approval rating in late 2021, he was engaged in a campaign to convince lawyer Oleksii Reznikov to become his minister of defense. A military veteran (he served in the Soviet Air Force in the 1980s) and lawyer, by late 2021 Reznikov was serving as the deputy prime minister, Minister for Reintegration of the Temporarily Occupied Territories of Ukraine. After initially refusing the president's offer of the Ministry of Defense, Reznikov eventually agreed to shift into this appointment and became the Ukrainian defense minister on 3 November 2021.[30]

Several months before the appointment of Reznikov, one final appointment by the president took place that would have a significant impact on the defense of Ukraine from February 2022. As part of the government's efforts to reform the Ukrainian military in the wake of its poor performance in 2014, the government separated operational from policy positions, like how many Western military organizations are structured. Concurrently, Ukraine wanted to shift from its Soviet military legacy and become more aligned with NATO structures and doctrine.[31]

To lead this reform from the military perspective, Zelenskyy chose the forty-eight-year-old Valerii Zaluzhnyi. A relatively junior general in the Ukrainian armed forces, Zaluzhnyi had begun life on a military garrison in Novohrad-Volyns'kyi, a town in the Zhytomyr region in northern Ukraine. Joining the armed forces as the old Soviet Union crumbled, throughout his career Zaluzhnyi showed an interest in Western military institutions. As a 2022 *Time* profile of Zaluzhnyi notes, "For a master's thesis, Zaluzhnyi analyzed U.S. military structure. Seeing how Ukrainian forces were still weighed down by the Soviet model that relied on rigid, top-heavy decision-making, he began to implement changes to mirror the forces of U.S. and NATO partners."[32] In July 2021, Zaluzhnyi was appointed as the commander in chief of the Ukrainian armed forces. The new defense minister assumed his appointment several months later. By the end of 2021, the three key elements of Ukraine's strategic leadership in this war—Zelenskyy, Reznikov, and Zaluzhnyi—were in place.

While President Zelenskyy has received acclaim for his leadership since the Russian invasion, it was this trinity of people who were responsible for the defense of Ukraine. A relatively new leadership team when the war began in February 2022, they oversaw the development and implementation of the Ukrainian strategy of corrosion examined in chapter 3. Each appointment has distinct roles in the Ukrainian polity. But their real power and impact resulted from their collaboration, at least until Reznikov and Zaluzhnyi were replaced in the war's second year.[33]

PUTIN

Unlike Zelenskyy, by February 2022 Vladimir Putin had been holding the reins of power in Russia for over two decades. Putin assumed his first appointment as prime minister in 1999, then served two terms as president from 2000 to 2008; and after a term as prime minister until 2012, he returned to the presidency an office that he has occupied since. There is a significant asymmetry in the levels of experience in government between the two men.

Mastery of Language

Putin too uses speeches and language as part of his approach to strategic leadership. He hardly projects the calm, charming, and articulate leader that Zelenskyy has since February 2022. But that does not mean he eschews this element of leadership—far from it. Putin has given multiple speeches before and during the war to justify his special military operations, and to laud the achievements of his soldiers.

Perhaps two interesting examples are his 9 May "Victory Day" speeches given in 2022 and 2023, speeches designed primarily for domestic audiences. In both, Putin directly linked the wartime sacrifices of the Soviet Union to contemporary operations in Ukraine. He told the soldiers assembled in their parade uniforms in Red Square in 2022, "You are fighting for the homeland, for its future, for no one to forget the lessons of World War II."[34] In both years Putin described how external forces pose an existential threat to the modern Russian state, as with the Soviet Union in World War II. More and more he identifies this threat as NATO, apparently in an effort to justify why the special military operation is taking so long. And unlike in his 2022 speech, in 2023 Putin used the term "war" to describe how Russia had been forced into the conflict by the West.[35]

In these speeches, and many others, Putin provided an insight into his worldview. It is one where the threat from fascists and Nazis was not extinguished on that first Victory Day in 1945. And Putin's perspective is that Russia faces an existential threat from the forces of NATO and the West. Unfortunately for Putin and the Russian people, his worldview and the war spawned by such views in Ukraine have done nothing to make his country more secure or more prosperous. His speeches have reinforced the words of Ukrainian president Zelenskyy in his Victory Day speech in 2022: "This is not a war of two armies. This is a war of two worldviews."

Putin's words and deeds have united Europe and many other nations to more vigorously oppose the overt and aggressive ambitions of authoritarians. Therefore, unlike with Zelenskyy, Putin's words and speeches may have only weakened the strategic position of Russia since 2022.

Use of Media

Putin, unlike Zelenskyy, often appears uncomfortable with modern media. He may appear on state TV and in videos that are transmitted over social media networks, but these are productions worthy of a more dreary and unimaginative age. He does not tweet personally; he prefers to use the various elements of his government that control Russian media to control the flow of information inside Russia and disseminate Russian narratives beyond its borders.

That doesn't mean he is uninterested in news or the media. Indeed, as a 2015 story by Jill Dougherty puts it, Putin is "a man at the center of an ever-churning machine processing vast amounts of news and data at his command." He views daily summaries of all forms of news media—foreign and domestic. And he has a distinctly different view of the media than that held by Zelenskyy and many others in the West.

At a 2013 news conference, he informed those present that "there should be patriotically minded people at the head of state information resources . . . people who uphold the interests of the Russian Federation. These are state resources. That is the way it is going to be."[36] He has become increasingly oppressive in the decade since. As Robyn Dixon explained in a 2022 *Washington Post* article, "He had worked to reverse the raucous freedoms of the 1990s and rebuild Russia in his vision of a great power. That meant tightening the screws, year by year, on the voices that might question his goals or his methods for achieving them."[37]

This trend has become even more severe since the beginning of the special military operation in Ukraine. In March 2022 he signed a law reasserting government control over major media corporations in Russia. The law incorporated passages that criminalize any reporting that contradicts the Russian government's version of events.[38]

Battlefield Visits

Putin has yet to conduct a frontline visit to his troops in the field, although he did undertake a short, evening visit to the ruined, Russian-occupied city of Mariupol in April 2023.[39] His apparent reluctance to visit frontline soldiers might be because of the threat from the Ukrainians. But it is possible that Putin could be under just as great a threat from his own soldiers, who have been poorly trained, equipped, and led during the war.

▓ ▓ Authenticity

Whereas Zelenskyy has demonstrated austerity and empathy during the war, Putin has shown neither. During a large war rally in March 2022, Putin wore an expensive Italian puffer jacket that cost roughly twenty-five times the average annual Russian's salary. These clothing choices were designed not only to solidify his status as a strong leader but also to combat information operations portraying Russia as a poor country. Regardless of the intentions surrounding Putin's fashion choices, they do send a message about how separate—and distanced—he is from the Russian people.[40]

▓ ▓ Collaborative Leadership

Putin, like Zelenskyy, has surrounded himself with a small team. In contrast to Zelenskyy, however, one might have to stretch the definition of "leadership team" to call it that. Putin has maintained a small coterie of advisers for many years. Among these are his defense minister, Sergei Shoigu, and Chief of the General Staff of the Russian armed forces, Valery Gerasimov.

But the Russian military of 2022 and 2023 was, like its Soviet ancestor, totally subordinated to the political leadership. This is different from the civil-military relationships that exist in democracies. At the start of the Russian invasion, all the key Russian military personnel had been in their appointments for many years, and all owed their positions, power, and wealth personally to Putin. As Lawrence Freedman has written, "They would not have been inclined to offer unwelcome advice, even if it had been sought. The incentives to offer only welcome advice permeated the command structure."[41]

And this culture of centralized command, not asking questions, and not offering alternative views flows down from the top. As Peter Mansoor and Williamson Murray write in *The Culture of Military Organisations*, "Militaries reflect the culture of the societies that create them."[42] Russian military culture, particularly that on display during their invasion and ongoing occupation of Ukraine, very much reflects Putin's centralized leadership philosophy.

Putin has steadily concentrated decision-making power in his own hands. As Catherine Belton has described in *Putin's People*, "Putin, by steadfastly eliminating all political rivals and concentrating power in his own hands, had boxed himself in to such a degree that there was almost no way out for him."[43] Likewise, Andrei Kolesnikov has written that "as with the Soviet Union under Stalin, one gets the impression that Russia today has no alternative to Putin." And when asked in late 2022 if he regretted anything about the special military operation in Ukraine, Putin acknowledged that the war was his own personal project, stating, "My actions were the right ones at the right time."[44]

A public demonstration of this concentration of power was the Russian Security Council meeting that was staged on television on 21 February 2022. Unlike the one that took place the previous year, when COVID-19 had prevented in person meetings, this one was held in person. While ostensibly it was a session to show the president of Russia receiving wise counsel on the situation in Ukraine from his closest advisers on national security, the reality was somewhat different. Mark Galeotti has described it thus: "In practice, it was an exercise in symbolic power and collective incrimination. One by one, they were expected to parrot Putin's own views and support his policies. No divergence from the script was acceptable . . . and the tsar needed not guidance from his underlings but their unflinching obedience."[45] This is vastly different from the approach Zelenskyy has taken during the war. For Zelenskyy, leaders like Reznikov, Umerov, Zaluzhnyi, and Syrskyi are (or have been) valuable advisers who inform (and at times privately challenge) Zelenskyy's decisions. They can also be trusted to execute their duties and "get on with the job" without constant reference back to their president.

Nothing could be further from this model than that in contemporary Russia. Putin is the key decision-maker, and all power of the state resides in him. To quote Mark Galeotti again, "Others in Russia are just extensions of Putin's will. Wherever his eye is focussed he is very powerful. Where it is not, other things happen."[46] And while the Prigozhin mutiny of June 2023 is likely to have temporarily weakened Putin's position, it is difficult to see a successor emerging in the short term.

Thus, the concentration of military and political power in a single individual guarantees neither timely decisions nor better ones. Lawrence Freedman explores this theme in *Command: The Politics of Command from Korea to Ukraine* (2002). In comparing authoritarian and democratic decision-making about war, Freedman finds that in democracies, "the advantage lies in their ability to recognize mistakes, learn, and adapt. Closed systems, in which subordinates dare not ask awkward questions, and in which independent initiative risk punishment, will suffer operationally."[47]

Where Zelenskyy appears accessible and authentic, Putin (at least from a Western perspective) appears closed off and cold. Putin, the older man who frequently uses historical narratives to justify his actions in the present, is contrasted with a younger and more vibrant Ukrainian leader who focuses on creating a better future through action in the here and now. Whereas Zelenskyy appears to work collaboratively with his national security team, Putin is almost tsar-like in his focus and inability to tolerate dissent.

Individual qualities have an impact on leadership styles. And leadership styles have an impact on how a nation develops and implements strategy. Strategy does not just "happen," nor is it possible to allow strategies free to be implemented without discipline or oversight. Strategy must be led, and Putin and Zelenskyy have demonstrated very different approaches to strategic leadership in this war. As historian Margaret MacMillan has written,

> In a great crisis, the eve of a war, it matters who has the final authority to say stop or go. It also matters who is leading the country that is under attack and how its leader chooses to respond. As modern history has amply demonstrated, the greatest conflicts, and their outcomes, have often been shaped as much by personal leadership as by objective factors such as resources or military strength.[48]

Both Zelenskyy and Putin understand the necessity to influence contemporary media. Both seek to use it to shape the views of their own people and those beyond their borders as part of their larger strategies for this war. But these two men, products of very different eras and systems, apply vastly different methods.

In his book *No Time for Spectators*, former chairman of the U.S. Joint Chiefs of Staff Martin Dempsey notes that "we often have the opportunity to make small impacts on people's lives, and every once in a while, if we are really lucky, we might have an opportunity to make a big impact."[49] Volodymyr Zelenskyy, former comedian and now wartime leader of a nation in peril, has provided the leadership that has made "a big impact" on his own people and many others beyond the borders of Ukraine since February 2022. He has an authority, in domestic and international affairs, that he has earned from the multitude of tough decisions he has faced and addressed since the 2022 Russian invasion.[50] His strategic leadership, with the support of his defense ministers and commander in chief, is likely to be studied for decades to come in a way similar to how historians explore the approaches of Lincoln and Churchill. And historians will probably study the leadership of Russia's Vladimir Putin for very different reasons.

7

LESSONS FROM UKRAINE

Strategy and Future War

RICHARD RUMELT, an American academic and a professor emeritus at the University of California, wrote a book called *Good Strategy, Bad Strategy: The Difference and Why It Matters* (2011).[1] It is an examination of the contemporary application of strategy, primarily in its application to business. Rumelt writes that a strategy is actually a hypothesis: "A new strategy is, in the language of science, a hypothesis, and its implementation is an experiment. As results appear, good leaders learn more about what does and doesn't work and adjust their strategies accordingly."[2]

As the preceding chapters demonstrate, the Russians, Ukrainians, the Americans, and the NATO alliance have all developed hypotheses they hoped would achieve strategic objectives but could not conclusively prove would actually work beforehand. These nations have learned from their successes and failures and adapted their strategy as the war has progressed.

The observations contained in this chapter are evolutions of existing knowledge. Wars are the aggregation of tactics, technologies, ideas, and strategies from previous conflicts. While there are some new technologies at play, including masses of autonomous systems, meshed civil-military sensor networks, and artificial intelligence, there are more continuities than changes apparent in this war. Therefore, observing this war against the context of previous conflicts is important. Sir

Michael Howard has described the necessity of context in "The Use and Abuse of Military History":

> Wars are . . . conflicts of societies, and they can be fully understood only if one understands the nature of the society fighting them. The roots of victory and defeat often have to be sought far from the battlefield, in political, social, and economic factors which explain why armies are constituted as they are, and why their leaders conduct them in the way they do. . . . Without some such knowledge of the broader background to military operations one is likely to reach totally erroneous conclusions about their nature, and the reasons for their failure and success.[3]

In presenting observations about strategy from the war in Ukraine, a degree of humility is necessary. As the war continues, many aspects of strategic decision-making and the interactions between belligerents and allies remain invisible to most observers. Many classified documents remain to be revealed. Nonetheless, there remains a responsibility for institutions and individuals in leadership positions to learn from such observations in the short term. Strategy is an undertaking that is about generating advantage over a competitor. Every bit of knowledge, even if incomplete, is valuable. It is therefore incumbent on us to learn what we can now if it enables generating military advantage in the future.

I propose that there are seven key observations on strategy from the war so far, and the following sections discuss each in turn.

- Strategy matters.
- Strategic assumptions drive success and failure.
- Leadership and will are essential.
- Strategy and influence are indivisible.
- Integration is vital.
- National resilience underpins national strategy.
- Strategy must constantly adapt.

STRATEGY MATTERS

As the Russians have rediscovered in Ukraine, getting strategy (and its underpinning assumptions) right is critical to effective military operations. The price of strategic incompetence is military organizations being used for unclear or unachievable political objectives, poorly resourced or out of balance in their capabilities, badly led, or a combination of all four. Ultimately, bad strategy is punished on the battlefield, as the Russians have experienced on multiple occasions in this war. And if there are enough of these battlefield defeats, they can eventually lead to national humiliation, disgrace, or defeat.

In the case of Russia, the opportunistic and narrow approach to strategy taken by Putin has led to a string of battlefield defeats, economic sanctions, and the humiliation of a nation that considered itself a superpower. It has also led to a reinvigoration of the NATO alliance. Putin appears to be a good opportunist but a poor strategic thinker.

Effective strategic thinking is more important than tactical excellence. Alan Millett and Williamson Murray have noted that "it is more important to make correct decisions at the political and strategic level than it is at the operational or tactical level. Mistakes in operations and tactics can be corrected, but strategic mistakes live forever."[4] For this reason, strategic effectiveness—getting the political outcomes and supporting strategy right—is of profound importance to twenty-first-century nations and their military institutions. Russia's special military operation debacle in Ukraine is an important case study of suboptimal thinking, planning, execution, and evolution of strategy in the twenty-first century.

Strategy (as a product) and strategic thinking (as a process) go hand in hand. The ability to produce good strategy is founded on nurturing the people and institutions that are able to engage in strategic thinking and then turn that into practical and achievable plans. These two approaches are often confused as being one and the same, but they are not. Strategic *planning* is an endeavor conducted within given constraints. It applies existing strategic direction to assist in applying resources, people, and institutions to realize a desired direction. It largely deals with addressing variations in the present rather than reimagining the future.[5]

On the other hand, strategic *thinking* challenges the parameters used for strategic planning. As Loizos Heracleous proposes, strategic thinking is about "discovering and committing to novel strategies which can rewrite the rules of the competitive arena and necessitates relaxing at least part of conventional wisdom."[6] Strategic thinking and planning are necessary elements in strategy, and in this war, the Ukrainians have demonstrated an edge in both.

The Ukrainian strategy of corrosion described in chapter 3 outlines the key elements of Ukrainian strategy over the first eighteen months of the war. During the eight years between the 2014 war and February 2022, the Ukrainians had been planning for the type of Russian operation that unfolded in 2022. The Ukrainian high command had been thinking, wargaming, and training for how they might defend against a Russian onslaught. This included combat forces, air defense, large stockpiles of munitions, and a strategy that incorporated a "defense in depth" with Territorial Defense troops, and small, mobile units of troops to target supply lines.[7]

The ultimate test of Ukrainian strategy has been in two different but related endeavors: first, on the battlefield; and second, in the strategic information and diplomatic arenas. In both areas, the Ukrainian strategy has proven to be generally more resilient and successful than that of the Russians. But it has not yet won them the war.

Effective strategic thinking and strategy development must align political objectives with the means available to achieve them. In other words, strategy needs to be resourced appropriately. Whether it is the allocation of personnel to the right areas of government and the military, or the provision of sufficient quantities of equipment and munitions, as strategist Bernard Brodie once wrote, "strategy wears a dollar sign."[8] Resourcing of strategy includes sustaining an industrial base that can expand when the occasion arises.

As such, good strategy in the military context should ensure a close alignment of military capability with political objectives. This is a key observation from the war. The Ukrainians better prepared their military for the type of war that was most likely—a Russian invasion. And when that invasion eventuated, they were better at adapting than the Russian military. The Russians, on the other hand, had a poorly aligned military posture and structure with the political demands of Putin in February 2022. Seth Jones has described this as a key observation that can be taken from the war: "The Russian invasion force was far too small to seize and hold territory."[9] This was also a key theme in John Lewis Gaddis' book *On Grand Strategy*, where he notes that "ends and means have to connect if anything is to happen."[10] And as Vladimir Frolov has written, "The discrepancy between the strategic goals and the means allocated for achieving those goals was the main cause of Russia's military failures from February through to September."[11]

With the poor assumptions about Ukrainian military capacity, and a willingness to fight baked into Russian military strategy, it was almost inevitable that there would be a misalignment between what Putin wanted and the Russian military's capacity to achieve it. And while some mitigation could be provided by the fact that the kind of war in Ukraine is not one that the Russians prepared for in their decade of transformation before February 2022, their adaptive processes since then have done a poor job of realigning their military and political objectives.

Two final aspects of the "strategy matters" observation should be emphasized.

First, good strategy accepts that war is possible. This is an essential starting point for useful national and military strategies. Too often, many in Western governments appear to wish away the possibility of large-scale war. John Mueller, for example, wrote in 1990, "War is apparently becoming obsolete, at least in the developed world: in an area where war was once often casually seen as beneficial, noble, and glorious, or at least as necessary or inevitable, the conviction has now become widespread that war would be intolerably costly, unwise, futile, and debased."[12] The actions of Russia in the past two years should disabuse many of the notion expressed by Mueller. Writing about the impact of war on the development of human societies, Ian Morris has described war as "something that cannot be wished out of existence, but that is because it cannot be done."[13]

The second aspect is that no individual weapon, institution, or idea is strategically decisive. There has been much reporting on "war-winning weapons" in particular during this war, or "war-winning" offensives. The introduction of the U.S. HIMARS long-range artillery rocket system in 2022 is one example of such unjustified exuberance, but so too were early reports of the Russian use of Iranian-made kamikaze drones.[14] There is little historical precedent that offers evidence for such a view, although there are many precedents for people thinking that such "silver bullets" are possible. The ideas of airpower theorists in the interwar period,[15] and the Nazis' "wonder weapons" in World War II,[16] were futile attempts at generating a quick, simple pathway to victory.

Good strategy eschews the myth of wonder weapons. But with effective strategy and the application of the right kind and quantity of human, material, and moral components, nations can give themselves a fighting chance of success.

STRATEGIC ASSUMPTIONS DRIVE SUCCESS AND FAILURE

Strategy matters, but so do the assumptions that underpin strategy.

While much is written about strategy, less is written about strategic assumptions, how to make them explicit, and how to test, modify, and discard them when required. For example, in the U.K. guide *Getting Strategy Right (Enough)*, uncertainty is acknowledged, but how assumptions might be developed and used as a foundation for strategy that reduces uncertainty is absent.[17] As Vincent Barabba and Ian Mitroff note in *Business Strategies for a Messy World*, "Everything that people and organizations do hinges on the robustness and validity of the assumptions that they make about themselves, others, and the world around them."[18]

In his handbook *Strategy and Defence Planning*, Colin Gray briefly explores strategic assumptions. He describes how "defence planning has always been extraordinarily vulnerable to potential errors in assumptions. . . . Defence planning is conducted for safe passage through the terra incognita of the future. Futurological net assessment of conflict requires the making of assumptions for every component vital to the analysis."[19] So making valid assumptions in strategy is hard. That doesn't absolve nations and institutions from doing their best to validate their assumptions that inform strategy and its implementation.

In the first eighteen months of the war in Ukraine, the assumptions on which the Russians based their military and national strategy were flawed. Putin expected that the war would resemble a large coup rather than a military campaign, that it would prove short, and that Russian forces would be victorious. When this did not eventuate, Putin then assumed that time was on his side and history would repeat itself. After his short wars in Chechnya, Georgia, and Crimea, European outrage and resolve had dissolved, mainly because of a hunger for cheap gas.[20] This assumption of the future resembling the past was not unreasonable, but it, like his other assumptions about the war, has turned out to be wrong. Other assumptions about Russian forces being welcomed by Ukrainians who desired the demilitarization and de-Nazification of Ukraine have proved similarly wrong.[21]

Russian assumptions about a rapid Ukrainian collapse underpinned their initial military strategy. Putin's desired political end state—a compliant Ukraine—relied on a decisive and quick military victory. Russian military planning, based on these bad strategic assumptions, was biased toward combat units around the borders of Ukraine.

The aim of showing off Russian combat power was to cower the Ukrainians into an accommodation. The Ukrainians missed this memo. As analysist Dara Massicot has written, "This operation is struggling because those who planned it are stuck at the intersection of Russian imperial hubris and Soviet-style secrecy. The Russians underestimated their opponents' will and capability to resist, just as they underestimated the Ukrainians' ability to assimilate western support."[22]

Jeffrey Edmonds has pointed out that "the fundamental mistake made at the leadership level, that carried down to the lowest ranks, was an underestimation of the lengths Ukraine's leadership, military, and people would go to defend it."[23] The assumptions that underpin strategy should be sound. They need to be evidence based and, if possible, tested.

Perhaps the best description of the importance of validating the assumptions underpinning strategy is provided by Edward Luttwak. In 1987, he published a book called *Strategy: The Logic of War and Peace*. In the book's conclusion he describes assumptions as "huge uncertainties of fact must be accepted in devising strategy." But because of the necessity of using assumptions to construct strategy, there is a permanent danger of errors and of those errors being systematized. In democratic systems, the interplay of bureaucracies as well as civil-military debate should cancel out the majority of these errors over time. But in regimes where there is minimal debate, these errors—or flawed assumptions—can have a profound and negative impact. This tendency to compound flawed assumptions through systematizing errors appears to be something that might be observed in the development and execution of strategy in contemporary Russia.[24]

Good strategic assumptions are also underpinned by good intelligence. There have been many examples of poor intelligence—in collection, analysis, and use—before and during the war. Before the war, both the Russians and the Ukrainians had active intelligence campaigns. The Russians undertook widespread infiltration of Ukrainian institutions, including their national intelligence apparatus and political system, in the hope that Russian forces would be welcomed into Ukraine. They did the same before 2014. An excellent RAND report on the 2014 war describes in some detail Russian intelligence operations that are almost a mirror image of what they conducted in the lead-up to this war.[25]

The Ukrainians collected extensive intelligence on the preparedness of Russian forces, finding a lack of logistic support and combat readiness before the war. The United States had a very active intelligence campaign and shared information with Ukraine and the Europeans in the lead-up to the war. It also used this intelligence to attempt to deter the Russian invasion. Since the war began, it is likely that many Ukrainian long-range strikes have utilized American or European intelligence.

There are exemplars of good and poor intelligence practice on all sides. But perhaps the most damaging has been the poor performance of Russian intelligence services in the lead-up to the war. They underestimated Ukrainian resolve and the competence of the Ukrainian armed forces. They overestimated the level of support for Russia among the political class in Ukraine. Their lack of strategic competence led Putin to make decisions about invading that were based on wrong assumptions, and the prosecution of a totally unnecessary war.

LEADERSHIP AND WILL ARE ESSENTIAL IN STRATEGY

The war in Ukraine has shown (again) that ambiguity and uncertainty are central to warfare, regardless of how many tweets and TV reports observers might view. The old idea of "the fog of war," described by Clausewitz in *On War*, has new meaning in a world where people can access all the information they desire without becoming any wiser about what is occurring in a conflict. Because of this, people and organizations also keep getting surprised. In war, surprise occurs at every level as the combatants—and national leaders—seek new sources of advantage. And the greatest source of advantage, in all forms of war and in every era of human existence, is good leadership.

This war has reinforced existing knowledge about the impact of good tactical leadership. On the one side, the Western-trained and -oriented Ukrainians (for the most part) have prepared their junior leaders—noncommissioned and officers—to take the initiative and lead their soldiers by example. The Russians, who decided to eschew the development of a professional NCO corps during their decade of reform from 2012 to 2022, demonstrated poor battlefield leadership at almost every level.

Good military leadership is vital. But effective national leadership is even more important in war. It is an essential part of executing strategy.

The most important leader in the Russo-Ukraine War has been President Zelenskyy. Underestimated by Western leaders and analysts before the war, he has unified his people, exhorted courage from his military, and inspired observers around the world. In doing so, he has reinforced the will of his people. This "will" is a vital aspect of executing strategy and winning wars. Clausewitz describes its centrality to war when he writes, "War is thus an act of force to compel our enemy to do our will."[26]

This will, as well as the time bought on the battlefield by Ukrainian soldiers, has had multiple impacts on the implementation of Ukrainian strategy. First and foremost, it has demonstrated to external observers that Ukraine is worth assisting. Many nations will assist others when they demonstrate a determination to help themselves first, and this is what Ukraine has done. The resulting external assistance has seen the development, implementation, and ongoing evolution of an immense international regime of sanctions against Russia. It has resulted in massive amounts of lethal and nonlethal aid to Ukraine, and an outpouring of moral and diplomatic support from many nations around the world.

The power of charismatic strategic leaders matters. As chapter 6 examined, the asymmetry in strategic leadership between Zelenskyy and Putin has probably had a significant impact on the war so far. Therefore, one key observation that might be taken from the war is that effective strategic leadership is powerful, and good strategy must be led.

STRATEGY AND INFLUENCE ARE INDIVISIBLE

The old saying that "information is power" has never been more applicable than in the contemporary era. Russia has ensured the Chinese Communist Party amplifying their strategic messaging.[27] At the same time, it has focused less on audiences in the West and more on those in India and Africa. As a 2022 OECD report notes, "Russian propaganda and disinformation activities are produced in large volumes and are distributed across a large number of channels, both via online and traditional media."[28]

Ukraine has also invested in a significant strategic influence campaign. It has run a model program to influence Western governments and solicit aid and diplomatic assistance. This government effort has been supplemented by the Ukrainian telecommunications industry keeping its phone and internet network functional, allowing citizen journalists to transmit images of the war, including Russian atrocities.

Support from nongovernment influence actors—including the global #NAFO (North Atlantic Fella Organization) movement—have provided important reinforcement to messaging from Ukraine, NATO, and the United States about the war and have been active in combating Russian misinformation. There are important lessons to learn from these nongovernment social media actors and more generally from citizen participation in information warfare.

A final observation on the information fight is the importance of deception and operational security (OPSEC). Ukraine has been effective at this, and while the flow of strategic influence material has been high, the flow of factual information has been much smaller. The Russians have not been as effective, and many Western-oriented social media platforms, satellite mapping, and open-source intelligence feeds have openly supported Ukraine.

Deception and OPSEC may be even more important in the modern world, where everything is theoretically visible. The meshing of civilian and military sensors, analysis, and dissemination in the past decade only reinforces the idea that the battlefield, and the world more broadly, is "transparent." And while people may be able to see more of the world, and the events that occur in it, than ever before, what can be seen and what is actually occurring are often two different things. And therein lies the importance of influence operations to deceive one's adversaries. Such arts will be vital to convince people they are not seeing what they think they are seeing. Strategic influence is now indivisible from strategy.

STRATEGIC INTEGRATION IS VITAL

The character of war has evolved since the beginning of the twentieth century. World War I was the first modern war that featured total national mobilization of military, industrial, and societal resources. As such, it required political and military leaders to be better at high-level strategic thinking. It also necessitated the closer integration of military and industrial outputs with political needs. This integrated political-military approach has only deepened across the following century.

One contemporary approach to strategic integration is explored in the 1999 Chinese book *Unrestricted Warfare*. It describes how "the new principles of war are no longer "using armed force to compel the enemy to submit to one's will" but, rather, are "using all means, including armed force or non-armed force, military and nonmilitary, and lethal and nonlethal means to compel the enemy to accept one's interests."[29] Or, as the more recent British *Integrated Operating Concept* notes, "maximizing advantage will only be realized through being more integrated: within the military instrument, vertically through the levels of warfare—strategic, operational and tactical; across government and with our allies; and in depth within our societies."[30]

Of the many issues that have contributed to Russia's physical battlefield woes in Ukraine, one of the most important has been the shortfalls in joint or combined-arms operations. Russia's poor level of coordination between its various services and ground combat branches has often led to battlefield defeats.[31] The Russians have at times committed forces piecemeal and demonstrated limited capacity for combined-arm maneuvers or air-land integration. The Ukrainians have done better at integration in the tactical arena, but heavy causalities and a gross disparity in armor and artillery have at times hampered their capacity for large-scale offensives or operational breakthroughs.

Higher-level integration—at the strategic level and the international level—is also crucial. The integration of all national efforts is a deliberate undertaking in the planning, execution, and evolution of strategy. This is not just because nations need to use resources efficiently but also because it provides for more resilient strategy, offering adversaries fewer weaknesses or seams to target and exploit.

In the main, the Ukrainians have done this competently over the course of the war. While there is no perfect approach in such an undertaking, they have been able to mobilize their people, industry, economy, military, and information resources for a total war effort to stave off national extinction.[32] For the Ukrainians, this national integrated approach has also featured the integration of commercial technologies into military operations, injected private social media commentators into the national influence campaign, and embraced private crowdfunding initiatives to complement government humanitarian and military needs.

The Russians have not demonstrated nearly as effective integration. From the start, the military means have never matched the desired political outcomes (take-over of Ukraine) and have had to be constantly pared back by Putin and his regime. At the operational level, the Russians began the war fighting separate campaigns in the North, Northeast, East, and South, as well as in the air and in the information domain. There was little evidence of coordination, prioritization, or main efforts. This situation has improved: unified commanders have been appointed (several times) during the war, and they have reduced their campaigns to those in the East and the South, but it is a poor showing from a nation that provided many of the theoretical foundations for contemporary military operational art.[33]

Finally, the integrated approach to strategy must be broader than national capacity—it must include alliances and coalitions. A lesson of the war has been the centrality of alliances and their contribution to security in the twenty-first-century security environment. A moribund NATO has since February 2022 been infused with energy and new purpose in the wake of the Russian invasion of Ukraine. While Ukraine is not a member of NATO, and the alliance has stopped short of deploying forces to Ukraine, it has demonstrated a resolve since 24 February that had been absent before then. Its July 2022 strategic concept reinforced both the contemporary and future roles of NATO, as well as its focus on supporting Ukraine to defeat Russia.[34] The 2023 NATO summit reinforced the ongoing support for Ukraine; its official communiqué noted that NATO remains "steadfast in our commitment to further step up political and practical support to Ukraine as it continues to defend its independence, sovereignty, and territorial integrity within its internationally recognized borders, and will continue our support for as long as it takes."[35]

This is an important lesson about why alliances—with the right purpose—remain an important element of how the West achieves collective defense for their sovereignty, and for democracy more broadly.

▥ NATIONAL RESILIENCE IS A FOUNDATION FOR STRATEGY

The previous chapters explored the Ukrainian and Russian embrace of mobilization of indigenous industry to sustain their war efforts. But in the modern era, no nation can be totally self-reliant. Ukraine has shown that despite the resilience of its military and populace, it needs outside assistance. Whether that assistance involves access to fuels (and additives), the foundations for medicines, or access to advanced weapon systems for defense, assured access to these in good times and bad is necessary.

The secretary of the U.S. Army, Christin Wormuth, noted after the Russian invasion of Ukraine had begun that "Ukraine underscores the importance of maintaining our industrial base and our munition stockpiles."[36] Or, as another article notes, "the biggest lesson the West needs to learn is to have massive stockpiles of artillery shells and missiles." War requires many resources. The shortfalls in artillery ammunition and precision missiles are exemplars of the expense of war and how shortchanging peacetime military institutions can impact those same organizations when they must go to war.

In July 2022, a report about NATO members' defense industries from the Washington, DC–based Center for Strategic and International Studies described how "many parts of NATO's diverse national systems of weapons development and production have very limited surge capability. It can take years for given countries to rebuild stocks of modern and critical weapons."[37] In the same month, the U.S. Government Accountability Office, in reviewing the American defense industrial base, described how the Department of Defense's (DOD) Industrial Base Policy office lacks a consolidated and comprehensive strategy to mitigate risks, and guide the investment in, the defense industrial base.[38]

The war in Ukraine has provided multiple observations about military industrial capacity. The conflict has seen a return to what the Royal United Services Institute (RUSI) has described as "industrial warfare."[39] It has become a massive consumer of people, equipment, fuel, and munitions. The resupply of ammunition has been a major undertaking for the Ukrainians and Russians, reminiscent of the British 1915 "shell crisis," which saw a shortage of artillery ammunition on the Western Front becoming a major political scandal.[40] Both sides have deployed large forces of both tube and rocket artillery. The use of the ammunition for these weapons has been prodigious, particularly during key phases of the 2022 midyear Donbas campaign and the 2023 Russian and Ukrainian offensives.

Western munitions and material production is increasing only slowly, despite the demand from Ukraine as well as the need to refill Western inventories of precision munitions and other equipment dispatched to Ukraine since 2022.[41] One year after the beginning of Russia's large-scale invasion of Ukraine, a report in *The Economist* noted,

> For at least the past five years, military planners have paid lip-service to the growing possibility of such a conflict in the future, with a revanchist Russia in Europe or in the Pacific with a China attempting to invade Taiwan. But it has not been reflected in either the stockpiling of essential munitions or the investment in the industrial capacity required to produce them at the rate that any war lasting more than a few weeks would demand.[42]

A fundamental reassessment is needed to understand the quantity and quality of munitions and weapon systems needed by European, American, and other nations in the event of a prolonged war in Ukraine, or in the event of another large-scale war occurring in Asia. The advent of a new war in Gaza in late 2023 has resulted in additional pressure on the West's industrial base and reinforced the imperative for change. Assumptions about the scale, duration, and intensity of warfare must be reset based on future industrial-scale war. They cannot be based on the past two decades of low-intensity counterinsurgency operations in places like Iraq, Afghanistan, and Africa. As Seth Jones has written, "The war in Ukraine has demonstrated that great-power wars—particularly wars of attrition—are industrial conflicts. The effort to deploy, arm, feed, and supply forces is a monumental task, and the massive consumption of equipment, systems, vehicles, and munitions requires a largescale industrial base for resupply."[43]

Preparing for such a conflict requires good strategy, the allocation of resources, the skilling of an expanded workforce, the construction of modern munitions production factories, and the expanded stockpiling of both precision and nonprecision munitions.

But national resilience is about more than access to commodities and weapons. As Ukraine has demonstrated, a terrestrial, sea cable, and satellite communications network is critical. So, too, are other aspects of resilience, including national unity, trust in government, and an enhanced capacity for responding to natural disasters.[44] Civil defense is also an important part of this national resilience model. It includes the physical elements, such as shelters and emergency services, as well as information aspects—national unity, trust in government, and keeping people informed (such as President Zelenskyy's daily speech).

Central to strategic resilience is ensuring strategy is resourced appropriately over the long term. This includes the allocation of personnel to the right areas of government and the military, or provision of sufficient quantities of equipment and munitions, and the protection of civilians and civil infrastructure. Resourcing of strategy includes sustaining an industrial base that can expand when the occasion arises, or when the need to deter an adversary is necessary.

STRATEGY MUST CONSTANTLY ADAPT

Strategy needs to be adaptive. As circumstances change, so too must strategy. War often tends toward escalation. This can be driven by a variety of factors, including the desire to generate new advantages by one side or the other, the geographical spread of conflict, the introduction of new technologies or warfighting concepts, the political or military outcomes of "sunk costs," battlefield defeats, and changes in the circumstances of alliances and security partnerships.

It is apparent that the Ukrainians have been able to evolve various aspects of their strategy more quickly than the Russians have. Partly this is because Ukraine faces an existential threat, and partly it is that the Ukrainian president, his cabinet, and his senior military leaders have an effective and reasonably open relationship. But they are also exposed to, and informed by, the mass of government and open-source information that floods into their offices daily.

On the other hand, President Putin appears to have been not as well informed about the progress and challenges of his military forces in Ukraine. As early as 30 March 2022, there were reports from the U.S. and European governments about a poor flow of information to Putin. As one White House briefing explained, "Russian President Vladimir Putin was misled by advisers who were too scared to tell him how poorly the war in Ukraine is going and how damaging Western sanctions have been."[45] And in a December presentation to the Reagan National Defense Forum in California, Avril Haines, the U.S. director of national intelligence, noted, "I do think he is becoming more informed of the challenges that the military faces in Russia, but it's still not clear to us that he has a full picture at this stage of just how challenged they are."[46]

This should not be surprising. As Murray, Knox, and Bernstein have explained in *The Making of Strategy: Rulers, States and War*, authoritarian states have long demonstrated the capacity for limiting the flow of information to leaders and self-deception. They write that "throughout the centuries, tyrannies have displayed the notorious tendency to punish the bearers of bad news, consequently, the willingness of their bureaucracies to analyze the world in realistic terms may be less than satisfactory."[47]

This situation is hardly conducive to building sufficient knowledge about the military situation in Ukraine for the Russian leader. He has therefore been at a distinct disadvantage in his ability to review and adapt his strategy compared to the leaders of Ukraine. But as explored in earlier chapters, Putin has slowly evolved Russia's strategy throughout the war, forcing the Ukrainians to adapt in kind. This is a topic we will return to in the second part of this book.

▨ A FINAL OBSERVATION: SURPRISE IS INEVITABLE

Once a war begins, it rarely proceeds as expected by the belligerents or outside observers.

While many citizens in the West were surprised that large-scale war was still possible in the modern world, it is likely that no one has been more surprised by how the war has gone than the Russian president. Vladimir Putin hardly expected an enlarged and unified NATO to emerge from the war. Nor did he expect the massive expansion in the size and quality of the Ukrainian armed forces that has taken place since February 2022. These have been major strategic surprises for Putin and his closest advisers.

Many politicians in Europe and in the West have also been surprised about the war's duration. This is less a reflection on the political class than it is on the education systems of Western nations. With a decrease in war studies and other humanities fields that teach history of warfare and human conflict, it was perhaps inevitable that there is a massive gap in knowledge about war and its impacts between two large, relatively wealthy and determined belligerents.[48]

All the same, other surprises have occurred. The Russian failure at Hostomel, the Kharkiv offensive in September 2022, the Kerch Bridge attacks in October 2022 and in 2023, and the Moscow Drone attacks in 2023 are all examples of surprise in this war. Further complicating strategic decision-making by Western leaders has been the surprise Hamas attacks against Israel on 7 October 2023, and the resulting war in Gaza.

The rise of crowdfunding military capability has been an interesting and pleasant surprise that has provided both humanitarian and military assistance to both sides. The continuous expansion in the use of autonomous systems has also delivered a surprising, and lethal, closing of the gap between detection and destruction of military units in the field. And finally, there has been a rediscovery of the centrality of leadership, at every level, in the conduct of the war.

Surprise is one of the great continuities in war. It is how adversaries seek to generate an advantage over each other. Surprise, and the shock that follows, allows greater destruction of an adversary's forces, or increases one side's leverage in bargaining over cease-fires or peace conditions. And despite the ongoing technological developments that transform military operations, surprise is here to stay. All the technology in the world does not prevent humans from innovating and thereby deceiving and surprising their enemies. As such, military leaders, institutions, and ideas must possess the ability to anticipate surprise at the strategic and tactical levels and, if surprised, be sufficiently resilient to survive and adapt.[49]

Part II

ADAPTATION

8

LEARNING IS HUMAN

The Adaptation Battle

IN THE LEAD-UP to the Ukrainian offensives of 2023, soldiers on the nation's eastern front were grimly holding ground around the city of Bakhmut. Other Ukrainian forces slowly, grindingly advanced on the Svatove-Kreminna line to the north. Casualties on both sides were high. The Russians, after their battlefield reverses in the second half of 2022, had managed to stabilize their front lines with the deployment of tens of thousands of newly mobilized troops. They were also able to inject some of the more elite professional units withdrawn from western Kherson while also degrading the capacity and strength of Ukrainian ground forces with Wagner Group human wave tactics.

Against this background, one British journalist was able to travel to the Ukrainian front lines and speak with a range of soldiers from different units. A key theme that emerged from his visit was that the Russians were reinvigorated, reinforced, and almost ready to commence further offensive operations in the East. But perhaps the most important theme that he took away from his interviews with soldiers was that the Russians appeared to have learned from their battlefield experiences in 2022. Replacing Wagner troops with regular Russian forces, the Russians were learning and adapting. As one soldier told the journalist Andrew Harding from the BBC, "We understand that Russia is learning every day and changing their strategy. And I think we need to learn faster."[1]

Other contemporary reports described how the Russians evolved their tactics on the eastern front in early 2023. The Russians started to form what they called Storm-Z units. In their original manifestation, these were integrated, combined-arms companies capable of undertaking tactical infiltration and assault operations against entrenched Ukrainian forces. Working in close cooperation with artillery and air support, these assault companies were designed to exploit weaknesses in the Ukrainian defensive lines. However, as Russian operations evolved in 2023, these units became where poor-performing soldiers, prisoners, and other dregs of the Russian system were sent. As one British intelligence report stated, "Storm-Z recruits have tumbled from elite status to fighting in what are effectively penal battalions."[2]

These Storm-Z units, using what has come to be described as "meat assaults," have been employed around Bakhmut and elsewhere. They have generally been used as expendable, first wave infantry. This is a form of adaptation, although for Western military professionals it is a distasteful one.[3]

It does, however, demonstrate that the Russian army has been able to learn and evolve its operations in Ukraine. This learning capacity, and the ability to share lessons across an institution, is at the heart of every successful military organization. Whether it is prewar innovation, tactical learning, or the constant adaptation to military strategy during a war, learning and adapting is an essential component in military operations. It is impossible for military institutions and their leaders to foresee every possible future contingency or to predict the reactions of an enemy. There is an infinite array of interactions and situations to consider, even in the smallest tactical actions. Uncertainty is part of the enduring nature of war. Because of this, an important design feature for military organizations in peace and war must be the ability to learn and to adapt to unexpected events.[4]

In a 1961 lecture on the applications of military history titled "The Use and Abuse of Military History," British soldier-scholar Sir Michael Howard explained, "[It] is not surprising that there has often been a high proportion of failures among senior commanders at the beginning of any war. These unfortunate men may either take too long to adjust themselves to reality . . . or they may have had their minds so far shaped by a lifetime of pure administration that they have ceased to be soldiers."[5] It is thus essential that effective military institutions possess a learning culture and the ability to learn and disseminate lessons so they can adapt.

The theory of adaptation has its origins in early developments in the biological sciences. When Charles Darwin produced his theory of evolution, a causal mechanism was developed to account for evolutionary changes.[6] Darwin, with his theory of natural selection, sought to understand and describe how new species emerge and how others disappear.[7] In the twenty-first century, research into adaptation has moved beyond the early work of Darwin. It has come to be applied across a variety of scientific endeavors. The theory of adaptation has become important in the examination of the optimum organization of societies, businesses, and other organizations as they attempt to improve their effectiveness in changing environments.

The competitive learning environment of military operations reinforces the requirement to develop and exploit the adaptive processes of military institutions. This adaptation occurs at multiple levels. It takes place with individuals at the individual level but also occurs at many levels in units, formations, and armies within military organizations. In military literature, the best-known adaptive cycle is Colonel John Boyd's OODA (observe-orient-decide-act) loop.[8] Other useful studies of military institutions that have been successful at adaptation include Aimée Fox's *Learning to Fight* as well as Murray and Millett's *Military Innovation in the Interwar Period*.[9]

But as Cohen and Gooch find in their 1990 book *Military Misfortunes*, not all learning or adaptation in wartime results in battlefield success. One reason is that some institutions are not able to efficiently absorb new technologies or ideas. Alternatively, some institutions fail to anticipate the range of future threats or are unable to assess which of the identified threats are the most serious.[10] A final reason for adaptive failure is that the enemy is actively seeking to interfere with its opponent's learning and adaptation processes.[11]

This adaptation battle has been taking place throughout the war in Ukraine. Both sides offer lessons in how contemporary military institutions might develop and sustain the learning culture that underpins adaptation—and success—at every level of military operations.[12] But that learning, and adaptation, begins well before the first shot is fired in a war.

LEARNING IN PEACE AND WAR

Wartime adaptation is founded on peacetime innovation and the form of learning culture that is established in military institutions. As such, as part of the exploration of adaptation in this war, it is useful to also review prewar innovation and reform that took place in the Russian and Ukrainian military institutions. The events of decades before the war can have a profound bearing on an organization's capacity to adapt in war.

One of the most important institutional responsibilities of senior leaders in military and national security institutions is providing the incentives for innovation during peacetime. This allows appropriate organizational constructs and cutting-edge technology to be combined to provide an advantage against adversaries in war. But it does require a cultural predisposition to learning and sharing lessons widely, accepting failure as an opportunity to learn, and a well-honed understanding of risk. In *The Culture of Military Learning*, Dima Adamsky writes of these prerequisites for adaptation, describing how "in the future, both state and nonstate actors will continue to develop military knowledge, and security experts will continue to uncover foreign military innovations. In each case there will be a need to figure out the tools of war (hardware) and anticipate their application (software). The task with regard to 'software' will be much more demanding, and a cultural approach will be indispensable for it."[13]

While the old saying "Adapt or die" has its place, large-scale collection, assessment, sharing, and absorption of lessons is challenging. This is especially true when one considers all the other challenges and demands placed on military institutions that are concurrently in the midst of fighting, planning for the next fight, and bringing in new members while steadily losing others to death, wounds, and sickness. At the same time, judgments must be made about which new ideas are likely to be successful and which will not. Institutional traditions, culture, and trust also have an impact.[14]

As difficult as learning and adapting in war may be, it is harder for a military force to win if it lacks a learning culture or possesses one that is suboptimal or poorly developed. Learning in, and from, war is a serious business that can have profound implications for military organizations in future conflicts. The lives of future service personnel, and the existence of nations, can depend on how well organizations learn and adapt.

Throughout this war the Ukrainians have demonstrated an effective learning culture. This learning culture, which incorporates a willingness to take risk and innovate and the capacity to rapidly absorb new technologies and integrate them into their operations, did not emerge fully formed on 24 February 2022. The Ukrainians learned from Russian operations in 2014, and their military operations in eastern Ukraine since. This provided a legacy capacity for learning and adaptation on which Ukrainian armed forces improvements in military effectiveness have been based since February 2022.

The Russians also brought with them a legacy learning culture, although it appears to be inferior to the Ukrainian model at the lower levels. This issue was covered in a 2022 report from the Royal United Services Institute, which notes, "Those who fail are usually replaced or threatened with punishment. Far from incentivizing success, this often leads to dishonest reporting in which the blame for failure is transferred onto others. This . . . obscures the actual operational problems that must be solved. These only become apparent when they can no longer be concealed, slowing the learning of lessons."[15]

The Russians clearly did learn from their operations in places such as Chechnya and Syria, but whether they learned the right lessons, or whether those lessons have been retained by the Russian military institution, might be questioned. It will be a topic for much research in the wake of this war. However, the Russians appear to have assumed they would be fighting the same Ukrainian army that existed in 2014. Thus, the Russian army's learning culture before the war was suboptimal. This afforded a poor foundation for learning and adapting once the war began.

ADAPTATION AND MILITARY EFFECTIVENESS

One of the implied outcomes of adaptation is that the effectiveness of military organizations and personnel is enhanced. Often, military innovation and military success are conflated in many studies of tactical and strategic innovation. However, this is not always the case. As such, a distinction is required between adapting and improving military effectiveness. Changing tactics, command, and support arrangements does not necessarily mean that an organization's overall performance will improve. As Michael Horowitz and Shira Pindyck have highlighted, assuming that adaptation and the improvement in military effectiveness are the same is problematic because "it conflates whether a military institution changes in some way, and whether that change leads to greater military effectiveness, which can depend on many other factors. A range of intervening variables may influence whether a given resource or capability produces battlefield outcomes."[16]

Adaptation and military effectiveness must be explored as related yet separate concerns.

Military effectiveness is a topic central to the design, functioning, and improvement of military organizations, the forces they deploy in combat, and the institutions that support these combat elements in many functions at different levels. In the 1980s, American scholars Allan Millett and Williamson Murray studied military effectiveness. The output of their work was a three-volume series of books on twentieth-century military effectiveness that was published in 1988. Exploring several countries and their performance during World War I, the interwar period, and World War II, each book applied a framework to explore different levels of military effectiveness. These historical periods chosen served the study well because they offered insights for the strategic competition between the United States and the Soviet Union at that time. More recently, a 2007 book from Risa Brooks and Elizabeth Stanley called *Creating Military Power: The Sources of Military Effectiveness* explored this topic.

Millett and Murray defined military effectiveness as "the process by which armed forces convert resources into fighting power."[17] Brooks and Stanley define military effectiveness as "the capacity to create military power from a state's basic resources in wealth, technology, population, and human capital."[18]

The military effectiveness of twenty-first-century military institutions is determined by their success in converting resources into the capacity to influence and fight within an integrated national approach. Adaptation, regardless of its level, should be contributing to the maintenance and improvement of military effectiveness. Has it done so for the forces engaged in the war in Ukraine? That key question will be explored in this second part of the book.

▨ FAILED ADAPTATIONS

While differentiating between adaptation and effectiveness is important, it is also important to ensure that the institutional processes of military organizations are informed by examples of failed lessons and failed "lessons learned" processes. Examples of failed attempts at organizational reform can sometimes be as informative as successful adaptations.

Failed historical adaptations are explored by David Barno and Nora Bensahel in *Adaptation under Fire*. In particular, they examine the World War II example of U.S. Army supplemental armor in 1944–45. This was a process of putting additional armor on U.S. main battle tanks to adapt to the increasingly penetrative power of the guns mounted on German tanks. It resulted in solutions that weighed the U.S. tanks down, placing a greater strain on their engines and running gear and decreasing their mobility, without significantly improving their survivability.[19] Barno and Bensahel note the connection between tactical and institutional adaptation, pointing out that some tactical problems cannot be overcome by tactical learning and adaptation alone. Some battlefield innovations are effective, but for other challenges, institutional adaptation is needed.

But even learning and adaptation at the institutional level wasn't always successful. Barno and Bensahel examine the development of the U.S. Army's main tank in World War II, the M4 Sherman:

> The U.S. Army in World War II stubbornly clung to its prewar views about how to employ tanks long after they should have been demolished by the experience of combat. Furthermore, infighting among different parts of the army's bureaucracy effectively stonewalled any new tank development during the entire war. . . . The U.S. Army's continued reliance on the M4 Sherman throughout World War II was an unmistakable failure of institutional adaptation.[20]

This is an example of a failure in the institutional learning system. But it also provides insights that might be used to improve an institution's ability to scan for areas where current capabilities are no longer relevant or require enhancement. Such knowledge might also be leveraged by organizations to use an adversary's cultural predispositions against them and induce failure in an enemy's lesson and learning system.

Ultimately, if the right questions are not being asked at the right levels, either adaptation will not occur or the adaptations that are attempted will not improve military effectiveness. As Williamson Murray has argued in *Military Adaptation in War*, "It is the asking of the right kinds of questions that is the essential first step to any successful adaptation to the problems raised by a particular conflict."[21]

The same applies for crafting bad assumptions when developing strategies and plans. Again, Murray has something to say on this matter: "All going-in assumptions are faulty to some degree. Therefore, one must assume the need to adapt to the actual conditions and the actual enemy."[22] If, however, for a range of reasons one fails to recognize the inaccuracy of starting assumptions in a war, adaptation will invariably be compromised.

Often the failure of adaptation comes down to a lack of flexibility within a given military culture. The concept of flexibility, when applied to military institutions, incorporates command, organizational doctrinal, technological, and cognitive aspects. In his 2007 study of military flexibility in the face of surprise, Meir Finkel writes that "when armies markedly improve their response skills and reaction time to technological and doctrinal surprise, most of the obstacles based on prediction and intelligence solutions become superfluous.... Military culture then appears to be of importance in establishing an infrastructure for the culture of flexibility."[23]

Not only can adaptation fail to improve the performance of an organization; it can also be detrimental to the institution as a whole. In 2022 Kendrick Kuo explored how military innovation can also hurt military effectiveness. Kuo's work contains many useful lessons for observing military affairs and drawing lessons on innovation and adaptation. Importantly, Kuo notes that "military innovation can be healthy insofar as it realigns military means with political ends. But ensuring the proper balance and integration of new and traditional capabilities involves calibrating the appropriate level of radicalness in an innovation process for an uncertain strategic landscape."[24]

As Kuo notes, conventional wisdom suggests that innovation always improves military performance. Militaries that oppose it apparently invite defeat, but those that are able to innovate are victorious. Innovation is considered a sign of organizational health because the ever-changing character of war constantly threatens to render existing capabilities obsolete. Conversely, misfortune comes to those who allow the march of historical change to overtake them. The notion that innovation and better military performance go hand in hand is thus intuitive but, as Kuo explains, also wrong.[25]

Under pressure to achieve battlefield success during war, or to promise cheaper more effective ways to achieve missions in peacetime, there is considerable pressure on military leaders at all levels to innovate. Not all these attempts at adaptation succeed. The war in Ukraine has seen all forms of adaptation, from those that have improved military effectiveness of the belligerents to those that have not. One example of an adaptation attempt that has not resulted in increased military effectiveness is the Russians' frequent changes in command.

During this war the Russian military has sought to adapt and improve its effectiveness through changes in commanders. This has occurred at the level of the overall command in Ukraine. Initially, there was no overall commander. Then, in early 2022, General Aleksandr Dvornikov was appointed. He was replaced in October 2022 by General Sergey Surovikin. In January 2023 Surovikin was in turn replaced by General Valery Gerasimov. Some have also speculated that General Gennady Zhidko may have also been in command at some point between the tenures of Dvornikov and Surovikin.

At the same time, the next level of command—the Russian military district commanders—has also seen frequent turnover. The Southern and Central Military District commanders have changed at least three times since the beginning of the war. The Western and Eastern Military District commanders have changed at least four times each.[26]

These changes are the result of both battlefield setbacks, as well as President Putin and Defense Minister Sergei Shoigu wishing to insulate themselves from the impacts of Russia's many reverses in fortune during its special military operation in Ukraine. And as Riley Bailey and Kateryna Stepanenko from the Institute for the Study of War wrote in April 2023, these frequent command rotations accord with Putin's overall approach to leadership within his regime: "Putin has long rotated personnel in government positions as a way to ensure that no one figure amasses too much political influence and to maintain support among competing factions. Putin also routinely avoids outright dismissing officials and instead temporarily demotes them in order to encourage them to seek to regain his favor and to retain options for future appointments."[27]

One of the key lessons from the recent war in Afghanistan is that short tours and rapid turnover in personnel—especially commanders—degrades the overall campaign effectiveness of a military institution.[28] In an article on the lessons of Afghanistan, John Sopko called the frequent changeover of command teams the "annual lobotomy" and described how "brief rotational deployments and frequent shifts in command contribute to a 'lack of proper continuity of effort, a breakdown, or gaps in critical U.S.-host country relationships, and a mutual lack of trust.'"[29] And so far in this war, the Russian practice of adapting its command and control of its military operations in Ukraine through frequent rotation has yet to drastically improve their performance. It is an example of how not every institutional adaptation succeeds.

▧ LEARNING FOR THE FUTURE: OTHERS ARE ALSO OBSERVING AND ADAPTING

The war in Ukraine has shown how a well-led and motivated military force might effectively disrupt or even defeat an adversary of much larger size and capacity. The power of contemporary defensive technologies and tactics means that defenders can inflict substantial costs, and prolong the duration, of an aggressor's military operation. There has been a reinvigorated exploration of the "primacy of the defense" in the past few years. In a 2018 article Major General Robert Scales (retired) of the U.S. Army wrote that "if the past is prologue and if a firepower-dominant battlefield favors the defensive, we are witnessing a figurative 'return to Gettysburg.' This fifth cycle now underway will likely make the offensive costlier and more difficult."[30]

Functions such as leadership, multidomain integration, signature management, closing "detection to destruction" times against an adversary, massed use of crewed and uncrewed systems, information operations, and industrial-scale warfare are all part of the defensive scheme that Ukraine has employed against Russia. The study of their approach will drive institutional adaptation in the military institutions of many nations. It is likely to drive changes in techniques, technologies, tactics, and organizations in many military organizations. As T. X. Hammes has written about the lessons from the war in Ukraine, "These game-changing capabilities are giving new and powerful advantages to defenders in ground combat. While this precept does not necessarily mean offense will be impossible, it will certainly be much more costly."[31]

In particular, the United States and the Chinese have been watching the Russo-Ukraine war carefully. Both have a long history of studying other people's wars to foster transformation in their own organizations. For the United States, the Arab-Israeli wars in the late 1960s and early 1970s were a catalyst for technological and doctrinal change. Concepts such as air-land battle resulted.

The U.S. Army, based on its desire to learn from the war, has dispatched teams to Eastern Europe to learn from the war. It also delayed the release of a new version of its Multi-Domain Warfare doctrine in order to incorporate lessons from the Russo-Ukraine War.[32] A variety of official publications as well as journals and blogs have recorded and proposed lessons from the war that range from urban operations and fires to tactics and logistics. The key, however, will be sifting through the myriad of lessons and deciding which are relevant primarily for Ukraine or the European theater, and which lessons might be more general and appropriate to other theaters, such as Asia and the Western Pacific.

Nations beyond Europe and North America are also watching the war and drawing their own conclusions. The People's Liberation Army (PLA) in China is watching and probably learning strategic and tactical lessons from the war in

Ukraine. In the past half century, the PLA has demonstrated expertise in studying foreign wars and applying the lessons to its own force design and procurement processes. The Chinese studied the 1991 Gulf War in great detail. It was a crucible event for the Chinese army. They appreciated that their large and low-technology military would not compete with the kind of connected, precision military that the United States deployed to Saudi Arabia, Kuwait, and Iraq. It is very likely that the observations and analysis of the war by the United States and China will result in adaptation to their weapons programs, warfighting concepts, organizations, and personnel training.[33]

As Toshi Yoshihara has written on Chinese studies of past wars, "Chinese findings from these retrospectives offer tantalizing hints of the PLA's deeply held beliefs, assumptions, and proclivities about future warfare, such as the penchant for striking first and attacking the enemy's vulnerabilities. . . . Policymakers should treat the lessons that Chinese strategists have learned as early warning signs of the PLA's future trajectory."[34] One important subject for review by the leadership of the People's Liberation Army will be their current warfighting doctrines to ensure these are updated and appropriate to the circumstances they are likely to face against the United States and its allies in any Indo-Pacific conflict. The Russians, who have undertaken major reforms of their doctrine in the past decade, were preparing for an environment where military operations would be conducted less to seize terrain and more to sap their will and endurance.

The Chinese are likely to draw lessons from the war in Ukraine about command and leadership, the integration and speed of joint operations, information operations, covert warfare to remove political leaders, and waging war at industrial scale.[35] But the People's Liberation Army is not the only military institution far from Europe that is studying the war.

Taiwan has also been watching closely.[36] After all, it is a small, young democracy adjacent to a large, authoritarian country that possesses territorial and political designs for the incorporation of its smaller neighbor. And like Russia, China repeatedly employs historical narratives to justify their argument that Taiwan is not a sovereign nation. The small island nation has much to learn from the behavior of Russia and the doughty defense of the Ukrainians.

In early 2023, the Taiwanese chief envoy to the United States, Bi-khim Hsiao, stated, "Everything we're doing now is to prevent the pain and suffering of the tragedy of Ukraine from being repeated in our scenario in Taiwan. So ultimately, we seek to deter the use of military force. But in a worst-case scenario, we understand that we have to be better prepared."[37]

Other members of the Taiwanese government have also spoken about the lessons they might draw from Ukraine, including Defense Minister Chiu Kuo-cheng, who has noted that "the Russia-Ukraine war has brought great lessons for [the Chinese]—they will definitely seek speed."[38] Other lessons will undoubtedly be integrated into Taiwanese force planning, including the application of precision munitions, large-scale use of autonomous systems, and enlarged stocks of critical weapons and fuel in order to buy time before allies might assist it.

And it may result in a more asymmetric approach to Taiwanese force structure. After decades of investing in conventional forces to deter China, a 2017 plan called the Overall Defense Concept from the then–chief of the Taiwanese armed forces described a shift to more indirect approaches to deterring a large and more advanced People's Liberation Army. As the Russians invaded Taiwan in February 2022, much of this concept lay unrealized due to interservice rivalries and institutional obstruction of eschewing conventional weapons. Considered too radical by many of Taiwan's senior miliary leaders, key elements of the Overall Defense Concept, including the more defensive, littoral approach using mines and missiles it described, might have been left on the drawing board if not for the war in Ukraine.[39]

The war in Ukraine has shocked the Taiwanese into rethinking their position. It has begun to revise its defense strategy, beginning a shift toward a revised military strategy that includes more of the asymmetric ideas described in the 2017 Overall Defense Concept.[40] Since the beginning of the February 2022 Russian invasion, Taiwan has revised its national service policies, extending it from four months to one year. But it is too early yet to assess the full impact of Ukraine and what Taiwan may have learned from it.[41]

But it is Ukraine and Russia who have the most at stake in current learning and adaptation efforts. As the war in Ukraine continues, both sides are observing the enemy, and their own operations, and then learning and adapting. Their battlefield interactions with each other and support from other nations, as well as new technologies and ideas, shape this learning and adaptation process and ensure that it is continuous. The following chapters will examine how Ukraine and Russia have learned during the war and how they have subsequently adapted their tactics, organizations, support mechanisms, and information operations, and even the ways they learn and share lessons.

9

THE POWER VERTICAL

Foundations of Russian Adaptation in Ukraine

AT LEAST IN THEORY, the Russian army had an excellent foundation for learning and adapting prior to its special military operation in Ukraine. But as the war has progressed and the Russian army has unveiled its tactics and methods to the world, theory and practice have diverged. The theories of war, and their implementation in wartime, can be extraordinarily difficult to align.

Since 1991, the former military forces of the Union of Soviet Socialist Republics (USSR) have undertaken multiple reform programs. These have been driven by the significant reduction in resources available to the military after the fall of the Iron Curtain, the lessons of the 1991 Gulf War, and other significant transformations in the technology and operating concepts of Western military intuitions. Changes in the political attention and advocacy received by Russian military organizations also had an impact.

The years between 1991 and 2008 were a grim time for the Russian army. While attempts were made in the aftermath of the Cold War to sustain a unified Commonwealth of Independent States military, the departure of Ukraine and other former Soviet republics required Russia to form its own military in 1992. The Russian army thereafter endured a decade and a half of downsizing, stagnant budgets, minimal investment in new equipment, and a reliance on the massive trove of vehicles and munitions accumulated during the Cold War. As Mark Galeotti has written, "For

most of the 1990s, the Russian military was led by political appointees more con-
cerned with protecting their positions and appeasing [President Boris] Yeltsin than
articulating some coherent vision for the country's armed forces. They ended the
decade scarcely any more reformed—just smaller—than when they had started."[1]

There were some attempts at reform during this time, however. From 1992, the army
attempted to restructure from its army-division-regiment structure to one that was
arranged around corps and brigades. A lack of funding, poor political oversight, and
internal resistance meant these reforms never fully materialized. Increasing criminal
behavior and corruption in the military also had a major impact on the resources
available for reform activities and distracted many military officers from their normal
duties. As one 1995 report put it, "The Russian Armed Forces is an institution increasingly defined by the high levels of military criminality and corruption embedded
within it at every level. Military crime is now directly associated with the Russian
Ministry of Defense, General Staff, and other senior staffs. . . . Individual military
criminals range from general- and field-grade officers to the newest conscripts."[2]

In 1997, newly appointed minister of defense Igor Sergeyev initiated further
reforms of the Russian military, particularly its ground forces.[3] A three-tiered
readiness system was announced, which contained units at constant readiness,
low-level readiness, or strategic reserve status. Sergeyev introduced other changes,
including reducing the size of the military and merging the air force and air defense
forces. In 1998, an economic collapse resulted in shortfalls in resources for reform,
as well as shortages of fuel for training. Leadership quality deficits and an open
rift in the military about the changes meant that within two years of commencing,
these reforms had stalled.[4]

Soon after Putin assumed power in 2001, he replaced Sergeyev with Sergei Ivanov.
A Putin confidant, Ivanov in 2003 issued a reform plan called *Urgent Tasks for the
Development of the Armed Forces of the Russian Federation*, which has also become
known as the Ivanov Doctrine.[5] Despite Ivanov's efforts to improve the overall
quality of the Russian military, they bore little fruit. According to Mark Galeotti,
"ultimately, Ivanov had made the intellectual case for reform, but was unable to
impose it on a recalcitrant High Command. . . . He was also too distracted with
other responsibilities, and lacked the specific skills to ensure that the money being
spent was being spent wisely. He had made a start, no more."[6]

Further reforms were initiated in the wake of the Russo-Georgia War in 2008.
This program, which Michael Kofman has described as "chaotic reform," commenced
in late 2008 under Minister of Defense Anatoly Serdyukov. The reforms initiated by
Serdyukov had a major impact on the Russian armed forces. Key outcomes included
the abandonment of the old Soviet mass mobilization model, the reduction in the
number of conscripts as a proportion of the overall military, and improvements in

readiness and mobility of military units.[7] These would all have an impact on the Russians invasion of Ukraine in 2022.

A new period of military reform commenced in 2012 when Serdyukov was replaced by Putin confidant Sergei Shoigu. In the same year, General Valery Gerasimov was appointed to serve as the Chief of the General Staff of the Russian armed forces. In the decade between their appointments and the invasion of Ukraine, Shoigu and Gerasimov undertook multiple activities to transform the Russian military into a more modern and capable force.

An important objective was rearmament. New hardware was procured to address shortfalls in the design, development, and issue of new equipment for the Russian armed forces in the 1990s. Increasing readiness was also a focus, with multiple exercises conducted to improve the availability and coordination of military forces. But perhaps the best-known reform was the creation of battalion tactical groups, partly to create permanently ready tactical forces and partly to address the inability to form high-readiness brigades. It was with these combined armed units that the Russian forces crossed the border into Ukraine in February 2022.

However, it was not only strategic reform activities that should have provided a foundation for adaptation for Russian forces before this war. Their adaptive stance was informed by their participation in multiple wars before their 2022 invasion of Ukraine. As the following summary of Russian military operations show, they had many opportunities in the first two decades of the twenty-first century to learn and evolve.

▓ CHECHNYA I

Like the Russian soldiers who invaded Ukraine in 2022, the Russian soldiers who advanced into Grozny, the capital of Chechnya, in December 1994 did not expect a fight. As Olga Oliker has written, "They were confident that their enemy, a rebel force seeking independence for Chechnya . . . was untrained and unorganized. Their commanding officer had told them there was nothing to worry about."[8]

The Chechens were prepared, however, and they inflicted terrible casualties on the Russian troops as they fought for control of the city. Eventually, in March 1995, the Russians gained control of the city, but at the cost of nearly 30,000 civilian lives. At least 3,000 Russian soldiers were also killed, according to figures released by the General Staff of the Russian armed forces.

Fighting elsewhere in Chechnya continued until August 1996, which included shelling and Russian air force bomber raids that destroyed large parts of Grozny. However, a cease-fire was brokered by President Yeltsin's national security adviser, and Russian forces were withdrawn by the beginning of 1997. A peace treaty between Russia and Chechnya was signed in May 1997.

This war, the first major conflict for the newly created, post-Soviet-era Russian military, was a humiliation for Russia. While well equipped, the forces that conducted operations in Chechnya were poorly trained, and their units were undermanned and outnumbered by Chechen rebels. Many battalions contained soldiers from multiple units who had little time to train together.[9] Russian operations also featured large-scale destruction of civilian areas, and there were allegations of widespread human rights abuses. One analyst described the war as follows: "Post-Soviet Russia fought its first war—the First Chechen War—in 1994–96. In effect, it lost: a nation with a population of 147 million was forced to recognize the effective autonomy of Chechnya, a country one-hundredth its size and with less than one-hundredth of its people. A mix of brilliant guerrilla warfare and ruthless terrorism was able to humble Russia's decaying remnants of the Soviet war machine."[10]

⬚ CHECHNYA II

Within two years of signing a peace treaty, Russian forces again invaded Chechnya. The rationale was the invasion of Dagestan by Chechen-based forces from the Islamic International Peacekeeping Brigade. However, a series of apartment bombings in Moscow and Volgodonsk in September 1999 was also used as a strategic justification for the second Russian operation in Chechnya.[11]

The Russians had studied the lessons of the first war in Chechnya and made efforts to improve their performance for the subsequent campaign from 1999. This included improved planning and training, the use of firepower, and the integration of forces on the ground and in the air.

On its second attempt, Russia commenced its invasion with a large aerial campaign in August 1999. This was followed by land operations of a much larger scale than its first operation. Up to 80,000 Russian troops were involved in a hard-fought campaign in Grozny as well as a mountain campaign. Despite efforts to learn from the first Chechen war, many Russian soldiers were still poorly prepared for urban combat, and many of the reforms in command and control eventually broke down as the campaign continued. Despite this, major combat operations were largely completed by the beginning of May 2000, although a counterinsurgency campaign followed for another nine years.[12]

⬚ RUSSO-GEORGIA WAR OF 2008

In August 2008, Russia conducted a five-day war against Georgia. While the Russian military overcame its tiny adversary, this brief conflict did reveal multiple deficiencies in the larger country's armed forces: first Russia's air force performed poorly. As Pallin and Westerlund note, "The Russian ability to combat enemy air defence . . . was clearly limited, even against a small and not particularly advanced adversary."[13] Advanced reconnaissance technologies were lacking, impacting on situational awareness. And the command and control mechanisms necessary for modern, unified, and joint military operations were lacking: different services were unable to integrate their operations.

One of the few positive takeaways from the war for Russia was that it generated significant self-critique and debate within the Russian military. The country's Chief of the General Staff at the time, General Makarov, described to foreign military attachés that "it is impossible to not notice a certain gap between theory and practice."[14] This kind of self-critique is vital if an institution wishes to learn from its wars and make changes to improve its performance. In the wake of the Russo-Georgia War, significant reform activity commenced in the Russian military, and Minister Serdyukov announced "New Look" reforms to the military in October 2008.[15]

▨ UKRAINE 2014

After Ukrainian president Viktor Yanukovych was removed from office by pro-Western forces, Russia sought to reassert its influence over Ukraine. Beginning in February 2014, Russia conducted two distinct campaigns in Ukraine. The first, between February and March 2014, saw the annexation of Crimea. The second, from February 2014 onward, included the political mobilization and conduct of combat operations in eastern Ukraine.

The Russian operation in Crimea resulted in a rapid seizure of the Ukrainian territory. The operation benefited from several unique circumstances, including the confined geography of Crimea, the proximity of the Russian Black Sea Fleet, and the historical and linguistic links between Russia and many of Crimea's inhabitants. The Russians also employed deception measures including using exercises to cover the move of units, and having Russian soldiers convince Crimean inhabitants that they were native self-defense forces. The Russians also exclusively used elite forces such as naval infantry, airborne forces, Spetznaz, and professional regular infantry for this phase of their Ukraine operation.[16] Supported by strategic information operations, the operation succeeded in rapidly seizing Crimea.

The Russian occupation of Crimea generated little resistance from the West. As Ukrainian historian Serhii Plokhy has written, "Numerous parallels have been drawn between the Crimean 'reunification' and the Austrian Anschluss. . . . In both cases there was hope that the aggressor would not go farther. It proved to be wishful thinking at its worst."[17]

The Russian campaign in eastern Ukraine was conducted differently. Exploiting protests that commenced in eastern Ukraine after Yanukovych was ousted, Russia initially undertook a political destabilization operation in the Donbas region. After the government of Ukraine launched an offensive against pro-Russian forces in

April 2014, Russia intervened that August with what it described as a "humanitarian convoy." In reality this was Russian military personnel, including artillery, to assist separatists in eastern Ukraine. These forces, in combination with militias from the Donetsk and Luhansk People's Republics, succeeded in recapturing much of the ground that the Ukrainian armed forces had secured in the preceding months.

Despite the Minsk I and Minsk II cease-fires, and over twenty subsequent cease-fire agreements, combat operations continued in the Donbas—with varying levels of Russian support—until the Russian major invasion of Ukraine in February 2022. Since then, this ongoing conflict has been absorbed into the larger conflict in Ukraine. The Donbas has been the scene of some of the most bitter fighting since February 2022.

The outcome of the 2014 Russian operations in Ukraine is best summarized by Sir Lawrence Freedman. Writing in late 2014, he describes how "Putin's power play in Ukraine was impulsive and improvised, without any clear sense of the desired end state. Putin offered no long-term vision for Ukraine."[18]

▓ THE INTERVENTION IN SYRIA (2015)

In 2015, Russia commenced military operations in Syria. While it had maintained a small presence in the country since the 1970s, 2015 saw a massive expansion of the Russian footprint there. President Putin, focused on promoting Russia's great power status, used the Syria intervention as part of this strategy. Anna Borshchevskaya has written, "Putin had multiple goals in Syria, but fundamentally, his September 2015 intervention was part of this same pursuit: the erosion of the U.S.-led global order."[19] There was also a firm belief among many in the national security community in Russia that if Syrian president al-Assad's regime fell, Syria would be dismembered and the resulting ISIS- and Al-Qaeda-led Sunni extremism could eventually threaten Russia's soft underbelly in the Caucasus.[20]

For the first time since the fall of the Soviet Union, Russian air, ground, and maritime forces all deployed and fought outside the borders of the old Soviet empire. And despite their aim to ensure the stability and survivability of the Syrian regime, Russia sought to keep its Syria operational footprint small. It has been estimated that the size of the Russian force did not exceed five thousand personnel, including contractors (the Wagner Group and other private military contractors).[21]

The Russian intervention turned the course of Syrian civil war decisively in favor of the al-Assad regime. As Michael Kofman has written, the Syrian operation will "influence an entire generation of military leadership" in Russia.[22] It was clear, at least in the early days of the special military operation in Ukraine, that the Syria experience had a heavy bearing on the most senior leaders of the invasion, most of whom had served in Syria.

At the time that Russian forces crossed the Ukrainian frontier in February 2022, Russian military forces were continuing to underpin the stability of al-Assad's regime in Syria. By late 2022, the Russian military had begun to draw down its forces in Syria, especially air defense units, to redeploy them to Ukraine.[23]

Despite the Russian achievements in Syria, the armed forces of Russia also demonstrated several traits that have relevance to the adaptive capacity of a military institution. Dima Adamsky has studied whether Syria was an indication of a change in Russian strategic culture.[24] He found that despite some shifts toward operational creativity and mission command in Syria, the overall Russian conduct in Syria indicated a steadiness rather than change in the Russian style of war and military thought. He explains,

> The campaign demonstrated such traditional traits as "a holistic approach to strategy and military operations"; a certain degree of recklessness, disconnect between theory and practice, and an inclination to stage events for show; a mix of pragmatic and messianic considerations behind the campaign design; "integral management style"; and the professional military virtue of "operational creativity." Thus, the analysis of the case study has supported the basic theoretical proposition that the strategic behaviour of a given actor is more likely to demonstrate continuity in the culture of war and military tradition, rather than a departure from earlier traits.[25]

Therefore, instead of driving significant reform in how the Russian military performed, the Syrian operation mainly reinforced its extant military culture. This is an important finding because it explains how the Russian military has sought to return to more traditional methods of war in Ukraine and has been slow to learn when the situation changes.

This should not be surprising. The Russian military was primarily engaged in counterinsurgency operations in Syria. It did not have to conduct the complex conventional operations that would test the full spectrum of combat, combat support, and combat service support functions. Additionally, nearly 40 percent of deployed personnel were officers and generals. This was a learning and development opportunity for the Russians and permitted many of its leaders to gain experience in distributed operations. It also field-tested evolved methods for applying fires and uncrewed aerial systems.[26] But it presented no fundamental challenges to the overall Russian system for raising, training, and employing military forces.

This examination of reform programs and operational commitments shows that the Russian military has had ample opportunity to hone its approach to institutional learning and adaptation over the last two decades. Indeed, some reforms in structure and personnel systems were linked to operational experiences, especially the first war in Chechnya, Georgia, and the Syria experience. These should have provided a good foundation for institutional learning once Russian forces crossed into Ukraine for their special military operation.

But other factors, as will be explored below, have also influenced Russian institutional learning and its foundation for adaptation in the Ukraine War.

▒ OTHER INFLUENCES ON PREWAR RUSSIAN MILITARY ADAPTATION

Not long before the war in Ukraine commenced, Russia analyst Timothy Thomas wrote that "Russia's military prowess has increased significantly ever since the appointments of Sergey Shoigu as Minister of Defense in 2012 and Valery Gerasimov's assignment as Chief of the General Staff in 2013. They have diligently worked to fulfill President Vladimir Putin's May 2012 edict that called for modernizing the Armed Forces by 2020."[27] However, this increase in military prowess has not been on full display in Ukraine. Consequently, we need to look beyond reform initiatives and military deployments to build a more accurate picture of Russian adaptive capacity, and the institutional constraints that accompanied the Russian invasion force into Ukraine. A range of institutional factors can prevent the full realization of operational learning and institutional transformation programs.

In some instances, deeply rooted ideas and cultures within military institutions can hinder or even stop military innovation. Multiple authors have explored this tendency in military organizations. These include Norman Dixon's 1976 book *On the Psychology of Military Incompetence* as well as more recent studies such as David Johnson's *Fast Tanks and Heavy Bombers*, Frank Hoffman's *Mars Adapting*, and Dima Adamsky's *The Culture of Military Innovation*.[28]

In other circumstances, the lack of an enduring learning culture can be a significant hindrance to adaptation at all levels. Learning needs to be practiced continuously at all levels of a military institution. As Meir Finkel describes it, self-improvement must be "a central motif in military activity."[29] Military personnel must be able to report and learn from mistakes without fear of punishment. After action reviews in the wake of combat must be undertaken as a deliberate and constant part of postbattle processes. Units must be trained and enabled to identify and share lessons with their adjacent units as well as their higher headquarters. All of these endeavors have been made much simpler in contemporary warfare through the application of digital networks and other communications and database technologies.

Poor force design is yet another factor in hindering the adaptive capacity of a military institution, even if it possesses the ability to identify shortfalls in performance. Some military organizations lack the ability to quickly adapt due to force structure choices made years before a conflict begins. For example, a force designed to primarily conduct light infantry counterinsurgency or peacekeeping operations will find it very difficult to adapt to combined-arms heavy conventional operations because it will not possess the equipment or doctrinal basis for rapid adaptation.

Despite the range of different military deployments undertaken by Russia in the past decade, learning and adaptation still appear to be a challenging endeavor within the Russian military institution. Adaptation has occurred in Russian strategy, tactics, and organizations since the beginning of the war. But the Russian formal and informal processes for learning, sharing lessons, and adapting appear to be slower and less systemically connected than those of Ukraine.[30] Overall, I propose that there are four important factors that have hindered—but not stopped—Russian adaptation in their Ukrainian special military operation: overly centralized control; force design shortfalls; a disconnect between theory and practice; and fear.

Ongoing Culture of Centralized Control

In his book on the Soviet invasion and occupation of Afghanistan, *The Great Gamble*, Gregory Feifer wrote that "an over centralized military command that reserved most decision making for the top was ineffective for taking quick actions and facilitating the rapid mobility needed."[31] This overcentralization is also reflected in a 2021 research paper from the Center for Naval Analyses titled "Russian Approaches to Competition." Its authors propose that decision-making in Russia was becoming increasingly centralized. Issues of strategy and military coordination were more often than not being decided in the Kremlin. While the integration of all aspects of nation power is an important function of governments and government agencies, not every decision can or should be made centrally. That can result in groupthink and can deny policymakers access to a fuller range of ideas than might be available in a more disaggregated decision-making culture.[32]

This centralization can also result in high workloads for the few at the center of decision-making, and lower productivity. The book *Russian Approaches to Competition* describes the situation thus: "This high degree of centralization leads to reliance on what is often termed the 'vertical of power,' or a hierarchical chain of authority that is built to provide for the disciplined implementation of decisions reached at the top."[33]

Ironically, during the first two terms of President Putin's rule, this resulted in as few as only half of his presidential decrees being carried out. Bureaucratic reluctance is shaped by normal institutional resistance to change as well as corrupt government officials' unwillingness to change their modes of revenue raising and acquisition of personal benefits. Reforms that improve efficiency in the Russian system are rare. As the authors of *Russian Approaches to Competition* note, "Russian institutional capacity is a significant inhibitor to seeing through a coherent approach or strategy."[34]

Until recently, Putin surrounded himself with three types of people: economic experts; cynical political fixers; and former and current security service and law enforcement personnel, known as the *siloviki*. But over time the first two groups were marginalized, and as a result the *siloviki*, particularly the more hardline personalities, gained the ascendency in Putin's inner circle of advisers. At the same time, he has convened his Security Council less often.[35]

Putin's isolation as an informed decision-maker became more pronounced during and after the COVID-19 pandemic. He sequestered himself in isolated locations, communicating with a small group of people via video-conferencing facilities. In an April 2023 speech the director of the U.S. Central Intelligence Agency, Bill Burns, described how Putin's "circle of advisers narrowed and in that small circle it has never been career-enhancing to question his judgment or his almost mystical belief that his destiny is to restore Russia's influence."[36]

The overcentralization of power in Russia has also led to the Russian president receiving less diverse views on strategy. He is less likely to be exposed to views that might counter his personally held beliefs. Over many years this has resulted in an atmosphere where few were willing to either warn him of the dangers of certain strategies, including military intervention. As former Russian diplomat Boris Bondarev has written, "Putin likes his foreign minister, Sergey Lavrov, because he is 'comfortable' to work with, always saying yes to the president and telling him what he wants to hear."[37]

And because Putin did not receive sufficient warning of the risks of military operations against Ukraine, he apparently believed that the Russian army would be unbeatable in military operations against its smaller neighbor. These bad strategic assumptions, discussed in part I of this book, underpinned the planning and early conduct of the war.[38] For many months into the invasion, Putin was still being deceived by his closest advisers. In a briefing by Defense Minister Shoigu two weeks after the invasion, at a time when the invasion was bogged down north of Kyiv, Shoigu informed Putin that "everything is going to plan."[39]

Boris Bondarev has also described this situation. A former Russian diplomat with twenty years' experience in the Russian Ministry of Foreign Affairs before his May 2022 resignation, he has written how the war is "a stark demonstration of how decisions made in echo chambers can backfire. Putin has failed in his bid to conquer Ukraine, an initiative that he might have understood would be impossible if his government had been designed to give honest assessments."[40] And if the Russian government functions in this manner, there is no prospect of its military institutions functioning in any way that is divergent from this centralized control model.

This culture of resistance to change, and the *power vertical,* is important to understand because it sets the example for how other government institutions operate at lower levels, including the Russian military. The Russian military has a very centralized command culture. This poses significant challenges to the identification of institutional problems as well as the development of solutions to those problems. This phenomenon in Russia is summed up by Dima Adamsky in *The*

Culture of Military Innovation: "The General Staff was not a futuristic crowd of military theoreticians but a 'brain' that commanded operations that it had planned singlehandedly and coordinated ground, air and naval forces on a number of fronts. It envisioned future war and then prepared, planned and executed it."[41]

Finally, these views were echoed by Owen Matthews in his 2022 book about the lead-up to the February 2022 Russian invasion of Ukraine, *Overreach*. Writing about the 21 February 2022 national security meeting where Putin conducted his final consultations about the pending war, Matthews describes how

> the most deluded and the most ideologically driven members of Putin's entourage were on the inside, while those with the most detailed and forensic real-world knowledge were on the outside. . . . Putin showed in his Security Council meeting that he was interested not in debate but in ritual public displays of approval. Dissent—such as Shoigu's misgivings about the wisdom of annexing Crimea in 2014—was no longer conceivable.[42]

There is a close link between societies and the military institutions they produce. They are not, and cannot be, entirely separate entities. After all, military institutions recruit from, live among, and service their communities. Sir John Hackett explored this theme in *The Profession of Arms* in 1983. He argued that "what a society gets in its armed services is exactly what it asks for, no more and no less. When a country looks at its fighting forces it is looking in a mirror; the mirror is a true one and face that it sees will be its own."[43]

If a political system is unable to listen to diverse views and consider a broader array of options, that has a knock-on effect within its military forces. This then becomes an obstacle to honest reflections on performance, learning, and adapting to improve military effectiveness. This is likely to have been a fundamental inhibitor to Russian strategic and military effectiveness in its war with Ukraine.

Force Design Shortfalls

The reforms undertaken by the Russian military prior to 2012 focused on the development of a more professional force, like its Western counterparts. The Russian army sought to consolidate units, formations, and equipment to form a smaller and more ready permanent military force. Like many Western military institutions, the Russian general staff believed that a smaller but better-equipped military would be able to respond to a broad variety of conflicts and security challenges.

The reforms designed to bring this new force into being were partially reversed after Gerasimov and Shoigu were appointed to their positions in 2012. These included the most resented yet least consequential cuts: reductions in the cohorts of Suvorovtsy and Nakhimovtsy, the cadets who attended the Suvorov Military Schools and Nakhimov Naval Schools.[44] Defense Minister Shoigu also expanded the number of military units, giving the appearance of a larger military and increased the number of military exercises. The number of contracted permanent soldiers never fully materialized, however, and the Russian military was left to rely on a mix of conscripts, contracted soldiers, and empty positions that would be filled through wartime mobilization. Michael Kofman and Rob Lee have described the outcome of this trade-off as follows:

> Russian ground formations were staffed somewhere between 70 to 90 percent. . . . A 3,500 sized brigade might only have 2,500 men at peacetime. When accounting for 30 percent conscripts likely to be in the unit, this meant that no more than 1,700 would be considered deployable. If actual readiness levels were being padded, or there were insufficient numbers of contract servicemen to fill out two battalion tactical groups, then the real number of forces available was even further reduced.[45]

Despite the best intentions of most commanders, conventional wars eventually are decided by who can produce the most material, who has the most strategic endurance (or will), and who is able to sustain larger forces in the field. The Russian force design choices in the lead-up to the 2022 invasion of Ukraine meant that the Russian military was compromised in its ability to deploy and sustain large-scale forces. And because it was so busy trying to raise new units and find replacements for its casualties in Ukraine, it had less capacity to undertake the learning and adaptation necessary on military operations. Force structure choices made long before the 2022 invasion were found to be wanting in the early days of the invasion, and problems were exacerbated by poor tactical employment of those forces. As Michael Kofman and Rob Lee have written, "The Russian campaign floundered not just because it pursued unrealistic political goals, but also because the plan for the invasion did not account for the choices made on force structure, and the limitations they imposed."[46]

Ultimately, the force design choices made years in advance of a war can have an impact on the ability of that force to learn and adapt when it goes to war. These choices, made by senior Russian leaders over the past decade, have had an impact on Russian adaptive capacity since 2022.

▓ ▓ Disconnected Theory and Practice

Another insidious yet all-too-common factor that has provided a set of obstacles to more effective adaptation by the Russian forces is a gap between military theory and practice. Closing the gap between theory and practice in military institutions is challenging even for the best military forces. The chasm between great theories and the implementation and practice of those theories has rarely stopped the Soviets or the Russians. The Soviets were very good at thinking innovatively, which manifested in ideas such as *operational theory* and the *military technological revolution* (MTR). But implementation left much to be desired.

The implementation of the MTR, and the need for flexibility and independent action, faced significant obstacles in a Soviet military that did not possess these qualities in abundance. As Dima Adamsky writes, "Rarely were the holistic and profound visions of Soviet theoreticians transformed into concrete, practical ideas."[47] This cultural trait was also apparent in the Russian operations in Syria, according to Adamsky.[48]

This issue has also been raised in a 2022 Royal United Services Institute (RUSI) report that explored shortfalls in Russian performance in Ukraine. Of particular note has been the difference between the theory and practice of battalion tactical groups (BTGs). The Russian army had insufficient personnel to man these new organizations before the war commenced, and this only got worse as they sustained casualties in Ukraine. As the RUSI report noted, "The battalion staff is insufficient to manage all the enablers that are assigned." Compounding this issue has been the design of the BTG, which is compromised after taking even small amounts of casualties.[49] Therefore, the BTG concept is both a shortfall in design and an example of theory being disconnected from practice.

▒ ▒ Fear

A final influence on the adaptive capacity of Russian individuals and institutions is fear. The Russian military has a reputation, based on strong evidence, of brutalizing its members. Long before Russian forces crossed the border into Ukraine, the Russian military possessed a culture of cruelty. As Gregory Feifer describes the circumstances of Red Army soldiers in Afghanistan in the 1980s, "Many young men's more immediate and important problems [was] abuse from their superiors."[50]

Systemic hazing also breeds fear. Despite some attempts to stamp it out, the military has a brutal hazing system known as *dedovshchina*. It is a tradition that encourages senior conscripts to beat, brutalize, or even rape younger soldiers.[51] In 2004, this practice was investigated by Human Rights Watch, which found that "under a system called dedovshchina, second-year conscripts force new recruits to live in a yearlong state of pointless servitude, punish them violently for any infractions of official or informal rules, and abuse them gratuitously. Dozens of conscripts are killed every year as a result of these abuses, and thousands sustain serious—and often permanent—damage to their physical and mental health."[52] Thousands of reports of abuse are made each year, and many soldiers also die at the hands of senior soldiers.[53] This creates a brutal culture, with knock-on effects for how Russian soldiers treat civilians and prisoners of war. And it ensures that a culture of fear pervades the lower ranks, one of the principal sources of innovation in military institutions.

But fear is prevalent in more senior ranks as well. Failure is rarely reported and almost never accepted. In his exploration of Russia's early operations in the war, Andriy Zagorodnyuk writes,

From now on, fear will shape every single decision made by Russian commanders in Ukraine. This will not be fear of losing precious lives or damaging Russia's national interests; it will be a very personal fear of retribution from a vindictive hierarchy seeking culprits to blame for the rapidly declining fortunes of the Russian army. This reaction speaks volumes about the dysfunctional leadership culture within the Russian military, where fear of failure has been the dominant instinct since Soviet times and can arguably be traced all the way back to the czarist era.[54]

This issue of fear was explored by a RUSI team in their preliminary findings of lessons from the war in November 2022. Their report found that the "reporting culture" of the Russian army was deficient because it "does not encourage honest reporting of failures."[55] Anyone who is perceived to have failed is normally replaced or punished. For more senior leaders in the army, failure can result in important missions being stripped from the organization they command. As the RUSI report notes,

> Far from incentivising success, this often leads to dishonest reporting in which the blame for failure is transferred onto others. This scapegoating of colleagues—endemic in the Russian special services but also in the military—obscures the actual operational problems that must be solved. These only become apparent when they can no longer be concealed, slowing the learning of lessons, but also leading to predictable and predicted vulnerabilities not being addressed.[56]

This is hardly a good basis for expecting soldiers and officers to honestly report problems, let alone propose new procedures or solutions to operational problems. Fear of reporting honestly and exposing bad news on the battlefield is a significant inhibitor in Russian battlefield and strategic adaptation.

HINDERING ADAPTIVE CAPACITY

Given their reform efforts, and their operational experience in the preceding decades, one would have expected a better performance from the Russian military in the early days of its new invasion of Ukraine in 2022. That they did not will be the subject of analysis for decades to come. But it is prudent to not underestimate the Russians' military capability or their ability to learn and adapt. As one study of initial lessons of the war pointed out, "There is a perception that the AFRF [Armed Forces of the Russian Federation] are systemically incompetent, irredeemably corrupt, that their weapons are ineffective and unreliable, and that the force is incapable of adapting. This narrative is dangerous, both because it is inaccurate, and also because it encourages complacency."[57] Therefore, in the following chapters we turn to an exploration of Russia's adaptive capacity during their Ukraine operations at the strategic, operational, and tactical levels.

10

DYSFUNCTIONAL WARFARE

Russian Adaptation in Ukraine

IN AN ARTICLE that explored the early days of the Russian February 2022 invasion of Ukraine, Professor Rob Johnson examined systemic weakness in the strategic and operational planning undertaken by the Russians in the lead-up to the war. He described dysfunctionality in the tactical-operational interface of Russian operations and concluded that "Russia's operational dysfunctionality has prevented military success [and] the political miscalculations made by the Kremlin have been even more significant. . . . The war remains an example of supreme folly conducted with shameful brutality."[1]

Despite this dysfunctionality, the Russian military has been able to adapt to the changing circumstances it has faced. While the performance of Russian forces in Ukraine has at times been professionally awful, it has still demonstrated learning at the unit and higher levels during the war. The Russians had to adapt their campaign within the first forty-eight hours because their attempt at a lightning conquest of Ukraine failed. Since then, the Russians have had to adapt at the strategic, operational, and tactical levels. The aim of this chapter is to explore Russian adaptation, with a focus on adaptation that has taken place at the war's strategic and operational levels.

STRATEGIC ADAPTATION

"Strategic adaptation" refers to the learning and adaptation that occurs at the strategic level or has an impact that affects the making of national and military strategy and the war's overall direction. In *Military Adaptation in War*, Williamson Murray describes how "adaptation at the strategic level may represent the easiest to recognise but the most difficult to accomplish."[2]

In a 2023 *Foreign Affairs* article, scholar of military innovation Barry Posen explored how the Russians had partially recovered in the preceding months from the setbacks of 2022. He describes how "the Russians continue to do many dumb things and indeed still do. But broadly speaking, the Ukrainians' intuition in the summer now appears correct: when it comes to overall military strategy, Moscow seems to have gotten smarter. . . . Russian strategic decisions are finally starting to make military sense."[3]

In addition to the adaptation to Russian strategy explored earlier in this book, there have been two important Russian strategic adaptations since the beginning of the war: the mobilization of the Russian population; and the movement toward a more unified approach to military command and control for the special military operation in Ukraine.

Mobilizing the People (Partially)

An important strategic adaptation, although an incomplete one, has been Russia's readoption of mobilization to replace combat losses, increase the size of its military, and expand the output of indigenous defense production. The term "readopt" is apt because mobilization was a central element in Soviet strategy to expand the size of its military forces during wartime. Soviet units were located across the breadth of the USSR, and throughout the Cold War they remained dependent on the mobilization of large numbers of reservists. This was driven by the need not only to balance NATO forces but also to prepare for a worst-case scenario, where the Soviet Union might be at war with NATO and China.[4]

This Cold War approach was founded on the experience of growing Soviet forces after the German invasion during World War II. While much of the Soviet Union's productive capacity had to be relocated farther east to avoid capture or destruction by German forces, by 1942 it had achieved a significant expansion. In 1942–43, the Soviets produced over 20,000 tanks, and over 100,000 artillery pieces, per year.[5]

At the end of World War II, senior Soviet military leaders believed that future wars were most likely to resemble the war just finished, although these would probably also include atomic weapons. Such wars would require large numbers of personnel arranged in Divisions and Army Groups, similar to the Soviet Army that had fought its way across Eastern Europe and into Berlin in 1945. But to sustain such a large force without bankrupting the Soviet Union, the Soviet leadership implemented a system of universal conscription. Military service was seen as an "obligation of citizenship," deferments were limited, and a high percentage of eighteen- to twenty-one-year-olds served as conscripts.[6] This, along with the bases, stored equipment, and expert cadre staff, allowed the Soviet military—especially its ground forces—to rapidly expand.[7]

The downsizing the Russian forces in the wake of the Cold War, and the professionalization reforms in the two decades before the invasion of Ukraine, removed much of the mobilization infrastructure. Physical infrastructure for expansion was either demolished or left to rot. Processes and procedures for military mobilization were forgotten or not updated. The 2009 New Look reforms played a key role in this process. At that time, many senior leaders believed that resources were being squandered on retaining a mass mobilization capability and that these resources could be better used by increasing the size and readiness of active units. As Sam Cranny-Evans explains in a 2022 report, "Many of the cadres responsible for maintaining the equipment and knowledge were disbanded after 2008, leading to a loss of equipment and capability."[8]

From 2014, Russia began to establish a voluntary military reserve force. Reservists began to participate in Russian military exercises shortly afterward. From 2021, the reserve force was renamed as the Special Combat Army Reserve. By some reports, this force began to be activated as early as August 2021, aiming for a strength of 38,000 personnel.[9]

At the time of its invasion of Ukraine, the Russian military had higher readiness but was a much smaller regular force than it possessed during the Soviet era. If Russia's original plan for taking over Ukraine had gone smoothly, this would have been fine for a short campaign of military intimidation to replace President Zelenskyy and install a Ukrainian government more favorable to Russia's interests. It did not work out that way. And in having to engage in sustained combat operations against the Ukrainian armed forces, the Russian military suffered levels of personnel and equipment losses that its New Look military was not designed to absorb.

By September 2022, even the most optimistic Russian government and military leaders could not avoid a key conclusion: Russia's standing military forces were not large enough to undertake a long-term campaign in Ukraine. Consequently, strategic adaptation was necessary in the Russian system for utilizing its citizens in wartime.

The first element of this strategic adaptation was the announcement of partial mobilization by President Putin on 21 September 2022: "I find it necessary to support the proposal of the Defence Ministry and the General Staff on partial mobilisation in the Russian Federation to defend our Motherland and its sovereignty and territorial integrity, and to ensure the safety of our people and people in the liberated territories."[10] This decree included the mobilization of personnel as well as measures to increase Russian industrial production to support the war. The process was initially chaotic. As Mark Cancian describes in a contemporary report on Russian mobilization, "The bureaucracy appears unready to handle the demands of such a complex effort."[11] But the process was eventually streamlined and at least 300,000 Russians were inducted into the army.[12] And while the Russian declared the mobilization had been completed by 1 November 2022, some experts believed that the Russians continued a less visible, smaller-scale continuous mobilization after that time.[13] This has been described by the Institute for the Study of War as "crypto-mobilization."[14]

A portion of the mobilized troops were deployed to Ukraine within a month of their enlistment. Some were sent to eastern Ukraine, while others were deployed to parts of Kherson west of the Dnipro River then held by the Russians. Many of the mobilized troops were employed as tactical rear guards during the Russian withdrawal from western Kherson in November 2022 in order to allow higher-quality Russian troops to escape.[15]

A second part of the Russian mobilization process was the January 2023 announcement of reforms to military force structure and the expansion of the military for large-scale, sustained military operations. The Russian defense minister, Sergey Shoigu, announced that he will implement large-scale changes to the military between 2023 and 2026. These include the expansion of the Russian armed services to 1.5 million and the formation of twelve new divisions.[16] But as Russian military expert Dara Massicot stated regarding these Russian plans in testimony to the U.S. Congress in February 2023, "Russia's combat potential is diminished due to the number and type of losses it has sustained in the first year of the war. . . . It is unlikely that Russia will be able to expand to that number in the next few years, short of multiple rounds of mobilization."[17]

While the Russian military has demonstrated the capacity to strategically adapt to its changed circumstances in Ukraine, these adaptations remain incomplete. The impact of mobilization, including the medium- and long-term impacts of PTSD on returning veterans, will play out over the coming years and decades. Dara Massicot has written that "Russia's looming troop-retention and veteran-treatment problems are already visible on the horizon, even though they have been delayed by policy. By invading Ukraine, Russia has created a wave of severe trauma that will soon crash over its own country."[18]

The ultimate impact of Russian short-term mobilization initiatives—positive or negative on the war overall—remains to be seen. Longer-term expansion plans, which will face significant obstacles due to ongoing losses in Ukraine, and the difficulties of replacing Russian equipment due to supply constraints, remain similarly in doubt. The true human cost of this strategic adaptation, which has resulted in many more Russian citizens being killed, wounded, and exposed to the traumas of combat, will manifest themselves in the coming decades.

More Unified Command and Control

The second Russian strategic adaptation has been the evolution of their command and control for the special military operation in Ukraine. In April 2022, the Russian president appointed a single overall commander for the Russian campaign, Colonel General Alexander Dvornikov.[19] Awarded the Hero of the Russian Federation title for his command role in Syria in 2015, Dvornikov had previously served as the commander of Russia's Southern military district. It was an adaptation of the initial dysfunctional command and control design and aimed to bring improved unity of effort to the war.

Dvornikov brought focus on the eastern front, but the battles there proved to be enormously expensive for the Russians in terms of manpower and material. Although they had been able to lure the Ukrainians into an attritional fight they could not afford for a short period, it came at the cost of thousands of Russians killed and wounded for the gain of minimal territory. And once the United States provided Ukraine with its long-range rocket artillery system, the High Mobility Artillery Rocket System (HIMARS), this eastern campaign was largely brought to a standstill by clever Ukrainian targeting of Russian logistics, artillery, and headquarters.

By September 2022, when the Ukrainians had launched offensives in Kherson and Kharkiv and also attacked the Kerch Bridge, the Russian president decided he needed a new commander. In October 2022, Russian General Surovikin was appointed. He had a long service history in the Russian army, having graduated from an officer training academy in Omsk in 1987 and served in Afghanistan, Chechnya, and Syria. He had a reputation for brutality.

Almost immediately after his assumption of command, Surovikin used his unified command powers to evolve the Russian campaign. He ordered a series of massed missile and drone attacks against Ukrainian civilians and civilian infrastructure. This campaign was focused on the systemic targeting, degradation, and destruction of Ukraine's power generation and distribution network. Coming as it did just before the onset of the Ukrainian winter, where temperatures can remain well below zero for long stretches of time, this immediately began to impose significant humanitarian suffering on the people of Ukraine.

It was a campaign with little military utility, although it forced the Ukrainians to move some of their air defense assets to defend critical power stations. In reality, the evolved Russian approach was a terror campaign. It was designed to cower the Ukrainian people and force its government into an accommodation with the Russian leadership. Sir Lawrence Freedman described this new Russian approach as "a coercive Russian strategy against Ukrainian society. . . . Russia is also trying to turn off the power and electricity in Ukraine. The Ukrainians cannot do the same against the Russians in terms of targeting infrastructure. The Ukrainians are winning on the battlefield, but they cannot hit back against the Russians on that strategic level."[20]

By early January 2023, the Ukrainians had not capitulated, and Russian forces had suffered defeats on the battlefield at both Kherson and Kharkiv. Russian forces had also suffered mass casualties during a rocket attack on a barracks in the small town of Makiivka.[21]

Putin decided again to adapt the command of the operation in Ukraine. This time it was a significant adaptation because he placed in charge the man who for the previous decade had been a Putin loyalist. On day 322 of the Russian invasion, the Russian Ministry of Defense announced that General Valery Gerasimov had been appointed as the "commander of the combined forces group for the special military operation in Ukraine." He was the end product of nearly a year of strategic adaptation in the command and control of the Russian special military operation.

▬

The Russian military, despite its strategic and battlefield shortfalls in this war, has nonetheless demonstrated the ability to adapt at the strategic level to continue what has become a national effort to subjugate Ukraine. However, the strategic level is not the only aspect of military endeavor where the Russian military has demonstrated the ability to learn and adapt since the start of their invasion of Ukraine. The operational level has also seen important adaptations.

▓ OPERATIONAL ADAPTATION

Operational adaptation is the learning and change that take place where military campaigns are planned, executed, and won or lost. Many draw a distinction between the operational level of war, and operational art. The operational level, described in the doctrinal manuals of many military institutions, is "the level of operations at which campaigns and major operations are planned, conducted and sustained to accomplish strategic objectives within theatres or areas of operations."[22] Operational art, on the other hand, is "the disciplines required to place military forces in an advantageous position to employ tactics to achieve strategic effects."[23]

Therefore, this is an adaptive process that occurs above the level of battles and tactical concerns but beneath the layer where military strategies are produced and enacted. It is the ability to learn and then improve military effectiveness for the employment of major forces in the achievement of strategic aims in a theater of war.[24]

Three key Russian operational adaptations are explored below: military objectives, force disposition, and logistics.

▨ ▨ Adapting Military Objectives

In military operations, the desired outcome must be simple, widely communicated and understood, and aligned with political objectives. Those political objectives must also be achievable within the resources, scale, and capacity of the military forces available to a nation.

Initial Russian war aims were very broad. Officially, Putin sought to "demilitarise and de-Nazify Ukraine."[25] This language, which appeared in Putin's speech to his nation on the eve of the invasion, has remained in use throughout his special military operation. Achieving that goal, however, would require the seizure of large parts of Ukraine's territory as well as its capital (Kyiv) and major cities in the Northeast, East, and South. The "demilitarization and de-Nazification" objective also saw Russia aiming to replace the democratically elected government with one more amenable to Moscow and to ensure that Ukraine would be unable to become a member of the European Union or NATO.

Subsequent discoveries of documents have revealed that the Russian government expected its military to be able to achieve this, and transition to an occupation footing, within about ten days of the invasion commencing.[26] In the initial phases of the war, the Russians sought to prosecute their war on four fronts on the ground, in Ukraine's North, Northeast, East, and South:

- The Northern Front, with three combined arms armies (the 29th, 35th, and 36th) commanded by Russia's Eastern Military District.
- The Northeastern Front, with two combined arms armies (the 41st and 2nd Guards) commanded by the Central Military District.
- The Eastern Front, with the 1st Guards Tank Army and two other combined arms armies (the 6th and 20th) commanded by the Western Military District.
- The Southern Front, with three combined arms armies (the 8th, 49th, and 58th) and air assault division and air assault brigade, commanded by Russia's Southern Military District.[27]

In addition to these ground assaults on four different axes, a campaign of air and missile attacks was conducted against Ukraine, and a strategic influence operation was undertaken.[28] It became clear early in the Russian special military operation that these were being run as their own separate wars by military districts rather than as subelements of a unified Russian campaign. While southern forces made good progress, those in the East and North quickly bogged down in close combat and attrition of logistic systems.

By March 2022, the Russians had to adapt and consolidate their aims to narrower objectives in the East. They redeployed their exhausted ground forces from the North of Ukraine back into Belarus and Russia. The Russians then began to redeploy those units to eastern Ukraine. It was apparent by April that the Russians, while they might still have long-term aspirations to subjugate Ukraine, had decided to narrow their short-term focus on the Donbas. The key military objective now shifted from capturing Kyiv and other key Ukrainian political centers to the attrition of the Ukrainian military.

Another aspect of adaptation to Russian military objectives that occurred in the first year of the war was the shift from offensive operations to defensive operations. From February 2022 until July 2022, the Russians largely held the strategic and operational initiative in the war. Despite setbacks in the North, they retained an offensive strategy and operational posture. After the grinding attrition of the Donbas campaign, however, the Russian forces enter an operational pause period. On 7 July 2022, the Russian Defense Ministry stated, "The units that performed combat missions . . . are taking measures to recover their combat capabilities. The servicemen are given the opportunity to rest."[29]

Not long afterward, the Ukrainians commenced offensive operations in Kherson, and in September they began their lightning offensive in Kharkiv. The Russians had to quickly adapt to assume an operational posture that placed them on the defensive. They remained on the defensive until the commencement of the Gerasimov-directed Russian offensive that was launched at the beginning of 2023.

The Russian plan had not anticipated drawn-out combat operations in Ukraine. When these combat operations eventuated in the North and the East, the Russians had little choice but to change their military objectives for the war—at least temporarily. And in adapting their military objectives, the Russians also had to change the disposition of their forces in Ukraine.

Adapting Force Disposition and Posture

From April 2022, the Russians adopted a more concentrated deployment in Ukraine, focusing on operations in the East, with smaller supporting efforts in the Northeast and South. The Russian operations around Kharkiv at this time appear to have been an economy of force mission, designed to keep Ukrainian forces pinned in the North so they could not be redeployed to the nation's southern or eastern regions.

The Russian occupation of Ukraine's southern territory provided a land bridge from Russia to Crimea. It also deprived Ukraine of the many mines, steelmaking facilities, and agricultural production from which it might earn export revenue. In the South, the Russians also captured many of Ukraine's seaports, further hindering export activity.

But it was in the East that the Russians focused much of their combat power in this next phase of the war, from April 2022. The Russian intelligence services had fostered and resourced separatist movements in the Donbas region since 2014. And

Putin fixated on the people of this region, and their protection from Nazis, in his speeches before the war.

This greater concentration of forces was hindered by shortfalls in Russian combat troops, however. The Russians entered the war with units not fully manned, particularly in infantry troops. As a result of the Kyiv campaign, they had lost a significant proportion of these troops. Therefore, in this second phase of the war the Russians adapted their operations to focus more on firepower and their advantage over the Ukrainians in numbers of artillery systems and quantities of munitions available. At one point, the Russians had a 12:1 numerical superiority over the Ukrainians in artillery systems, and it told on the battlefield. Heavy Russian barrages resulted in some of the highest daily casualty figures of the war for the Ukrainian armed forces.[30] It also forced them to slowly give up ground in the East, including the key city of Severodonetsk.[31]

This shift to the East of Ukraine led to some tactical success for the Russian forces. This Eastern Front campaign did for a time draw the Ukrainians into an attritional fight, often resulting in over one hundred killed in action per day on both sides. However, the Russians were also suffering large numbers of casualties, and because of their continued shortfalls in infantry, they were expending massive amounts of artillery munitions. Although they were able to capture the final Ukrainian-controlled city in Luhansk, Severodonetsk, in late June 2022, the costs of Russia's Luhansk operations did not justify the small amount of territory its army secured.[32]

While the Russian military had adapted their tactics and the geography of their deployed forces, their operational successes remained minimal. They had captured territory but had not broken the Ukrainian armed forces. And despite an operational pause in the wake of the Luhansk operation, Russian forces since then have made minimal battlefield progress in the East. Their 2023 offensive, overseen by General Gerasimov, gained little ground and wasted an enormous number of lives and a massive quantity of munitions and equipment.

But Gerasimov's offensive in 2023 did buy time for another significant operational adaptation—the development of very extensive defensive works in southern Ukraine. In late 2022, then–overall Russian commander General Surovikin initiated the construction of obstacles, including minefields, antitank trenches, and strongpoints, to defend southern Ukraine. The Russians spent over six months developing this scheme of defense, which was initially designed to stop Ukrainian forces overwhelming exhausted Russian forces in the wake of the Kharkiv and Kherson offensives.

Built across one thousand kilometers of southern (and eventually eastern) Ukraine, the Russians have constructed the most extensive defensive layout in the world in decades, which has come to be described as the Surovikin Line. A report from the Center for Strategic and International Studies described this as "one of the largest defensive systems in Europe since World War II."[33] The obstacle zones built by the Russians contain fortified forward security zones as well as main defensive lines. The depth of the Surovikin Line varies but can be many kilometers deep. It contains antitank obstacles, mined trenches, minefields, and trenches manned by Russian soldiers as well as many reinforced strong points.[34]

This very long, and quite deep, zone of obstacles and defending troops poses multiple challenges to the attacking Ukrainians.

First, Russian observation of the entire defensive scheme is pervasive. As examined elsewhere in this book, the war has seen a steady integration of sensors in a new-era meshed civil-military framework. The Russians employ drones, electronic warfare (EW), counterbattery radars, dismounted and mounted reconnaissance soldiers and sensors, civil information, and satellite collection to produce a near real-time picture of the battle space. This poses major issues for any combined arms–breaching activities by the Ukrainians.

Second, with pervasive observation along the defenses, this has simplified the use and prioritization of Russian fire support. Artillery, long-range rockets, attack rotary and fixed-wing aircraft, loitering munitions, scatterable mines, and electronic warfare have all been prepared, and used, to prevent a Ukrainian breakthrough in the initial phase of their 2023 offensive.[35]

Finally, the Russians have improved the quality of the forces defending the South. In accordance with their defensive doctrine,[36] the Russians have executed a defensive regime composed of static and mobile elements. While there remain many mobilized troops who are of a lower quality than the best Russian forces, these are buttressed with higher-quality elite troops that act as mobile reserve forces. The mobile elements include airborne and mechanized Russian army units as well as artillery batteries that move depending on where Ukraine might be attacking. These elite forces are often held just behind the main defensive positions as well as areas well to the rear and have been employed effectively in response to where a Ukrainian breakthrough appears possible.[37]

These defenses have played a major role in slowing down the Ukrainian 2023 advances in the south of Ukraine and have been a successful operational adaptation for the Russians.

One other event has had a major impact on Russian operational adaptation. Mid-2022 saw the introduction of HIMARS, allowing the Ukrainians to make longer-range and more precise strikes on high-value Russian targets. Not only did this have an impact on the conduct of Russian operations; it also drove adaptation in how the Russians supported their forces in Ukraine. The adaptation of Russian logistics is the focus of the final operational-level adaptation examined in this chapter.

▓ ▓ Logistics and National Support

In an early 2023 article, Brad Martin asked an important question about the trajectory of the war in Ukraine: "Will logistics be Russia's undoing in Ukraine?"[38] It is an important topic, because the longer this war continues, the ability of nations to mobilize their tactical, operational, and national logistic support bases will have a greater impact on the battlefield and beyond.

Logistic support takes many forms in war. It is the basic provision of food, water, fuel, repair parts, and ammunition to soldiers and their vehicles engaged in battlefield operations or preparing for them. It is the logistic support by units behind the lines that undertake recovery, repair, and maintenance of vehicles; treatment and evacuation of human casualties; or the forward movement of ammunition and a range of other commodities. Logistic support also includes the national industrial capacity of nation to procure or manufacture the myriad of things that soldiers and other service personnel use during peacetime and in wars. This includes everything from uniforms, small arms, ammunition, and fuel to tanks and fighter aircraft.

Finally, support can have a more international dimension, with nations purchasing—or being gifted—military and logistic support for their essential wartime needs. Whether it is the Lend-Lease program of World War II, the reequipping of the Iraqi and Afghan armies in the wake of the post-9/11 American interventions in their nations, or the provision of military assistance to Ukraine in this war, international support can play a crucial role in wars and the survival of nations.

But it was battlefield logistics early in this current war that drew the attention of military historians and analysts as well as the media more broadly. Indeed, one of the many surprises in this war has been a reinvigoration of the study of military logistics.

On 24 February 2022, Russian forces conducted air mobile operations to capture Antonov Airport, as well as a ground invasion focused on the envelopment and capture of Kyiv. The Russian forces, having planned a short ten-day war, had not forward-deployed many of its normal logistic units. In short, they did not expect to have to fight their way to Kyiv, so they carried their normal three to five days' worth of supplies in the expectation that intermediate logistic hubs would resupply them either on the way to Kyiv or in Kyiv itself.

However, within several days, Russian ground forces found that they were having to fight for every kilometer of ground in a slow, grinding advance on their objective. Added to this, the Russians had failed to secure the Hostomel Airport and establish the forward logistics hub that would be required to support ground forces on the approach to Kyiv. Once the airfield was secured, supplies would have been flown in. But this plan did not succeed.

Therefore, the Russian high command hastily concocted an alternative scheme to send more logistic forces forward on the ground. It was the first, but not the last, instance of Russian adaptation to their operational logistics plan. And as discussed in chapter 8, not all adaptations are successful. This one certainly was not.

Unfortunately, the majority of vehicles used in this grand logistics convoy of February and March 2022 were restricted to the few sealed roads leading south. The result was a massive sixty-four-kilometer traffic jam of military vehicles north of Kyiv.[39] This was too tempting a target for the Ukrainian military: regular and volunteer units conducted hit-and-run attacks, destroying vehicles and supplies and further worsening the shortages of fuel, ammunition, and food for troops in the vanguard of the slow Russian advance.

This logjam of vehicles, artillery, and tanks was captured in satellite pictures and broadcast around the world. Very quickly, commentators were discussing Russian military logistics in news reports and journal articles about the war. Logistics, which rarely receives much attention even from many military organizations, was suddenly of key interest to laypeople and experts alike in their examination of the newly begun Russian invasion.

But what is the genesis of these Russian challenges with military logistics?

The old Soviet military system saw the ground forces organized to fight in echelons.[40] While one echelon was fighting, another was being prepared to replace it and exploit its gains. Each echelon had some integral logistic support, but combat units were not expected to be self-sustaining for long periods of time. Once the initial echelon was replaced on the battlefield, it would be reinforced, reequipped, and resupplied from the Material Technical Support Brigades that were integral to each army group.

After the Soviets finalized their replacement of pack and cart transport with automotive transport in the 1950s, logistic support was based primarily on railway systems and pipelines, with some augmentation by trucks at lower levels.[41] Trains were the foundation on which Soviet, and now Russian, logistic support is based. The reliance on these means of moving supplies forward has meant that Russian expeditionary operations beyond its near abroad are difficult. It has also meant that Russia's Material Technical Support organizations have sustained units for the construction of railways and pipelines to carry fuel and water.[42] Separate railway troops dedicated to the maintaining and protecting railway lines are attached to military districts.

Soviet doctrine emphasized high readiness and the mobility of logistics elements, but they did not incorporate large fleets of road transportation vehicles.[43] Trucks are the foundation of Western military logistics. Truck-based logistics provides a more flexible and adaptive way of supporting operations, because trucks are not restricted to certain railway routes. The Russian ground forces have only enough trucks to allow a ground force to "meet its logistic requirement more than 90 miles beyond supply dumps."[44] Designed for Soviet operations that would thrust into Western Europe during the Cold War, the system based on railways and pipelines demonstrated its weaknesses during the Russian invasion of Ukraine. It has been easy to identify the vehicles, easy to predict their routes, and easy to interdict and destroy them.

Magnifying these logistic challenges have been the reforms undertaken in the Russian army from 2012 onward. The legacy Soviet concept for military logistics was replaced with a leaner model. This largely was a result of the Russian Federation deciding that older mass mobilization models were neither affordable nor desirable, which impacted the overall structure of the Russian military, including their logistic support organizations.[45]

The logistic reforms after 2012 did not significantly interfere with the organizational bias toward railway-centric logistic support to military operations. The reforms did, however, reduce the size of military logistics units and the number of storage bases. They also incorporated outsourcing of functions such as daily fuel deliveries and maintenance.[46] Some of these reforms were subsequently reversed due to complaints from military commanders about the feasibility of contractors undertaking maintenance on the battlefield.

Contemporary Russian maneuver brigades may have only about 75 percent the number of vehicles as Western brigades, but they sometimes have up to three times as much artillery. This imposes a significant logistic challenge on combat forces, particularly in haulage of ammunition. As the Russian ground forces entered Ukraine in 2022 from the north, east, and south, they did so with Material Technical Support organizations that were generally smaller than their Western counterparts. Whereas a U.S. battalion would possess a logistic support company, a Russian battalion (or battalion tactical group) would have something the size of a platoon.[47] This, and the doctrinal reliance on railways, would have a major impact on Russian ground force logistics throughout 2022.

The logistics challenge was compounded by Russian units being generally under-strength in infantry when they crossed the Ukrainian frontier.[48] A consequence of infantry shortages for the Russian military technical support units was that there were no spare combat forces to conduct rear-area security operations. This is an important mission in any conflict, but especially during offensive operations. As the forward troops advance, increased territory must be secured, and the lines of support back to home logistic bases are extended. This territory needs to be defended to prevent air and ground attacks on logistics units, headquarters, and areas where reinforcement troops or reserves are held.

In the march south to Kyiv by the Russian ground forces, there were few Russian combat units for this mission. The Ukrainians identified this weakness quickly, allowing them to attack these rear areas as well as railways, using a mixture of drones, mortars, and artillery as well as special and conventional forces. This reduced the resupply of forward units and degraded their ability to fight and advance. It resulted in the breakdown in tactical cohesion of Russian forces and had an impact on morale. As Skoglund, Listou, and Ekstrom describe, this led to "logistics culmination" and eventually allowed the Ukrainians to undertake a counteroffensive to push the Russians back north into Belarus.[49]

The change in military objectives, and reconcentration of Russian forces in eastern and southern Ukraine, led to additional adaptations in the conduct of Russian military logistics. Not only were Russian forces more concentrated in fewer parts of the country, but they were also closer to large Russian supply bases in Russia. Additionally, Russian forces had been conducting support to operations in Crimea and the Donbas since 2014, so there was a more extensive and practiced approach for Material Technical Support operations in these areas.[50]

Despite the severe difficulties encountered by Russian ground forces in northern Ukraine in the war's early weeks, the Russian military had demonstrated some agility and adaptation in the conduct of logistic support. Throughout the Russian mid-2022 offensive operations in eastern Ukraine, their logistic network was able to sustain the supply of combat units and the resupply of ammunition to Russian artillery units.

While the deployment of HIMARS to eastern Ukraine resulted in the destruction of multiple Russian logistics nodes, until the operational pause in July 2022 the Russian logistic network allowed their combat forces to maintain an overwhelming superiority in firepower. But the Russians adapted to the new, longer-range Ukrainian rocket systems. Logistics nodes were pushed back farther from the front and more dispersed. Supply bases were better camouflaged. Greater use was made of trucks to supplement rail networks. At the same time, the Russians evolved both the firing sequences and the processes involved in linking their reconnaissance and artillery units to increase the effectiveness of artillery units if supply was constrained.[51]

The Russian military logistics system is an example of an adaptation that, at minimum, sustained the battlefield effectiveness of Russian ground forces. As such, it must be viewed as a successful adaptation by the Russians.

▬

The headline of a 2020 article in *The Economist* declared, "Russian Military Forces Dazzle after a Decade of Reform." The piece then proceeded to describe how lavish funding and political attention had led to a Russian military institution that was not only better equipped but "also fleet footed" and enjoyed the advantage of being "blooded in battle."[52]

Since their invasion of Ukraine in February 2022, the Russian military forces have hardly dazzled the world with their prowess in combat. Indeed, for much of the war, the Russians have been a force that shows little resemblance to the one described in that 2020 article in *The Economist*. But that is often the case in war and in combat. As multiple historical examples have shown, from the well-equipped French army before World War II to the allegedly elite Republican Guard in Iraq in 1991, military institutions that appear impressive in peacetime may fail miserably in combat. But they can redeem themselves if they either possess—or develop—a learning culture when war breaks out.

For Russia, there is evidence that they have been able to learn throughout their special military operation in Ukraine. They have evolved their strategy, particularly with regard to the geographic scope of their operations and the increased use of long-range strike weapons.

But they have also learned and adapted at the operational level. They have changed their force constructs, their objectives, and the way they command their forces. Importantly, they have learned hard lessons about logistic support, particularly after the introduction of the U.S. HIMARS system in 2022. They have learned and adapted as a result.

As we shall see in the following chapter, their learning and adaptation—albeit somewhat unevenly across the entire force—has extended down into the realms of combat and tactics. And while the Russian military has learned and adapted at the tactical level, that change has come at a very high price.

II

NOT IDIOTS

Russian Combat Adaptation

IN HIS BOOK *On Tactics: A Theory of Victory in Battle*, B. A. Friedman describes tactics as "an arrangement of military forces in such a way to defeat an enemy. . . . The tactician must be prepared to confront the enemy in combat."[1] Friedman then breaks down tactics into four physical elements (maneuver, mass, firepower, and tempo), four mental elements (deception, surprise, confusion, and shock), and, finally, one moral element (cohesion).[2] To wield these as a single unified battle plan requires a military leader to possess experience, training, and tactical acumen.

Tactical acumen is essential to the effectiveness of military organizations in a theater of war. At the most basic level of military operations, armies, navies, air forces, and their supporting elements must be able to fight and win battles. The tactical level of war is dedicated to the planning and employment of military forces in battles, engagements, and other activities to achieve military objectives. In the contemporary era, these tactical actions are normally undertaken within joint task forces, but not always. In some circumstances, military activities by a single service might be undertaken.[3]

Tactical adaptation is the sum of actions that underpin learning and improvement on the battlefield, the dissemination of those lessons to other battlefield elements, and the training that prepares reinforcements and new units. Five key Russian tactical adaptations have occurred since the beginning of their invasion of Ukraine:

combat and tactics adaptation, human-machine teaming, signature management, air-land integration, and air defense operations.

COMBAT ADAPTATION AND TACTICS

The Russians have adapted their ground combat tactics throughout the war. Early on, the Russians sought to conduct sweeping maneuvers that coordinated airborne operations with ground offensive operations. Russian air-land integration and ground combined-arms tactics were poorly executed, however. The shortfalls in infantry and the armor-heavy "thunder runs" of Russian tanks toward Kyiv early in the war demonstrated either a lack of tactical competence or an impatience on the part of commanders to take the time to orchestrate the various elements of the combined-arms team on the ground. This permitted the Ukrainians to attack Russian logistics and rear areas while also killing many of the dismounted infantry soldiers of the Russian invading force. It ultimately led to the Russian retreat from Kyiv and Kharkiv.[4]

The disastrous crossing of the Siverskyi Donets River by Russian forces in May 2022 was another example of poor Russian tactical integration in their combat operations. Over the course of a full day on 11 May 2022, the Russian attempt to cross the river was repulsed by Ukrainian forces. They lost over a quarter of personnel committed to the crossing and nearly 80 percent of their armored vehicles.[5] It was a decisive defeat, indicative of an army that was still coming to grips with modern surveillance and targeting, along with the complex integration of ground and air units when crossing obstacles.

This also drove the Russians to adapt their design for battle in the Donbas. Instead of more maneuverist tactics, they adopted an attritional model. The Russians turned to massed artillery guided by unmanned aerial vehicles (UAVs) to "lead the way" in their offensive thrusts. It resulted in the Russians advancing more slowly, and they exercised more caution in order not to expose their logistics to attack.[6]

The introduction of HIMARS by Ukraine in mid-2022 forced more Russian adaptation. Russian logistics units had to disperse and to shift farther from the frontlines. This made resupply of their artillery and forward combat units slower and riskier. As Ukrainian defense minister Reznikov stated in a May 2023 interview, "I have to give them credit . . . they learn very well. When we started using HIMARS, they moved all their control points and warehouses 120 kilometers away so that we cannot reach them."[7]

Russia's conduct of the withdrawal from Kherson in October and November 2022 also shows that they had learned from their withdrawals in the wake of Ukrainian Kharkiv offensive. The Russian forces were able to undertake a large-scale river crossing operation and extract a large portion of the Russian forces that were deployed in southern Ukraine.[8] As one review of the operation recounts,

The Russians succeeded in withdrawing two army-sized groupings from the Dnipro right bank: the Crimea-based 22nd Army Corps in the south; and a mixed northern grouping comprising formations from 35th Combined Arms Army and 49 CAA. 42,370 troops got away. . . . 253 tanks and almost 400 armored personnel carriers of various types were also evacuated alongside several thousand wheeled vehicles. A Russian Army got away, and a Russian President escaped a humiliating defeat on the battlefield.[9]

Another combat adaptation emerged with the deployment of Wagner Group mercenaries in late 2022, particularly in the Bakhmut area of eastern Ukraine. Their adaptation was essentially a return to human wave attacks (later described as meat assaults) that have featured in conflicts such as the Iran-Iraq War. These tactics were also used by the Soviet Union during World War II, particularly with their penal battalions.

This was not just the simple application of human wave tactics, however. It was a more sophisticated adaptation to tactics where the initial human waves were just the first echelon of multiple attacks. Each successive echelon featured more experienced and capable troops. The Wagner Group, which had actively recruited convicts from the Russian penal system, used convicts as first wave troops, and their main role was to force Ukrainian defending forces to reveal their positions. Each successive wave would target the newly revealed Ukrainian positions to claw out small gains. Eventually, the better-trained and more experienced Wagner Troops would exploit any gains that these human wave attacks achieved.[10]

The Economist, in examining this adaptation in Russian tactics described the Russian approach as "sending small packets of 'disposable' infantry, a handful of men at a time, often under the influence of amphetamines, to 'skirmish . . . until killed.' It is not so much a human wave as a human trickle. But it reveals Ukrainian positions and consumes Ukrainian ammo. Then larger groups of better-trained assault infantry move in, backed up by armor, mortars and artillery."[11]

This adaptation was, however, a stopgap for a Russian army that was by late 2022 an exhausted and depleted force. Once mobilized troops began to arrive toward the end of that year, the pressure on the Russian army eased. But with many mobilized Russian army troops being poorly trained, it was inevitable that some form of this concept of employment by a Russian army that sees many of its personnel as "single-use soldiers" would feature in other Russian operations.[12] These tactics were used in the 2023 Gerasimov-led Russian offensive in eastern Ukraine. But this campaign made little progress and eventually petered out in the face of Ukrainian defenses and a dawning Ukrainian midyear offensive.

In early 2023, further combat adaptation appeared with new Russian assault methods that incorporated infiltration tactics. This approach had its origins in the search for breakthroughs on the Western Front in World War I. While the Germans are given credit for this, the tactics originated elsewhere. A French army officer, Captain André Laffargue, was wounded in 1915 and during his convalescence wrote a pamphlet called *The Attack in Trench Warfare*. Published in 1916, the pamphlet described a system of infiltration to be employed by well-trained volunteers using automatic weapons, mountain guns, and other weapons to move swiftly through an enemy's defensive positions.

Not long after its publication, a copy of Laffargue's pamphlet was discovered in a captured German trench. While it was translated into German and distributed widely, it is not referred to in later German tactical doctrine. However, the Germans became quite adept at such battlefield tactics. The Germans developed a new tactical approach that incorporated surprise, penetration at weak points, exploitation, fire support, and momentum.[13]

But despite the effectiveness of these tactics, there was a major problem with them. The new German tactics were not aligned with an operational approach that could exploit these new tactics. They could create gaps in an enemy defensive line but could not then move a force through this hole in order to exploit the breakthrough by attacking targets deep in the enemy's rear. And not only was there a lack of capacity; senior military commanders also did not appear to have a desire to do so. As German commander Ludendorff told one of his army group commanders, "I forbid myself to use the word 'strategy.' We chop a hole. The rest follows."[14]

Good tactics are wasted without operational art or good strategy.

As Gudmundsson writes in *Stormtroopers Tactics*, "In 1918, the German infantry could use stormtroopers tactics to tear gaps. As long as following formations relied on muscle power for mobility however, these holes could never be turned into war winning victories."[15] If the Russian army was to start using these tactics in the East, it would also need to address other, related issues.

The first of these was to implement a wide-scale retraining and reequipping program if it was to employ these tactics widely. This would have included troops in theater and those that are being trained at home. The challenge of doing this in a system that is under great pressure and that has lost many of its middle and junior leaders was significant. It is not clear that any wide-scale retraining took place outside of a few elite units.

A second and more important challenge was that the Russian military needed a plan to exploit the "gaps" that might be created through such tactics. Russian exploitation of these tactical gaps would require strong, armored reserve forces that have the leadership, authority, and agility to penetrate deep into Ukrainian territory. Such an operational penetration would aim to dislocate large parts of the Ukrainian defensive scheme of maneuver while destroying HQ, logistics, reserve troops, and longer-range artillery.

It is not apparent that the Russian army possessed the ability to create tactical "break-ins" and then conduct operational exploitation. They suffered significant losses in personnel, leaders, and equipment up to the end of 2022. And even if the Russians were able to concentrate these mechanized reserves, it is highly probable that these would be detected and interdicted by Ukrainian long-range strikes using missiles, drones, and artillery. So while the Russians demonstrated organizational learning with infiltration tactics, it remained an incomplete adaptation. The lack of any major successes in the Russian offensive of early 2023 tends to indicate that these new tactics did not result in breakthrough military capabilities.

A final tactical adaptation is the Russian employment of armor, which has evolved significantly since their initial operations in February 2022. Initially applied as part of battalion tactical groups in company-sized organizations to penetrate Ukrainian defenses, the Russians discovered that these companies lacked mass and thus experienced large casualties. And while the Russian persisted in attempting to use larger formations of tanks to generate tactical breakthroughs, the destruction of a Naval Infantry Brigade and the loss of dozens on armored vehicles during the Battle of Vuhledar in February 2023 appears to have put an end to the Russian employment of tanks in this manner.[16]

Instead, the Russians have adapted the tactics for tanks and other armored vehicles to embrace three kinds of mission. First, they are used as very precise, stand-off fire support to mounted and dismounted attacks on Ukrainian defensive positions. While this has been a role of tanks in previous conflicts, it had not been a primary focus of the Russian army in this conflict until significant losses force a refocus on tactics. Even older T-55 and T-62 tanks can be used effectively in this role.

Second, Russian tanks are also used to conduct short, rapid raids on Ukrainian positions. Tanks are used as part of a combined-arms system where Russian dismounted troops cause casualties to Ukrainians, forcing them to rotate units. Tanks are then employed during these combat rotations to inflict even more casualties. In these raids, normally undertaken at night with tanks that possess better thermal sensors, the vehicles rapidly approach their target, fire multiple rounds, and then withdraw.[17]

Finally, Russian tanks are being used as indirect fire support to Russian combat units and formations. This is generally the case where the allocation of artillery ammunition for Russian formations is low. Although this form of fire support in military operations is inefficient, this role is included in the tank doctrine of some nations, and tanks have been used in this way in previous conflicts. And this form of fire support is very mobile and more survivable than most artillery systems.

Evolving and improving tactics does not always lead to winning wars. But on the other hand, it is difficult to win wars if you cannot win battles, and the combat adaptations undertaken by the Russian army in 2022–23 will make them a more difficult adversary for the Ukrainian armed forces.

▓ RUSSIAN HUMAN-MACHINE TEAMS EVOLVE

A growing part of combat on both sides in this war has been the use of uncrewed platforms and autonomous systems. With losses running into the thousands per month, the Russo-Ukraine war is witnessing the industrial-scale use of autonomous systems. There has been a rapidly expanding number of lethal and nonlethal missions for them, as well as counter-drone systems to combat them.

Both sides are employing many different military and civil aerial systems. Drones have been used for reconnaissance, correcting indirect fire (artillery, mortars, and tanks) and employed as loitering munitions. Where Russian artillery units owned their own UAVs, they have been highly effective in adapting their operations to close the time between the detection of a target and the execution of fire missions against those targets. This improvement in the responsiveness of artillery has meant that the Russians have been able to engage Ukrainian targets within three to five minutes of detection.[18]

The Russians have also evolved the use of drones for pre-attack reconnaissance. Instead of the headlong rush into combat that many Russian units, particularly armored units, conducted in the early days of the war, many have evolved their tactics to lead with aerial autonomous systems to feel the way and pinpoint Ukrainian defensive positions. Tanks are often held back and used as indirect fire support rather than being used in the initial assault against Ukrainian positions. Often this fire support is coordinated by using drones.[19]

One expert on drone operations, Samuel Bendett, has written that "prior to the war, the Russian military saw uncrewed systems playing a growing role in battlefield information gathering and management, support to command and control (C2), and the targeting process."[20] These predications have come to fruition in Ukraine. As Elisabeth Gosselin-Malo has written, "In terms of the emerging capabilities of loitering munitions, the Russo-Ukrainian war is serving as a proving ground before our eyes."[21] Drones have come to play an increasingly important role in the Russian reconnaissance strike and fire complex. But it is not only autonomous or remotely piloted drones that have been adapted to speed up the detection to destruction cycle in Ukraine. Loitering munitions are also playing an increasingly significant function.

Loitering munitions, such as the Russian ZALA Lancet drone, can loiter for around an hour and be used to attack armored vehicles, artillery, and logistics nodes. Another type, the KYB, is a semi-autonomous system for attacking fixed sites. The Russians first used these drones in Syria and have honed their use throughout their operations in Ukraine, including for counter-battery operations that attack

Ukrainian artillery.[22] Increasingly they are being used for longer-range strikes, in which the Russians use Iranian loitering munitions such as the Shahed drone against infrastructure targets.[23]

The growing use of drones has been an important adaptation in Russian combat operations. It is likely that these aerial systems will continue to proliferate and become more effective and survivable as the war progresses. Indeed, the growth in their use has been exponential so far in this war. This has required Russia to source commercial drones from China, particularly different DJI variants, as well as military kamikaze drones from Iran, such as the Shahed drones.[24]

The Russians also intend to also deploy autonomous systems in the land environment. In February 2023, Dmitry Rogozin, a former Roskosmos (Russian space agency) director, announced that several Marker uncrewed ground vehicles (UGVs) had been dispatched to eastern Ukraine.[25] Able to be fitted with machine guns, antitank weapons, and grenade launchers, this type of UGV would provide a useful capability in combat and as a support platform (such as counter-UAV operations) if it proves effective. If the utility of such UGVs can be proven in Ukraine, they will proliferate there as well as in other future conflicts around the globe.

For the most part, however, uncrewed systems in the ground environment have been remotely operated rather than autonomous. One example is the Uran-6 demining vehicle. Remotely operated by Russian army engineers, it has been used in multiple locations to clear Ukrainian minefields. A second example, used for the first time in June 2023, was a remotely operated Russian T54/55 tank that was packed with explosives and driven at Ukrainian defensive positions.[26] Although it exploded short of its objective, the huge number of such older vehicles in storage in Russian indicates that there will be further such applications for remotely operated explosive vehicles in this conflict.

▓ SIGNATURE MANAGEMENT ADAPTATION

From the beginning of the war, Russian armored vehicles, headquarters, and logistics locations have been important targets for the Ukrainian armed forces. And because the Ukrainians have targeted them, the Russian military in Ukraine has sought to reduce their vulnerability by making them harder to find and harder to kill. Signature management has been an important element of this desire to improve survivability

Almost since the beginning of the war, the Russians have sought to upgrade the protection afforded to the various types of armored vehicles, and even light wheeled vehicles. This is a response to the massive inflow of Western antivehicle and antiarmor systems.[27] These have supplemented the weapons Ukraine already deployed before the invasion, which included the Soviet-era RPG-7 as well as the Ukrainian-developed Stugna-P and RK-3 Corsar antitank missiles.

This menagerie of threats to Russian vehicles of all types has driven adaptation through the survival instinct of Russian soldiers at the tactical level. One example was the improvised armor applied to light-skinned trucks after the initial few weeks of the war saw huge numbers of Russian logistic vehicles attacked during the advance on Kyiv. This makeshift armor has included solutions such as logs and sandbags attached to the outside of vehicle cabs. But it has also included more sophisticated, artisanal approaches in which steel metal and parts of other armored vehicles are added to the light skins of wheeled support vehicles.[28]

Another approach has also appeared to increase the survivability of the Russian army's heavier armored vehicles: bar armor. Also known as slat armor or cage armor, this concept first appeared on German tanks in World War II: the Germans used wire mesh or steel plate on the sides of their tanks to reduce the penetrative power of antitank rifles, bazookas, and tank rounds. This form of stand-off armor has also been used in more recent times by the Israeli Army as well as by coalition forces deployed in the second Iraq War.[29] One news organization dubbed the use of such an approach "hillbilly armor."[30]

Even before the war began in February 2022, many Russian tanks and self-propelled artillery began to sprout cages attached to the top of their turrets. This was a counter to the top-attack technique used by many Western antiarmor missiles over the past several decades. As with other armies that have applied this technique, it was designed to deflect incoming antitank missiles or tank projectiles: the cage designers hoped that such "armor" would crush the fuses of antitank weapons before they hit the tank's main armor or that the bars of the cage would denotate them before they reached the tank or other type of armored vehicle. In other instances, static armored vehicles have used cages that are not connected to the vehicle but enclose it almost entirely to protect it from loitering munitions and small, armed UAVs.[31]

This tactical adaptation has had some effectiveness, depending on the type of antitank weapon used and the range it is fired from. Modern, sophisticated Western antitank missiles such as the NLAW and the Javelin detonate well above an enemy tank turret using a shaped explosive charge. A superheated jet of molten metal simply slices through the cage and easily penetrates the light armor at the top of the turret. However, smaller bomblets dropped by drones may be prematurely detonated by the cages, giving them some utility on a battlefield where drones carrying bomblets and loitering munitions have become almost ubiquitous.[32]

In the war's second year, the Russians improved the survivability of their armored vehicles by changing their detectability at longer range. This has been achieved, first, through the use of thermal protection systems. Several captured Russian tanks, including an abandoned T-90M tank, have been fitted with thermal reduction systems including the Nakidka signature reduction material.[33] This material has been complemented with modifications to the engine deck of tanks to reduce thermal emissions. Russian tanks and other armored vehicles have also begun to operate in the periods around dusk and dawn. This ensures that the heat signature of the vehicles is much closer to ambient temperatures, making them harder to detect at medium and long ranges and thus complicating their engagement by modern antitank missiles.[34]

Russian headquarters have also adapted to reduce their signatures and improve their survivability on a battlefield with ubiquitous sensors. The introduction of HIMARS in 2022 saw the destruction of multiple Russian tactical headquarters that remained within the range of this new system. One example of the impact is the Ukrainian targeting of the various Russian headquarters west of the Dnieper River in 2022. Over an eight-month period, the Ukrainians attacked the headquarters of Russia's 8th Combined Arms Army, 49th Combined Arms Army, 22nd Army Corps, 76th Guards Air Assault Division, and 247th Guards Air Assault Regiment, along with subordinate command posts, over twenty times. This particular example has been repeated across Ukraine, resulting in the death of multiple Russian generals and other senior officers, degrading Russian operational cohesion and depriving formations of their key leaders and planners.[35]

The meshing of various sensors, human intelligence, and new long-range strike capabilities introduced a new tactical and operational vulnerability for the Russian army in Ukraine. This necessitated changes in the headquarters' location: they were pushed back out of the range of these long-range rocket systems. Those that could not be pushed back, such as battalion and brigade command posts, were hardened significantly and constructed underground. And to enhance their survivability, headquarters have reduced their electromagnetic emissions by using field cables and relay vehicles and exploiting the Ukrainian telecommunications system.[36]

▓ AIR-LAND INTEGRATION

Another Russian adaptation has been the improved integration of ground and air operations. The initial phase of the war saw a variety of strikes against Ukrainian radars, air defense, logistics, and airfield targets. Russian military forces used ballistic missiles and cruise missiles for many of these strikes. And if not for dispersal of Ukrainian military assets in the hours and days before the beginning of the Russian invasion, they may have had a decisive effect on the Russian advance on Kyiv and the course of the war more broadly.

Unfortunately for the Russians, the Ukrainians had shifted enough of what the Russians would have considered high-value targets. This is one reason the Ukrainians were able to weather the early Russian air campaign. In addition, after the initial strikes against Ukrainian targets, the Russian air force failed to exploit the successes it had achieved. The Russians certainly had a significant overmatch in tactical and fighter aircraft, with an advantage ratio of 15:2 at some stages. They also possessed a qualitative edge with their Su-35 and Su-30 fighters and their long-range radar-guided missiles.[37] That they did not conduct a strike campaign after their initial attacks hindered the ground campaign and ceded Ukrainian airspace back to the Ukrainians.

Over three hundred modern Russian combat aircraft were based within range of Ukraine. But as Justin Bronk has pointed out, they appear to have "largely stayed on the ground throughout the first four days of fighting. This has allowed the Ukrainian Air Force to continue flying low-level defensive counter-air and ground-attack sorties."[38] In the first eighteen months of the war, Russian aircraft have not regained the ability to operate in Ukrainian-controlled airspace due to Russia's inability to suppress the increasingly integrated and capable Ukrainian air defense system.

At the same time, the Russian military forces were unable to effectively coordinate ground and air operations as part of a unified campaign. Instead, as one study of Russia's Ukraine campaign notes, "the timid air offensive has seemed haphazard and often unrelated to ground operations, resorting to less risky, but also less precise, night-time punishment strikes on infrastructure targets. Subpar air-ground coordination was identified as a weakness after Russia's attack on Georgia in 2008 and was thought to have since been rectified as part of Russia's reform effort, but this seems not to have been the case."[39]

The later Russian operations in the East have demonstrated a degree of learning in the conduct of air-land integration. The Russian air force sortie rate increased, and it was able to concentrate its efforts to support Russian army ground operations in the East. But air-land integration, honed to an art by Western military organizations, remains underdeveloped by the Russian military, and this hinders Russian ground force operations.[40]

This has necessitated adaptation on the Russians part and has resulted in their using more expensive cruise and ballistic missiles for what otherwise would have been missions conducted by crewed aircraft using precision munitions. Perhaps realizing the expense and lack of decisive results from this approach, the Russians have also been employing cheaper Iranian drones in more focused attacks on Ukrainian infrastructure since October 2022.[41]

In mid-2023, the Russian military formed an air strike task force, building on its lessons from the war so far. According to British intelligence, in May 2023 the Russia air force created a new attack aviation group, which they code-named "Shtorm," for operations in the skies over Ukraine. The unit is believed to consist of at least one squadron of Su-24 Fencer and Su-34 Fullback fighter-bombers, along with a squadron of attack helicopters. As the British intelligence report of the time explains, this new group indicates that the "Russian assesses its regular air force squadrons have severely underperformed in their core function of conducting airstrikes on Ukrainian lines."[42]

▨ AIR DEFENSE OPERATIONS

During the Cold War the Soviet Union had a sophisticated and (for its time) well-integrated air defense capability. The Soviet Union devoted huge resources toward the development and sustainment of a very effective, networked air defense system for its homeland and deployed combat forces. A 1981 study described how the "Soviet Union has a decent, effective air defense system which, in fact, shows some innovation."[43] By the end of the Cold War, the Soviet Air Defense Troops (VPVO) possessed over two thousand interceptor aircraft, eight thousand surface-to-air missile launchers, and half a million troops.[44]

Despite the significant cutbacks in Soviet and Russian forces in the wake of the Cold War, the Russian army retained an array of very capable air defense radars and weapons. Many of these have been deployed for its special military operation in Ukraine.

Over the course of this war, the Russians have learned to better connect the various battlefield and strategic sensors to tighten the air defense of their borders as well as above military forces deployed in Ukraine. Early in the war, poor coordination saw Ukrainian air force aircraft able to successfully strike Russian ground combat formations. The Russian military, however, rapidly adapted its air defense network for forces deployed inside Ukraine, as well as for its key bases in Russia being used to support Russian forces in Ukraine. The goal has been to improve defense against both crewed Ukrainian combat aircraft and the increasing hordes of uncrewed aerial systems deployed by the Ukrainian armed forces.

A 2023 report by the Royal United Services Institute has noted that "Russian air defenses have become significantly more robust since the autumn of 2022."[45] Air defense systems such as the SA-21 (also known as the S-400 Triumf) and SA-23 (also known as the S-300) long-range air defense systems are concentrated around high-value targets such as higher headquarters and logistics hubs. Combined with long-range, ground-based air search radars, these have been very effective at denying airspace to Ukrainian aircraft and missiles. These have been complemented with shorter-range missile systems such as the SA-15 (also known as the Tor missile system) and SA-22 (also known as the Pantsir). Connecting these missile systems and radars within an air defense network has been a useful and effective adaptation for Russian air defenses during their invasion of Ukraine.[46]

But it is not only existing air defense missile and radar systems that have been key to the survivability of Russian units on the ground. Counter-drone capabilities have been significantly enhanced as well, improving the overall Russian air defense environment.

The Russians have deployed a high density of electronic warfare systems to support combat operations and counter-drone activities. One major electronic warfare systems, the truck-mounted Shipovnik-Aeroare, has been deployed every ten kilometers along the Russian front line. This system can quickly detect Ukrainian UAVs and suppress their control signal within a minute.[47] The Russian approach has incorporated the simultaneous deployment of the Krasukha-2/4, R-330Zh Zhitel, and RB-301B Borisoglebsk-2 ground-based electronic warfare systems, which use a combination of jamming and spoofing. Each is able to target a different part of the electromagnetic spectrum. These systems have also been employed by the Russian military to conduct reconnaissance of Ukrainian radio communications, followed by interference once targets are identified.[48]

The Krasukha-2 electronic warfare system consists of three vehicles based on the Kamaz-6350 truck. It is able to jam airborne warning and control systems at ranges of up to 250 kilometers but can also interfere with airborne radars used on radar-guided missiles. The truck-based R-330Zh Zhitel system can interfere with satellite communications equipment, navigation systems, and mobile phones within a thirty-kilometer (twenty-mile) radius. Although these systems were not designed initially for the conduct of counter-drone operations, they have been adapted and usefully employed in this battlefield role.[49]

Supplementing these large and capable systems are smaller man-portable systems that have been issued to many Russian combat and support units. Systems such as the LPD-802 electronic warfare gun and Serp-VS5 antidrone system provide local defense against reconnaissance and strike drones.[50]

Finally, the Russians have been using GPS jamming during their operations in Ukraine. From mid-2022 onward, reports emerged that Russian GPS jammers were affecting the accuracy of the rockets fired by HIMARS. This jamming is part of the wider Russian response to the longer range and better precision of the HIMARS capability.[51]

Although this system is not perfect, it has limited the freedom of movement of Ukrainian aircraft and missiles in the proximity of Russian forces.[52] This has proven to be an important adaptation that has enhanced the survivability and effectiveness of Russian logistics as well as its higher-level command and control.

▬▬▬

John Jessup has described how "the Soviets entered the Second World War in chaos and panic and came out of it as a victorious, major world power."[53] Depending on how well the Russians continue to adapt, this situation may well be reversed as a consequence of their decision to invade Ukraine in 2022. They could conceivably have entered the war in Ukraine as a major power and could come out of it in panic and chaos.

But so far the Russians have demonstrated the ability to learn and to adapt at the strategic, operational, and tactical levels. While this has been uneven, and not always evident across the breadth of Russian military operations, there is sufficient evidence that learning and evolution are taking place. There is also some evidence that while fear, centralized control, and other factors inhibit some tactical learning and the overall speed of Russian adaptation, Russia's institutional mechanisms for adaptation are quite effective once engaged. Their ability to scale up the employment of small Iranian drones and proliferate improved electronic warfare systems to counter Ukraine's drones and precision munitions in 2023 are examples of this institutional adaptation. This military capability will be central to Russia's ongoing ability to conduct operations in Ukraine. The longer the war lasts, the better the Russians are likely to get at adapting, and this will reduce any advantage Ukraine may have in this aspect of the war.

Notwithstanding the Russians' ability to learn and adapt, it is also clear that the Ukrainians have also been quick studies in modern war. Indeed, since the beginning of the Russian invasion, they have demonstrated the ability to learn on the battlefield and evolve. They have also shown a knack for the rapid assimilation of new equipment such as HIMARS and Western armored vehicles and have then applied these systems with great tactical competence.

But this adaptive capacity—evident at multiple levels—did not emerge from nowhere on 24 February 2022. It has been founded on a decade of reforms and battlefield learning in the Donbas as well as a range of other factors. It is this foundation for Ukraine's individual and institutional adaptation that is explored in the following chapter.

12

UKRAINIAN POST-2014 REFORMS

The Basis of Wartime Adaptation

MILITARY INSTITUTIONS almost always get the next war wrong.

This characteristic is one of the enduring features of human conflict. Many of the factors behind it are beyond the control of military organizations. For this reason, individuals within military forces—especially the most senior leaders responsible for preparing for future conflict—face a daunting balancing act. They must, on the one hand, avoid repeating the errors of past wars through ignorance of those errors. On the other hand, they must understand which theories of war from the past remain relevant and which ones have been rendered obsolete by new theories, technologies, or political circumstances.[1] This has been true throughout the different conflicts of the twentieth century and will likely remain true for the conflicts to come in this century and beyond.[2]

Some have described the significant changes in the past several centuries as military revolutions or revolutions in military affairs. There is a rich scholarship on the origins of the theory of revolutions in military affairs. It was first developed in the 1970s by the Soviet military as a way of describing how new sensors, computers, and precision weapons were influencing late twentieth-century military thought. This concept, first described by Soviet military theorists as a military technological revolution, soon evolved into one called revolutions in military affairs (RMA), and the name has stuck. From the 1990s onward, the concept has been a byword for the exploration of new ideas and technologies to generate an advantage over an enemy state. Inherent in the RMA concept are theories related to technological change, the evolution of military systems, operational innovation, and organizational adaptation.[3]

Until the First Industrial Revolution, developments in tactics and equipment moved at a very slow pace. But with the technologies introduced during the industrial revolutions, social and technological change also sped up the pace of military developments. And while military change was hastened in peacetime, war turbocharged it. Thus, military organizations needed to improve their ability to recognize that their environment had evolved and to then make the most efficient and effective changes to ensure they remained competitive within that new environment.

Military institutions that could develop and implement the processes for empirically based peacetime innovation stood a better chance of being able to adapt effectively in war. Military organizations needed not only to increase their physical capacity in peacetime but also to build the intellectual capacity to adapt and succeed during conflict. As Williamson Murray and Barry Watts have written, "Military organizations that have trouble being scrupulous about empirical data in peacetime may have the same difficulty in time of war."[4] Bad intellectual habits can carry over from peacetime into times of conflict. But good habits and incentives in a military institution that enable innovation can underpin effective military adaptation during war. As Murray writes in *Military Adaptation in War*, "The evidence would indicate that serious intellectual effort during peacetime in thinking through what the past and present suggest about the future plays an important role in how well military organizations are able to adapt in conflict. Without that effort, there is unlikely to be a baseline from which to plot out intelligent course for adaptation."[5]

Much has been written since February 2022 about the capacity of the Ukrainian armed forces to learn and adapt in combat. Admittedly, the Ukrainian approach to adaptation has been an uneven process and has required formal processes as well as many grassroots efforts by deployed forces to learn and share lessons. The sometimes chaotic process of Ukrainian adaptation was foreseen by Murray and Watts when they wrote that "genuine innovation, like democracy, is unlikely to be a tidy process. . . . Indeed, attempts to eliminate the inherent messiness may be one of the surest ways to kill innovation."[6]

To understand how Ukraine has adapted, it is important to first explore the foundations created in peacetime for Ukraine's wartime adaptive stance. As such, this chapter provides the underpinning for subsequent examinations of Ukrainian tactical, operational, and strategic adaptation during the war.

▧ A NEW UKRAINIAN MILITARY

A key foundation for Ukrainian adaptation after the Russian 2022 invasion was the reforms to the Ukrainian military over the decade that preceded the invasion. The declaration of sovereignty for Ukraine in 1990 with the dissolution of the Soviet Union included provision for the formation of Ukrainian armed forces, separate from the military of the Commonwealth of Independent States. In 1992 Ukraine possessed one of the largest armies in Europe. With over 230,000 troops (and 1 million reservists with recent military service), 6,300 tanks, 1,100 combat aircraft, and over 2,000 artillery pieces, it was—at least on paper—a very powerful military institution.[7]

However, with NATO now a security partner and Russia less of a perceived threat, Ukraine saw little need for such a large standing military. It therefore launched a series of reforms that restructured and downsized its military. It also renounced the use of nuclear weapons.[8]

As part of its decision to not retain Soviet-era nuclear weapons, in 1994 Ukraine signed a memorandum with Russia, Britain, and the United States in Budapest to provide security assurances and to assist its entry into the Nuclear Non-Proliferation Treaty.[9] The commitments within the agreement (officially called the Memorandum on Security Assurances in Connection with Ukraine's Accession to the Treaty on the Non-proliferation of Nuclear Weapons) were violated by Russia when it annexed Crimea in 2014 and conducted its campaign of aggression in eastern Ukraine.[10]

Until the Russian military operations against Ukraine in 2014, three priorities guided the operations of the Ukrainian armed forces: deployment of forces on peacekeeping missions, combating terrorism threats, and preparing for a local war. However, a lack of resources often prevented the Ukrainians from fully realizing these three objectives. As Denys Kiryukhin has written, by 2013 "its main defense forces were in a deplorable state. . . . Ukrainian military had downsized compared to its Soviet predecessor, comprising 184,000 soldiers, roughly 700 tanks, 170 combat aircraft, and 22 warships."[11]

By the time Russian operations against Ukraine commenced in 2014, the smaller country's military was described by Ukraine's General Viktor Muzhenko as "an army in ruins," one that was "depleted, neglected and underfunded."[12] The Russian annexation of Crimea and operations in the Donbas resulted in an abrupt change in approach by the Ukrainian government toward its military institutions.

After the 2014 Russian invasion, the Ukrainian government undertook multiple steps to reform its military. Exploiting a window of opportunity provided by the first Minsk cease-fire in September, the Ukrainian armed forces conducted a partial mobilization to increase its size by more than 100,000 personnel. Concurrently, an eighteen-month-long period of conscription service was introduced.

Several Western nations also commenced training missions to build the capability and professionalism of Ukrainian armed forces personnel. The U.S. Army established a joint multinational training group based on the 7th Army Training Command, and in 2015, Canada established Operation Unifier to train Ukrainian military personnel.[13] At the same time, Ukrainian personnel were for the first time welcomed on NATO courses conducted throughout Europe.

Despite these changes, challenges remained. A 2016 RAND report on security sector issues in Ukraine described a range of problems. It portrayed the Maidan Revolution (also known as the Revolution of Dignity) as a foundation for reforms in a system that had "resisted them for a quarter of a century." Further, the report unearthed significant issues with command and control clarity in government and the military, coordination across different branches, and deficiencies in warfighting capability and the use of resources.[14]

In 2016, the Ukrainian *Strategic Defense Bulletin* described reforms that would be needed to achieve NATO standards. Its State Program for the Development of the Armed Forces (2017–20), issued not long afterward, outlined the implementation steps for this aspiration. Another important transformation was the 2018 Law on National Security, which provided the groundwork to simplify Ukraine's defense planning and to entrench civilian control over the military forces.[15]

Between the 2014 Russian operations in Ukraine and the 2022 full-scale invasion, planned changes for the Ukrainian military to respond to Russian aggression were described in multiple strategic documents. The first was their *National Security Strategy*, initially published in 2015 and updated most recently in September 2020.[16] The strategy describes three core principles of Ukrainian national security policy: deterrence, the development of capabilities to deter military aggression against Ukraine; resilience, the ability of society and the state to quickly adapt to security environment changes and remain functioning; and cooperation, including development of relationships with foreign partners, especially with the EU, NATO, and the United States.[17]

According to the strategy, Russia was recognized as an "aggressor state, a source of long-term systemic threats to Ukraine's national security" that conducts "hybrid" aggression against Ukraine. This is unlikely to change in the future, even in the event of a Ukrainian victory in this war.

A second important document that informs reform is the *Ukrainian Military Doctrine*, published in September 2015. The policy contained within focuses on blunting Russian aggression and better aligning with NATO.

A third document was the *Strategic Defense Bulletin*, a detailed explanation of best practices in a range of military endeavors and the efficient application of resources to meet outcomes in accordance with these best practices. Finally, the country has adopted a State Program for the Development of the Armed Forces, an ambitious program to ensure that the Ukrainian military meets NATO standards.[18]

During this time, the Ukrainians also published their first cyber strategy. Endorsed by the Ukrainian president in 2016, it was designed to respond to the lessons of constant Russian cyberattacks during and after their 2014 operations to seize Crimea and the Donbas. These Russian cyber operations had targeted government and private infrastructure. The new strategy outlined key objectives such as the protection of information and infrastructure, and responsibilities and arrangements for international cooperation on cybersecurity.[19] This international cooperation resulted in networks that were energized to assist Ukraine to enhance and adapt its cyber defenses once the Russians attacked in 2022.

The cyber strategy led Ukraine to examine distributing its digital operations and data not just across Ukraine but internationally. At that time, due to a Ukrainian data protection law, data had to be kept inside Ukraine. A week before Russia invaded, however, the Ukrainian Parliament amended the law, allowing Ukraine to transfer the data of over one hundred agencies into the cloud with the assistance of the private sector. Not only did this enhance Ukraine's cyber resilience; it has also made Russian targeting much more difficult throughout the war.[20]

Despite setting objectives in their strategic documents, the Ukrainians before the war at times failed to fully fund reform programs. In 2021 Nicolo Fasola and Alyssa Wood wrote, "Ukraine's programmatic documents, though logical enough, fail to provide specific guidance for the armed forces on how they should function within the new and prevailing Euro-Atlantic political framework. Furthermore, the National Security Strategy and the Strategic Defense Bulletin set ambitions that exceed Ukraine's reach."[21]

Notwithstanding this critique, there were injections of resources into the Ukrainian military in the wake of the 2014 Russian operations in Crimea and the Donbas. In October 2014, the Ukrainian government announced a fivefold increase in the defense budget by 2020.[22] There were increases by the Ukrainians over the five-year period from 2017 to 2021, but not of this magnitude. The armed forces budget, which is made up of a General Fund and a Special Fund (foreign donations), increased from 68.5 Ukrainian hryvnia in 2017 to 126.6 Ukrainian hryvnia in 2021.[23] And while financial allocations don't tell the entire story of an institution undergoing reform, changing an organization without increased resources is difficult.

With this better funding Ukraine boosted the size and combat readiness of the military. Since 2014, the number of military personnel in the Ukrainian armed forces rose by 36 percent, to 250,000. The Ukrainian army also moved to a contract service model, and it began designing and running more exercises with foreign military institutions to enhance the quality of combat training for its personnel.[24] At the same time, though, it remained equipped mainly with older Soviet-era matériel.

A NEW STRATEGY—2021

Reform of the Ukrainian military, along with wider national security affairs, continued up to the beginning of the war in 2022. In July 2021, President Zelenskyy signed new laws that provided for further expansions in the size of the armed forces, which were primarily focused on filling positions in the newly created Territorial Defense Corps. This legislation also created a new "national resistance framework"—the Law on the Fundamentals of National Resistance—to provide a formal network to resist foreign forces in the event of an invasion.[25]

The same year, the president of Ukraine endorsed a new *Military Security Strategy for Ukraine*. This replaced the Ukrainian military doctrine that had been released in September 2015. The new strategy continued to assume the threat posed by Russia was the primary challenge that would need to be addressed by the Ukrainian armed forces. The principal objective for Ukraine described in the strategy was to deter Russia from further escalation of the war it had begun in 2014. This was to be achieved by increasing the cost of a potential offensive and occupation to an unacceptable level. The Ukrainian concept of deterrence against Russia would also be supplemented with diplomatic activities as well as implementing a comprehensive security concept that integrates military and nonmilitary activities such as propaganda and cyber warfare.

An important part of the 2021 military strategy was direction to adapt the structure and equipment of the Ukrainian armed forces to put greater emphasis on antiaircraft and tactical missile forces, the wide application of drones and autonomous systems, and the increased use of satellite communications. Further, networking and sharing information across the battle space was emphasized, as was the conduct of asymmetric operations against their most likely enemy.[26] Since February 2022, the Ukrainian armed forces have largely stuck to this prescription in their defensive operations against the invading Russian force.

Another interesting aspect of the 2021 *Military Security Strategy* was its narrative about how Ukraine envisioned a future defense of the nation. The Ukrainians anticipated the conduct of a four-stage war campaign, which they laid out in the strategy. The first stage would see regular and territorial military forces being employed to deter Russian offensive actions using asymmetric operations. The second stage would see these initial forces being reinforced by reserve forces and the formation of resistance elements in areas that the enemy was able to occupy.

A third stage would include a general mobilization as well as requests for foreign military support. The fourth and final stage would be postwar stabilization.[27] Like the prioritized capabilities, the stages described in the 2021 *Military Security Strategy* show a close alignment with how Ukraine has fought the war so far.

A final point should be made in this discussion about Ukrainian military developments in the lead-up to the 2022 Russian invasion. The strategic objective of the Ukrainian government with its reform of the military was not to fight a war but to deter one. The Ukrainian Ministry of Defense's White Book, its annual update on military developments, described in 2021 how "in 2021, the Armed Forces managed to deter the escalation of the Russian armed aggression."[28] As such, the Russian invasion of 2022 was a failure of deterrence. Despite their best efforts, Russia and its leader were not deterred from invading their neighbor. That is a valuable lesson for other countries: sometimes authoritarian nations can't be deterred.

BUILDING A BASELINE FOR WARTIME ADAPTATION

What insights might be drawn from Ukraine's reforms before the Russian invasion of February 2022? There are several observations that might inform military innovation and reform programs in the West.

First, adaptation begins long before wars do. The aggregation of actions, programs, initiatives, and legislative changes in the years leading up to 2022 have underpinned Ukrainian strategy and adaptation in the war. A principal driver was the 2014 Russian invasions of Crimea and the Donbas. These Russian military and information operations fundamentally reshaped how the Ukrainian government and military perceived its threat environment.

Even before this, the Ukrainians understood their principal threat would be Russia. Russian actions in 2014 only crystalized for many the menace that Russia posed to the security, and the very existence, of a sovereign Ukraine. As security expert Hanna Shelest writes in a November 2022 report for the European Council on Foreign Relations:

> Since 2014, the country has transformed its armed forces, upgrading logistics and communications and empowering midlevel officers; put in place a network of reservists; and taken measures to ensure Ukrainian society's broader resilience to crises. It built this approach both on the adoption of NATO best practices and on a unique movement of volunteers who raise funds to support the war effort, merging defence and measures to increase national resilience into a single system.[29]

The 2014 Russian operations against Ukraine highlighted numerous flaws in Ukraine's military and national security posture. The combination of these two elements drove reforms that ensured that Ukraine possessed many of the necessary elements to learn and adapt when the war came in February 2022. As Shelest notes toward the end of her report, "The lessons Ukraine learned in 2014 were vital in 2022, and the lessons Ukraine and its European and NATO partners learn in 2022 may be just as important for the next crisis."[30]

A second observation is that while military initiatives were an important part of Ukraine's adaptive stance leading into the war, a range of other plans and strategies that could be grouped under a broad heading of "national resilience" were also crucial to Ukraine's ability to survive the initial Russian onslaught and then adapt to conditions as they evolved. Indeed, as part of the Joint Forces Operation that was formed in the wake of the 2014 Russian invasion, military and law enforcement agencies were placed under this unified command.

This was accompanied by other initiatives, including hardening critical infrastructure against cyberattacks and building the capacity for civil defense. The 2016 cybersecurity strategy for Ukraine applied the lessons of Russian cyberattacks in 2014 (and afterward) to describe key outcomes desired as well as delineate the responsibilities of the key agencies involved in implementing the strategy. These efforts to update and harden Ukraine from a cyber perspective have provided for resilient national communications networks during the war and have helped to minimize the impact of ongoing Russian cyberattacks on Ukrainian infrastructure. Russia was not able to generate a cyber advantage because Ukraine had learned and adapted from Russian attacks conducted in 2014 and 2016. The Ukrainian government had hardened likely targets of Russian cyberattacks, improved its detection and response capabilities, and formed partnerships with other nations to share information and techniques. As an assessment by the Center for Strategic and International Studies in 2022 states, "No defense is perfect, but Ukraine's efforts have so far been able to thwart the Russian cyberattacks."[31]

A third observation that could be made of preparations before the war is that none of the foregoing was simple, neat, or tidy. Part of the untidiness is inherent in reform programs, which must shift attitudes and change organizational structures and processes. Since 2014 the Ukrainian government has driven a wide range of reforms that include realigning command and control around NATO standards, reequipping, and adopting new training approaches fostered by NATO mentors in Ukraine. Shifting from decades of Soviet-era doctrine, ideas, and cultures is not a simple task. Despite the logic and government intention to shift to NATO models, this was still a difficult and ongoing reform agenda when the Russians launched their assaults of 24 February 2022. However, it did provide a foundation for the massive influx of NATO equipment, and for the training it received from NATO countries, after the Russian large-scale invasion.

There is no perfect preparation for war. However, preparation of capabilities and the nurturing of innovation can ensure that a nation and its military can be better prepared to learn and adapt when war does come.

And while the activities described in this chapter provided a foundation for the Ukrainians to adapt after the Russian invasion, there were few indications to external observers of the Ukrainian armed forces of the capacity for adaptation that has been demonstrated since February 2022. This is mainly because before the war, despite the many lessons that could be gleaned from the 2014 war, the Ukrainian armed forces were not studied as closely by Western analysts in think tanks and military organizations as the military forces of Russia were.

With the range of reforms initiated in the wake of the Russian 2014 seizure of Crimea and the Donbas, the Ukrainian leadership created the incentives to nurture innovation. This process accelerated once the Russians invaded. The Ukrainians have demonstrated a commitment to learn and change in the face of the Russian threat. In the following chapter, we will explore the nature of those changes. At the strategic, operational, and tactical levels, the Ukrainian government, its military, and its citizens have demonstrated an adaptive spirit that has enabled them to surprise the world with their resilience and capacity to hold off, and sometimes defeat, the Russians in many facets of modern war.

13

THE ASYMMETRIC HORIZON

Ukrainian Adaptation in War

VOLODYMYR HORBULIN is somewhat of a living legend in Ukraine. An engineer, he began his career designing missiles and eventually worked on the design of intercontinental missiles for the Soviet Union during the Cold War. Afterward Horbulin headed the Ukrainian National Space Agency and was responsible for the Sea Launch multinational consortium, which launched rockets from a mobile, ocean-based platform between 1999 and 2014. He has served as the secretary of the Council of National Security for the Ukrainian president in the 1990s and has been an adviser to several Ukrainian presidents on national security matters.

He is also an author. One of his publications is a 2020 book called *How to Beat Russia in the War of the Future*, a detailed examination of Ukrainian security challenges. In it Horbulin proposed, "Achieving military parity with Russia is unreal for Ukraine, at least in the foreseeable future. . . . Having an economic potential incomparable with that of Russia and therefore a completely different level of military appropriations, Ukraine must learn to use alternative possibilities, including developing asymmetric sources of counteraction to possible full-scale aggression."[1]

His prescriptions for Ukrainian military strategy have proved prophetic. Throughout the war, Ukraine has applied indirect or asymmetric strategies to defend its people and its territory. The Ukrainian strategy of corrosion, explored in part I, appears to be a real-time manifestation of Horbulin's ideas. One of the most crucial asymmetries that Ukraine has developed with Russia during the war has been adaptation.

▩ STRATEGIC ADAPTATION

In chapter 10, I defined strategic adaptation as the learning and adaptation that occurs at the strategic level and has an impact on the development and implementation of national and military strategy and the direction of the war overall. Like Russia, Ukraine has undertaken a variety of strategic adaptations since the beginning of the large-scale Russian invasion in February 2022. These have been conducted on the foundation of its overall war strategy.

Strategic adaptation, at least in theory, aims to increase the strategic effectiveness of the institution undertaking such changes. This concept of strategic effectiveness is an important one when we explore Ukraine's constant innovation to improve its performance against the Russian military as well as its global influence campaigns. Ukraine needs to be better than Russia at developing, implementing, and evolving strategy. While it does not have to be better by much, it does need to consistently test its approach and assumptions about its strategy to ensure that it stays ahead of Russian strategic thinking and action. Strategic competence is underpinned by a combination of, first, political effectiveness, where Ukraine gains and retains matériel and political and financial support from the West while also making sure the right resources are dedicated to appropriate warfighting elements; and, second, the most effective use of their military apparatus to "secure by force national goals set by the political leadership."[2]

Adaptation is made more difficult by the inherent messiness of military operations, particularly large-scale combat operations that absorb masses of personnel and national resources. Rarely is the picture of the war, regardless of what level it is observed from, sufficiently clear to make definitive judgments on what success will look like. It is a matter of experience, judgment, and risk-taking by leaders. As Eliot Cohen puts it, "Military power is at best a rough and imprecise instrument, used painfully and with unpredictable results. . . . It is however indispensable."[3]

As difficult as it may be to measure the effectiveness of military strategy and its subordinate operations, judgments must still be made about what is working and what is not. Institutional emphasis is required for those systems, processes, weapons, and organizations that are most likely to generate advantage against an adversary. As Stephen Biddle has written, "Military effectiveness matters chiefly because it shapes military outcomes; other things being equal, effective militaries ought to win more often than ineffective ones."[4]

Two strategic adaptations have been central to the ongoing improvement of Ukraine's strategic effectiveness in this war: a transition to a NATO-style military; and the development of a national integrated air, missile, and drone defense network.

▨ ▨ Transition to a NATO-Style Military

An important strategic adaptation by Ukraine has been their transition from Soviet-era weapons and support approaches to NATO systems. This process commenced well before the war. In the mid-1990s the Ukrainian government adopted a policy of moving toward a military organization more closed aligned with NATO processes, equipment, and organizations.

However, these reforms moved slowly before the 2014 Russian invasion. As Jack Detsch notes in a 2023 essay, "The reformist fervor found in Ukraine's streets hadn't yet trickled into the military. It was top heavy and junior officers feared that they might take the fall if things went wrong on the battlefield."[5] And as Margarita Konaev and Owen Daniels write in "Agile Ukraine, Lumbering Russia," "Underfunded, poorly trained, and crippled by corruption, the Ukrainian military failed to repel the Russian-backed separatists in the Donbas in 2014 and could not regain lost ground."[6] The foundations for strategic adaptation in the Ukrainian military were slow to take root in the initial years after independence. But the 2014 Russian invasion changed this, and the United States has played a critical role in the post-2014 reforms.

The United States is a key partner in Ukraine's transition effort. Since before the 2014 Russian invasion, Ukraine received assistance under Building Partner Capacity and Defense Institution Building authorities of the U.S. Department of Defense. It also obtained support through International Military Education and Training programs, where Ukrainian personnel undertook professional military education at U.S. defense institutions. After the 2014 Russian invasion, the United States provided nonlethal security assistance, including body armor, helmets, vehicles, night vision equipment, radios, patrol boats, counter-mortar radars, and other associated military equipment.[7]

In a September 2021 announcement, the United States and Ukraine also announced a strategic partnership that would encompass a range of defense coop-eration programs, including cyber defense and industry reforms, collaboration in research and development, and security assistance in the form of Javelin antitank missiles.[8] In the second half of 2021, with increased Russian military deployments in the proximity of Ukraine's borders, U.S. and other foreign assistance was increased. U.S. assistance packages in August and December 2021 included, for the first time, lethal military assistance.

Other NATO countries also play a role in assisting Ukraine to move from its Soviet-era roots to a more NATO-aligned military institution. Missions undertaken by the United Kingdom and Canada, as well as NATO training schools in Europe, have provided assistance in the training, education, and professional development of Ukrainian military personnel.

Notwithstanding this assistance, before the 2022 Russian invasion there had been limited progress in the matériel shift to NATO-aligned military forces in Ukraine. In 2021, its armored vehicle fleet consisted largely of upgraded Soviet-era T-64, T-72, and T-84 main battle tanks as well as multiple variants of Soviet-era armored personnel carriers and infantry fighting vehicles. Although not yet obsolete, they were not first-rate modern armored vehicles. The air force was equipped with Soviet legacy fighters, such as the MiG-29 Fulcrum, Su-27 Flanker, Su-24 Fencer, and Su-25 Frogfoot. In 2021, none of these aircraft could have been considered state of the art in military aviation.[9]

The reformation of Ukrainian artillery is one example of the shift from older Soviet technology to more modern NATO-standard equipment and munitions since the start of the war. As the Russians raced to capture Kyiv, foreign assistance began to flow. That aid began with a trickle of handheld missile systems, but eventually the United States and Europe dispatched artillery and munitions. Among the capable artillery systems provided over the first year were over four hundred towed guns, including the U.S. M777 155 mm towed howitzer (provided by multiple countries), as well as older 105 mm howitzers such as the British L119 and American M119.

Eventually, self-propelled artillery such as the M109 self-propelled 155-meter system, the German Pz2000 self-propelled gun, and the French CAESAR 155 mm 6-by-6 self-propelled gun began to arrive. This influx of towed and self-propelled gun systems changed the balance of Soviet-era and NATO systems by the end of 2022. Given the significant battle damage and losses of Ukrainian army systems in the first year of the war, NATO-provided artillery have ensured that Ukraine has not totally ceded the field in artillery to the Russians in the first, and very destructive, year of the war.

The arrival of the HIMARS-fired GMLRS missiles in mid-2022 further improved the situation for Ukrainian fire support. At the same time, the introduction of digital systems to better coordinate and prioritize the use of artillery and to speed up the time to bring Russian targets under fire enhanced the tactical effectiveness of the Ukrainians.

Here I have examined in detail only the example of Ukrainian artillery, but a similar situation has also occurred in other military endeavors of the Ukrainian armed forces. Air defense and armored vehicles are two other areas where there has been a massive influx of Western systems, adding to the speed of the transition to NATO standards for the Ukrainians.

But it is not just the physical war matériel that has driven change. There has also been an acceleration in the intellectual aspects of NATO alignment as well, and ideas about the employment of artillery have also evolved. Challenges with the supply of ammunition to gun lines, and the very long front line, have meant that Ukrainian artillery have been more dispersed than Soviet (or even Western doctrine) proscribes. As a consequence, the Ukrainians had little choice but to shift from an approach that used massed fires to one where precision was used more widely. Precision munitions provided by European and U.S. partners, including the GPS-guided M982 Excalibur and SMArt 155 systems, have permitted this shift to precision-based fire support to combat forces. Additionally, many of these munitions have longer ranges than Soviet legacy munitions, allowing the Ukrainians to hold at risk a larger number of (and more senior) Russian headquarters and logistics establishments.[10]

This intellectual shift has also been a result of many nations providing training for Ukrainian soldiers and officers since the beginning of the war. While much of this training assistance comprises technical training on new equipment—everything from artillery to main battle tanks to Patriot air defense systems—NATO training assistance has been much broader and substantial.

Operation Interflex, a UK-led training mission that coordinates the training of Ukrainian soldiers across multiple countries, including some from faraway Australia and New Zealand, trained over ten thousand Ukrainians in 2022 alone.[11] This training program was expanded in 2023 to include the training of Ukrainian marines as well as fighter pilots.[12]

In Europe, the United States and NATO established the Joint Multinational Training Group–Ukraine to coordinate other training of Ukrainian military personnel. Under this program, Ukrainian unit groups have been trained not only on U.S.-provided equipment but also in calling for artillery fire and medical training as well as in combined-arms combat planning and execution.[13] These training missions serve an immediate requirement for the Ukrainian armed forces in providing the skilled soldiers that an already overburdened Ukrainian military training system may not be able to provide. But at the same time, NATO ideas about command and control, battlefield discipline, mission command, and junior leadership are inherent aspects of much of the training being provided. This will underpin the intellectual transition of the Ukrainian military from older Soviet doctrines and training methods to more Western-aligned approaches.

Reinforcing the Ukrainians' intellectual shift was the impetus of former Commander in Chief Valerii Zaluzhnyi. Zaluzhnyi spent the formative years of his military career in the post-independence Ukrainian armed forces. Like many of his peers, he made his name from 2014 onward, during the fighting in the Donbas. His consideration of Western military thinking was clarified during his time at the National Defense University of Ukraine, where he wrote a thesis comparing the U.S.

and Ukrainian militaries. One of the key conclusions of his study was that Ukraine's military paled in comparison to the U.S. armed forces in leader development.[14]

The zeal with which Zaluzhnyi pursued a post-Soviet military was evident in the wake of the Russian invasion of 2022. In a May 2023 interview he noted, "The most important thing is that I try to change the culture within the Armed Forces of Ukraine. To change it. So that everyone listens to the opinion of the subordinate. My subordinates know that if I find a little representative of some Soviet Army, somewhere at any post I will not be looking into the matter for too long."[15]

From 2017 until 2023, the NATO support to Ukraine was undertaken under the auspices of the NATO-Ukraine Commission. However, the 2023 Vilnius NATO summit saw this commission replaced with a new NATO-Ukraine Council, where Ukraine now participates in NATO discussions as an equal participant. This represents a deepening relationship that also encompasses an array of working groups on topics such as logistics, training, and air defense.[16]

The physical and intellectual transition of the Ukrainian armed forces remains an incomplete undertaking, however. Some old Soviet ideas and processes remain. But results on the battlefield, and leadership from strategic leaders such as Zaluzhnyi, are steadily ensuring that the strategic adaptation of the Ukrainian armed forces to be a NATO-like military continues apace.

Integrated Air, Missile, and Drone Defense

The Ukrainian armed forces have assembled an increasingly effective integrated air, missile, and drone defense system over the course of the war. With a stated intention of "closing the skies,"[17] this air defense system is now capable of detecting and intercepting simple drones as well as the most sophisticated of Russian missiles. It has provided vital air cover for military forces in the field, high-value targets such as headquarters and logistics nodes, and civilian infrastructure and cities.[18] But it has taken trial, error, and much adaptation to get to this point. Adaptation has taken place in several pulses of innovation in response to Russian changes in tactics with the use of their drones and strategic missile forces.

When Russian invaded in February 2022, the Ukrainian air defense system consisted of Soviet legacy systems, including a few of the S-300 (SA-12 Gladiator for NATO) long-range systems, less than a dozen TorM short-range systems, and a variety of point defense weapons, including SA-8 Gecko, SA13 Gopher, and SA-19 Grison systems.[19] These missile launchers, and their associated radars and command support systems, were complemented with old ZSU-23-4 Shilka self-propelled antiaircraft guns as well as towed 23 mm and 57 mm antiaircraft guns.

To inform these engagement systems, air situational awareness was vital. Ukraine possessed a myriad of air defense radar systems, including those that were integral to its S-300, 2K12 Kub, Tor, and Buk-M1 air defense capabilities. But Ukraine also possessed another means of generating situational awareness in the air domain: it had joined the NATO Air Situation Data Exchange program in July 2006. This program, designed to improve awareness and aviation safety through air situation data, no doubt provided vital early warning and location data for the Ukrainians in the early hours of the war. According to NATO, it has continued to collaborate closely with the Ukrainian military to provide the most relevant air situational awareness data possible throughout the war.[20]

In the first days after the Russian invasion began, jamming equipment and aerial decoys deployed by the Russian military were effective at degrading the Ukrainian air defense system. The Ukrainians had anticipated that their air defense network was the primary target for early Russian strikes and had relocated many of their radars and engagement systems. However, Russian strikes using ballistic and cruise missiles were still able to target and destroy many of the Ukrainian air defense radars that were a vital component of their national air defense system. Concurrently, surface to air missile systems such as the SA-11 and S-300 were attacked and destroyed in the country's North and South. Consequently, ground-based air defense in the first days of the war was relatively ineffective, and overall defense of the air domain was carried out by Ukrainian air force fighters such as their aging MiG-29s.[21]

The Ukrainian air defense network thereafter was able to repair damaged sensors and engagement systems, as well as redeploy them to new positions to avoid follow-up strikes by the Russians. Concurrently, the Russians experienced significant electronic fratricide with the systems that had previously been effective at degrading Ukrainian air defense capabilities. As Justin Bronk has reported, Russian "electronic warfare assets began to greatly scale back their operations after the first two days. This allowed newly relocated Ukrainian SAM systems to regain much of their effectiveness."[22]

The Russian air, missile, drone, and electronic warfare capability, at least on paper, should have overwhelmed Ukrainian air and missile defense capabilities in the early days of the Russian invasion. But because of the rapid Ukrainian repairs and adaptation to their deployment locations, and Russian communications and electronic warfare problems, the Ukrainian air defense system was able to survive and regain a level of effectiveness. Even when the Russians began to evolve their approach to use hunting parties of Orlan-1 UAVs to unmask Ukrainian radars to be attacked, the Ukrainians were able to adapt by moving their air defense assets farther back from the front lines.[23]

The next pulse of innovation from the Ukrainians occurred when Russia shifted focus to launching missile attacks against Ukraine's energy and transportation sectors and blatant terror attacks against civilians in mid-2022. Attacks on oil refineries caused fuel shortages throughout Ukraine over the northern summer. Russian missile strikes also aimed to slow down the flow of military aid from the West to Ukraine through attacks on Ukraine's rail infrastructure. The effects of this next series of Russian strikes were mitigated through an evolved Ukrainian air defense network, as well as adaptations in the Ukrainian logistics network to make targeting it more difficult.

A third pulse of adaptation took place when the Russians evolved their strategy in the wake of the appointment of General Surovikin in October 2022 and began to target civilian facilities across Ukraine, including the power and water network. Using their depleted stocks of cruise and ballistic missiles, as well as their newly acquired Iranian Shahed 136 loitering munitions, the Russian strikes commenced on 10 October 2022: eighty-three missiles and drones were launched at various targets.[24] While forty-three were shot down by the Ukrainian air defense system, the other forty found their targets and caused civilian deaths and damage to civilian infrastructure.[25]

This prompted the Ukrainian president to reemphasize the need for sophisticated Western air defense systems. Speaking to a meeting of G7 leaders on 11 October, he declared, "It is important that we have sufficient missiles for the air defense and antimissile systems provided and that these systems are integrated with our defense system."[26]

The Ukrainians also adapted to use fighter aircraft to shoot down some incoming missiles and drones to preserve the rapidly dwindling numbers of air defense missiles. But this was a losing battle for the Ukrainians. Their stocks of air defense missiles were smaller than Russian stocks of missiles and Iranian drones. Russia launched over 150 missiles and drones in the first three days of its October 2022 assault.[27] And at least in the case of the Iranian drones, these were much cheaper (around US$20,000 each) to shoot at a target than the air defense missile that was used to destroy them.[28] This reflected a cost-imposition strategy by the Russians, and if the Ukrainians did not adapt their approach, they would expend their missiles and the Russians would have much more freedom in Ukrainian skies. This in turn would be disastrous for the defense of critical civilian and military infrastructure as well as military units in the field.

The Ukrainians then developed additional mobile antidrone teams and expanded the air defense reporting network through the deployment of a mobile phone app, developed by Ukraine's tech industry, that permitted civilians to report sightings of Russian drones and missiles. Released in October 2022, the air defense app added another layer to Ukrainian air situational awareness.[29] The app was yet another example in this war of the meshing of civilian and military intelligence collection, analysis, and dissemination.

Since October 2022, the performance of the Ukrainian air defense network has improved considerably. Using data collected from Ukraine's National Security and Defense Council and the General Staff of the Ukrainian armed forces, American Ian Williams has published an analysis showing that Ukraine improved its interception of Russian missiles from around 10 percent between February and July 2022 to 75–80 percent by December 2022.[30]

While significant learning and adaptation by Ukrainian air defense operators has contributed to this improvement in performance, another important contribution has been the adaptation of the Ukrainian air defense network in late 2022 driven by the arrival of several more-advanced Western air defense systems. The Ukrainians were initially provided with older U.S. Hawk air defense missiles; later, the newer German IRIST and U.S. National Advanced Surface-to-Air Missile Systems (NASAMs) air defense systems began to be absorbed into Ukraine's armed forces. Both IRIST and NASAMs possess their own radars, fire control centers, and missile launchers, each of which added a layer of capability and redundancy to the Ukrainian armed forces' approach to air defense. These were enhanced with the even more capable Patriot air defense system in 2023.[31]

These longer-range systems have been supplemented with mobile teams that are equipped with cheaper antimissile and drone systems. A menagerie of such weapons systems are now used by the Ukrainians. There are self-propelled systems, including the armored German Flakpanzer Gepard, the Strela-10, U.S. antidrone 30 mm gun trucks, and ZSU 23-4; and more improved systems, such as 12.7 mm machine guns bolted to the trays of offroad vehicles.[32] Short-range air defense missiles include the Mistral, Igla, Strela-2, and Stinger human-portable air defense weapons.

Electronic warfare systems also feature heavily in Ukraine's evolved air defense environment. A range of antidrone detection systems, jammers, and spoofing systems, both human-portable and heavier, have been provided by foreign donors of military assistance. And finally, the Ukrainians are acting as a testing ground for other more advanced antidrone and antimissile systems provided by the United States, such as mobile counter-UAS laser-guided rocket systems.[33]

This adaptation has even extended to the mating of Soviet and Western equipment on a single air defense platform. The Soviet-era Buk medium-range tracked air defense system was in service with the Ukrainian armed forces before the Russian invasion. But the heavy Russian missile attacks on Ukraine from October 2022 meant that stocks of the missiles fired by the Buk launchers, the 9M family of medium-range missiles, became severely depleted. As a result, the United States assisted Ukraine to mate the U.S. RIM-7 missile to the Buk launcher in early 2023. Although the RIM-7 missile has a shorter range than the 9M missile it replaced, it remains a very capable missile and is held in large numbers by Western military organizations.[34]

Brought together and networked by secure, digital command and control architectures, the Ukrainian air defense network could probably be described now as the most effective in existence anywhere in the world. Not for many decades has a single country come under such sustained attack from the air from such a diversity of different aerial weapon systems. The Ukrainians have had to learn and adapt since the beginning of the war to reach this point.

By May 2023, due to the effectiveness of the Ukrainian air defense system, over 90 percent of missiles and drones were being shot down.[35] Perhaps the contemporary effectiveness could be exemplified by a 28–29 May 2023 series of raids on the Ukrainian capital. Russia fired several barrages of missiles and drones at the Kyiv region. These included Iskander ballistic missiles Kh-101 and Kh-555 cruise missiles and Iranian Shahed drones. Across three separate raids, 87 Shaheds, 40 cruise missiles, and 11 ballistic missiles were fired at Kyiv. Only 6 of the 148 missiles and drones reached their targets.[36]

The adaptations to the Ukrainian air defense network have had a strategic impact on the war. They have ensured that Ukrainian military operations are able to be conducted with less molestation from Russian missiles, drones, and aircraft. This has reduced Russia's capacity to surveil the Ukrainians and has enhanced the Ukrainian military's freedom of movement. Russian crewed aircraft now rarely fly over Ukraine. This very effective air defense environment has reduced the threat to Ukrainian civilians and civil infrastructure. Not only is this an important moral and humanitarian outcome; it also helps Ukrainian factories that are supporting the war effort stay open.

These strategic adaptations have been underpinned by Ukraine's ability to solicit military aid from abroad. This has included cutting-edge Western military equipment and munitions as well as additional items of Soviet-era equipment and ammunition. Led by its former defense minister, Oleksii Reznikov,[37] Ukrainian delegations scoured the world seeking military equipment, ammunition, and matériel to keep Ukraine's military supplied with the equipment required to defend its territory and to conduct the offensives required to recapture Ukrainian lands from the Russians.

The strategic adaptations described above would also have been more difficult to achieve without the meshing of many civilian and military sensors since the start of the war. A significant transformation in itself, a variety of military and commercial technologies have been used in generating situational awareness for Ukrainian forces, as well as in the dissemination of that knowledge.

OPERATIONAL ADAPTATION

Without the crucible of combat, even the very best doctrinal foundations can be found wanting. Institutions must accept that the initial clashes with an enemy during wartime will highlight areas that were given the wrong emphasis, or aspects of war that they entirely missed. It is impossible for a military institution to anticipate every eventuality. Throughout the war, the Ukrainian armed forces have undertaken a range of adaptations to their force posture, structure, and processes to enhance their operational effectiveness. One in particular stands out: long-range strike.

Striking Farther

Long-range strike has been a key adaptation for the Ukrainians since the beginning of the Russian invasion. Initially founded on ground-based rocket launchers, Ukraine has over the course of the war expanded its long-range strike arsenal to include armed drones, truck-launched antiship missiles (the Neptune), new cruise missiles from the United Kingdom and France, and uncrewed maritime strike vessels.[38]

From the middle of 2022, the Ukrainian armed forces have demonstrated the ability to absorb and use very precise, long-range rocket systems against the Russians. The High Mobility Artillery Rocket System (HIMARS), an American truck-mounted rocket launch platform, began to be deployed to Ukraine in June 2022. It is a lighter, more deployable version of the older, tracked M270 Mobile Rocket Launch System (MLRS) that was used to great effect during the 1991 and 2003 Gulf Wars.[39] Since the arrival of the HIMARS, however, several countries including the United Kingdom and Germany have also provided MLRS platforms to Ukraine. The HIMARS and MLRS fire the same rockets.

Because of their long range and precision, the HIMARS and MLRS are weapons for attacking targets deep behind the front line of fighting. This makes them more of an operational level tool than a tactical one, where artillery is still the predominant form of fire support. These rockets fired by the HIMARS and MLRS, almost exclusively the Guided Multiple Launch Rocket System (GMLRS), have been used to destroy critical Russian communications nodes, Russian army headquarters and command posts, locations where reserve Russian troops are housed, and important logistics facilities. These targets have been constantly attacked by the Ukrainians since the introduction of the HIMARS and MLRS.[40]

Because the HIMARS and MLRS system is mobile, its launchers can quickly stop, fire their rockets at their designated targets, and then move away before Russian counterbattery fires can destroy them. This ensures that these long-range strike weapons are very survivable as Russians continue to improve the linkage between their reconnaissance drones and their artillery units.[41] Perhaps the most important impact of these two long-range rocket launchers is that it has allowed the Ukrainians—after a bloody campaign in the Donbas in mid-2022—to return to fighting the Russians at a distance and where they are weakest. Because the strategy of corrosion, described in chapter 3, seeks to avoid bloody, attritional ground fighting until absolutely necessary, it relies on this approach.

This was a critical adaptation in the East, where the Russians had changed tactics to concentrate their forces in single large offensive. The Russians used their firepower advantage in the Donbas and forced the Ukrainians into an attritional battle for that region. This relentless, crunching attrition is Russia's preferred way of fighting, but it is a form of war that the Ukrainians cannot afford to wage. The introduction of HIMARS changed the battlefield calculus in the fight for Ukraine.[42] The introduction of the longer-range U.S. Army Tactical Missile System (ATACMS) missiles in 2023, however, did not have a similar effect. Despite a very effective strike on Russian helicopter bases in Luhansk and Berdyansk in October 2023, it is apparent that these missiles were not provided in sufficient quantities to have a decisive impact on the war.[43]

Along with the physical impacts, these long-range rockets have had a psychological effect on the Russians. More of the Russian force is now at threat of attack from the longer-range and more precise GMLRS rockets. Russian soldiers see their impact both firsthand and on social media. The Russians had to quickly adapt, and dispersing their already tenuous logistic system has made them even less efficient. However, Russian adaptations to counter the accuracy of HIMARS rockets with electronic warfare have been more effective.[44]

These ground-based systems have not been the only new long-range strike weapons deployed by the Ukrainians. In 2023, their ability to strike the Russians was enhanced with long-range aerial weapons. Initially, the Ukrainians modified old Soviet-era Tu-141 Strizh surveillance drones to conduct strike operations. The Strizh looks more like a cruise missile than a traditional reconnaissance drone. It is a rocket launched from a trailer and flies a predetermined course at transonic speed.[45] After some modification by the Ukrainians, these stopgap cruise missiles were used in long-range strikes on the Engels and Dyagilevo Air Bases inside Russia in December 2022.[46]

In 2023, a newer aerial long-range strike capability entered the Ukrainian inventories. The provision of the U.K.-built Storm Shadow missile was announced by the British prime minister in May 2023.[47] The Storm Shadow is a stealthy missile launched from fighter aircraft and able to hit targets over 250 kilometers from its launch point. The Storm Shadow is designed to strike high-value targets with its

400-kilogram penetrating explosive warhead.[48] The missile considerably extends the ability of the Ukrainian armed forces to strike operational-level Russian targets and will force the Russians to further adapt, dispersing and defending their high-value headquarters and logistics nodes.

Ukraine has also been developing indigenous solutions to its long-range strike requirements. In attempting to narrow the chasm between its long-range capabilities and those of Russia, Ukraine has expanded its array of indigenous drone programs for reconnaissance and attacking enemy fixed targets, vehicles, and other drones. One Ukrainian company, AeroDrone, has stated that one of its models, called Enterprise and based on the frame of a light aircraft, can fly over three thousand kilometers.[49] Notwithstanding the provision of Western longer-range strike missiles such as Storm Shadow, it is likely that Ukraine will continue to develop its own strike drones as the war continues. In late 2023, reports emerged of a long-range attack drone, called the Beaver, being developed by Ukraine.[50]

A final adaptation that has allowed the Ukrainians to strike farther, and in different domains, has been their development and combat use of uncrewed surface vessels, also known as kamikaze boats.

In October 2022, the Ukrainians conducted a surprise attack on the Russian Black Sea fleet with up to seven uncrewed surface vessels, supported by eight uncrewed aerial vehicles. An *Admiral Grigorovich*–class frigate and a Russian navy mine countermeasure (MCM) ship were reportedly attacked by the Ukrainian kamikaze boats. In the wake of the attack, the Russian Ministry of Defense acknowledged only that there had been minor damage to the MCM vessel. Subsequent attacks were conducted in March, April, and May 2023, although there is believed to have been little damage caused by the Ukrainian kamikaze boats in these attacks.[51] In the wake of the July 2023 attack on the Kerch Bridge, the Ukrainian minister for digital transformation, Mykhailo Feorov, claimed that Ukrainian naval drones were responsible.[52]

Developed to interdict Russian naval vessels in the Black Sea and to prevent missile-carrying warships leaving the Russian naval base in Sevastopol, the Ukrainians have developed at least three uncrewed surface vessels (USVs). The first is a 5-meter-long surface vessel that looks much like a covered speedboat. With an explosive warhead of up to 200 kg and an operational radius of nearly 400 kilometers, these USVs were the ones involved in the October 2022 attack at Sevastopol.[53]

A second USV developed by Ukraine is a semisubmersible vessel that is smaller than the larger surface USV used in the October Sevastopol attacks. Little is known about this vessel. A third vessel is the Toloka armed uncrewed underwater vehicle (UUV). A vessel with a tubular body and a large keel and horizontal stabilizers amidships, it was revealed in April 2023.[54] Designed as a family of one-way kamikaze submersibles for attacking Russian warships, the Tolokas have a range of one hundred to almost two thousand kilometers depending on the variant.[55]

This family of maritime strike vessels is an exemplar of the Ukrainians adapting their strategy to embrace an indirect approach against a conventional navy. The Russian Black Sea Fleet is a powerful combination of surface, submarine, and support vessels operating out of the base at Sevastopol in occupied Crimea. With almost no likelihood of developing its own conventional naval fleet to fight the Russians, the Ukrainians have developed uncrewed capabilities. While ostensibly designed to sink or damage Russian surface warships, they are also intended to have the psychological effect of dissuading the Russian ships from putting to sea. Given that many of the missile attacks aimed at Ukraine originate from warships in the Black Sea, Ukraine is hoping to drastically reduce the effectiveness of Russia's Black Sea fleet in a manner similar to how the Royal Navy kept the German high seas fleet in port for the second half of World War I.

Despite these adaptations to long-range strike by the Ukrainians, the long-range strike capability offered by the rockets fired from the HIMARS and M270 MLRS, aerial systems, and kamikaze boats systems are not wonder weapons. They are having an ongoing effect but will not in themselves win this war. Military forces are complex organizations with many different capabilities in function, range, scale, and impact. Long-range strike is just part of a highly networked, sophisticated system of humans, machines, and information that Ukraine needs to win this war.[56] And to win this war, Ukraine needs to engage in close combat and win battles. Adaptation in this realm is the topic of the next chapter.

14

THE LAST FULL MEASURE

Ukrainian Tactical Adaptation

THE UKRAINE WAR has seen some of the bitterest combat since World War II. Infantry, tanks, artillery, attack helicopters, combat engineers, and fixed-wing aircraft of various types have fought at different ranges. Sometimes combat has been beyond the sight of participants, as it often is with aerial combat or artillery duels on the ground. And sometimes it has been very up close and personal for the combatants, with urban fighting and trench warfare engagements taking place at nearly point-blank range between tanks and dismounted troops, overseen by the ubiquitous presence of lethal drones and sensors.

No other endeavor forces people to make such brutal, rapid choices about life and death. There have been thousands of combat engagements over the course of this war so far, taking place within hundreds of battles and many campaigns in northern, eastern, and southern Ukraine as well as in the skies above it and in cyberspace.

Tactical excellence is a foundational capability in effective military institutions. At this level of war, adaptation provides a firm base for learning and the evolution of battlefield proficiency. Tactical adaptation also incorporates the distribution of tactical observations and lessons to both combat forces as well as military training, education, and doctrine institutions that prepare reinforcements, new units, and new institutional tactics.

Three important Ukrainian tactical adaptations have occurred since the February 2022 Russian invasion: adaptation in tactics, the proliferation of autonomous system, and digitized battle command and control.

ADAPTATION IN TACTICS

The Ukrainian army began to adapt their tactics during the Russian advance on Kyiv. Using precision weapons from the West, such as the Javelin and NLAW, as well as their own stocks of Soviet-era antitank and antivehicle missiles, the Ukrainians conducted the stalking and ambushing of Russian mounted columns. These dismounted antiarmor tactics were so successful early in the war that the Javelin missile became of the early iconic weapons of the war. Ukrainian influence operations thereafter featured images of Mary Magdalene, dubbed St. Javelin, holding a Javelin missile.[1]

Just as effective has been the Saab Bofors Dynamics Next Generation Light Anti-Tank Weapon. Collaboratively designed by Britain and Sweden, it is a lighter and cheaper version of the Javelin missile. Designed for shorter-range engagements than the Javelin missile, Ukraine's armed forces have estimated that this single weapon is responsible for the destruction of between 30 and 40 percent of Russian armor in the early months of the Russian invasion.[2]

The Ukrainian adaptations resulted from their exploitation of a paucity of Russian rear-area security, a slow Russian shift from coup de main to combat operations, and massive military traffic jams to fight the Russians in the rear areas. The resulting attrition in Russian armor, logistics, and command nodes saw a steady corrosion of Russian combat power and morale. The Ukrainians, understanding they had to assume the defensive for the initial phase of the war, used these small-scale tactics in other battles, including their monthslong defense of Mariupol in 2022.[3]

This approach was hardly new. During the 1973 Yom Kippur War, the Israeli army faced the Soviet-made AT-3 Sapper antitank missiles employed by the Arab armies. In one battle alone, on 8 October 1973, the Israeli 162nd Armored Division lost 83 of its 183 tanks in a frontal armored assault against Egyptian forces. In the first three days of the war, the Israelis lost over 350 tanks in the Sinai. Meir Finkel, in *On Flexibility*, describes how the antitank missiles represented a significant tactical surprise for the Israelis on the Sinai front during the war, particularly in its use in vast numbers in Egypt's scheme of defense.[4] However, innovation in combined-arms tactics including dismounted infantry and a more integrated use of artillery and smokescreens saw the survivability of Israeli armor improve.[5] The tank versus antitank missile is not a new tactical conundrum for armies, and multiple solutions exist to ensure the survivability of armored ground forces.

The combination of these new-era precision human-portable systems, clever Ukrainian small unit tactics, and the Russian unpreparedness for wide-scale combat at the start of the invasion resulted in Ukrainian tactical adaptation. But as with all adaptation, eventually the enemy learns enough about their opponents' new tactics to adapt its own approach. And that is exactly what occurred when the main Russian effort in this war shifted to the east.

But not all adaptation in Ukraine's tactics has been at the small team level. Since the beginning of the war, the Ukrainian ground forces have been slowly improving their capacity to undertake larger-scale combined-arms operations. This means operations—both defensive and offensive—at the battalion (or battle group) and brigade levels. It is not a simple undertaking and has at times been challenged by a lack of time for collective training.

Ukrainian learning has also been influenced over the institutional struggle about whether the Ukrainian ground forces culture should be Soviet legacy or more Western oriented. This battle for the soul of the Ukrainian ground force's command culture has been explored by several academics. In 2023, an adjunct fellow at the Center for a New American Security explored the conflict between Soviet models of centralized command and the Western approach of more disaggregated, mission command models. He notes,

> Part of Ukraine's armed forces, in particular the ground forces, risk back-sliding to their old and inflexible ways. One reason is the large number of casualties incurred among NATO-trained Ukrainian soldiers in the first months of the war, and the consequent mobilisation of a large number of retired Ukrainian officers steeped in rigid Soviet military thinking. But that is only part of the explanation. In fact, Soviet influences have always been more prevalent than many observers have realized.[6]

Even after eighteen months of exposure to Russian modes of command on the battlefield, which emphasize centralization of control and minimal trust in subordinates, some Ukrainian commanders have continued to eschew the methods of mission command taught in most Western military institutions. As Sam Skove writes in an April 2023 article, the Ukrainian officer corps remains "rife with Soviet style thinking."[7] And in a mid-2023 article for *War on the Rocks*, two U.S. military trainers who had just returned from Ukraine describe how the Ukrainian military still has challenges with mission command and combined-arms training.[8]

To be fair to the Ukrainians, it is very difficult to transition from Soviet-era approaches to full-on NATO methods in a short period of time. There is an old saying that nothing is harder to change in a military institution than an idea. Even Western military institutions struggle with effective combined-arms operations. The journey to build effective joint operations and institutions has taken decades. But the Ukrainians have come some way since the beginning of the war.

One example of this progress was the Ukrainian offensive conducted in Kharkiv in September 2022.[9] Coordinating the sequential employment of multiple brigades after months of careful reconnaissance, deception, and other preliminary activities, the Ukrainians were able to conduct a successful offensive to recapture large swaths of Ukrainian territory around Kharkiv, the country's second-largest city. Panicked Russian troops withdrew from large parts of northeastern Ukraine, leaving behind masses of equipment and munitions. It was also a strategic shock to the Russian government, which shortly afterward announced the partial mobilization of Russian forces.

But as successful as this offensive was, it was also a learning experience. The Kharkiv offensive was the first major ground offensive that the Ukrainian armed forces had conducted since gaining their independence in 1991. Ukrainian troops had to clear Russian soldiers from entrenched positions and to do so while under almost constant surveillance. And it took five days of hard fighting and massive artillery barrages by the Ukrainians before the initial Russian defenses started to give way and then break. After this point, the Ukrainians formed what Liddell Hart described as an "expanding torrent," one that saw the Ukrainians capture the key centers of Kupiansk and Izium and push the Russians all the way back to the Russian border.[10] But even then, Russian forces were able to shell the advancing Ukrainians all the way.[11]

This offensive demonstrated that Ukraine was learning about combined-arms operations. It had required a more intricate coordination of artillery, combat forces, and surveillance activities as well as the ability to quickly exploit battlefield opportunities. There was much improvisation, but that is the norm for combined-arms operations.[12] However, the vast majority of activities in this offensive occurred at the platoon and company levels. It was a step toward more integrated combined arms fighting capabilities, but an incomplete journey.

The offensive also demanded detailed planning and reconnaissance to finalize the assault routes that would best exploit Russian weaknesses in northeastern Ukraine. With the planning led by the commander of the operation, General Oleksandr Syrskyi, the Ukrainians gained critical experience in planning more sophisticated combined-arms operations than they had at the beginning of the war. Speed, surprise, firepower, and decisive action were key to the plan and how it eventually unfolded. As Syrskyi later explained, "Everything depended on the first day—how far we could break through. The farther we went, the less they could do, the more their units would be cut off and isolated under psychological pressure."[13]

And with this improvement in combined arms offensive capacity came a strategic impact: Ukraine's supporters for the first time witnessed how Ukraine could and would fight to regain its territory. As one contemporary account noted, "The Kharkiv offensive revealed the inability of an undermanned and underequipped Russian force to hold territory across a vast front. It shocked the Kremlin, and it proved to Ukraine's supporters that they were not wasting billions in weapons and economic aid."[14]

As the Kharkiv offensive played out, the Ukrainians were mounting a larger-scale offensive in the Kherson region.[15] A large and complex operation against a well-prepared, capable, and larger Russian force that was defending the territory west of the Dnipro River, the campaign to liberate this Ukrainian territory was a significant step up in difficulty, and bloodiness, from the Kharkiv offensive. Where the Kharkiv offensive had seen the employment of around six to eight Ukrainian maneuver brigades (as well as several territorial brigades in support),[16] the longer Kherson offensive that continued into November 2022 involved more than double that number, with territorial brigades and artillery units in addition to this number.[17]

This demonstrates learning and adaptation in the Ukrainian armed forces in their higher-level ability to coordinate tactical ground force operations. Over a period of nine months, the Ukrainians had progressed from the ad hoc command and control that drove the coordination of the defense of Kyiv to larger-scale maneuvers in the Kherson offensive.

But challenges remained. The tension between Soviet and Western command approaches remained. Ukrainian ground operations remained focused on platoon- and company-level maneuvers, and operations above this level were conducted sequentially rather than in an integrated fashion. Logistic support to combat forces remained difficult, and the supply of ammunition for Ukrainian artillery units was constrained if not constant.

As explored in the previous chapter, fire support, out of necessity and from operational learning, shifted more toward precision engagements. At the same time, the preparation of brigade staffs in the planning and execution of combined arms operations was stepped up by NATO countries.[18] Information about this training came to light in the wake of the April 2023 Discord leak of secret U.S. government briefing slides. The slides identified Western-supported collective training (training of units, not individuals) in progress for Ukrainian ground forces on four types of main battle tank (Challenger, Leopard 2, T-72, and T-64) as well as infantry fighting vehicles (BMP, Marder, and M2 Bradley), armored personnel carriers (M-113, Viking, and XA-185), and different variants of the M109 self-propelled howitzer.[19]

The 2023 Discord leaks also identified locations where this collective training was being conducted (including Britain, Germany, Poland, Ukraine, and Finland), although some of this information—such as U.S. Army training in combined-arms operations—had been available in the press since at least December 2022.[20] The U.S. Army had been providing the training at its Grafenwoehr training area in Germany from late 2022 and continued to do so into 2023. In May 2023, it was also revealed that an entire Ukrainian brigade had been reequipped and training in combined arms operations in Sweden.[21]

At the same time, the Ukrainian commander in chief was adamant about the transition of the Ukrainian armed forces from their Soviet origins. He stated openly, "My subordinates know that if I find a little representative of some Soviet Army, somewhere at any post I will not be looking into the matter for too long."[22] But the vestiges of Ukraine's Soviet past remain. In a 2023 critique of the Ukrainian military, Glen Grant wrote,

> Despite the victories and amazingly stubborn defenses in places like Bakhmut, not all is good with the management of the Ukrainian conduct of war. . . . A further challenge from this is that there is an increasing difference in leadership abilities within the system. The best are getting better daily and more western in their approach, but some commanders remain Soviet to the core. The worst commanders . . . are increasingly turning to bureaucracy and rules to avoid responsibility and to cover up their obvious gap in leadership abilities.[23]

While the commander in chief may be focused on removing Soviet influences, it will be difficult to transform an institution as large as the Ukrainian armed forces from Soviet to NATO methodologies rapidly. Change is occurring, but expecting instant change and improvement in military effectiveness is unrealistic in a human organization.

The ultimate effectiveness or otherwise of these Ukrainian adaptations could be assessed by the conduct of the initial stages of the 2023 Ukrainian offensive. It was a campaign that had been planned for some time. In a September 2022 article, then Ukrainian commander in chief General Zaluzhnyi wrote that "the only way to radically change the strategic situation is undoubtedly for the Ukrainian Army to launch several consecutive, and ideally, simultaneous counter strikes throughout 2023. It would be hard to overestimate their military, as well as political and informational, significance."[24]

While Ukraine was able to put a large number of brigades into the field and conduct combined-arms operations, these remained mainly at platoon, company, and sometimes battalion levels. There is little evidence, at this point, of ground maneuvers being conducted by multiple brigades in an integrated fashion. There was a disparity in the quality of cohesive offensive action, with older units proving to be better than newly formed (but better-equipped) brigades.[25] Additionally, the scale and depth of Russian defenses, and the improvements in Russia's capacity to defend its ground, provided significant challenges. It certainly resulted in a much slower offensive than many expected; even President Zelenskyy described the initial phase of the Ukrainian offensive as "slower than desired."[26] And it resulted within the first weeks of the 2023 southern offensive in Ukrainian units disaggregating into platoon-sized forces conducting small-scale attacks, often supported by just a couple of tanks, to seize the next tree line.

The learning and adaptation of the Ukrainian ground forces' tactics provide the two bookends of the story told in this book of the first eighteen months of the war. In February 2022, the Ukrainian armed forces were able to defend their nation against the Russian onslaught, although they lost over 20 percent of their territory in doing so. Since that time, the Ukrainians have fought, learned, adapted, and demonstrated an increasingly competent—but still evolving—combined-arms combat ability.

Ultimately, it was the learning and adaptation in the war's first year that underpinned the planning and initial conduct of the 2023 Ukrainian offensives. But given the planning, leadership, and combat problems experienced by several Ukrainian brigades in June 2023, the Ukrainians still had a ways to go in demonstrating the capacity for large-scale combined arms maneuver.

The Ukrainian adaptation in this war has had many components so far. One of them has been their embrace of new technologies in combat and support operations. The rise of autonomous and uncrewed systems, and their role in surveillance and strike operations, is perhaps one of the most important.

AUTONOMOUS SYSTEMS: CLOSING THE DETECTION-TO-DESTRUCTION GAP

Peter Singer's book *Wired for War* examines the growth of autonomous systems in warfare. There Singer notes, "The revolution in robotics is forcing us to reexamine what is possible, probable, and proper in war and politics. The wars of the future will feature robots of a wide variety of sizes, designs, capabilities, autonomy, and intelligence. . . . The systems and stories captured in this book are just the start of a process that will be of historic importance to the story of humanity itself."[27]

The war in Ukraine has furthered the understanding of the potential of autonomous systems in war. Although both sides understand the advantages that autonomous and uncrewed systems bring to the battlefield, there are still often shortfalls in the quantity of drones needed. This gap has often been filled by crowdsourcing and civilian volunteer efforts. Commercial drones have driven both demands, and the increasing level of capability, of the integration of drone operations into recon, surveillance, and strike operations in Ukraine.[28]

One campaign, called *Army of Drones*, has provided over three thousand drones for the Ukrainian armed forces.[29] In an environment where the combat losses of drones can run into hundreds each week, the rapid production and procurement of drones is a vital part of war mobilization.[30] As T. X. Hammes has written, "The increasing capabilities of commercial drones are changing the game of how militaries will use this technology. . . . An increasing range of long-endurance, commercial drones carrying commercial surveillance payloads such as these will allow even smaller states access to affordable intelligence, surveillance, and reconnaissance (ISR) and attack."[31] And while commercial drones are now used in the hundreds and thousands, they are only part of the story of the growth of autonomous systems used by the Ukrainians. Numerous military drones, which are hardened against electronic warfare and have greater range and a greatly increased ability to deliver lethal effects, have also entered service during this conflict.

In Ukraine, drones have been used for reconnaissance and correcting indirect fire (artillery, mortars, and tanks) and as loitering munitions. Increasingly they are being used for longer-range strikes. The Russians have done this since the start of the war. The Ukrainians, although lacking the same depth of missile reserves, have begun to undertake their own long-range strikes on maritime and ground targets.

But the most ubiquitous are those drones used by tactical forces to seek out the enemy. Either the information gathered is used to call in artillery or missile strikes, or the drones themselves are used as attack systems by dropping munitions or as kamikaze drones. They have been responsible for drastically reducing the time between detection and destruction in tactical activities. As a British report noted in 2022, Russian times for detecting and then engaging a target are about three to five minutes.[32] Ukrainian engagement times are reportedly much faster. In some instances, once a drone is overhead, those who are being observed (or targeted, in the case of a loitering munition) can have as little as a minute to live.

Along with their battlefield impacts, the influx of drones has had an organizational effect. Institutionally, the Ukrainian armed forces initially absorbed the capacity of multiple different drones into their existing force structure. The drones were generally just an addition to unit organizations. In 2023, however, the Ukrainians decided to augment this approach of issuing drones to combat units by forming special drone attack companies.[33] These attack companies would be undertaking reconnaissance as well as lethal strike operations. Sixty companies were formed in the first half of 2023. This, and the need to provide more drones to more combat units being formed for the 2023 offensives, necessitated a step-up in training, so ten thousand drone operators were trained.[34] It also required a more accelerated approach to drone procurement.

To enable this, the Ukrainian government has also worked to remove bureaucratic obstacles to the development and production of drones for the Ukrainian armed forces. In March 2023, the government of Ukraine issued a decree to remove some of the red tape associated with bidding for their armed forces' contracts for drones.[35] Deputy Prime Minister Mykhailo Fedorov, who oversees innovation and technology, noted that "instead of spending months on unnecessary paper and bureaucratic work (we will have) accelerated admission of drones to operation, their purchase, and delivery to the front."[36]

Some of the drones in these new companies have been undertaking counter-drone operations: for the first time, drones are being used in combat against other drones. As an article in *Scientific American* put it in April 2023, "A new epoch in air warfare is emerging: drone-on-drone combat."[37] Ukraine has begun to deploy purpose-designed drones that could engage or even capture Russian drones. This drone capture mission, recorded on multiple online videos, is likely to become part of the role set of autonomous systems given the potential for intelligence exploitation of enemy drones.[38]

The employment of loitering munitions is another area of adaptation by the Ukrainian armed forces. These munitions were initially developed by Iran, the United States, and Israel in the 1970s and 1980s. In testimony before the U.S. Congress in March 1975, U.S. Air Force Brigadier Lovic Hodnette testified, "We don't want a man in the loop. We want to let it go, find a radar, and hit it and never come back. We don't want the manpower, the logistics, to bring it back. It's a one-way mission."[39]

This type of weapon is a unique form of UAV that carries a warhead and is able to "loiter" in an area before finding a target and diving into it. In many respects, it is a small, uncrewed version of the kamikaze aircraft used by the Japanese military in the Pacific War.[40] A May 2023 study published by the Vertical Flight Society describes over two hundred types of these one-way uncrewed systems being developed in over thirty nations.[41] But although these kinds of weapons have been used by military organizations for several decades, the Ukrainian armed forces did not have any in their inventory at the beginning of the war.

The Ukrainians were fast learners, however. The first loitering munitions were dispatched to Ukraine as part of a March 2022 military assistance package announced by the U.S. government. This was further clarified in April 2022, when the U.S. Department of Defense announced it had provided seven hundred Switchblade 600 loitering munitions to Ukraine.[42] Since that time, these munitions have been part of nearly every assistance package dispatched by the Americans to Ukraine. Not only do they make up for shortfalls in artillery ammunition; they also provide a different attack vector against Russian vehicles, equipment, and headquarters, which can be difficult to defend against. And while a variety of loitering munitions are now employed by the Ukrainians, they have supplemented these foreign munitions with a program that uses first-person view (FPV) racing drones that are converted into small, hard-to-intercept loitering munitions. These drones are easy and cheap to produce and are provided by the hundred to Ukrainian combat units.[43]

Finally, the Ukrainians have adapted to improve the survivability of their drones against Russian counter-drone operations. They have done so to ensure that their losses are more sustainable, to enable drones to more successfully conduct their reconnaissance or strike missions, and to ensure the survivability of drone operators on the battlefield. As a recent RUSI report noted, "Russian electronic warfare (EW) remains potent, with an approximate distribution of at least one major system covering each 10 km of front. These systems are heavily weighted toward the defeat of UAVs and tend not to try and deconflict their effects. Ukrainian UAV losses remain at approximately 10,000 per month."[44]

Countering autonomous systems has generally been a "lagging capability" in this war, but both the Ukrainians and Russians have been sprinting to improve their ability to intercept, capture, and destroy drones, as well as trace the location of drone operations centers and attack them. Russia has actively sought to counter the Ukrainian adaptations to absorb a range of different military and civilian uncrewed aerial systems. The Russians have instituted an integrated system that employs a mix of electronic warfare, along with missile systems and connected sensors, to degrade Ukraine's battlefield and strategic use of drones and loitering munitions.[45]

A variety of approaches have been adopted to ensure the survivability of drones and their operators. Hardening drones against electronic attack is a partial solution, although this can add weight and is not an effective solution for some smaller and lightweight drones. Mobile drone operations centers are also used, and communications links have been encoded. By understanding how their own learning and adaptation processes function, military institutions can also influence their adversary's ability to adapt. This theory of *counteradaptation* has played out in the real world in Ukraine alongside the adaptive processes of Ukraine and Russia.[46] A key lesson from this adaptation battle is that military forces require a new generation of counter-autonomy systems that are cheaper to purchase and deploy widely.[47]

In *Wired for War*, Peter Singer writes that "revolutionary new technologies are not only being introduced to war, but used in ever greater numbers, with novel and often unexpected effects."[48] This has played out in Ukraine. Both Russia and Ukraine have massively expanded the number and type of drones they deploy as well as the kinds of missions they undertake. Drones are now attacking drones, and in one incident in mid-2023, a Ukrainian drone was used to recover a Russian drone from a minefield. This is indeed a novel effect. There are sure to be other new and unexpected uses of battlefield drones. But ultimately, this hardening of the entire drone capability will be a core aspect of the adaptation battle in Ukraine—and in future wars.

▪ DIGITAL BATTLE COMMAND AND CONTROL

The application of drones, and the significant expansion in their use, could not have occurred without the adaptations in Ukrainian command and control systems that have taken place before and during the war. These digital systems, some civilian and some military, have connected operators to drones and have been vital in the sharing of information collected by autonomous systems in a manner that enables its rapid exploitation.[49]

Ukraine has become a testing ground for Western weapons, munitions, and ideas about warfighting. Much attention is given to systems such as HIMARS, the Patriot air defense system, or armored fighting vehicles. Less attention is given to the technologies that connect these weapons and their human users in a warfighting network. But it is these systems, the contemporary digitized battle command and control systems, that have seen considerable development during war. The deployment of digital command and control, supported by artificial intelligence, in the Ukrainian armed forces has been an important adaptation and has enhanced their tactical effectiveness.

Digital battle command and control systems have been evolving in Western military institutions since the development of the U.S. Air Force's development of the Semi-Automatic Ground Environment (SAGE), which was designed to coordinate the air defense of North America in the 1950s. At the heart of SAGE was a processor known as Whirlwind. This was later placed into production as the IBM AN/FSQ-7 and changed how the U.S. military establishment thought about computer-based information sharing and coordination of military activities.[50]

On the ground, because of limitations in the mobility and energy needs of early computers, the deployment of computer-based command and control took until the deployment of blue force trackers by the U.S. Army in 2002.[51] Blue force tracking systems generally comprise a Global Positioning System receiver, a computer to display location information, and a satellite terminal and antenna. More recent iterations of blue force tracking and other digital battle command and control systems also include software that can be used to distribute and receive orders, enable collaborative planning, coordinate and prioritize artillery, undertake terrain 3D analysis, and enable more timely logistic support.

For Ukraine, the introduction of sophisticated digital command and control systems has underpinned their ability to respond to the Russian invasion. It is an adaptation that has enabled commanders to connect with subordinate units and has sped up the transmission of tactically useful information.

One important system, the Delta digital C2 system, was developed by Ukraine's Defense Ministry with assistance from NATO, and the initial version was tested in 2017. Part of the rationale for it was to transition Ukrainian forces toward more distributed modes of decision-making and away from the centralized command culture of the Soviet military. Delta combines real-time mapping with pictures and locations of enemy units. This information is then combined with other intelligence feeds to help commanders decide where and how Ukrainian troops should attack Russian forces.

Delta's first combat test was during the initial Russian thrust toward Kyiv in February 2022. It allowed the Ukrainian armed forces to plot and track thousands of Russian targets. This information was then used to coordinate attacks on Russian logistics and other targets. Delta was continuously improved, with more than thirty upgrades during the war, and was used to assist commanders and troops in the Kherson region in late 2022.[52]

Delta also uses artificial intelligence (AI) both to assist analysis and to speed relevant information to the right users. Employing software developed by Palantir and connected to NATO battle command systems, Delta is widely available and used in Ukrainian units.[53] Its use has evolved over the course of the war to refine software versions and enhance user effectiveness.

The Ukrainians have also integrated AI into their digital command and control system by employing it for geolocation and analysis of open-source data in order to identify Russian units, weapon and sensor systems, and the disposition of Russian formations. This is perhaps its most significant application at present, and the most widely used product: companies like Maxar Technologies and Planet Labs produce satellite imagery that is provided to Ukraine in an almost continuous stream. And as Sam Bendett has written, "Neural networks are used to combine ground-level photos, video footage from numerous drones and UAVs, and satellite imagery to provide faster intelligence analysis and assessment to produce strategic and tactical intelligence advantages."[54] AI's facial recognition capabilities have also been used to identify dead Russian troops and to find Russian assailants.[55]

These new-era digitized command and control systems are used for other functions as well. When Russia first invaded Ukraine in 2014, the Ukrainian ground forces not only were deficient in weapons but also faced challenges with inaccurate fire from legacy artillery systems, old maps, soldiers with poor training, and a deficit in geospatial intelligence. In the wake of the initial Russian operations against Ukraine, the League of Defense Enterprises of Ukraine was formed to rapidly coordinate defense contractors and information technology companies for national security requirements. One outcome of this collaboration was the Geographic Information System of Artillery, or GIS Arta.

GIS Arta applies a bottom-up approach to select battlefield targets. UAVS, dismounted human forward observers, and other reconnaissance elements are able to input details of an enemy target over an encrypted network in real time. GIS Arta works on a network that uses satellite, internet, and radio communications on a wide variety of commonly available devices. Most users of GIS Arta work with it through an Android app on their smartphones. Given the real-time nature of the system, it facilitates rapid target verification and subsequent decision-making about priorities and the means of engaging the target. The GIS Arta's interfaces essentially mean that it connects everything from an individual smartphone to the most sophisticated weapons system, such as the Multiple Rocket Launcher System.[56]

Most impressive is that this adaptation to older "call for fire" doctrines means that the detection-to-destruction time for an enemy target can be as little as one minute. This is a significant reduction in time for directing friendly artillery, and it can enhance the chances of destroying enemy targets and provide the wherewithal for a friendly commander to dictate battlefield tempo.

Other digital command and control aids have also been introduced during the war. These include the Kropyva intelligence mapping application, which plots information from UAVs and other collection assets. It is used on handheld tablets and computers by forward combat units to plot enemy and friendly locations.[57] A final adaptation is the ComBat Vision military intelligence system, which ingests data on locations and the appearance of objects and individuals and classifies them along with embedded geographic data, then provides this for further analysis by humans or other computer programs.[58]

There are three reasons these software innovations are important tactical adaptations for Ukraine. First, they allow for the Ukrainians to be nimbler than their larger but slower-moving Russian adversary. In essence, the digital C2 systems allow Ukrainian forces to connect, decide, and act more quickly than the Russians, and to generate an operational tempo that forces the Russians to respond to Ukrainian initiatives. Even junior Ukrainian soldiers are able to enter data in these systems about Russian troop locations.

This ensures a more accurate portrayal of the battle space for commanders, and those responsible for prioritizing systems such as artillery. This portrayal of the battle space includes not only information on the enemy but also important geospatial information. Such systems, deployed widely in a military organization, also speed up the flow of information from the collectors to the users of relevant battlefield information. This might include intelligence staffs, headquarters planners, or those who are being tasked with the coordination of artillery, air strikes, or electronic attack missions.

Second, digital C2 is very adaptive and can be updated regularly. This is an important characteristic because the Russians actively seek to interfere with Ukrainian digital C2 systems. The adaptability of digital C2 allows it to be updated and its security strengthened as the Russians work to counter its impact. The Ukrainians, partnering with commercial entities throughout the war, have been able to rapidly update and improve their digital command and control systems.

Finally, these systems are important because they make the Ukrainian armed forces more efficient. Not only do many battlefield functions speed up, generating a tempo advantage over the Russians, but they also facilitate better prioritization of scarce resources and the conduct of logistics and personnel reinforcements. In some respects, access to the data in these new-era digital battle command systems provides every individual in the battle space with their own support staff to aid in decision-making. This has greatly enhanced the tactical and operational effectiveness of the

Ukrainians in this war. The possession and effective exploitation of such systems by other military institutions will be a crucial aspect of future military effectiveness.

▬▬

An institution's adaptive capacity—its ability to adapt on the battlefield and as an institution—is critical to success in war. As Barno and Bensahel write in *Adaptation under Fire*, "Adaptation has always been necessary to bridge the gap between the type of war that was predicted and the inevitably different realities of an actual war."[59]

While they are separate systems, the tactical adaptations explored in this chapter are intimately connected. New drones have necessitated adaptation in tactics and combined-arms operations by the Ukrainian armed forces. In turn, connecting this all up has necessitated changes in command and control, which have been founded on the development and ongoing innovation in digital command and control systems across the Ukrainian military.

But as the initial Ukrainian attacks in southern Ukraine in June 2023 demonstrated, there is also a limit to what Michael Horowitz calls "adoption capacity" when organizations are adapting.[60] The Ukrainians have undertaken an enormous range of strategic, operational, and tactical adaptations in this war, and many of these have made Ukraine's military a more effective institution. But even the best military organizations can only change so much, particularly under the competing pressures of defending their homeland; quickly expanding their military; transitioning from Soviet to NATO equipment, doctrines, and cultural and historical preferences; and responding to political objectives. The shortfalls in combined arms capacity above company level and the ability to integrate the operations of multiple brigades in combat demonstrate that Ukraine's combat adaptation is an ongoing and incomplete journey.

Succeeding in the adaptation battle is a core part of war. It is the most human of endeavors. As T. X. Hammes has written, "Emerging technology is vital to each capability, but, like the development of the blitzkrieg or carrier aviation, these transformational capabilities can only be realized by combining several technologies effectively and implementing them in coherent, well-trained operational concepts."[61] Creativity, innovation, and a tolerance of failure are important components of a successful, adaptive military institution. It demands good leadership, experimentation, and the humility to learn lessons from the mistakes and successes of others.

And it demands an institutional acceptance of the fact that given the enemy's ability to evolve, the task of adaptation is never finished.

15

RACE TO THE SWIFT

Adapting for Future War

IN THE 1980S, Richard Simpkin wrote several books on the future of land warfare. A retired British Army officer who had served in North Africa during World War II, Simpkin also played a role in developing the British Army's main battle tank during the Cold War, the Chieftain. After retiring from the army in 1971, Simpkin turned to thinking and writing about modern warfare and the impacts of new technologies.

Focusing on Soviet military operations, mechanized warfare, and the human dimension of warfare, Simpkin made a significant contribution to thinking about modern war in the latter stages of the Cold War. His best-known work of this period is a book titled *Race to the Swift: Thoughts on Twenty-First Century Warfare*, which was designed to reset military thinking to ensure that Western nations in the 1980s avoided getting trapped in the age-old problem of preparing to fight the last war. As Don Starry notes in the book's foreword, "Military establishments demonstrate a marvelous propensity for summing up at the close of each armed confrontation and forthwith setting about getting ready to fight over again, better, the conflict from which they just emerged."[1]

While some of Simpkin's predications have not aged well, such as rotary-wing aircraft becoming the primary battlefield system, there are few books that do a better job of combining a historical review of warfare with the exploration of the interaction of trends in technology with strategy, policy, and military doctrine.

Simpkin's focus on a confrontation with the Soviets in central Europe also now seems eerily relevant again.

Ultimately, Simpkin's book is about institutional adaptation in military organizations.

The aim of this chapter is the same. What are the observations from the war in Ukraine, and the key adaptations, that can assist in Western military forces building and retaining a winning edge in the years ahead?

American scholar Frank Hoffman, in *Mars Adapting: Military Change during War*, notes that "the ultimate test of military preparation and effectiveness does not end once a war begins. On the contrary, history strongly reflects the enduring phenomena of learning and implementing change during war.... The requirement that a force must adapt while it is in combat is built into the inherent nature of war."[2] This chapter offers five key observations from Ukraine that might assist in improving the capacity of other military forces.

OBSERVATION I: MILITARY INSTITUTIONS MUST ESTABLISH EFFECTIVE LEARNING CULTURES BEFORE WARS

While tactical adaptation is important, a strategic process for adaptation is also necessary. Drawing lessons from combat, analyzing them, developing solutions to new problems, and then ensuring that solutions—doctrinal, training, technological, or otherwise—are integral to military success in war. While it is possible such a system could emerge during a conflict, the existence of one beforehand, as part of an integral learning culture, is a superior and more efficient approach.

These learning cultures must be rigorous enough to ensure that there is not a "one size fits all" approach. By that, I mean that learning from one war cannot be the sole data point for institutional change. It can inform larger programs of military transformation, but the context of every war is different. As Sir Michael Howard reminds us, we must study military history in depth, breadth, and context. He writes in "The Use and Abuse of Military History" that "the roots of victory and defeat often have to be sought far from the battlefield, in political, social, and economic factors which explain why armies are constituted as they are, and why their leaders conduct them in the way they do."[3]

The Russians appear to have made this mistake in the wake of their Syrian operations. They probably took away the right lessons for a similar operational deployment elsewhere, but those lessons were largely irrelevant to the preparation for, and conduct of, larger-scale conventional conflicts like their special military operation in Ukraine. The war in Syria was an intervention at the invitation of a host government to suppress the population. The Russians did not engage in large-scale ground operations. Many lessons from the Syrian conflict were immaterial to their invasion of Ukraine. Many Western observers of the Russian military did not make this connection in the lead-up to the war in Ukraine.

At the same time, two decades of low-level counterinsurgency warfare has not provided a useful foundation for the future of Western military institutions. While it may have been one of the three "theories of war" that Simpkin explored in *Race to the Swift*, Western governments must be careful about what lessons they take from these conflicts. Rarely were Western forces challenged in the air or at sea during their post-9/11 operations in Iraq and Afghanistan. The scale and tempo of these operations were similarly unhelpful when thinking about many future contingencies. Most Western military institutions have ongoing reform or transformation programs, and there is much they can learn from comparing Russian efforts to change their military institution from 2008, and their operations in Ukraine.

Context matters. Always.

OBSERVATION 2: ADAPTATION AND INNOVATION ARE NOT THE SAME AS ENHANCING EFFECTIVENESS

Not all innovation succeeds. Both sides have made efforts at innovation that either have not produced the desired results or that the enemy has been able to rapidly respond to, ensuring that those innovations do not provide a new source of advantage.

While the Russian military has adapted in many areas since commencing its February 2022 invasion of Ukraine, we should make a clear distinction between adapting and improving military effectiveness. Changing tactics and command and support arrangements does not necessarily bring about improvement in an organization's overall performance. Despite the variety of adaptations explored above, it is unclear that these have led to a commensurate improvement in Russian military capability against Ukraine. Indeed, there is evidence that their adaptive processes have been too slow to make measurable improvements and that some adaptations have been counter to a more effective military campaign.

Military effectiveness is a topic that is at the heart of the design, functioning, and improvement of military organizations, the forces they deploy in combat, and the institutions that support them at different levels. Every good military institution, while absorbed with the day-to-day challenges of fighting in wartime or training in peacetime, also invests in improving its military effectiveness.

In the 1980s, American scholars Allan Millett and Williamson Murray undertook a study of military effectiveness. The output of their work was a three-volume series of books on twentieth-century military effectiveness that was published in 1988. Exploring several countries and their performance during World War I, the interwar period, and World War II, each volume used a framework to explore different levels of military effectiveness. These historical periods served the study well because they offered insights for the strategic competition between the United States and the Soviet Union at that time. More recently, a 2007 book from Risa Brooks and Elizabeth Stanley called *Creating Military Power: The Sources of Military Effectiveness* has explored the same topic.

Millett and Murray defined military effectiveness as "the process by which armed forces convert resources into fighting power."[4] Brooks and Stanley define military effectiveness as "the capacity to create military power from a state's basic resources in wealth, technology, population, and human capital."[5]

In essence, the military effectiveness of twenty-first-century military institutions and forces is determined by how successful their process is to convert resources into the capacity to influence and fight within an integrated national approach. Adaptation, regardless of its level, should be contributing to the maintenance and improvement of military effectiveness. The question is, has it done so for the belligerents during the war in Ukraine?

Three notable examples indicate that despite a range of adaptations, a military institution may still not improve some aspects of its military effectiveness.

First, the ability of the Russians to seize terrain has not improved significantly since the first days of the invasion. The Battle of Bakhmut, which has raged from August 2022, has been a slow-moving meat grinder for the Russians. While some small-unit infiltration tactics have been on display, the Russians have continued to conduct the same kind of firepower-heavy and human wave attacks over many months. The more recent Battle of Vuhledar was also a demonstration that Russian conventional forces had learned little in the preceding year of combat: a frontal attack across open ground using armored vehicles that employed elements of the 155th Guards Naval Infantry Brigade and the 40th Naval Infantry Brigade was repulsed by the Ukrainians in February 2023. There were significant Russian casualties, and over thirty damaged and destroyed Russian armored vehicles littered the battlefield afterward.[6]

Russian ground forces have adapted. They did not significantly improve their effectiveness in combat during offensive operations.

Second, while Ukraine has undertaken a myriad of changes and adapted at the tactical, operational, and strategic levels since February 2022, these have not driven major improvements in their ability to expand the level at which they can conduct effective combined-arms maneuvers. The Kharkiv and Kherson offensives, while effective, generally saw the Ukrainians fight at platoon and company battles, within their battalion or brigades. Despite the training of battalion and brigade staffs in combined-arms maneuvers over the winter of 2022, the array of other training and operational imperatives for the Ukrainian ground forces—including being rearmed with Western equipment, forming new brigades, and having insufficient time for collective training and shortages of experienced midranking combat leaders—appears to have denied them significant improvements in their ability to integrate combined arms, particularly at the battalion and brigade levels.

The failed Ukrainian attacks in the first month of the Ukrainian 2023 offensive have provided multiple examples of this failure to progress to higher-level integrated combined-arms maneuvers. There has been a huge amount of adaptation by the Ukrainians, as the previous chapters have discussed. But it has not helped them conduct the integrated brigade and above maneuvers that were necessary to penetrate the extensive Russian defensive works in southern Ukraine.[7]

A third example is that the Russian air campaign has not become significantly more effective or efficient in the period since the beginning of the operation. Indeed, Ukrainian airspace is something that Russian crewed aircraft avoid, with the exception of battlefield helicopters and some low-flying ground attack aircraft. The overall command and control of aviation has continued to be managed by ground-based units and prioritized largely by ground tactical objectives.[8] There have been some adjustments to more focused strike campaigns that target strategic infrastructure, but this has absorbed large numbers of expensive and hard-to-replace missiles such as their short-range ballistic Iskander missiles and their air- and sea-launched Kalibr cruise missiles.[9] As Mike Pietrucha has written, the Russians lacked an air campaign plan and have therefore "largely returned to the three areas where the Russian military is most comfortable: flying artillery support, artillery spotting, and the haphazard employment of long-range weapons against civilian targets."[10] And because of the Russian failure to effectively adapt to this environment, Ukraine's success in defending its air space challenges the current Western airpower paradigm and provides "an alternative vision for pursuing airspace denial over air superiority."[11]

Military forces must improve both their combat performance and their ability to detect change, develop solutions, and disseminate them widely. Adaptation occurs with an aim to enhance the effectiveness of military organizations at different levels but does not always succeed.

▨ OBSERVATION 3: BUILDING MILITARY EFFECTIVENESS THROUGH ADAPTATION IS NOT JUST ABOUT TECHNOLOGY

Technology plays an important part in war, competition, deterrence, and a wide variety of other national security endeavors. While an array of new technologies has improved the capacity of combatants in Ukraine, this is not a new aspect of military affairs. The fields of metallurgy, chemistry, ballistics, and electronics have been central to the technological breakthroughs underpinning military revolutions and other enhancements over the past two centuries.[12]

Several key technologies have stood out since the beginning of the war in Ukraine.

First, communications technologies featured right from the beginning of the war. As the Russian forces crossed the borders from Belarus and Russia into Ukraine, Russia undertook a large-scale cyberattack against the ViaSat KA-SAT network to degrade Ukraine's national and military command and control.[13] Shortly after the Russian invasion had begun, Ukrainian officials acknowledged the impact of the Russian cyberattack, noting that it was "a huge loss in communications at the beginning of the war."[14] Not only did this highlight the risk of low cybersecurity for space assets; it also made clear to Ukrainian leaders the need for a more robust communications network. This led to an array of measures, the most prominent of which has been the adoption of Starlink satellite communications. This is now pervasive at all levels of the Ukrainian military institution given its mobility, simplicity of use, security, and resilience.[15]

Second, commercial surveillance and analytical tools, sometimes referred to as open-source intelligence, have played a significant role. The war in Ukraine has broken down many of the barriers between the classified world of intelligence collection, assessment, and dissemination and the many unclassified capabilities resident in the commercial sector. As such, a high-tech, meshed sensor and assessment environment has developed over the course of the war. Augmented by artificial intelligence provided by vendors such as Palantir, huge amounts of commercial and classified data can now be assembled, assessed, and disseminated more quickly than has been possible before. It has enhanced the transparency of the physical battlefield, if not the intentions of those serving in and leading military organizations. Key functions beyond battlefield application of AI have included the gathering of information on war crimes,[16] water level modeling after the destruction of the dam in Kherson in June 2023, and analysis supporting humanitarian and reconstruction operations.[17]

Third, uncrewed and autonomous systems have seen a Cambrian explosion in the quality and quantity of UAVs employed during the war. From dozens, and perhaps hundreds, of systems at the beginning of the war, thousands of autonomous systems—principally in the air domain—are now employed at any one time in the war. There exist multiple layers of capability, range, resilience, and lethality in these systems, and there is a mix of commercial off-the-shelf systems, modified commercial systems, and military platforms. These have been important in surveillance, in closing the time between the detection and destruction of enemy units, and in the ability to conduct longer-range and more lethal strikes against battlefield organizations. They have been vital in the air and at sea.

However, none of these new technologies would have had the impact they have without a variety of human interventions. These interventions generally fall into one or more of three types: new ideas, new (and evolved) organizations, and training.

All of the technologies explored above were initially applied in traditional ways, and then, gradually, new forms of application arose due to battlefield or strategic imperatives. Whether it was the employment of Starlink satellite communications to replace battlefield radios to enhance soldier survivability, the addition of munitions to commercial drones, or new tactics in the application of drones, the adoption of new ideas and adaptation of older ideas generated by humans have been central to realizing the benefits pf new technologies.

At the same time, new organizational constructs have been important in the adaptation of military capabilities during the war. Examples of new or evolved institutions during the war include the Russian Storm-Z units, drone attack companies formed by the Ukrainians to support each brigade, and the air defense organizations established to undertake counter-drone operations against autonomous systems attacking military and civilian targets.

The performance of newly formed Ukrainian brigades in mid-June 2023 is a demonstration that the best equipment does not guarantee effective military performance. Although equipped with the most modern Western tanks, infantry fighting vehicle (IFVs), and other equipment, newly formed brigades were not able to plan or execute combined-arms operations against the Russian forces in southern Ukraine. Initial attacks consisted of platoon- or company-level actions, but combined-arms battle group or brigade attacks appeared to be beyond the competency level of these new formations. In the West, it takes experienced army formations months to progress from platoon- to brigade-level activity in a training year. Expecting this capacity from newly formed brigades, with soldiers just out of their short recruit training, was a bridge too far, and it showed in battlefield results.[18]

Ultimately, technology plays second fiddle to human ideas, institutions, and training. This is not a new observation. In 1993, the founding director of the U.S. Office of Net Assessment, Andrew Marshall, wrote that "the most important competition is not the technological competition. The most important goal is to be the best in the intellectual task of finding the most appropriate innovations in the concepts of operation and making organizational changes to fully exploit the technologies already available."[19] And as Paul Scharre has written more recently, "How technology is used reflects the values, whether conscious or unconscious, of its creators and users."[20] As exciting as the appearance of new technologies in war may be, their successful absorption and employment by military institutions will always rely on new and evolved ideas and institutions.

▨ OBSERVATION 4: ADAPTATION PROCESSES NEED TO CLOSE THE INTERVAL BETWEEN NEW TECHNOLOGIES AND NEW MODES OF EMPLOYMENT

There is almost always a time lag in the process between introduction of new technologies and the introduction of the new doctrines and institutions that best exploit it. There are multiple historical examples where the introduction of new technologies has not yielded immediate advantage for one side or the other because it was used in accordance with older doctrines.

In *The Diffusion of Military Power*, Michael Horowitz proposes what he calls the "adoption capacity theory," which "makes clear the distinction between interest in responding to an innovation and the substance of that response."[21] The adoption capacity of organizations and nations can either see a rapid process of adaptation that generates military advantage, or the ignoring of key innovations until it is used against them. Both the cost of new technologies and an institution's organizational capital—which includes critical task focus, experimentation, and organizational age—have a major influence on the update of innovation and the process of adaptation. But whether an institution or a nation has high or low adoption capacity, there is generally a lag between when the need for change is identified and when that change is implemented.

One of the earliest examples of this was the introduction of an early firearm called the arquebus. Introduced in the sixteenth century and used in the firing of volleys, its users were generally defenseless during the long process of reloading the weapon in battle. And because of the noise it made, the weapon generated more terror than casualties. It was not until approximately fifty years after its introduction that the tactic of the *countermarch* truly exploited the capabilities of the arquebus. The countermarch was a tactical formation, borrowed from a tactic used by Roman legions, where the front rank fires its weapons and then moves to rear to reload while successive ranks repeat that process. Tactics and organization took time to catch up with, and improve the employment of, new technology.[22]

This process of technology leading new ways of war has been repeated throughout history. The mass slaughter by machine guns and artillery during World War I was largely a result of prewar thinking being applied to capabilities of new age weaponry. As Hew Strachan has explained, "All armies in the decade before the First World War confronted the problem of how to mount an attack across a fire-swept battlefield."[23] Debates over the use of aircraft carriers and submarines in the interwar periods, only settled in the heat of the battles in the Atlantic and the Pacific, tracked a similar course.[24] There is almost always an interval between when new military technology is available and when it is used at its most effective. Changes only take place once it becomes apparent that new weapons and new technologies demand adaptation.[25]

This is an aspect of the war where the Ukrainians appear to have developed a relative advantage over the Russians. The Ukrainians, in the lexicon of Michael Horowitz, appear to have developed a better adoption capacity than their enemy, excelling at the more rapid assimilation of new technologies and weapons. Their employment of drones, development and deployment of digitized command and control, and rapid absorption and employment of the U.S.-provided HIMARS long-range rocket artillery system are three examples.

One other example stands out in the Ukrainians' ability to rapidly absorb new technology into their order of battle and use it innovatively: the introduction of Patriot missiles.

First developed and issued to U.S. Army formations in the 1980s, the Patriot is the backbone of the U.S. Army's air and missile defense network. The Patriot capability is made up of a family of different components, including command and control units, radars, a family of interceptor missiles, and support equipment. At the end of 2022, the U.S. government decided to provide the Patriot capability to Ukraine. At a cost of approximately $1 billion per unit, it is an effective but very expensive capability.[26]

In a January 2023 article, one military commentator described the U.S. decision to send Patriot missiles to Ukraine thus: "Patriot systems are as likely to stop the drone threat as a water balloon is to stop a forest fire. The mismatch is too great."[27] Another article described this as "symbolic but not a gamechanger."[28] However, the Ukrainians proved to be very quick studies of the new system. By March 2023, the Ukrainians undergoing training on the Patriot air defense system were completing their training much quicker than normal: while the training for U.S. Army soldiers normally takes up to a year, the Ukrainians were able to gain competency in operating the system in under ten weeks.[29]

By May 2023, the new Patriot battery had been dispatched to Ukraine. The Ukrainians were able to quickly insert the new sensors and interceptor missiles into their integrated air and missile defense system, which was described in chapter 13. On 15 May 2023, the Ukrainian Patriot operators defeated a barrage of Russian missiles, including the "unbeatable" Kinzhal ballistic missiles.[30]

In a very short period of time, the Ukrainians had absorbed this new technology into their organization and adapted it for the Soviet-NATO air defense network they had developed. This small lag in time between the receipt and successful employment of a new technology has provided a crucial missile defense capability for Ukraine. But beyond the war in Ukraine, Western military institutions must evolve methods to ensure that there is only a small gap between new technologies and the development of new doctrines and organizations to employ them.

OBSERVATION 5: THE "LETHALITY VERSUS DISPERSION" ADAPTATION BATTLE CONTINUES

In his book *The Evolution of Weapons and Warfare*, Trevor Dupuy includes a graph that projects the relationship between the increasing lethality of military systems and the increasing dispersion of military forces, particularly over the last five hundred years. This lethality-dispersion relationship—in some respects a "law" that applies to the military just as Moore's Law applies to computer memory—is another long-term trend that has driven adaptation during the war in Ukraine.

The meshed intelligence sensor-assessment-dissemination framework that has evolved in Ukraine has provided a level of visibility over the battlefield that is possibly unprecedented in warfare. Anyone with a mobile communications device has the ability to access near-real-time mapping or assessments on the war. They can simultaneously monitor dozens of journalists and news organizations providing news and commentary, as well as the thousands of citizen journalists that have covered various aspects of the war.

This level of transparency extends beyond the visible spectrum for observers. With the right sensors and technologies, a range of signatures has become easier to detect and monitor. Electronic warfare has been used extensively for geolocation, jamming drone controls and battlefield communications, and spoofing enemy radio networks or sensors. Thermal sensors have become almost ubiquitous, from expensive military models on the battlefield to the more strategic feeds such as the NASA Fire Information Resource Management System (FIRMS), available online.[31]

All of these sensors are layered to provide a useful picture of troop locations, movements, supply and transport chokepoints, convoys, and artillery unit locations. Both sides have used a sensor network to attack troop concentrations and logistic supply locations. Another vulnerable yet valuable military target is headquarters. The electronic emissions of headquarters can be easily detected and will stand out in any network analysis of enemy communications. The Ukrainians and Russians have sought out and attacked headquarters throughout the war, resulting in the deaths of many senior officers on both sides.[32]

At the same time, the number of systems that both sides possess to engage and destroy the enemy has also expanded. Not only have longer-range artillery systems been deployed and used to good effect, but a broad range of lethal autonomous systems has also been employed across the battle space. Explored in both the Russian and Ukrainian chapters on tactical adaptation, modified commercial drones as well as a variety of loitering munitions have closed the time between detection and destruction and opened up the number of targets able to be struck at short notice.

The impact of this improved battlefield transparency, and the ability to strike targets more quickly, have meant that the "lethality versus dispersion" battle continues. Both the Russians and the Ukrainians have dispersed their forces across a wide swath of eastern and southern Ukraine while also utilizing a variety of deception and camouflage regimes to decrease the chances of detection and improve survivability.

Both sides have therefore adapted by dispersing high-value targets, hardening them physically (especially by burrowing underground) and minimizing their electronic signatures through the use of satellite bearers for communications, hard-wired networks, and runners. And while the immediate imperative drives ongoing adaptation by the Ukrainians and Russians to improve the survivability and resilience of their headquarters and command and control systems, it also provides an array of insights for other military institutions.

Headquarters sizes, mobility, and physical hardening will be an important imperative for future military operations. At the same time, reducing the number of headquarters staff through reach-back and more automation of headquarters functions by using artificial intelligence will also be part of the response to ensure the survivability of battlefield commanders and their headquarters. And finally, redundant command and control nodes as well as a broader implementation of decentralized or mission command will be important contributors to the resilience of future military headquarters. Similar methods will also need to be applied to logistics locations, troop concentrations, and fires units such as artillery to improve their ability to survive and be effective on the modern battlefield.

In *War Made New* (2006), Max Boot described adaptation and transformation in military institutions as "a sudden tempest which turns everything upside down."[33] He returned to this theme in 2023, when he explored Russian military doctrine and the Russian military capacity to learn and adapt from its experiences in this war:

> The Russian military has also done far worse than most analysts expected in part because it was simply not prepared for the kind of war it is fighting. That's not uncommon in military history. Even so, the best armies adapt on the fly. That's what the U.S. Army and Marine Corps did during the Iraq War: They had not trained to fight insurgents, but they learned hard lessons and, in 2006, produced a counterinsurgency field manual. . . . The Russian armed forces haven't shown that kind of ability to improvise. They continue to stick with what isn't working. The Russian conduct of this war is not only a moral failure but also an intellectual one.[34]

> Every military institution develops its combat power through the melding of physical, moral, and intellectual capabilities. These vary from country to country, and even between different services in a single nation. But if one is left underdeveloped, it has an impact on the other two aspects of warfighting capability.

This has been the experience of both sides in the war in Ukraine since February 2022. In cases where either side has invested in the intellectual rigor to investigate and implement new methods and organizational constructs to better absorb new technologies, they have generally been more successful on the battlefield. This demonstrates, again, the importance of an adaptive stance within military institutions, which allows them to respond to surprise and engage in the learning and improvement—at all levels—that are essential to winning battles and wars.

The preceding chapters have described adaptation at the strategic, operational, and tactical levels for both the Ukrainians and Russians during this war.

Strategic-level adaptation is often held hostage to the political realities of war. Politics and policy drive military strategy. Therefore, if strategic adaptation is to take place, some of the fundamental assumptions held by political leaders about the objectives and kind of war being fought must also adapt. Because the interactive nature of war forces changes in the overall environment, this reevaluation of assumptions must be an ongoing process by the most senior leaders of a nation, informed by the military advisers. It is apparent in this war that the political leadership of Ukraine is better placed to undertake this ongoing reevaluation than the more centralized approach taken by President Putin and his small circle of advisers.

At the same time, strategic adaptation is predicated on understanding one's adversary and continuing to build that knowledge as the war develops. Again, the Ukrainians appear to have had a much better understanding of their adversary before the war. The Ukrainian president speaks fluent Russian and worked extensively in Russia before his election. The Ukrainian commander in chief, Valery Zaluzhnyi, stated in a 2022 interview with *Time* magazine, "I was raised on Russian military doctrine, and I still think that the science of war is all located in Russia. . . . I learned from Gerasimov. I read everything he ever wrote."[35]

The Russians, at least in the early parts of the war, did not appear to have been as diligent in studying their Ukrainian adversary. As we have explored at length in the preceding chapters, the Russians made many unfounded assumptions about Ukrainian capability and willpower. Not only did this have terrible repercussions on the battlefield and in strategy; it has also compromised Russia's ability to adapt more effectively at the strategic level.

But there is one area of strategic adaptation where Russia probably leads Ukraine. Russia, which has a much larger economy and a significant industrial base, appears able to undertake systemic adaptation at a scale that is beyond Ukraine. While Russia may be slow to adapt, once it does adapt it is able to do so in a very systemic and large-scale way. Its employment of Iranian-made (and other non-Russian-made) drones, FPV uncrewed aircraft, and protective cages for equipment are three examples of this. This Russian capacity for systemic, top-down adaptation will only improve as the war continues.

At the operational and tactical levels, adaptation remains vital. But new technologies have not made this process any simpler. The fog and friction of war may have been described by Clausewitz two hundred years ago, but they remain impediments to learning and adaptation in the modern era. Understanding exactly what has occurred on the battlefield, and why it occurred, and then using that information to improve one's military effectiveness remains a substantial and difficult undertaking.[36]

As the examples in the preceding chapters have shown, the modern battlefield remains chaotic, deadly, and often very dispersed. The technological developments of the past half century have had a significant impact on our ability to see the battle space and to quickly undertake operations to kill, destroy, or maim an opponent's forces. But it has not in any way allowed humans to see into the minds of their enemy. Computer simulations and clever algorithms may provide well-informed simulations of potential outcomes for future operations. But one can understand the true will, steadfastness, and endurance of one's enemy only after combat has been joined.

Therefore, a final insight is that war remains a human occupation, just as it was when the first caveman picked up a rock and threw it at his neighbor. War remains, at heart, about imposing one's will on another. To do that by successfully adopting new technologies also demands guile, surprise, shock, determination, resilience, and professionalism. And underpinning that are the very human traits of learning and adaptation.

CONCLUSION
Ukraine and the Future of Conflict

WORLD WAR I is a popular metaphor often used by journalists and some analysts writing about the war in Ukraine. The imagery of Ukrainian and Russian soldiers living and fighting in a dense network of trenches in southern and eastern Ukraine has been compared to the appalling conditions in muddy trenches that soldiers endured for years on the Western Front during World War I.

In a July 2023 update on the war, *The Economist* magazine wrote of the war in Ukraine as a mix of "Silicon Valley and the Somme."[1] In a December 2022 article, Radio Free Europe described how "rain-filled trenches, mud, and shredded trees in Ukraine have drawn comparisons on social media with photos from World War I."[2] Anatol Lieven, writing for *Foreign Policy*, described how "we should also not need historians of the future, or the lessons of the World War I, to tell us that hubris invariably leads to nemesis."[3]

None of these comparisons with a war a century earlier is necessarily wrong. There are many parallels between the Great War of 1914–18 and the war spawned by Russia's invasion of Ukraine. One key parallel is that in the lead-up to both wars, many assumed that a large-scale war in Europe was simply not possible. Historian Margaret MacMillan has written that "in 1914 and 2022 alike, those who assumed war wasn't possible were wrong."[4] And as MacMillan notes, Ukraine has (again) exposed the fallacy of assuming wars between major powers will be short: "Equally dangerous was the aggressors' assumption that a war would be short and decisive. In 1914, the major powers had only offensive war plans, predicated on quick victories. . . . Putin made much the same mistake."[5]

The points made by MacMillan represent continuities in warfare. The features she describes have been present in many other conflicts besides World War I and the war in Ukraine. Besides these, there are other important continuities apparent throughout this war. During the modern era, many have sought to make the case that today's governments, unlike those before them, are more rational and less likely to engage in warfare. Before World War I, Norman Angell noted in *The Great Illusion* that "military power is socially and economically futile, and can have no relation to the prosperity of the people exercising it; that it is impossible for one nation to seize by force the wealth or trade of another—to enrich itself by subjugating, or imposing its will by force on another; that, in short, war, even when victorious, can no longer achieve those aims for which peoples strive."[6] Despite the best intentions of authors like Angell, the future of humans was always more likely to resemble the past. As Colin Gray writes in *Strategy and Defence Planning*, "It is a reasonable assumption that future strategic history will resemble the past and present. Because it rests upon the evidence of 2,500 years, this is not a recklessly bold claim."[7]

One reason there are so many continuities in war is that every conflict is primarily an aggregation of the ideas, organizations, technologies, and tactics that have worked in previous wars. Each contains a variety of different historical layers that inform, shape, and sometimes strangle the effectiveness of military organizations. There are seven important continuities that have—again—risen to prominence during the war in Ukraine.

First, war remains central to human affairs—and humans are central to war. Competition is an enduring aspect of human existence on earth. The prevalence of war may decline for years or decades, but war remains a characteristic in the interplay of nations, groups of nations, and nonstate entities. And there are still those who believe war is the best way to get what they want. There are always leaders and influential people who want what others have. It appears that humankind is cursed to periodically produce, and enable, those who cannot be deterred and who view warfare as a useful way of gaining power, wealth, or respect in international affairs.

Humans have also proven to be central to all aspects of war in Ukraine. While there are many old technologies at play, along with some new ones we have explored in this book, humans remain at the heart of military operations as well as to the broader conduct of a national war effort. Only humans can devise the different tactics required for changing situations on the battlefield and develop the right mix of people, ideas, organizations, and technologies for each specific scenario or military activity. Even with the amazing advances in artificial intelligence in the past decade and more recent advances in generative artificial intelligence, human creativity, spirit, cohesion, and courage remain essential characteristics of successful nations and military institutions.

Human commitment, expertise, and sacrifice—as well as brutality and cowardice—have been on display throughout the war in Ukraine. No technology can replace the human capacity for providing exemplary behavior that can inspire fellow soldiers or citizens to greater heights of performance and duty.

A second continuity is surprise. This is usually defined as striking at a place, time, or location in a manner for which an adversary is not prepared. British scholar Sir Lawrence Freedman, writing about surprise, describes how "a surprise attack, conceived with cunning, prepared with duplicity and executed with ruthlessness, provides international history with its most melodramatic moments." Ultimately, surprise is designed to shock an adversary and overwhelm them when they are at their weakest, or when they least expect it. The war in Ukraine has delivered many surprises.[8] This includes Ukraine's initial surprise that Russia did not only invade in the Donbas region, and Russia's initial surprise at the resistance offered by Ukrainian military forces during its initial assaults in February 2022.[9] Other surprises have included

- Defeat of Russian army at the gates of Kyiv. As the Russian invasion of Ukraine commenced, many Western commentators believed that Ukraine would not be able to hold out against the Russians for more than a few days. However, Ukrainians were able to hold, and then force the withdrawal of, the Russian forces north and northeast of their capital. It was a strategic surprise for the Russians and for the West, which thereafter significantly increased military assistance to Ukraine.
- The first Kerch Bridge attack. On 8 October 2022, the Kerch Bridge from Russia to occupied Crimea was blown up, and both the railway bridge and the roadway were extensively damaged. This had a significant impact on traffic between Russia and Crimea, and the bridge took months to repair.
- The 2022 Kharkiv offensive. In September 2022, the Ukrainian armed forces achieved tactical and strategic surprise against Russian forces in the Kharkiv region. The Ukrainians attacked a sparsely defended area and achieved a significant penetration into Russian rear areas, which they were able to exploit over several weeks.
- The 2023 Belgorod incursions. In May and June 2023, armed groups deployed from Ukraine into the Russian Belgorod region. Former Russian president Dmitry Medvedev blamed Ukraine for the attacks. And while they achieved only minor tactical outcomes, the incursions caused shock in senior levels of the Russian government and necessitated a reassessment of Russian military dispositions.

- Moscow drone attacks. In May 2023, several unidentified drones flew across Moscow airspace. Eventually, all of them crashed or were shot down. The drones resulted in minor damage but generated worldwide headlines, as did subsequent attacks throughout 2023.
- Ukrainian offensive of 2023. The initial attacks of the Ukrainian ground forces in southern Ukraine were unsuccessful. That newly formed brigades with limited collective training failed should not have been a surprise. But given the high expectations raised (fairly or unfairly) before these offensives, the lack of success in the South could be described as a strategic surprise for politicians and citizens in the West.

Many have been surprised by the Russian tactical and strategic incompetence demonstrated so far. While the Russians have demonstrated the ability to learn, as explored in various parts of this book, the baseline for this learning was far lower than analysts predicted before the war. Research into Russian military reforms in the decade before the war did not grasp the array of weaknesses that lay just beneath the surface of the Russian military institution.

The West has been surprised—as have the Russians—by the resilience of alliances like NATO and institutions such as the European Union in their ongoing support for Ukraine. One of Putin's assumptions going into this war was that the West would not respond decisively and would instead treat this Russian invasion similarly to the one in 2014. But NATO reacted in a more meaningful way than the Russians expected. Since the February 2022 Russian invasion, NATO has become reinvigorated, with newfound purpose, and has even added Sweden and Finland as members. Putin, who launched this war partially because of the threat he perceived from NATO, has instead driven its expansion.

Regardless of the sophistication and cutting-edge technologies of military and intelligence organizations, humans' agency and their desire to surprise their enemies is relentless. It is an enduring part of warfare that military institutions must be prepared to counter through adaptation and leadership.

A *third continuity of war,* demonstrated in Ukraine, is the centrality of alliances and military partnerships in building and sustaining an effective fighting force. Throughout history, tribal leaders and contemporary statemen have increased the military potential of the nations they lead by entering into partnerships with other countries. Since the Russian assault that began on 24 February 2022, a dilapidated NATO institution has been imbued with renewed energy and purpose. Although Ukraine is not a member of NATO, and the alliance has not deployed forces into Ukraine itself, NATO has demonstrated significant resolve and massive support for Ukraine. This is a modern demonstration of why alliances remain a crucial part of how nations achieve collective defense for their sovereignty and prosperity.

A fourth continuity is that strategy matters. The war in Ukraine has provided strategic theorists, academics, politicians, and military leaders with a wealth of observations on the development and execution of strategy. It is perhaps one of the most important lessons that could be drawn from this current war.

As I explored in the first part of this book, the war has offered examples of effective strategy development and the implementation of that strategy. At the same time, there have been examples of poor strategic thinking, strategy making, and execution. The case studies of strategy in this book, from the Ukrainians, Russians, Americans, and NATO, represent only an early survey. As the war continues and as more documents are released in its wake, more lessons will become apparent.

An important part of strategic thinking and planning is getting one's assumptions right. Assumptions matter greatly in strategy. The Russians appear to have been worse at this process than the Ukrainians. The Russian president assumed that Ukraine would not fight for long, that the Ukrainian government would flee, and that the West would not provide assistance beyond that provided after Russia's 2014 operations in Ukraine. The Ukrainians have made him pay for his poor assumptions.

Strategy is also a competitive art. Good strategy aims to generate a relative advantage over an opponent. As such, Ukraine has demonstrated a competent national capacity for integrating their national assets into a single unified strategy to defend against the Russian invasion. The Ukrainian strategy of corrosion described in chapter 3 has seen them attack many different components of Russian fighting power in the physical, intellectual, and moral dimensions. In military operations, strategic influence activities, the mobilization and unification of their people, and the solicitation of foreign assistance, Ukraine has shown a strategic prowess not anticipated by Western strategists before this war. They certainly appear to be better strategic thinkers than the Russians. Given the stakes involved in this war, it could be the difference between national survival and extinction.

Yet another continuity in war that has been apparent in Ukraine is the necessity of good leadership. The war has demonstrated (again) that ambiguity and uncertainty are defining elements of conflict. For this reason, nations and military forces also keep being surprised (see continuity number 2 above). The most effective technique to prevent, or react to, surprise is good leadership. This has been on display most compellingly from President Zelenskyy. The Ukrainian president has shown courage and empathy and has led those who need him most—the Ukrainian people. Zelenskyy's resolve has underpinned building an immense international regime of sanctions against Russia. It has also resulted in significant military, humanitarian, and economic assistance to Ukraine.

Since the beginning of the war, the impact of good combat leadership has also been clear. Western-trained and -oriented Ukrainians have (in the main) prepared their junior leaders—senior soldiers, both noncommissioned and officers—to take the initiative and lead their soldiers by example. The Ukrainian military leaders have generally prepared, deployed, and led their forces to defend against the Russians in the North, South, and East. But the pressures of expanding their force quickly appear to have resulted in multiple instances of poor combat leadership in newly formed brigades during the initial phase of the 2023 Ukrainian offensive. This, again, proved the necessity of the selection and preparation of combined-arms leaders well in advance of military operations.

The Russians have demonstrated poor battlefield leadership at many levels. The Russian high command initially decided to fight multiple separate ground wars in the South, East, and North—as well as an air war—without a unified command structure. At the lower levels, they have committed forces piecemeal, have failed to provide adequate logistic support or properly equip many mobilized soldiers, and have constantly reinforced failure, doing the same things over and over yet expecting different outcomes. Worse, the Russian leadership has endorsed the deliberate targeting of civilians as a systemic campaign to kill and terrorize Ukrainian civilians as part of their de-Nazification propaganda.

However, on other occasions, Russian battlefield leadership has been adequate for the circumstances. This includes their eventual capture of Bakhmut and the defense of southern Ukraine in 2023.

As it has been through the ages, good leadership is still a central component of successful military institutions. That is one of the great continuities of war.

A sixth continuity has been the industrialization of war. Ever since steam-driven engines revolutionized manufacturing in the 1800s, the power of civil industry has been applied to nations' warmaking capacity. The Royal United Services Institute, which has explored this issue in the context of the war in Ukraine, described in 2022 how industrial-scale war has reemerged from the twentieth-century history books to once again "plague the 21st century."[10] As I wrote in my assessment of lessons from the war in August 2022, "This is an unwelcome development for democratic nations which have eschewed large military institutions since the end of the last Cold War. At the same time western nations reduced the size of their military forces, they also consolidated and reduced the scale of the military industrial capacity."[11] Consequently, nations such as America, Germany, France, and Britain have had to rely on drawing down their own war stocks of equipment and munitions to provide military assistance to Ukraine.

The situation at the beginning of the war with Western defense industry was grim. The production of munitions was small-scale, even in the United States, and reliant on a highly skilled but small workforce of experts. Additionally, most nations assumed that the war would not last long and therefore delayed any expansion of industrial capacity into 2023. But as we have witnessed in conflicts in the twentieth century, there is a time lag between identifying the need for increased defense production and realizing expanded capacity. Western governments have been provided with the warning to do so as part of this war. As they did in the global conflicts of last century, nations will need to expand defense industrial production and construct military forces of the size necessary to deter the aspirations of Russian and Chinese leaders.[12]

Fortunately, there is a profusion of literature that will assist to kick-start this process. Over the past two decades, military institutions have conducted a myriad of studies on mobilization issues. Additionally, books and think tank reports have also explored this subject from a variety of angles in both historical and contemporary contexts. Historical studies are contained in the official histories of World War II for the United States, Australia, and others. Books on mobilization lessons from this historical period include Richard Overy's *Why the Allies Won*, Arthur Herman's *Freedom's Forge*, and Paul Kennedy's *Engineers of Victory*.[13]

Among the publications exploring contemporary mobilization and defense industrial capacity are Seth Jones' *Empty Bins in a Wartime Environment*, Cynthia Cook's *Reviving the Arsenal of Democracy*, Peter Layton's *National Mobilisation during War: Past Insights, Future Possibilities*, the RAND Corporation's *Defence Mobilisation Planning Comparative Study: An Examination of Overseas Planning*, and the U.S. Department of Defense's *Securing Defense-Critical Supply Chains*.[14] There are also other publications and resources available to inform governments, military institutions, and civil industry on this subject, including hearings by different government bodies, in addition to the knowledge available on previous mobilization efforts.[15] The key will be for governments to invest in defense industrial capacity, which requires political risk and huge financial investments.

A final continuity that has again become apparent during this war is the importance of adaptation. The topic of adaptation was the subject of part II of this book. Both the Ukrainians and Russians have demonstrated the ability to learn and adapt throughout the war. This capacity has often been uneven and is not always systemic in nature. Not every unit on the battlefield learns at the same speed, and often the most important lessons are slow to be transmitted throughout the military institutions of both nations.

However, adaptation has been established as one of the crucial strategic, operational, and tactical capabilities of both sides in the war. An adaptation battle at multiple levels is ongoing, and it can inform military institutions in Europe and beyond about the modern conflict and potential evolution in the future of warfare. All that remains to be said of this important continuity in war is that military institutions must nurture the development of an institutional learning capacity before conflicts if they wish to adapt effectively during war.[16]

UKRAINE IS ALSO CHANGING THE CHARACTER OF WAR

Humans, and the ideas and institutions they produce, are central components in all the continuities described in the preceding section. In this regard, what military scholars describe as the enduring nature of war—the human, political elements that result in uncertainty and a contest of wills—encompasses these continuities.

At the start of this chapter, comparisons were made between the war in Ukraine and World War I. Another important similarity between World War I and the Russo-Ukraine War is that both occurred as a massive advance in technology began to impact societies around the world, leaving military institutions reaching for new ways of thinking about, and organizing for, war.

In *The Vertigo Years*, Philipp Blom describes how

> speed and exhilaration, anxiety and vertigo were recurrent themes of the years between 1900 and 1914, during which cities exploded in size and societies were transformed, mass production seized hold of everyday life, newspapers turned into media empires. . . . Rapid changes in technology, globalization, communication technologies and changes in the social fabric dominated conversations and newspaper articles; then as now, the feeling of living in an accelerating world, of speeding into the unknown, was overwhelming.[17]

World War I, which occurred in the later stages of the Second Industrial Revolution, eventually brought about a massive shift in how military institutions thought about strategy, as well as the domains where they fought and the tactics they employed.

A similar sense of accelerating change pervades today's societies. Technologies such as artificial intelligence, autonomous systems, and dense, meshed communications networks are revolutionizing how societies work and how businesses function. And as before and during World War I, military institutions are often lagging in their appreciation of the complexity and implications of many of these new technologies.

In this respect, both World War I and the current war in Ukraine function as a hinge between two eras, with transformational change in societies and military affairs being driven by new-era technologies.

The participants in World War I had to come to grips with a variety of new means that could be applied to increasing the strategic, operational, and tactical effectiveness of military forces. These new means included wireless communications, airplanes, the internal combustion engine, and new mass manufacturing techniques that could sustain millions of troops in the field for much longer than had ever been possible before.

The participants in the current war in Ukraine have had to adapt to new-era communications such as Starlink satellite communications, and an environment where sensors are ubiquitous, access to information (both good and bad) is near universal, the sky is crowded with uncrewed and autonomous vehicles roaming in search of targets to spy on or attack, and the Black Sea is increasingly the hunting ground for Ukrainian uncrewed naval vessels.[18] In such an environment, as with the Western Front of a century ago, it takes time for new ideas, new organizations, and new leadership modes to be developed and spread widely through military institutions.

The war in Ukraine has resulted in innovative combinations of old and new warfare techniques. As such, the world has borne witness to many ancient features of war, such the destruction or pillaging of cities; the rape, kidnapping, and murder of civilians; the employment of state and nonstate combatants in physical combat and information warfare; and the conduct of psychological operations to erode the will of combatants and civilians alike. But it has also seen the clever application of newer technologies in combination with new ideas and military organizations. In doing so, it has reflected how U.S. strategist Andrew Marshall described the development of new sources of military advantage: "The most important goal is to be the best in the intellectual task of finding the most appropriate innovations in the concepts of operation and making organizational changes to fully exploit the technologies already available and those that will be available in the next decade or so."[19] Crucially, some of the innovations that have emerged during this war are likely to drive changes in the character of war. These include meshed intelligence systems, new forms of strategic influence, and a Cambrian explosion in autonomous systems for wartime use.

Meshed Civil-Military Intelligence

Military institutions have always relied on good communications and networks to keep themselves informed about the strength and locations of their enemy, supply locations, routes, and information about themselves. The development of the internet and satellite communications has enabled the construction of dense networks that permit humans and military institutions to communicate instantly, maintain awareness of the world around them, and access a quantity and quality of information that is unprecedented in human history. Military and civil communication networks play an important function in military operations. Networks carry and fuse sensor data used by analysts and commanders and provide the entry point for those who might wish to interfere with the perceptions of military staff and commanders by inserting false data or cutting that data off altogether.

The concept of network-centric warfare (NCW) originated in the systems work of Admiral Owens in the 1990s. It was a concept for military operations that quickly spread and drove doctrinal development in the United States and beyond.[20] Technology since the original work on NCW has developed at a rapid pace. The military and other networks of the third decade of the twenty-first century are more capable, and generate more data, than the visionaries of NCW imagined.

Now the interaction and meshing of military and civilian networks, as well as sensors, has come to the fore. One example is online analysts' use of the U.S. National Aeronautics and Space Administration (NASA) Fire Information and Resource Management System (FIRMS), freely available online, to assess the level of artillery fire missions in Ukraine.[21] Open-source satellite data is also playing a role not just in Ukraine operations but also in measuring more strategic activities. Data from civilian technologies can provide a signature that might be exploited by unfriendly actors. The ability to track Strava users, which led to the mapping of several U.S. facilities overseas before the war, has also led to a Russian submarine captain being identified and shot dead at his home base in July 2023.[22] This is yet another example of civilian sensors and technologies being meshed with military activities.

Many civilian, open-source sensors employ older versions of military technology. And as NASA's FIRMS demonstrates, these provide only rough approximations of events that might be related to military activity. But intelligence activities require assembling multiple layers of information to build a complete picture or hypothesis of what those layers mean. The ability of open-source sensors, often used by civilian intelligence agencies such as Bellingcat or the Institute for the Study of War, to detect military activity means that military institutions must be even more careful and clever with their signatures in the twenty-first century.

This civil-military intelligence mesh extends beyond sensors. Over the last decade, there has been expansion in civil intelligence analysis that uses the data collected by these networks. Military intelligence has long focused on a cycle that includes the collection, analysis, and dissemination of usable information. Now, multiple civilian intelligence agencies operate in parallel—and sometimes in partnership—with military and other government intelligence agencies.

The products of the meshed civil-military intelligence analysis have been employed throughout the war used by military and other national security organizations. They have also been used by media organizations and private citizens, as well as different government agencies to supplement more classified sources. Additionally, these assessments are widely used in combat units in Ukraine to supplement intelligence from official sources that is either slower in dissemination or of lower quality.[23]

Another type of participation in meshed civil-military intelligence operations during the war in Ukraine has been online hackers. Independent hackers and hacker teams have undertaken operations on behalf of both sides of the conflict. For example, reports early in the war suggested that Ukraine had been able to build an army of civilian volunteer hackers that was over 400,000 strong.[24] These hackers have allegedly been employed combating Russian misinformation, attacking Russian websites, and defending against what has been described as Russia's aggressive and systemic efforts to generate a wartime cyber advantage.[25]

Finally, this meshing of civilian and military approaches has seen the development of much-improved digitized command and control. As discussed in part II of this book, digital systems, some civilian and some military, have connected operators to drones and been vital in the sharing of information collected by autonomous systems in a manner that enables its rapid exploitation.[26]

For Ukraine, the introduction of sophisticated digital command and control systems has improved their ability to respond to the Russian invasion. These systems permit commanders' connection with subordinate units and speed up the transition of tactically useful information. They also ensure a more accurate depiction of the battle space for commanders. The Ukrainians, partnering with commercial entities throughout the war, have been able to rapidly update and improve their digital command and control systems. These systems are also crucial because they make military organizations more efficient. They not only speed up many battlefield functions but also facilitate better prioritization of scarce resources and the conduct of logistics and personnel reinforcements.

At the same time, there has been a democratization of access to these systems. Previously accessed by commanders and staffs, digitized command and control systems are now used by any Ukrainian soldier with access to a smart device. This permits a broader range of information to be input into command and control systems, while also increasing the number of people who have access to the insights and battle space visibility that such systems provide. The possession and effective exploitation of such systems by other military institutions will be a crucial aspect of future military effectiveness.

In a 2023 article for *Foreign Affairs*, Amy Zegart examines the transformation of open-source intelligence that has occurred since the beginning of the war in Ukraine. Zegart depicts a new environment of meshed civilian and military collection, analysis, and dissemination of intelligence and concludes, "Secret agencies are no longer enough. The country faces a dangerous new era that includes great-power competition, renewed war in Europe, ongoing terrorist attacks, and fast-changing cyberattacks. New technologies are driving these threats and determining who will be able to understand and chart the future. To succeed, the U.S. intelligence community must adapt to a more open, technological world."[27] Every nation that values its sovereignty will need to consider, learn, and adapt to this new era in intelligence collection, assessment, and dissemination. Military, government, and civilian collection, analysis, and dissemination of intelligence is fundamentally changing and is in turn driving a change in the character of strategic competition and war.

▨ ▨ Strategic Influence Operations

A second fundamental shift in war that has occurred since February 2022 has been in the conduct of strategic influence operations. Wars have always involved a complicated balance of physical, intellectual, and moral forces. Influencing the thinking and actions of enemy commanders and political leaders is a central aspect of what Clausewitz described as the "battle of wills." The actions undertaken as part of influence activities include disinformation, subterfuge, propaganda, and military deception.

However, as wars shifted from limited military affairs to the total wars that evolved in the twentieth century, their center of gravity moved from military forces and geography to populations. And as this occurred, a new relationship developed between military operations, the media, and the influence of civil populations. As Alexander Lovelace has described in *The Media Offensive*, from World War I onward public opinion began shaping military action, and "this blending of war, politics and public opinion created new opportunities for commanders."[28]

New technologies have enhanced the reach and lethality of military forces while also delivering the technological means to target and influence different civilian populations in a way not previously possible. The ability to influence leaders, their advisers, and the inhabitants of different countries is now more sophisticated, more targeted, and more pervasive than ever before. Modern states, corporations, and nonstate actors can devise and test strategic messages—targeting different groups with different narratives—through the internet and social media, adjusting and retargeting millions of users with extraordinary speed.

An important observation from this war is that strategic influence operations can be successfully undertaken by democracies. In the lead-up to the 24 February 2022 Russian invasion of Ukraine, U.S. intelligence agencies used sensitive sources and reporting in an attempt to preempt a Russian invasion of Ukraine.[29] The release of secret intelligence was designed to discredit Russian narratives about the reason for the war as well as crowd the information space to degrade the impact of Russian influence campaigns.

Ukraine has implemented a continuously evolving program to influence Western governments and gain aid and diplomatic assistance since the beginning of the Russian invasion. Social media is central to this because of its demonstrated capacity to penetrate and influence the perceptions of humans. There has been a massive expansion in strategic influence activities by the Ukrainians and other actors. It has influenced Western support for the war, and the increase in military and economic assistance to Ukraine, since the beginning of the war.

Russia has also demonstrated an effective capacity for strategic influence, which has reinforced views in the Global South that "this is not their war." Using trading ties as a foundation, the Russians have been able to minimize support for Ukraine from nations in Africa, South America, and South Asia.[30] As one Lowy Institute article notes, "For the Global South, the Russian invasion of Ukraine is an expensive distraction, taking away attention and funding from the problems that matter to them. They're unconvinced by arguments that Russia's invasion undermines global norms, considering this to be hypocritical and selective, since conflicts elsewhere have not received the same attention."[31]

The blending of military operations, diplomacy, and strategic influence operations has been conducted by the Ukrainians and Russians, with varying degrees of success, since the beginning of the war. The reach and sophistication of the influence activities in particular herald a transformation in how nations conduct themselves in international affairs, and a significant evolution in how military institutions must prepare for, fight, and influence during future wars.

Autonomy and Counter-Autonomy

Autonomous or uncrewed systems, and robots in human-robot teams, have a wide variety of military applications. Human-robot combinations will be useful in training establishments to improve training outcomes and provide the testing ground for best practice in developing human-robot tasking relationships. In logistics, robots will have utility in performing tasks that are dirty, dangerous, or repetitive (e.g., contaminated areas; urban, deep sea and subterranean environments; densely protected military sites) but also in more mundane applications such as vehicle maintenance and repair, and basic logistics and movement tasks.

Several trends in uncrewed systems have emerged from the war in Ukraine. First, they have proved their utility across a range of lethal and nonlethal missions in Ukraine. We should expect to see further proliferation after this war. They are too cheap, too available, and too capable for military and other national security institutions to ignore. Second, there has also been a wide-scale use of commercial uncrewed systems to supplement the missions undertaken by military-grade systems. Both Ukraine and Russia have supplemented their military systems with a range of different commercial UAVS. Many of these have been provided by civilian crowdfunding efforts.[32]

Another trend is that counter-autonomy has been a "lagging capability." Despite early warning in multiple open-source and classified resources about the future use of autonomous systems, counter-autonomy has not kept up with deployment of uncrewed systems. It is hard to believe, but commercial drones dropping grenades and mortar bombs is still widely practiced in Ukraine. Military organizations will have to develop a new generation of counter-autonomy systems that are cheaper to purchase and deploy widely than it would be to purchase and deploy the uncrewed systems they defend against. They might even be a future "cost imposition" capability against the use of uncrewed systems.

But the application of uncrewed systems has largely been about aerial operations, with some use of uncrewed naval attack vessels by Ukraine commencing in late 2022. Given efforts by Ukraine and Russia to develop ground combat autonomous systems, new forms of combat that incorporate remote controlled or autonomous ground combat vehicles may appear on the battlefield in the near future. If those efforts prove successful, they will influence military institutions in the West and beyond.[33]

Uncrewed systems are now used in their thousands across the breadth and depth of the war in Ukraine. The systemic integration of uncrewed systems—across the domains—in the tactics of both belligerents is ongoing and is subject to frequent adaptation. As such, there is much for military organization across the world to learn from this war with regard to autonomous systems, how to employ them, and how to counter their effects. It is a significant transformation in the character of war. The warfighting concepts, organizations, and training approaches will need to evolve to ensure that we can exploit lethal and nonlethal uncrewed systems across all domains.

A SMALL PART OF A BIGGER STORY

As I wrote in the introduction, this book comprises only a small part of the much larger story of the Russian "special military operation" in Ukraine, and the Ukrainian response to that invasion. The war has demonstrated, again, that large-scale conflict is always a potential outcome when nations cannot peacefully reconcile their desires and differences. Humans remain competitive animals, willing to kill and destroy in order to get what they want. This is hardly a new lesson, but it is one that most Western polities have been shocked to relearn since February 2022.

This is an important lesson for all nations. Governments can't ignore or short-change deterrence or preparation for war. And they cannot avoid killing and destroying other humans in waging wars forced on them. War means combat. For nations that wish to protect what they have, or defend others, placing their citizens in close combat is the ultimate expression of national will. It means soldiers fighting on and under the ground, aviators killing other aviators, and naval vessels sinking and damaging other naval vessels.

There is too much evidence from over five thousand years of human conflict to suggest otherwise. What does this mean? It means that when they build military institutions, nations must focus on the core skill of combat. This combat must be aligned with strategy and politics and is the core of military institutions and the profession of arms.

And as we have also relearned during this war, technology is important but does not solve problems by itself. Many commentators have expressed a desire to find a breakthrough technology in this war that would equip Ukraine with a decisive advantage over the Russians. Whether it was Javelin antitank missiles in March 2022, or the June 2022 arrival of HIMARS in Ukraine, the search for technological silver bullets has been a feature of this war and of those that have gone before. The unfortunate reality is that no such thing exists. Machines and weapons do not think, fight, or triumph in conflict—humans do. This war has offered multiple observations on the human ingenuity, teamwork, and leadership that remains the key to success in both deterring wars and winning them. This too is an important lesson from the war in Ukraine.[34]

Ultimately, while there are some elements of the war that are driving a change in the character of war, there are very few new elements in the war. This conflict would be recognizable to a soldier from the Eastern or Western Front in Europe in World War II or even the Pacific War. Many features of the war in Ukraine—trench warfare, armored conflict, fear, comradeship, cowardice, good and bad leadership—would be familiar to soldiers in the industrial-era conflicts of the twentieth or even nineteenth centuries.

And while this may prove a forlorn hope, perhaps we can now also dispense with the notion that wars between large countries can be kept short. The war in Ukraine has already demonstrated that the idea of short, lovely wars is thoroughly bankrupt.

As I write the final words in this book, hundreds of thousands of Ukrainians continue to give their "last full measure of devotion" in the defense of their nation. They are fighting, bleeding, and learning in order to defend their nation and their culture. But at the time these words were written, Ukraine still faced significant obstacles to taking back territory in its East and South. Russian defensive works in southern Ukraine have proved extraordinarily difficult to penetrate, and the Russians have conducted a very competent scheme of defensive maneuvers with a mix of mobilized, "meat," and elite troops.

On the other hand, the performance of newly formed Ukrainian brigades showed that the best equipment does not guarantee mission success on the battlefield. Equipped with the most modern Western tanks, IFVs, and other equipment, several new Ukrainian brigades foundered through their first hours and days in combat. They were not able to plan or execute combined-arms operations against the Russian forces in southern Ukraine. While older brigades equipped with Soviet equipment made useful advances around Bakhmut, newly formed brigades with first-rate equipment but a dearth of experience or cohesion bogged down in the Russian defenses in 2023.

While this book can only cover part of the war, there are a myriad of old and new observations to be drawn from it. These observations should inform Western military and national security institutions as they attempt to deter—and prepare for—conflicts against the authoritarian powers. We must ensure that the sacrifices of the Ukrainian soldiers and the Ukrainian nation are honored not only through our support for them but also through our preparations to minimize the opportunities for predatory authoritarians to force similar catastrophes on other democratic nations in the future.

▰▰ NOTES

INTRODUCTION

Epigraph: James Sherr and Igor Gretskiy, *Why Russia Went to War: A Three-Dimensional Perspective* (Tallinn, Estonia: International Centre for Defence and Security, January 2023), 1.

1. Oliver Slow, "Ukraine Counter-offensive Actions Have Begun, Zelensky Says," BBC News, 11 June 2023, https://www.bbc.com/news/world-europe-65866880; "Video: Zelensky Confirms Counteroffensive against Russia," ABC News, 11 June 2023, https://www.abc.net.au/news/2023-06-11/zelensky-confirms-counteroffensive-against-russia/102467644.
2. Serhii Plokhy, *The Russo-Ukrainian War* (London: Penguin Books, 2023), 295.
3. This account and the images from Kalanchack are available at the Twitter feed of MilitaryLand.net, posted at 7:02 PM on 23 February 2022, https://twitter.com/Militarylandnet/status/1628937603163496454?s=20.
4. Since I began writing this book, Twitter has been rebranded as "X." I have retained the name used during my research.
5. Jack Watling, Oleksandr V. Danylyuk, and Nick Reynolds, "Preliminary Lessons from Russia's Unconventional Operations during the Russo-Ukrainian War, February 2022–February 2023," Royal United Services Institute, 29 March 2023, 20–22, https://rusi.org/explore-our-research/publications/special-resources/preliminary-lessons-russias-unconventional-operations-during-russo-ukrainian-war-february-2022.
6. Rob Johnson, Martijn Kitzen, and Tim Sweijs, *The Conduct of War in the 21st Century: Kinetic, Connected and Synthetic* (London: Routledge, 2021), 6.
7. Victor Davis Hanson, *The Father of Us All: War and History, Ancient and Modern* (New York: Bloomsbury, 2010), 17.

8. Vladimir Putin, "On the Historical Unity of Russians and Ukrainians," President of Russia, 12 July 2021, http://en.kremlin.ru/events/president/news/66181.

9. Putin.

10. Vladimir Putin, "Address by the President of the Russian Federation," President of Russia, 24 February 2022, http://en.kremlin.ru/events/president/transcripts/67843.

11. The ten-day campaign is based on captured Russian documents used as source material in Mykhaylo Zabrodskyi et al., "Preliminary Lessons in Conventional Warfighting from Russia's Invasion of Ukraine: February–July 2022," Royal United Services Institute, 30 November 2022, https://rusi.org/explore-our-research/publications/special-resources/preliminary-lessons-conventional-warfighting-russias-invasion-ukraine-february-july-2022.

12. Zabrodskyi et al., 11.

13. David Barno and Nora Bensahel, *Adaptation under Fire: How Militaries Change in Wartime* (New York: Oxford University Press, 2020), 9–10.

14. U.S. Army, *Establishing a Lessons Learned Program*, Notebook 11–33 (Fort Leavenworth, KS: Center for Army Lessons Learned, 2011), 3.

15. Toshi Yoshihara, *Chinese Lessons from the Pacific War: Implications for PLA Warfighting* (Washington, DC: Center for Strategic and Budgetary Assessments, 2023), ii.

16. Margarita Konaev and Owen Daniels, "Agile Ukraine, Lumbering Russia," *Foreign Affairs*, 28 March 2023, 2, https://www.foreignaffairs.com/ukraine/russia-ukraine-war-lumbering-agile.

17. Yalda Hakim, "Ukraine War: Zelensky Admits Slow Progress but Says Offensive Is Not a Movie," BBC News, 21 June 2023, https://www.bbc.com/news/world-europe-65971790#; Michael Kofman and Rob Lee, "Ukraine Struggles to Scale Offensive Operations," *War on the Rocks* podcast, 20 July 2023, https://warontherocks.com/2023/07/ukraine-struggles-to-scale-offensive-combat-operations/.

18. Zabrodskyi et al., "Preliminary Lessons in Conventional Warfighting."

19. Michael Kofman et al., *Lessons from Russia's Operation Crimea and Eastern Ukraine* (Santa Monica, CA: RAND Corporation, 2017), xii.

20. Don Starry, "To Change an Army," *Military Review*, March 1983, 20–27.

21. Aimée Fox, *Learning to Fight: Military Innovation and Change in the British Army, 1914–1918* (Cambridge: Cambridge University Press, 2017), 250.

22. Lawrence Freedman, "The Meaning of Strategy, Part 1," *Texas National Security Review* 1, no. 1 (November 2017): 90–105, https://tnsr.org/2017/11/meaning-strategy-part-origin-story/.

23. Lawrence Freedman, *Strategy: A History* (Oxford: Oxford University Press, 2013), 610.

24. This term has been used in multiple publications, including Patricia Kim, "China's Choices and the Fate of the Post-Post–Cold War Era," Brookings Institution, 8 March 2022, https://www.brookings.edu/blog/order-from -chaos/2022/03/08/chinas-choices-and-the-fate-of-the-post-post-cold-war-era/; Thomas Henriksen, "Confronting the Post-Post–Cold War World," *Hoover Digest*, Hoover Institution, 30 April 2001, https://www.hoover.org/research /confronting-post-post-cold-war-world; and Alexander Ward, Matt Berg, and Lawrence Ukenye, "Goodbye, Post–Cold War Era!," *Politico*, 12 October 2022, https://www.politico.com/newsletters/national-security-daily/2022/10/12 /goodbye-post-cold-war-era-00061441.

25. Michael Howard, "The Use and Abuse of Military History," lecture to the Royal United Service Institute on 18 October 1961, reprinted in *Parameters* 11, no. 1 (1981): 13.

CHAPTER 1. A NEW STATE NATIONAL SECURITY POLICY

1. Peter Layton, *Grand Strategy* (San Bernadino, CA: 2020), 1–3.

2. Hal Brands, *What Good Is Grand Strategy?* (Ithaca, NY: Cornell University Press, 2014), 3.

3. Samuel Charap et al., *Russian Grand Strategy: Rhetoric and Reality* (Santa Monica, CA: RAND Corporation, 2021), xiii.

4. Edward Luttwak, *The Grand Strategy of the Soviet Union* (New York: St. Martin's, 1983), 1.

5. Glenn Diesen, *Russia's Geoeconomic Strategy for Greater Eurasia* (New York: Routledge, 2018); Ofer Fridman, *Strategiya: The Foundations of the Russian Art of Strategy* (London: Hurst and Company, 2021); Oscar Jonsson, *The Russian Understanding of War: Blurring the Lines between War and Peace* (Washington, DC: Georgetown University Press, 2019); Glen E. Howard, *Russia's Military Strategy and Doctrine* (Washington, DC: Jamestown Foundation, 2018); Andrew Monaghan, *Russian Grand Strategy in the Era of Global Power Competition* (Manchester: Manchester University Press, 2022); Roger Kanet, ed., *Routledge Handbook of Russian Security* (New York: Routledge, 2019); Lawrence Freedman, *Ukraine and the Art of Strategy* (Oxford: Oxford University Press, 2019).

6. Charap et al., *Russian Grand Strategy*; Michael Kofman, Anya Fink, Dmitry Gorenburg, Mary Chesnut, Jeffrey Edmonds, and Julian Waller, *Russian Military Strategy: Core Tenets and Operational Concepts* (Arlington, VA: Center for Naval Analysis, October 2021); Michael Kofman, "Drivers of Russian Grand Strategy," *Frivarld*, no. 6, Stockholm Free World Forum (2019), https://frivarld.se/wp -content/uploads/2019/04/Drivers-of-Russian-Grand-Strategy.pdf; Ian Morris, "The Russian Grand Strategy Guiding the Invasion of Ukraine," *Time*, 5 March 2022, https://time.com/6155129/russian-strategy-guiding-invasion-ukraine/.

7. Kofman, "Drivers of Russian Grand Strategy."

8. Robert Pearson, "Four Myths about Russian Grand Strategy," Center for Strategic and International Studies, 22 September 2020, https://www.csis.org/blogs post-soviet-post/four-myths-about-russian-grand-strategy.

9. Andrew Monaghan, "Putin's Russia: Shaping a 'Grand Strategy'?," *International Affairs 89*, no. 5, Royal Institute of International Affairs (September 2013): 1223–26.

10. Monaghan.

11. Charap et al., *Russian Grand Strategy*, 11.

12. Charap et al., 31–32.

13. Condoleezza Rice, "The Making of Soviet Strategy," in *Makers of Modern Strategy: From Machiavelli to the Nuclear Age*, ed. Peter Paret (Princeton, NJ: Princeton University Press, 1986), 675.

14. Mark Galeotti, "Russia's New National Security Strategy: Familiar Themes, Gaudy Rhetoric," *War on the Rocks*, 4 January 2016, https://warontherocks.com/2016/01 /russias-new-national-security-strategy-familiar-themes-gaudy-rhetoric/.

15. Russian Federation, *On the National Security Strategy of the Russian Federation* (Moscow: Ministry of Foreign Affairs, July 2021), 8–9.

16. Julian Cooper, "Russia's Updated National Security Strategy," *NATO Defence College*, 19 July 2021, https://www.ndc.nato.int/research/research.php?icode=704.

17. Shane Harris et al., "Road to War: U.S. Struggled to Convince Allies, and Zelensky, of Risk of Invasion," *Washington Post*, 16 August 2022, https://www .washingtonpost.com/national-security/interactive/2022/ukraine-road-to -war/?itid=sf_world_ukraine-russia_russia-gamble_p002_f001.

18. Vladimir Putin, "Address by the President of the Russian Federation," President of Russia, 21 February 2022, http://en.kremlin.ru/events/president/transcripts /67828.

19. David Remnick, "Putin's Pique," *New Yorker*, 17 March 2014, https://www .newyorker.com/magazine/2014/03/17/putins-pique; also quoted in Charles Cogan, "You Have to Understand, George. Ukraine Is Not Even a Country," *Huffington Post*, 16 May 2014, https://www.huffpost.com/entry/you-have -to-understand-ge_b_4976198.

20. Vladimir Putin, "On the Historical Unity of Russians and Ukrainians," President of Russia, 12 July 2021, http://en.kremlin.ru/events/president/news/66181.

21. James Sherr and Igor Gretskiy, *Why Russia Went to War: A Three-Dimensional Perspective* (Tallinn, Estonia: International Centre for Defence and Security, January 2023), 5–6.

22. Putin, "Address by the President of the Russian Federation," 21 February 2022.

23. Ailing Tan, "China Buys a Record Amount of Russian LNG as Oil and Coal Purchases Also Surge," Bloomberg, 21 December 2022, https://www.bloomberg.com/news/articles/2022-12-21/china-buys-a-record-amount-of-russian-lng-as-oil-and-coal-purchases-also-surge#xj4y7vzkg.

24. Israel's diplomatic approach to the Russian invasion is examined in David Daoud, "Israel Won't Stick Out Its Neck for Ukraine. It's Because of Russia," Atlantic Council, 13 April 2022, https://www.atlanticcouncil.org/blogs/menasource/israel-wont-stick-out-its-neck-for-ukraine-its-because-of-russia/. The Indian stance is explored in Ashley Tellis, "'What Is in Our Interest': India and the Ukraine War," Carnegie Endowment for International Peace, 25 April 2022, https://carnegieendowment.org/2022/04/25/what-is-in-our-interest-india-and-ukraine-war-pub-86961; and Janis Lazda, "India's Stance on the Ukraine War Makes Little Sense," Politico Europe, 17 October 2022, https://www.politico.eu/article/indias-stance-on-the-ukraine-war-makes-little-sense/.

25. Vladimir Putin, "Address by the President of the Russian Federation," President of Russia, 24 February 2022, http://en.kremlin.ru/events/president/transcripts/67843.

26. Margaret MacMillan, "Leadership at War: How Putin and Zelensky Have Defined the Ukrainian Conflict," Foreign Affairs, 29 March 2022, https://www.foreignaffairs.com/articles/ukraine/2022-03-29/leadership-war.

27. Mykhaylo Zabrodskyi et al., "Preliminary Lessons in Conventional Warfighting from Russia's Invasion of Ukraine: February–July 2022," Royal United Services Institute, 30 November 2022, 7–8, https://rusi.org/explore-our-research/publications/special-resources/preliminary-lessons-conventional-warfighting-russias-invasion-ukraine-february-july-2022.

28. One example of media coverage of the visible Russian buildup is Shane Harris and Paul Sonne, "Russia Planning Massive Military Offensive against Ukraine involving 175,000 Troops, U.S. Intelligence Warns," Washington Post, 3 December 2021, https://www.washingtonpost.com/national-security/russia-ukraine-invasion/2021/12/03/98a3760e-546b-11ec-8769-2f4ecdf7a2ad_story.html.

29. Harris et al., "Road to War."

30. Robert Dalsjö, Michael Jonsson, and Johan Norberg, "A Brutal Examination: Russian Military Capability in Light of the Ukraine War," Survival 64, no. 3 (2022); 7–28; Harris et al., "Road to War."

31. Per Skoglund, Tore Listou, and Thomas Ekström, "Russian Logistics in the Ukrainian War: Can Operational Failures Be Attributed to Logistics?," Scandinavian Journal of Military Studies 5, no. 1 (2022): 99–110.

32. Zabrodskyi et al., "Preliminary Lessons in Conventional Warfighting," 10.

33. Trevor Dupuy, *Understanding War: History and Theory of Combat* (New York: Paragon House, 1987), 34.

34. Allan Millett and Williamson Murray, "Lessons of War," *National Interest* 14 (Winter 1988): 83–95.

35. Vladimir Putin, "New Year Address to the Nation," President of Russia, 31 December 2022, http://en.kremlin.ru/events/president/transcripts/70315.

36. Ishan Tharoor, "Putin Makes His Imperial Pretensions Clear," *Washington Post*, 13 June 2022, https://www.washingtonpost.com/world/2022/06/13/putin-imperial-russia-empire-ukraine/.

37. Lawrence Freedman, "The Problem with Donbas," *Comment Is Freed*, 31 March 2022, https://samf.substack.com/p/the-problem-with-the-donbas?utm_source=twitter&s=r.

38. Mick Ryan, "Vladimir Putin's Plan A in Ukraine Failed, but His Revised Theory of Victory Is Coming Into View," Australian Broadcasting Corporation, 12 July 2022, https://www.abc.net.au/news/2022-07-12/russia-ukraine-putins-revised-theory-of-victory/101227820.

CHAPTER 2. BUMBLING ALONG

1. Mick Ryan, "The Ingenious Strategy That Could Win the War for Ukraine," *Sydney Morning Herald*, 17 May 2022, https://www.smh.com.au/world/europe/the-ingenious-strategy-that-could-win-the-war-for-ukraine-20220517-p5alz4.html.

2. Mick Ryan, "Vladimir Putin's Plan A in Ukraine Failed, but His Revised Theory of Victory Is Coming Into View," Australian Broadcasting Corporation, 12 July 2022, https://www.abc.net.au/news/2022-07-12/russia-ukraine-putins-revised-theory-of-victory/101227820.

3. Sidarth Kausal and Joe Byrne, "The War in Ukraine, One Year On," Royal United Services Institute, 24 February 2023, https://www.rusi.org/explore-our-research/publications/commentary/war-in-ukraine-one-year-on.

4. Radio Free Europe / Radio Liberty, "Russian Military Official Shifts Rhetoric, Says Army Now Focusing on 'Liberation' of Eastern Ukrainian Regions," 25 March 2022, https://www.rferl.org/a/russia-ukraine-goals-scaled-back/31770879.html.

5. Ryan, "Vladimir Putin's Plan A in Ukraine Failed."

6. Ryan.

7. Mykhaylo Zabrodskyi et al., "Preliminary Lessons in Conventional Warfighting from Russia's Invasion of Ukraine: February–July 2022," Royal United Services Institute, 30 November 2022, 15, https://rusi.org/explore-our-research/publications/special-resources/preliminary-lessons-conventional-warfighting-russias-invasion-ukraine-february-july-2022.

8. Zabrodskyi et al., 39.

9. Ryan, "Vladimir Putin's Plan A in Ukraine Failed."

10. Australian Broadcasting Corporation, "General Who Led Syrian Bombing Campaign Is New Face of Russia's War in Ukraine," 21 October 2022, https://www.abc.net.au/news/2022-10-21/russia-war-has-a-new-face-syrian-bombing-leader-segei-surovikin/101564804.

11. Mick Ryan, "A New Russian Strategy Is Emerging in Ukraine—but Alone, It's Not Enough to Win the War," Australian Broadcasting Corporation, 25 October 2022, https://www.abc.net.au/news/2022-10-25/russias-new-military-strategy-in-ukraine/101570630.

12. Shane Harris et al., "U.S. Has Viewed Wreckage of Kamikaze Drones Russia Used in Ukraine," *Washington Post*, 20 October 2022, https://www.washingtonpost.com/national-security/2022/10/20/russia-iran-kamikaze-drones/.

13. Data on the Shahed 136 drone sourced from "Shahed 136," *Military Today*, https://www.military-today.com/aircraft/shahed_136.htm.

14. Ryan, "A New Russian Strategy Is Emerging in Ukraine."

15. Surovikin was subsequently implicated in the Prigozhin mutiny of mid-2023. He was relieved of his command and disappeared from public view until he reappeared in September 2023.

16. Tim Lister, "Putin Burns Through Another Top Ukraine Commander as Armed Forces Chief Is Handed 'Poisoned Chalice,'" CNN, 12 January 2023, https://edition.cnn.com/2023/01/11/europe/russia-valery-gerasimov-ukraine-commander-intl/index.html.

17. Mark Galeotti, "FY23 SCSS#4, 17 January 2023: 'Ukrainian Victory!,'" *In Moscow's Shadows* podcast, 17 January 2023, https://inmoscowsshadows.wordpress.com/2023/01/18/fy23-scss4-17-january-2023-ukrainian-victory/.

18. Anna Reid, "Putin's War on History," *Foreign Affairs* 101, no. 3 (May/June 2022): 54.

19. Reid, 55.

20. Vladimir Putin, "Address by the President of the Russian Federation," President of Russia, 21 September 2022, http://en.kremlin.ru/events/president/news/69390.

21. Timothy Snyder, "How to Talk about the War?," *Thinking About*, 6 March 2022. https://snyder.substack.com/p/how-to-talk-about-the-war.

22. Grigor Atanesian, "Russia in Africa: How Disinformation Operations Target the Continent," BBC News, 1 February 2023, https://www.bbc.com/news/world-africa-64451376; Shannon Bond, "A Pro-Russian Social Media Campaign Is Trying to Influence Politics in Africa," NPR, 1 February 2023, https://www.npr.org/2023/02/01/1152899845/a-pro-russian-social-media-campaign-is-trying-to-influence-politics-in-africa.

23. The 23 February 2023 vote saw 141 nations in favor of the resolution, 7 against, and 32 abstentions. United Nations, "UN General Assembly Calls For Immediate End to War in Ukraine," UN News, 23 February 2023, https://news.un.org/en/story /2023/02/1133847.

24. Igor Gretskiy, *Russia's Propaganda War: Russia's War in Ukraine Series No. 9* (Tallinn, Estonia: International Centre for Defence and Security, August 2022), 1.

25. Carl Miller, "Who's Behind #IStandWithPutin?," *The Atlantic*, 5 April 2022, https:// www.theatlantic.com/ideas/archive/2022/04/russian-propaganda-zelensky -information-war/629475/.

26. Fiona Hill and Angela Stent, "The Kremlin's Grand Delusions," *Foreign Affairs*, 15 February 2023, https://www.foreignaffairs.com/ukraine/kremlins-grand -delusions; Vladimir Putin, Presidential Address to Federal Assembly, 21 February 2023, http://en.kremlin.ru/events/president/news/70565.

27. Gretskiy, *Russia's Propaganda War*, 2–3.

28. Guy Faulconbridge, "Putin Casts War as a Battle for Russia's Survival," Reuters, 26 February 2023, https://www.reuters.com/world/europe/putin-russia-must -take-into-account-nato-nuclear-capability-state-tv-2023-02-26/.

29. Karoline Hird et al., "Russian Offensive Campaign Assessment," Institute for the Study of War, 27 February 2023, https://www.understandingwar.org /backgrounder/russian-offensive-campaign-assessment-february-27-2023.

30. Alexander D. Chekov, "War of the Future: A View from Russia," *Survival* 61, no. 6 (December 2019–January 2020): 34–37.

31. Michael Kofman et al., *Russian Military Strategy: Core Tenets and Operational Concepts* (Arlington, VA: Center for Naval Analysis, October 2021), 13.

32. Putin, "Address by the President of the Russian Federation," 21 September 2022.

33. Vladimir Putin, response to question during Valdai International Discussion Club, 27 October 2022: "Valdai International Discussion Club Meeting," President of Russia, http://en.kremlin.ru/events/president/news/69695; Associated Press, "Putin says 'no need' for using nuclear weapons in Ukraine" *PBS News Hour*, 27 October 2022, https://www.pbs.org/newshour/world /vladimir-putin-rules-out-using-nuclear-weapons-in-ukraine.

34. Guy Falconbridge, "Russia's Putin Issues New Nuclear Warnings to West over Ukraine," Reuters, 22 February 2022, https://www.reuters.com/world/putin -update-russias-elite-ukraine-war-major-speech-2023-02-21/; Putin, Presidential Address to Federal Assembly, 21 February 2023.

35. Pierre de Dreuzy and Andrea Gilli, "Russia's Nuclear Coercion in Ukraine," *NATO Review*, 29 November 2022, https://www.nato.int/docu/review/articles /2022/11/29/russias-nuclear-coercion-in-ukraine/index.html.

36. Owen Matthews, *Overreach: The Inside Story of Putin and Russia's War against Ukraine* (London: Mudlark, 2022), 306.

37. Trevor Dupuy, *Understanding War: History and Theory of Combat* (New York: Paragon House, 1987), 31–35.

38. Kateryna Stepanenko and Frederick W. Kagan, "Russian Offensive Campaign Assessment," *Institute for the Study of War*, 22 January 2023, https://www .understandingwar.org/backgrounder/russian-offensive-campaign-assessment -january-22-2023.

39. Mike Eckel, "Russia Proposes Major Military Reorganization, Conscription Changes, Increase in Troop Numbers," *Radio Free Europe*, 23 December 2022, https://www.rferl.org/a/russia-military-reorganization-expansion/32190811 .html; Anders Anglesey, "Russia Will Struggle to Staff and Equip Any Expanded Army: U.K.," *Newsweek*, 22 January 2023, https://www.newsweek.com/russia -will-struggle-staff-equip-any-expanded-army-uk-1775586.

40. Valery Zaluzhny, "The Commander-in-Chief of Ukraine's Armed Forces on How to Win the War," *The Economist*, 1 November 2023.

41. Heather Ashby et al., "Amid War in Ukraine, Russia's Lavrov Goes on Diplomatic Offensive," United States Institute for Peace, 25 August 2022, https:// www.usip.org/publications/2022/08/amid-war-ukraine-russias-lavrov-goes -diplomatic-offensive.

42. Guy Faulconbridge, "Putin Says Tactical Nuclear Weapons to Be Deployed in Belarus in July," Reuters, 10 June 2023, https://www.reuters.com/world/europe /russia-deploy-tactical-nuclear-weapons-belarus-july-putin-says-2023-06-09/.

43. Anna Maria Dyner, "New Military Doctrine of the Union State of Belarus and Russia," Polish Institute of International Affairs, 15 February 2022, https://www.pism.pl /publications/new-military-doctrine-of-the-union-state-of-belarus-and-russia.

44. Brad Dress, "Why Belarus Matters for the Russia-Ukraine War," *The Hill*, 21 December 2022, https://thehill.com/policy/defense/3783470-why-belarus -matters-for-the-russia-ukraine-war/; Alesia Rudnik, "Will Putin Force Belarus to Join the Russian Invasion of Ukraine?," Atlantic Council, 22 December 2022, https://www.atlanticcouncil.org/blogs/ukrainealert/will-putin-force-belarus -to-join-the-russian-invasion-of-ukraine/.

45. Eugene Rumer, "Putin's Long War," Carnegie Endowment for International Peace, 9 December 2022, https://carnegieendowment.org/2022/12/09/putin -s-long-war-pub-88602.

46. Anjana Pasricha, "India Remains Steadfast in Partnership with Russia," Voice of America, 20 December 2022, https://www.voanews.com/a/india-remains -steadfast-in-partnership-with-russia/6883794.html.

47. Rajan Menon and Eugene Rumer, "Russia and India: A New Chapter," Carnegie Endowment for International Peace, 20 September 2022, https://carnegieen dowment.org/2022/09/20/russia-and-india-new-chapter-pub-87958.

48. Vladimir Putin speech of 21 September 2022, reported by *Washington Post* staff, "Putin's National Address on a Partial Military Mobilization," *Washington Post*, 21 September 2022, https://www.washingtonpost.com/world/2022/09/21/putin -speech-russia-ukraine-war-mobilization/.

49. Dara Massicot, "Why Vladimir Putin Is Likely to Be Disappointed," *New York Times*, 17 October 2022, https://www.nytimes.com/2022/10/17/opinion/russia -ukraine-military-putin.html?smid=tw-nytopinion&smtyp=cur.

50. British Ministry of Defence, *Intelligence Update: Update on Ukraine*, 11 February 2023, https://twitter.com/DefenceHQ/status/1624306543276527616.

51. David Axe, "Russia Sent 70-Year-old T-55 Tanks to Ukraine without Even Upgrading Them," *Forbes*, 14 April 2023, https://www.forbes.com/sites/davidaxe /2023/04/14/russia-sent-70-year-old-t-55-tanks-to-ukraine-without-even -upgrading-them/?sh=46daf4e134d2; Thomas Newdick and Tyler Rogoway, "Signs Point to Russia Sending Ancient T-54 Series of Tanks to Ukraine," *The Warzone*, 22 March 2023, https://www.thedrive.com/the-war-zone/signs-point -to-russia-sending-ancient-t-54-series-of-tanks-to-ukraine.

52. Mick Ryan, "The West Needs to Boost Its Industrial Capacity Fast," *Engelsberg Ideas*, 24 November 2022, https://engelsbergideas.com/notebook/the-west-needs -to-boost-its-industrial-capacity-fast/; Alex Vershinin, "The Return of Industrial Warfare," Royal United Services Institute, 17 June 2022, https://www.rusi.org /explore-our-research/publications/commentary/return-industrial-warfare.

53. Evgeney Gontmakher, "The Russian Economy Mobilizes for War," *Geopolitical Intelligence Services AG*, 5 December 2022, https://www.gisreportsonline.com/r /russia-economy-mobilization/.

54. Elisabeth Braw, "Putin's Mobilization Will Further Upend the Russian Economy," *Politico Europe*, 3 October 2022, https://www.politico.eu/article/putins -mobilization-will-further-upend-the-russian-economy/.

55. Kofman et al., *Russian Military Strategy*, 13–14.

56. *Forbes Ukraine*, https://forbes.ua/ru/profile/metinvest-218.

57. Simeon Djankov and Oleksiy Blinov, "Assessment of Damages to Ukraine's Productive Capacity," Centre for Economic Policy Research, 21 September 2022, https:// cepr.org/voxeu/columns/assessment-damages-ukraines-productive-capacity.

58. Andrew David et al., *Russia Shifting Import Sources amid U.S. and Allied Export Restrictions* (Washington, DC: Silverado Policy Accelerator, January 2023), 2–6.

59. World Bank, "The World Bank in Ukraine: Recent Economic Developments," 10 October 2023, https://www.worldbank.org/en/country/ukraine/overview#3.

60. Brad Roberts, "On Theories of Victory, Red and Blue," Livermore Papers on Global Security No. 7, Lawrence Livermore National Laboratory Center for Global Security Research, Livermore, CA, June 2020, 91.

61. Royal College of Defence Studies, *Getting Strategy Right (Enough)* (London: Ministry of Defence, 2017), 20.

62. Frank Hoffman, "The Missing Element in Crafting National Strategy: A Theory of Success," *Joint Forces Quarterly* 97 (March 2020): 56.

63. Anthony Cordesman and Hy Rothstein, "Conclusion: Can We Learn from the Assessment of War?," in *Assessing War: The Challenge of Measuring Success and Failure*, ed. Leo Blanken et al. (Washington, DC: Georgetown University Press, 2015), 319.

64. Colin Gray, *War, Peace and Victory: Strategy and Statecraft for the Next Century* (New York: Simon and Schuster, 1990), 38–39.

65. Karoun Demirjian, "G.O.P.'s Far Right Seeks to Use Defense Bill to Defund Ukraine War Effort," *Washington Post*, 12 July 2023, https://www.nytimes.com/2023/07/12/us/politics/defense-bill-republicans-ukraine-war.html; Andy Cerda, "More than Four-in-Ten Republicans Now Say the U.S. Is Providing Too Much Aid to Ukraine," Pew Research Center, 15 June 2023, https://www.pewresearch.org/short-reads/2023/06/15/more-than-four-in-ten-republicans-now-say-the-us-is-providing-too-much-aid-to-ukraine/.

66. Ryan, "Vladimir Putin's Plan A in Ukraine Failed."

67. Nicolas Camut, "Zelenskyy Predicts 'Peacetime' Next Year as Putin Warns War Will Be 'Long Process,'" *Politico Europe*, 7 December 2022, https://www.politico.eu/article/zelenskyy-predicts-peace-time-next-year-as-putin-says-war-will-be-a-long-process/.

68. Ken Bredemeier, "Putin Sees Long War in Ukraine, but No Need Now for Additional Soldiers," Voice of America, 7 December 2022, https://www.voanews.com/a/putin-sees-long-war-in-ukraine-but-no-need-now-for-additionalsoldiers-/6866606.html; Rumer, "Putin's Long War."

69. Paul Kirby, "Ukraine War: EU Set to Miss Target of a Million Shell Rounds," BBC News, 14 November 2023, https://www.bbc.com/news/world-europe-67413025.

70. Max Boot, "NATO Is More Unified Than Ever. But What about Those Tanks?," *Washington Post*, 23 January 2023, https://www.washingtonpost.com/opinions/2023/01/23/nato-unity-ukraine-tanks-lloyd-austin/.

71. North Atlantic Treaty Organization, *Vilnius Summit Communiqué*, adopted by Heads of State and Government at the NATO Summit in Vilnius, 11 July 2023, https://www.nato.int/cps/en/natohq/official_texts_217320.htm.

72. Owen Matthews, *Overreach: The Inside Story of Putin's War against Ukraine* (London: Mudlark, 2022), 380.

CHAPTER 3. INCREASE THE ENEMY'S SUFFERING

1. Colin Gray, *The Future of Strategy* (Cambridge: Polity, 2015), 23.
2. Carl von Clausewitz, *On War*, ed. and trans. Michael Howard and Peter Paret (Princeton, NJ: Princeton University Press, 1976), 87.
3. Volodymyr Zelenskyy, *Speech by the President of Ukraine at the 58th Munich Security Conference*, Munich, 19 February 2022, https://www.president.gov.ua /en/news/vistup-prezidenta-ukrayini-na-58-j-myunhenskij-konferenciyi-72997.
4. Volodymyr Zelenskyy, "Address by the President of Ukraine," Kyiv, 24 February 2022, https://www.president.gov.ua/en/news/zvernennya-prezidenta -ukrayini-73137.
5. Zelenskyy, "Address by the President of Ukraine."
6. Volodymyr Zelenskyy, "Ukraine Has Always Been a Leader in Peacemaking Efforts; If Russia Wants to End This War, Let It Prove It with Actions," speech by the President of Ukraine at the G20 Summit, Kyiv, 15 November 2022, https:// www.president.gov.ua/en/news/ukrayina-zavzhdi-bula-liderom-mirotvorchih -zusil-yaksho-rosi-79141.
7. Volodymyr Zelenskyy, "New Year Greetings of President of Ukraine Volodymyr Zelenskyy," Kyiv, 31 December 2022, https://www.president.gov.ua/en/news /novorichne-privitannya-prezidenta-ukrayini-volodimira-zelens-80197.
8. Gordon Craig, "Delbruck the Military Historian," in *Makers of Modern Strategy from Machiavelli to the Nuclear Age*, ed. Peter Paret (Princeton, NJ: Princeton University Press, 1986), 340–42.
9. Lawrence Freedman, *Ukraine and the Art of Strategy* (Oxford: Oxford University Press, 2019), 46.
10. Thomas Bruscino, "Reflections on Military Strategy: Killing Annihilation vs Attrition," War Room, U.S. Army War College, 14 August 2020, https://warroom .armywarcollege.edu/articles/annihilation-attrition/.
11. This example is used in the *Cambridge Dictionary* online: s.v. "corrosion," accessed 28 November 2023, https://dictionary.cambridge.org/dictionary /english/corrosion.
12. Citizen participation in warfare through taxation is explored in Sarah Kreps, *Taxing Wars: The American Way of War Finance* (Oxford: Oxford University Press, 2018).
13. Von Clausewitz, *On War*, 92.
14. Von Clausewitz, 92.
15. But this was not the case for the 2023 counteroffensive in the South, where Ukrainian forces attacked a very heavily defended Surovikin Line.
16. Mick Ryan, "The Ingenious Strategy That Could Win the War for Ukraine," *Sydney Morning Herald*, 17 May 2022, https://www.smh.com.au/world/europe

/the-ingenious-strategy-that-could-win-the-war-for-ukraine-20220517-p5alz4
.html.

17. Paul Sonne et al., "Battle for Kyiv: Ukrainian Valor, Russian Blunders Combined to Save the Capital," *Washington Post*, 24 August 2022, https://www
.washingtonpost.com/national-security/interactive/2022/kyiv-battle-ukraine
-survival/?itid=sf_world_ukraine-russia_russia-gamble_p002_f001.

18. The term "fighting power" was used by Martin van Creveld in his book *Fighting Power: German and U.S. Army Performance, 1939–1945* (London: Praeger, 1982). The term was also used to describe the combination of the physical, intellectual, and moral aspects of preparing an Army for war in Australian Army, *Land Warfare Doctrine 1: The Fundamentals of Land Power 2017* (Canberra: Australian Army, 2017), 37–39.

19. The tensions I refer to came to the surface in late 2023 after the Ukrainian commander in chief, General Zaluzhnyi, used the term "stalemate" in an interview with *The Economist*. The Ukrainian president responded with a public rebuke of his senior military commander and adviser, stating, "Time has passed, people are tired, but this is not a stalemate." Anders Anglesey, "Zelensky Shuts Down His Own Commander's War Comments," *Newsweek*, 5 November 2023.

20. President Zelenskyy replaced his defense minister, Oleksii Reznikov, with Rustem Umerov in late 2023.

21. Eliot Cohen, *Supreme Command: Soldiers, Statesmen and Leaders in Wartime* (New York: Free Press, 2002), 225.

22. Gray, *The Future of Strategy*, 23.

23. J. C. Wylie, *Military Strategy: A General Theory of Power Control* (Annapolis: Naval Institute Press, 1989), 14.

24. Von Clausewitz, *On War*, 81.

25. Australian Defence Force, *Leadership* (Canberra: Commonwealth of Australia, 2021), 47.

26. Mick Ryan, "Ukraine Can Win This War—on These Five Conditions," *Sydney Morning Herald*, 19 August 2022, https://www.smh.com.au/world/europe
/ukraine-can-win-this-war-on-these-five-conditions-20220817-p5bajr.html.

27. Mick Ryan, "A Tale of Two Speeches," *Futura Doctrina*, Substack, 4 January 2023, https://mickryan.substack.com/p/a-tale-of-two-speeches.

28. This blurring of hard and soft power is explored in Jennifer Kavanagh, "The Ukraine War Shows How the Nature of Power Is Changing," Carnegie Endowment for International Peace, 16 June 2022, https://carnegieendowment.org/2022/06/16
/ukraine-war-shows-how-nature-of-power-is-changing-pub-87339.

29. Mick Ryan, "Ukraine Must Maintain Western Attention to Win This War," *Sydney Morning Herald*, 14 June 2022, https://www.smh.com.au/world/europe/ukraine
-must-maintain-western-attention-to-win-this-war-20220614-p5atgf.html.

30. David Gioe and Ken Stolworthy, "Democratised and Declassified: The Era of Social Media War Is Here," *Engelsberg Ideas*, 24 October 2022, https://engelsbergideas.com/notebook/democratised-and-declassified-the-era-of-social-media-war-is-here/; Amy Zegart, "Ukraine and the Next Intelligence Revolution," *Foreign Affairs*, 20 December 2022, https://www.foreignaffairs.com/world/open-secrets-ukraine-intelligence-revolution-amy-zegart.

31. Jake Harrington, "Intelligence Disclosures in the Ukraine Crisis and Beyond," *War on the Rocks*, 1 March 2022, https://warontherocks.com/2022/03/intelligence-disclosures-in-the-ukraine-crisis-and-beyond/; Julian E. Barnes and Adam Entous, "How the U.S. Adopted a New Intelligence Playbook to Expose Russia's War Plans," *New York Times*, 23 February 2023, https://www.nytimes.com/2023/02/23/us/politics/intelligence-russia-us-ukraine-china.html; Ken Dilanian et al., "In a Break with the Past, U.S. Is Using Intel to Fight an Info War with Russia, Even When the Intel Isn't Rock Solid," NBC News, 6 April 2022, https://www.nbcnews.com/politics/national-security/us-using-declassified-intel-fight-info-war-russia-even-intel-isnt-rock-rcna23014.

32. Matt Burgess, "Ukraine's Volunteer 'IT Army' Is Hacking in Uncharted Territory," *Wired*, 27 February 2022, https://www.wired.co.uk/article/ukraine-it-army-russia-war-cyberattacks-ddos.

33. Kavanagh, "The Ukraine War Shows How the Nature of Power Is Changing."

34. Elisabeth Braw, "Ukraine's Digital Fight Goes Global: The Risks of a Self-Directed, Volunteer Army of Hackers," *Foreign Affairs*, 2 May 2022, https://www.foreignaffairs.com/articles/ukraine/2022-05-02/ukraines-digital-fight-goes-global.

35. Paul Adams, "How Ukraine Is Winning the Social Media War," BBC News, 16 October 2022, https://www.bbc.com/news/world-europe-63272202.

36. *The Economist*, "The Invasion of Ukraine Is Not the First Social Media War, but It Is the Most Viral," 2 April 2022, https://www.economist.com/international/the-invasion-of-ukraine-is-not-the-first-social-media-war-but-it-is-the-most-viral/21808456.

37. Mark Scott, "The Shit-Posting, Twitter-Trolling, Dog-Deploying Social Media Army Taking On Putin One Meme at a Time," *Politico Europe*, 31 August 2022, https://www.politico.eu/article/nafo-doge-shiba-russia-putin-ukraine-twitter-trolling-social-media-meme/.

38. Ryan, "Ukraine Must Maintain Western Attention to Win This War."

39. Volodymyr Zelenskyy, "We Stand, We Fight, and We Will Win. Because We Are United. Ukraine, America and the Entire Free World," address in a joint meeting of the U.S. Congress, 22 December 2022, https://www.president.gov.ua/en/news/mi-stoyimo-boremos-i-vigrayemo-bo-mi-razom-ukrayina-amerika-80017.

40. Mick Ryan, *War Transformed: The Future of 21st Century Great Power Competition and Conflict* (Annapolis: Naval Institute Press, 2022), 84.

41. North Atlantic Treaty Organization, *Commitment to Enhance Resilience*, issued by the Heads of State and Government participating in the meeting of the North Atlantic Council in Warsaw, 8–9 July 2016, https://www.nato.int/cps/en/natohq/official_texts_133180.htm.

42. Decree of the President of Ukraine No. 479/2021, on the decision of the National Security and Defense Council of Ukraine dated 20 August 2021, "On the Introduction of the National Stability System," Government of Ukraine, 27 September 2021, https://www.president.gov.ua/documents/4792021-40181; Hanna Shelest, "Defend. Resist. Repeat: Ukraine's Lessons for European Defence," *Policy Brief*, European Council on Foreign Relations, 9 November 2022, https://ecfr.eu/publication/defend-resist-repeat-ukraines-lessons-for-european-defence/.

43. Ivo Juurvee, "Civil Defence in Ukraine: Preliminary Lessons from the First Months of War," International Centre for Defence and Security, Estonia, November 2022, https://icds.ee/wp-content/uploads/dlm_uploads/2022/11/ICDS_Analysis_Civil_Defence_During_the_War_in_Ukraine_Ivo_Juurvee_November_2022.pdf.

44. One example of this work on a Ukrainian insurgency is Emily Harding, "Scenario Analysis on a Ukrainian Insurgency," Center for Strategic and International Studies, 15 February 2022, https://www.csis.org/analysis/scenario-analysis-ukrainian-insurgency.

45. Ryan, "The Ingenious Strategy That Could Win the War for Ukraine."

46. Ryan, "The Ingenious Strategy That Could Win the War for Ukraine."

47. The Russian use of human wave attacks, mostly with Wagner convict recruits or newly mobilized Russian army soldiers, is described in multiple sources. David Axe, "Russian Mercenaries' Human Wave Tactics Push Back Ukrainian Troops in Soledar," *Forbes*, 12 January 2023, https://www.forbes.com/sites/davidaxe/2023/01/12/russian-mercenaries-human-wave-tactics-push-back-ukrainian-troops-in-soledar/?sh=785e0d867701; Veronika Melkozerova, "Zelenskyy Slams Kremlin for Sacrificing Troops in the 'Meat Waves' of Bakhmut," *Politico Europe*, 20 December 2022, https://www.politico.eu/article/volodymyr-zelenskyy-ukraine-war-bakhmut-russia-sacrificing-troops-meat-waves/.

48. Ryan, "Ukraine Can Win This War."

49. Andrius Sytas, "Baltic States Sending Anti-tank, Anti-aircraft Missiles to Ukraine," *Sydney Morning Herald*, 22 January 2022, https://www.smh.com.au/world/europe/baltic-states-sending-anti-tank-anti-aircraft-missiles-to-ukraine-20220122-p59qcq.html.

50. Canada provided one of the largest training teams to Ukraine in the period from 2015 to 2022. In the Canadian military, it was known as Operation Unifier. Government of Canada, "Operation Unifier," last updated 28 November 2023, https://www.canada.ca/en/department-national-defence/services/operations

/military-operations/current-operations/operation-unifier.html. NATO also played an important role, commencing training in 2014. Its mission was (eventually) expanded in the wake of the Russian invasion. Associated Press, "EU Approves Ukraine Training Mission, Arms Funds," 17 October 2022, https://apnews.com/article/russia-ukraine-nato-foreign-policy-european-union -c000ba896559eee256e83769011e0c41.

51. One example of this economic aid is the World Bank assistance announced in August 2022: World Bank, "World Bank Mobilizes $4.5 Billion in Additional Financing for Vital Support to Ukraine," 8 August 2022, https://www.worldbank .org/en/news/press-release/2022/08/08/world-bank-mobilizes-4-5-billion-in -additional-financing-for-vital-support-to-ukraine.

52. Ryan, "Ukraine Can Win This War."

53. Shane Harris and Dan Lamothe, "Intelligence-Sharing with Ukraine Designed to Prevent Wider War," *Washington Post*, 11 May 2022, https://www.washington post.com/national-security/2022/05/11/ukraine-us-intelligence-sharing-war/; Anna Mulrine Grobe, "How U.S. Military Aids Ukraine with Information, Not Just Weaponry," *Christian Science Monitor*, 13 June 2022, https://www .csmonitor.com/USA/Military/2022/0613/How-US-military-aids-Ukraine-with -information-not-just-weaponry; Julian E. Barnes, Helene Cooper, and Eric Schmitt, "U.S. Intelligence Is Helping Ukraine Kill Russian Generals, Officials Say," *New York Times*, 4 May 2022, https://www.nytimes.com/2022/05/04/us /politics/russia-generals-killed-ukraine.html.

54. Julian E. Barnes and Helene Cooper, "Ukrainian Officials Drew on U.S. Intel- ligence to Plan Counteroffensive," *New York Times*, 10 September 2022, https:// www.nytimes.com/2022/09/10/us/politics/ukraine-military-intelligence.html.

55. Sanya Mansoor, "Why U.S. HIMARS Rockets Are Becoming Increasingly Decisive for Ukraine," *Time*, 5 January 2023, https://time.com/6244479/himars -rockets-ukraine-russia/.

56. Christoph Trebesch et al., "The Ukraine Support Tracker: Which Countries Help Ukraine and How?," Working Paper, Kiel Institute for the World Economy, February 2023, 2.

57. Jonathan Masters and Will Merrow, "How Much Aid Has the U.S. Sent Ukraine? Here Are Six Charts," Council on Foreign Relations, 22 February 2023, https://www .cfr.org/article/how-much-aid-has-us-sent-ukraine-here-are-six-charts; Chris- tina Arabia, Andrew Bowen, and Cory Welt, "U.S. Security Assistance to Ukraine," Congressional Research Service, 27 February 2023, https://crsreports.congress .gov/product/pdf/IF/IF12040.

58. Anthony Cordesman, "United States Aid to Ukraine: An Investment Whose Benefits Greatly Exceed Its Cost," Center for Strategic and International Studies,

22 November 2022, https://www.csis.org/analysis/united-states-aid-ukraine-investment-whose-benefits-greatly-exceed-its-cost.

59. Organization for Security and Co-operation in Europe, *Report on Violations of International Humanitarian and Human Rights Law, War Crimes and Crimes against Humanity* (Vienna: Office for Democratic Institutions and Human Rights, July 2022), https://www.osce.org/files/f/documents/3/e/522616.pdf.

60. "Ukraine President Orders General Mobilisation," *DW*, 25 February 2022, https://www.dw.com/en/ukraine-president-orders-general-mobilization/a-60908996.

61. Thomas Laffitte, "Ukraine's Defense Industry and the Prospect of a Long War," Foreign Policy Research Institute, 21 September 2022, https://www.fpri.org/article/2022/09/ukraines-defense-industry-and-the-prospect-of-a-long-war/; Tom Balmforth and Max Hunder, "War Spurs Ukraine to Ramp Up Defence Industry, Including 'Army of Drones,'" Reuters, 12 November 2022, https://www.reuters.com/world/europe/war-spurs-ukraine-ramp-up-defence-industry-including-army-drones-2022-11-11/.

62. Anna Pogrebna et al., "Ukraine Introduces New Rules for Reservation (Exempting) of Employees from Mobilisation," *Lexology*, 6 February 2023, https://www.lexology.com/library/detail.aspx?g=e24bf2ca-bf94-406d-ac62-46f3bcc3edce.

63. Anthony Burke, "Jus Ad Bellum (Just War Theory)," in *Key Concepts in Military Ethics*, ed. Deane-Peter Baker (Sydney: Sydney University Press, 2015), 105–15.

64. Matthews, *Overreach*, 286.

65. Volodymyr Zelenskyy, "It Is Time to Do Everything to Make the War Crimes of the Russian Military the Last Manifestation of This Evil on Earth," address by the President of Ukraine, 3 April 2022, https://www.president.gov.ua/en/news/chas-zrobiti-vse-shob-voyenni-zlochini-rosijskih-vijskovih-s-74053.

66. *Report of the OSCE Moscow Mechanism's Mission of Experts Entitled "Report on Violations of International Humanitarian and Human Rights Law, War Crimes and Crimes against Humanity Committed in Ukraine (1 April—25 June 2022)"* (Warsaw: Organization for Security and Co-operation in Europe Office for Democratic Institutions and Human Rights, July 2022).

67. Mick Ryan, "A 'Just War': West Has a Moral Obligation to Help Defeat Russia," *Sydney Morning Herald*, 19 July 2022, https://www.smh.com.au/world/europe/a-just-war-west-has-a-moral-obligation-to-help-defeat-russia-20220719-p5b2vx.html.

68. Michael Walzer, *Just and Unjust Wars: A Moral Argument with Historical Illustrations* (New York: Basic Books, 1977), 3.

69. Mick Ryan, "How Ukraine Is Winning the Adaptation Battle against Russia," *Engelsberg Ideas*, 24 August 2022, https://engelsbergideas.com/essays/how-ukraine-is-winning-in-the-adaptation-battle-against-russia/.

70. Mykhaylo Zabrodskyi et al., "Preliminary Lessons in Conventional Warfighting from Russia's Invasion of Ukraine: February–July 2022," Royal United Services Institute, 30 November 2022, 51, https://rusi.org/explore-our-research /publications/special-resources/preliminary-lessons-conventional-warfighting -russias-invasion-ukraine-february-july-2022.

71. Aimée Fox, *Learning to Fight: Military Innovation and Change in the British Army, 1914–1918* (Cambridge: Cambridge University Press, 2018).

72. Brad Roberts, "On the Need for a Blue Theory of Victory," *War on the Rocks,* 17 September 2020, https://warontherocks.com/2020/09/on-the-need-for-a -blue-theory-of-victory/.

73. The doubts of some Ukrainian senior leaders, including the president, about Russian intentions to invade are examined by several publications. These doubts receded in January 2022 when it became clear the Russians were in all probability going to cross the border into Ukraine. Shane Harris et al., "Road to War: U.S. Struggled to Convince Allies, and Zelensky, of Risk of Invasion," *Washington Post,* 16 August 2022, https://www.washingtonpost.com/national-security /interactive/2022/ukraine-road-to-war/?itid=sf_world_ukraine-russia_russia -gamble_p002_f001; and Serhii Plokhy, *The Russo-Ukrainian War* (London: Penguin Books, 2023), 142–49.

74. Zelenskyy, "Ukraine Has Always Been a Leader in Peacemaking Efforts."

CHAPTER 4. A GRANDER VIEW

1. William Shakespeare, *Henry VI Part 3,* 2.2.177–78.

2. Robert Heinl, *Dictionary of Military and Naval Quotations* (Annapolis: Naval Institute Press, 1966), 336.

3. Antoine de Jomini, *The Art of War* (London: Greenhill Books, 1996), 360.

4. Winston Churchill, "An Address to the House of Commons" (13 May 1940), reprinted in *Blood, Toil, Tears and Sweat: The Speeches of Winston Churchill,* ed. D. Cannadine (Boston: Houghton Mifflin, 1990), 149.

5. Dwight Eisenhower, *Crusade in Europe* (New York: Doubleday and Company, 1948), 167.

6. *Cambridge Dictionary,* s.v. "victory," https://dictionary.cambridge.org/dictionary /english/victory.

7. Cian O'Driscoll, *Victory: The Triumph and Tragedy of Just War* (Oxford: Oxford University Press, 2020), 5.

8. Barack Obama: "'Victory' Not Necessarily Goal in Afghanistan," Fox News, 23 July 2009, www.foxnews.com/politics/2009/07/23/obama-victory-necessarily -goal-afghanistan/.

9. Joint Chiefs of Staff, *DOD Dictionary of Military and Associated Terms* (Washington, DC: Department of Defense, November 2021).

10. Beatrice Heuser, *The Evolution of Strategy: Thinking War from Antiquity to the Present* (Cambridge: Cambridge University Press, 2010), 471.

11. B. H. Liddell Hart, "The Objective in War," *Naval War College Review* 5, no. 4 (December 1952): 1.

12. Heuser, *The Evolution of Strategy*, 442.

13. Beatrice Heuser, "Victory, Peace and Justice: The Neglected Trinity," *Joint Forces Quarterly*, no. 69 (Second Quarter 2013): 11.

14. Gabriella Blum, "The Fog of Victory," *European Journal of International Law* 24, no. 1 (2013): 393.

15. Brad Roberts, *On Theories of Victory, Red and Blue*, Livermore Papers on Global Security No. 7 (Livermore, CA: Lawrence Livermore National Laboratory Center for Global Security Research, June 2020), 91.

16. Carl von Clausewitz, *On War*, ed. and trans. Michael Howard and Peter Paret (Princeton, NJ: Princeton University Press, 1976), 81.

17. Volodymyr Zelenskyy, "Ukraine Has Always Been a Leader in Peacemaking Efforts; If Russia Wants to End This War, Let It Prove It with Actions," speech by the President of Ukraine at the G20 Summit, 15 November 2022, https://www.president.gov.ua/en/news/ukrayina-zavzhdi-bula-liderom-mirotvorchih-zusil-yaksho-rosi-79141.

18. North Atlantic Treaty Organization, *Vilnius Summit Communiqué*, adopted by Heads of State and Government at the NATO Summit in Vilnius, 11 July 2023, https://www.nato.int/cps/en/natohq/official_texts_217320.htm.

19. Transcript of the IMFC Press Briefing, International Monetary Fund, 21 April 2022, https://www.imf.org/en/News/Articles/2022/04/21/tr220421-transcript-of-the-imfc-press-briefing.

20. Christoph Trebesch et al., "The Ukraine Support Tracker: Which Countries Help Ukraine and How?," Working Paper, Kiel Institute for the World Economy, February 2023, 30–32.

21. A good resource for a holistic examination of the economic impacts of Russia's invasion of Ukraine is Paul Welfrens, *Russia's Invasion of Ukraine: Economic Challenges, Embargo Issues, and a New Global Economic Order* (Cham, Switzerland: Palgrave Macmillan, 2022).

22. Trebesch et al., "The Ukraine Support Tracker," 11–13.

23. Oleksandra Betliy, "Ukraine Needs a Financial Lifeline, Too," Carnegie Endowment for International Peace, 5 December 2022, https://carnegieendowment.org/2022/12/05/ukraine-needs-financial-lifeline-too-pub-88569.

24. Vladyslav Davydov, "Rebuilding Ukraine: How Will Policy-Makers Shape the Country after the War?," *Economics Observatory*, 7 March 2023, https://www.economicsobservatory.com/rebuilding-ukraine-how-will-policy-makers-shape-the-country-after-the-war.

25. World Bank, "Updated Ukraine Recovery and Reconstruction Needs Assessment," press release, 23 March 2023, https://www.worldbank.org/en/news/press-release/2023/03/23/updated-ukraine-recovery-and-reconstruction-needs-assessment.

26. World Bank Group, *Ukraine Rapid Damage and Needs Assessment, February 2022–February 2023* (Washington, DC: World Bank, March 2023), 10–14.

27. Cynthia Cook, "Rebuilding Ukraine after the War," Center for Strategic and International Studies, 22 March 2022, https://www.csis.org/analysis/rebuilding-ukraine-after-war.

28. Outcome Document of the Ukraine Recovery Conference URC2022, "Lugarno Declaration," Lugarno, 4–5 July 2022, https://www.eda.admin.ch/eda/en/fdfa/fdfa/aktuell/dossiers/urc2022-lugano.html.

29. Torbjörn Becker et al., *A Blueprint for the Reconstruction of Ukraine* (London: Centre for Economic Policy Research, 2022); Ronja Ganster et al., *Designing Ukraine's Recovery in the Spirit of the Marshall Plan: Principles, Architecture, Financing, Accountability: Recommendations for Donor Countries* (Washington, DC: German Marshall Fund of the United States, September 2022).

30. Julia Friedrich and Theresa Lutkefend, *The Long Shadow of Donbas: Reintegrating Veterans and Fostering Social Cohesion* (Berlin: Global Public Policy Institute, 2021), 3.

31. Kateryna Odarchenko, "Will Ukrainian Refugees Return Home?," Wilson Centre, 19 August 2022, https://www.wilsoncenter.org/blog-post/will-ukrainian-refugees-return-home.

32. One year after the Russian invasion, insecurity clouds return intentions of displaced Ukrainians, UNHCR, 23 February 2023, https://www.unhcr.org/news/unhcr-one-year-after-russian-invasion-insecurity-clouds-return-intentions-displaced-ukrainians.

33. Stanley Hoffmann, "Collaborationism in France during World War II," *Journal of Modern History* 40, no. 3 (September 1968): 375–95.

34. Human Rights Council, *Report of the Independent International Commission of Inquiry on Ukraine*, 15 March 2023, https://www.ohchr.org/sites/default/files/documents/hrbodies/hrcouncil/coiukraine/A_HRC_52_62_AUV_EN.pdf.

35. Thomas Schelling, *Arms and Influence* (New Haven, CT: Yale University Press, 2008), 31.

CHAPTER 5. STRATEGY FOR THE WEST

1. Richard Foster, Andre Beaufre, and Wynfred Joshua, eds., *Strategy for the West: American-Allied Relations in Transition* (London: Macdonald and Company, 1974), 3–5.

2. Mick Ryan, "How Ukraine Can Win a Long War: The West Needs a Strategy for After the Counteroffensive," *Foreign Affairs*, 30 August 2023, https://www.foreignaffairs.com/ukraine/win-long-war-strategy-counteroffensive.

3. Anthony Cordesman, "How? (and Does?) the War in Ukraine End: The Need for a Grand Strategy," Center for Strategic and International Studies, 24 February 2023, https://www.csis.org/analysis/how-and-does-war-ukraine-end-need-grand-strategy.

4. Kemal Dervis, "What Are the West's Strategic Goals in the Ukraine War?," Brookings Institution, 29 August 2022, https://www.brookings.edu/opinions/what-are-the-wests-strategic-goals-in-the-ukraine-war/.

5. Missy Ryan and Annabelle Timsit, "U.S. Wants Russian Military 'Weakened' from Ukraine Invasion, Austin Says," *Washington Post*, 25 April 2022, https://www.washingtonpost.com/world/2022/04/25/russia-weakened-lloyd-austin-ukraine-visit/.

6. White House, *National Security Strategy, October 2022* (Washington, DC: U.S. Government, 22), 26.

7. White House, *National Security Strategy, October 2022*, 11.

8. Steven Pifer, "U.S. National Interests Are Best Served by Stopping Vladimir Putin in Ukraine," Atlantic Council, 10 November 2022, https://www.atlanticcouncil.org/blogs/ukrainealert/us-national-interests-are-best-served-by-stopping-vladimir-putin-in-ukraine/.

9. White House, *U.S. National Security Strategy, October 2022*, 25–26; White House, "Remarks by President Biden and President Zelenskyy of Ukraine in Joint Statement," Mariinsky Palace, Kyiv, Ukraine, 20 February 2023, https://www.whitehouse.gov/briefing-room/speeches-remarks/2023/02/20/remarks-by-president-biden-and-president-zelenskyy-of-ukraine-in-joint-statement/; White House, "Remarks by President Biden Ahead of the One-Year Anniversary of Russia's Brutal and Unprovoked Invasion of Ukraine," Royal Castle in Warsaw, Poland, 21 February 2023, https://www.whitehouse.gov/briefing-room/speeches-remarks/2023/02/21/remarks-by-president-biden-ahead-of-the-one-year-anniversary-of-russias-brutal-and-unprovoked-invasion-of-ukraine/.

10. Joseph Biden, "What America Will and Will Not Do in Ukraine," *New York Times*, 31 May 2022, https://www.nytimes.com/2022/05/31/opinion/bidenukraine-strategy.html.

11. Christina Arabia, Andrew Bowen, and Cory Welt, *U.S. Security Assistance to Ukraine* (Washington, DC: Congressional Research Service, 5 October 2023), 1–2, https://crsreports.congress.gov/product/pdf/IF/IF12040.

12. Shane Harris et al., "Road to War: U.S. Struggled to Convince Allies, and Zelenskyy, of Risk of Invasion," *Washington Post*, 16 August 2022, https://

www.washingtonpost.com/national-security/interactive/2022/ukraine-road
-to-war/?itid=sf_world_ukraine-russia_russia-gamble_p002_f001.

13. Matthew Susses and Michael Clarke, "Nuclear Weapons and National Security: From the Cold War to the 'Second Nuclear Age' and Beyond," in *The Palgrave Handbook of National Security*, ed. Michael Clarke et al. (Cham, Switzerland: Palgrave Macmillan, 2022), 306.

14. Biden, "What America Will and Will Not Do in Ukraine."

15. David Anger and Jim Tankersley, "U.S. Warns Russia of 'Catastrophic Consequences' if It Uses Nuclear Weapons," *New York Times*, 25 September 2022, https://www.nytimes.com/2022/09/25/us/politics/us-russia-nuclear.html.

16. Molly Hunter and Patrick Smith, "U.S. Envoy to U.N. Sends Russia a Strong Warning against Nuclear Escalation," NBC News, 10 November 2022, https://www.nbcnews.com/news/world/us-envoy-un-sends-russia-strong-warning-nuclear-escalation-rcna56335.

17. The United States provided a small number of ATACMS to Ukraine in October 2023. Lolita Baldor, "Ukraine Uses US-Provided Long-Range ATACMS Missiles against Russian Forces for the First Time," AP News, 18 October 2023, https://apnews.com/article/atacms-ukraine-longrange-missiles-5fd95f32449d14da22b82d57d6ccab22.

18. These U.S. sanctions are described in full at the U.S. Department of the Treasury website, https://home.treasury.gov/news/press-releases/jy1296.

19. Kristin Archick, *Russia's War against Ukraine: European Union Responses and U.S.-EU Relations* (Washington, DC: Congressional Research Service, February 2023), 3.

20. Ricardo Barrios, *China-Russia Relations* (Washington, DC: Congressional Research Service, February 2023), 2.

21. The increasing effectiveness of the Ukrainian air, missile, and drone defense network is explored in part 2 of this book.

22. Jack Watling, *The Ukraine War Has Found the Machinery of Western Governments Wanting* (London: Royal United Services Institution, August 2023).

23. Volodymyr Zelenskyy, "We Have to Liberate Ukraine and Europe, Because When the Russian Weapon Shoots at Us, It Is Already Pointed at Our Neighbours," address by the President of Ukraine at the Munich Security Conference, 17 February 2023, https://www.president.gov.ua/en/news/treba-zvilniti-ukrayinu-ta-yevropu-bo-koli-rosijska-zbroya-s-81061.

24. Erlingur Erlingsson and Fridrik Jonsson, "Western 'Self-Deterrence' Is Aiding Putin's War of Aggression," *Just Security*, 15 March 2023, https://www.justsecurity.org/85460/western-self-deterrence-is-aiding-putins-war-of-aggression/.

25. Paul Sonne and John Hudson, "U.S. Has Sent Private Warnings to Russia against Using a Nuclear Weapon," *Washington Post*, 22 September 2022,

https://www.washingtonpost.com/national-security/2022/09/22/russia-nuclear
-threat-us-options/.

26. "Nato Alliance Experiencing Brain Death, Says Macron," BBC News, 7 November 2019, https://www.bbc.com/news/world-europe-50335257.

27. Fabrice Pothier, "Five Challenges That NATO Must Overcome to Stay Relevant," International Institute for Security Studies, 4 April 2019, https://www.iiss.org /blogs/analysis/2019/04/five-challenges-for-nato.

28. Brian Michael Jenkins, "Consequences of the War in Ukraine: NATO's Future," *RAND Blog*, 2 March 2023, https://www.rand.org/blog/2023/03/consequences -of-the-war-in-ukraine-natos-future.html.

29. North Atlantic Treaty Organization, "Comprehensive Assistance Package for Ukraine, Fact Sheet," July 2016, https://www.nato.int/nato_static_fl2014/assets /pdf/pdf_2016_09/20160920_160920-compreh-ass-package-ukraine-en.pdf.

30. North Atlantic Treaty Organization, "Relations with Ukraine," 22 February 2023, https://www.nato.int/cps/en/natolive/topics_37750.htm.

31. "Charter on a Distinctive Partnership between the North Atlantic Treaty Organization and Ukraine," signed 9 July 1997 by the Government of Ukraine and NATO members, North Atlantic Treaty Organization, last updated 4 March 2009, https://www.nato.int/cps/en/natohq/official_texts_25457.htm.

32. North Atlantic Treaty Organization, *NATO 2022 Strategic Concept*, adopted by Heads of State and Government at the NATO Summit Madrid, 29 June 2022, 2, https://www.nato.int/strategic-concept/.

33. North Atlantic Treaty Organization, *NATO 2022 Strategic Concept*, 4.

34. Jamey Keaten, "NATO Working 'Every Day' to Avoid War with Russia, Jens Stoltenberg Says," Associated Press, 9 December 2022, https://globalnews.ca /news/9337987/nato-ukraine-russia-jens-stolenberg/.

35. UK Ministry of Defence, "Operation Interflex: UK Training of Ukrainian Recruits," Joint-forces.com, 10 November 2023, https://www.joint-forces.com /uk-operations/68782-operation-interflex-uk-training-of-ukrainian-recruits.

36. Government of Canada, "Canadian Donations and Military Support to Ukraine," last modified 28 November 2023, https://www.canada.ca/en/department -national-defence/campaigns/canadian-military-support-to-ukraine.html; Pjotr Sauer, "Belgian Buyer of Europe's Spare Tanks Hopes They See Action in Ukraine," *The Guardian*, 1 February 2023, https://www.theguardian.com/world/2023/jan/31 /ukraine-europe-tanks-belgian-buyer-oip; Nicolas Camut, "France, Australia to Supply Ammo for Ukraine," *Politico Europe*, 31 January 2023, https://www.politico .eu/article/australia-france-ukraine-155mm-ammunition-caesar-howitzer/.

37. Catherine Belton and Emily Rauhala, "Europe's Military Industrial Capabilities Fall Short of Ukraine's Needs," *Washington Post*, 19 May 2023, https://www

.washingtonpost.com/world/2023/05/18/europe-weapons-military-industrial
-base/.

38. North Atlantic Treaty Organization, "NATO Force Model," accessed 28
November 2023, https://www.nato.int/nato_static_fl2014/assets/pdf/2022/6
/pdf/220629-infographic-new-nato-force-model.pdf.

39. Paul Belkin, *Russia's Invasion of Ukraine: NATO Response* (Washington, DC:
Congressional Research Service, March 2022), 1–3.

40. North Atlantic Treaty Organization, *Cyber Defence*, 23 March 2022, https://
www.nato.int/cps/en/natohq/topics_78170.htm.

41. North Atlantic Treaty Organization, *NATO 2022 Strategic Concept*, 6–7.

42. North Atlantic Treaty Organization, *NATO 2022 Strategic Concept*, 7.

43. Lorne Cook, "NATO Chief Warns Russia Not to Cross 'Very Important Line,'"
Associated Press, 14 October 2022, https://apnews.com/article/russia-ukraine
-putin-nato-government-and-politics-moscow-4b8db123007dde5c1f859bb813
4b7dd5.

44. Government of Germany, "Policy Statement by Olaf Scholz, Chancellor of
the Federal Republic of Germany and Member of the German Bundestag,"
27 February 2022, Berlin, https://www.bundesregierung.de/breg-en/news
/policy-statement-by-olaf-scholz-chancellor-of-the-federal-republic-of-germany
-and-member-of-the-german-bundestag-27-february-2022-in-berlin-2008378.

45. Government of Germany, "Speech by Chancellor Scholz at the Munich Security
Conference," 17 February 2023, Munich, https://www.bundesregierung.de/breg
-en/search/speech-by-chancellor-scholz-at-the-munich-security-conference
-on-17-february-2023-in-munich-2166536.

46. There is significant literature on alliance decision-making, and the tensions
around priorities and resources, during World War II to reinforce this point.
It is described in the memoirs of many wartime political and military leaders.
Sources on this subject include Christopher Thorne, *Allies of a Kind: The United
States, Britain and the War against Japan, 1941–1945* (Oxford: Oxford University
Press, 1978); David Stone, *War Summits: The Meetings That Shaped World War II
and the Postwar World* (Washington, DC: Potomac Books, 2005); and Maurice
Matloff, *Strategic Planning for Coalition Warfare, 1943–1944* (Washington, DC:
Center of Military History, U.S. Army, 1953).

47. Associated Press, "Moscow Drone Attack Exposes Russia's Vulnerabilities, Fuels
Criticism of Military," 31 May 2023, https://apnews.com/article/russia-ukraine
-war-drone-attack-moscow-defenses-4cd363fc7288998f0af26a8d8a8fe87c;
Anotoly Kurmanaev, "Moscow Drone Strikes a Psychological Blow, Russian Nationalists Say," *New York Times,* 30 May 2023, https://www.nytimes
.com/2023/05/30/world/europe/russians-war-moscow-drone-strike.html.

48. China's strategy for Ukraine is described in the Chinese government paper titled "China's Position on the Political Settlement of the Ukraine Crisis" (released in 2022), last updated 24 February 2023, https://www.fmprc.gov .cn/eng/zxxx_662805/202302/t20230224_11030713.html. China's strategy for Ukraine is also explored in Bruno Macaes, "An Insider's Perspective on China's Strategy in Ukraine," *Time*, 20 March 2023, https://time.com/6264512/insiders -perspective-on-chinas-strategy-in-ukraine; and Ved Shinde, "What Does China Want in Ukraine?," *The Interpreter*, Lowy Institute, 12 April 2023, https://www .lowyinstitute.org/the-interpreter/what-does-china-want-ukraine.

CHAPTER 6. A COMEDIAN AND A LONG TABLE

1. Bernard Montgomery, *The Path to Leadership* (London: Collins, 1961), 10.
2. Martin Van Creveld, *Command in War* (Cambridge, MA: Harvard University Press, 1985), 270.
3. Carl von Clausewitz, *On War*, ed. and trans. Michael Howard and Peter Paret (Princeton, NJ: Princeton University Press, 1976), book 1, chap. 3: "On Military Genius," 100.
4. Clausewitz, 102.
5. Mick Ryan, "The Keys to Effective Leadership," Strategy Bridge, 29 March 2016, https://thestrategybridge.org/the-bridge/2016/3/29/the-keys-to-effective -leadership.
6. Lawrence Freedman, *Command: The Politics of Military Operations from Korea to Ukraine* (London: Penguin Random House UK, 2022), 493–94.
7. BBC News, "Ukraine Election: Comedian Zelenskyy 'Wins Presidency,'" 22 April 2019, https://web.archive.org/web/20190421173305/https://www.bbc.com /news/world-europe-48007487.
8. Zelenskyy states in his speech, "Your applause is pretty light. . . . I guess not everyone likes what I'm saying?" Volodymyr Zelenskyy, "Volodymyr Zelen- skyy's Inaugural Address," 20 May 2019, https://www.president.gov.ua/en/news /inavguracijna-promova-prezidenta-ukrayini-volodimira-zelensk-55489.
9. Zelenskyy, "Volodymyr Zelenskyy's Inaugural Address."
10. Radio Free Europe / Radio Liberty, "Ukrainian President Signs 'Anti-oligarch Law,'" 5 November 2021, https://www.rferl.org/a/ukraine-zelenskiy-anti-oligarch law/31548053.html
11. Statista, "Do You Approve or Disapprove of the Actions of the President of Ukraine Volodymyr Zelenskyy?," 19 September 2023, https://www.statista .com/statistics/1100076/volodymyr-Zelenskyy-s-approval-rating-ukraine/.
12. "Socio-political Moods of the Population of Ukraine," Kyiv International Insti- tute of Sociology, 19 October 2021, https://www.kiis.com.ua/?lang=eng&cat =reports&id=1063&page=1.

13. Mykhailo Minakov, "Just Like All the Others: The End of the Zelenskyy Alternative?," Wilson Center, 2 November 2021, https://www.wilsoncenter.org/blog-post/just-all-others-end-Zelenskyy-alternative.

14. Volodymyr Zelenskyy, "Address by the President of Ukraine," 24 February 2022, https://www.president.gov.ua/en/videos/zvernennya-prezidenta-ukrayini-2017.

15. Owen Matthews, *Overreach: The Inside Story of Putin and Russia's War against Ukraine* (London: Mudlark, 2022), 216.

16. John F. Kennedy, *Remarks on Signing Honorary Citizenship for Sir Winston Churchill*, 9 April 1963, from the archives of the John F. Kennedy Presidential Library and Museum, https://www.jfklibrary.org/asset-viewer/archives/JFKPOF/043/JFKPOF-043-032.

17. Arkady Ostrovsky, *Preface: We Are All Here*, in Volodymyr Zelenskyy, *A Message from Ukraine: Speeches 2019–2022* (London: Hutchieson Heinemann, 2022), ix.

18. "Speech to U.S. Congress by Volodymyr Zelenskyy," *New York Times*, 21 December 2022, https://www.nytimes.com/2022/12/21/us/politics/Zelenskyy-speech-transcript.

19. Volodymyr Zelenskyy speech to the 2022 Grammy Awards, quoted in Tatiana Serafin, "Ukraine's President Zelenskyy Takes the Russia-Ukraine War Viral," *Orbis* 66, no. 4 (Fall 2022): 460.

20. Eliot Cohen, *Supreme Command: Soldiers, Statesmen and Leadership in Wartime* (New York: Free Press, 2002), 132.

21. Cohen, 224.

22. Kirstin Ferguson, *Head and Heart: The Art of Modern Leadership* (Melbourne: Viking, 2023), 166.

23. Australian Defence Force, *Leadership* (Canberra: Commonwealth of Australia, 2021), 11.

24. Volodymyr Zelenskyy, "Emotional Moment President Zelenskyy Tears Up When Asked about His Family," *The Telegraph*, posted 24 February 2023, YouTube video, 1:34, https://www.youtube.com/watch?v=FCxRLC4wEDE.

25. Volodymyr Zelenskyy, "'Very Difficult to Talk': Visibly Emotional Zelenskyy Shocked by Bucha Horror," *Daily Mail*, posted 4 April 2022, YouTube video, 2:28, https://www.youtube.com/watch?v=ndNyE7foNVs.

26. Matthews, *Overreach*, 286.

27. Cohen, *Supreme Command*, 2.

28. Cohen, 209.

29. Cohen, 118.

30. Radio Free Europe / Radio Liberty, "Ukrainian Lawmakers Approve Reznikov as New Defense Minister," 4 November 2021, https://www.rferl.org/a/ukraine-new-defense-minister/31545565.html.

31. David Herszenhorn and Paul McLeary, "Ukraine's 'Iron General' Is a Hero, but He's No Star," *Politico*, 8 April 2022, https://www.politico.com/news/2022/04/08/ukraines-iron-general-Zaluzhnyi-00023901.

32. Simon Shuster and Vera Bergengruen, "Inside the Ukrainian Counterstrike That Turned the Tide of the War," *Time*, 26 September 2022, https://time.com/6216213/ukraine-military-valeriy-Zaluzhnyi/.

33. Reznikov was replaced with Rustem Umerov in late 2023.

34. Vladimir Putin, "Victory Parade on Red Square: Speech Marking the 77th Anniversary of Victory in the 1941–1945 Great Patriotic War," Moscow, 2022, http://www.en.kremlin.ru/events/president/transcripts/68366.

35. Nick Mordowanec, "How Putin's Victory Parade Speech Changed Drastically from Last Year," *Newsweek*, 9 May 2023, https://www.newsweek.com/putin-victory-day-parade-speech-compared-last-year-1799245; Vladimir Putin, "Victory Parade on Red Square: Speech Marking the 78th Anniversary of Victory in the 1941–1945 Great Patriotic War," Moscow, 2023, http://www.en.kremlin.ru/events/president/transcripts/71104.

36. Jill Dougherty, "How the Media Became One of Putin's Most Powerful Weapons," *The Atlantic*, 12 April 2015, https://www.theatlantic.com/international/archive/2015/04/how-the-media-became-putins-most-powerful-weapon/391062/.

37. Robyn Dixon, "Long before His War in Ukraine, Putin Waged War on Russian Journalists," *Washington Post*, 24 September 2022, https://www.washingtonpost.com/world/2022/09/24/russia-media-putin-war-repression/.

38. Maya Vinokour, "Russia's Media Is Now Totally in Putin's Hands," *Foreign Policy*, 5 April 2022, https://foreignpolicy.com/2022/04/05/russia-media-independence-putin/.

39. Sarah Fowler and James Landale, "Putin in Mariupol: What the Russian President Saw on His Visit," BBC News, 19 March 2022, https://www.bbc.com/news/world-europe-65007289#.

40. Fernando Alfonso, "Putin's Puffy Coat and Zelenskyy's T-Shirts Show the Power of Fashion in War," NPR, 22 March 2022, https://www.npr.org/2022/03/22/1087983743/putin-coat-Zelenskyy-shirts-fashion-statement-russia-ukraine-war.

41. Freedman, *Command*, 399.

42. Peter Mansoor and Williamson Murray, eds., *The Culture of Military Organizations* (Cambridge: Cambridge University Press, 2019), 456.

43. Catherine Belton, *Putin's People: How the KGB Took Back Russia and Then Took On the West* (New York: Farrar, Straus and Giroux, 2022), 498.

44. Andrei Kolesnikov, "Putin's Stalin Phase," *Foreign Affairs*, 8 November 2022.

45. Mark Galeotti, *We Need to Talk about Putin* (London: Ebury Press, 2019), 143.

46. Mark Galeotti, "All Hail the Tsar?," *In Moscow's Shadows* podcast, 7 May 2023, https://podcasts.apple.com/us/podcast/in-moscows-shadows/id1510124746?i =1000612035443.

47. Freedman, *Command*, 514–15.

48. Margaret MacMillan, "Leadership at War: How Putin and Zelenskyy Have Defined the Ukrainian Conflict," *Foreign Affairs*, 29 March 2022, https://www.foreign affairs.com/articles/ukraine/2022-03-29/leadership-war.

49. Martin Dempsey, *No Time for Spectators: The Lessons That Mattered the Most from West Point to the West Wing* (Arlington, VA: Missionday, 2020), 210.

50. This issue of authority that is earned and not granted is explored in Freedman, *Command*, 515.

CHAPTER 7. LESSONS FROM UKRAINE

1. Richard Rumelt, *Good Strategy, Bad Strategy: The Difference and Why It Matters* (London: Profile Books, 2011).

2. Rumelt, 234.

3. Michael Howard, "The Use and Abuse of Military History," *Royal United Services Institute Journal* 107, no. 625 (1962): 7.

4. Allan Millett and Williamson Murray, "Lessons of War," *National Interest* 14 (Winter 1988): 83–95.

5. Mick Ryan, *Thinking about Strategic Thinking: Developing a More Effective Strategic Thinking Culture in Defence* (Canberra: Australian Defence College, 2021), 5.

6. Loizos Heracleous, "Strategic Thinking or Strategic Planning?," *Long Range Planning* 31, no. 3 (1998): 484.

7. Mark Galeotti, *Putin's Wars: From Chechnya to Ukraine* (London: Bloomsbury, 2022), 345.

8. Bernard Brodie, *Strategy for the Missile Age* (Princeton, NJ: Princeton University Press, 1959), 358.

9. Seth Jones, "Russia's Ill-Fated Invasion of Ukraine: Lessons in Modern Warfare," Center for Strategic and International Studies, 1 June 2022, https://www.csis .org/analysis/russias-ill-fated-invasion-ukraine-lessons-modern-warfare.

10. John Lewis Gaddis, *On Grand Strategy* (London: Penguin Books, 2019), 12–13.

11. Vladimir Frolov, "New Commander, New Goals for Russia in Ukraine," Carnegie Endowment for International Peace, 1 November 2022, https://carnegie endowment.org/politika/88301.

12. John Mueller, "The Obsolescence of Major War," *Bulletin of Peace Proposals* 21, no. 3 (1990), 321.

13. Ian Morris, *War: What Is It Good For?* (London: Profile Books, 2014), 391.

14. Raphael Cohen and Gian Gentile, "'Wonder Weapons' Will Not Win Russia's War," *RAND Corporation*, 10 November 2022, https://www.rand.org/blog/2022/11/wonder-weapons-will-not-win.html.

15. For example, Giulio Douhet argued that using aircraft to gain command of the air, and then bombing enemy cities and factories, would shatter civilian will to continue a war. Giulio Douhet, *The Command of the Air*, trans. Dino Ferrari (Washington, DC: Office of Air Force History, 1983).

16. Michel van Pelt, "Germany's Wonder Weapons," in *Rocketing into the Future: The History and Technology of Rocket Planes* (Chichester, U.K.: Praxis, 2012), 57–106.

17. U.K. Government, *Getting Strategy Right (Enough)* (London: Royal College of Defence Studies, 2017), 20–21.

18. Vincent Barabba and Ian Mitroff, *Business Strategies for a Messy World: Tools for Systemic Problem-Solving* (New York: Palgrave Macmillan, 2014), 23.

19. Colin Gray, *Strategy and Defence Planning: Meeting the Challenge of Uncertainty* (Oxford: Oxford University Press, 2014), 63.

20. As Lawrence Freedman has written, "Western countries stayed well clear of the fighting. The response to Crimea's annexation was limited economic sanctions and efforts to isolate Russia diplomatically." Lawrence Freedman, *Ukraine and the Art of Strategy* (Oxford: Oxford University Press, 2019), 171.

21. Owen Matthews, *Overreach: The Inside Story of Putin's War against Ukraine* (London: Mudlark, 2022), 352–56.

22. Dara Massicot (@MassDara), "Three takes on Russian military performance in 100 words or less. Thanks @marceldirsus! Mine: Russia's operation in Ukraine is struggling because those who planned it are stuck at the intersection of Russian imperial hubris and soviet-style secrecy," Twitter, 2:33 PM, 26 April 2022, https://twitter.com/MassDara/status/1519052044065255425.

23. Jeffrey Edmonds, "Start with the Political: Explaining Russia's Bungled Invasion of Ukraine," *War on the Rocks*, 28 April 2022, https://warontherocks.com/2022/04/start-with-the-political-explaining-russias-bungled-invasion-of-ukraine/.

24. Edward Luttwak, *Strategy: The Logic of War and Peace* (Cambridge: Belknap Press of Harvard University Press, 2001), 265.

25. Michael Kofman et al., *Lessons from Russia's Operations in Crimea and Eastern Ukraine* (Santa Monica, CA: RAND Corporation, 2017).

26. Carl von Clausewitz, *On War*, ed. and trans. Michael Howard and Peter Paret (Princeton, NJ: Princeton University Press, 1976), 75.

27. Samantha Hoffman and Matthew Knight, *China's Messaging on the Ukraine Conflict* (Canberra: Australian Strategic Policy Institute, May 2022); Maria Repnikova and Bret Schafer, *How the People's Republic of China Amplifies Russian Disinformation*, Briefing at U.S. Department of

State, 27 April 2022, https://www.state.gov/briefings-foreign-press-centers/how-the-prc-amplifies-russian-disinformation.

28. Julio Terracino and Craig Matasick, "Disinformation and Russia's War of Aggression against Ukraine: Threats and Governance Responses," Organization for Economic Co-operation and Development, 3 November 2022, 3, https://www.oecd.org/ukraine-hub/policy-responses/disinformation-and-russia-s-war-of-aggression-against-ukraine-37186bde/.

29. Qiao Liang and Wang Xiangsui, *Unrestricted Warfare* (Beijing: PLA Literature and Arts Publishing House, February 1999), 7.

30. U.K. Ministry of Defence, *Integrated Operating Concept* (London: U.K. Ministry of Defence, 2021), 9.

31. Justin Bronk, "The Mysterious Case of the Missing Russian Air Force," *Royal United Services Institute*, 28 February 2022, https://rusi.org/explore-our-research/publications/commentary/mysterious-case-missing-russian-air-force.

32. The mobilization of people for military service has at times been problematic, however. In August 2023, President Zelenskyy removed 112 military commissars, who were responsible for military recruiting, because of corruption and inefficiency.

33. As B. A. Friedman argues in *On Operations*, though, the assumption that operational art originated with the Russians in the early twentieth century is mistaken. Its theoretical underpinnings can be found in the Napoleonic Revolution, which drove change in the character of war in the early nineteenth century, and the Prussian and German military reforms of the mid- to late nineteenth century. B. A. Friedman, *On Operations: Operational Art and Military Disciplines* (Annapolis: Naval Institute Press, 2021), 11–29.

34. North Atlantic Treaty Organization, *NATO 2022 Strategic Concept*, adopted by Heads of State and Government at the NATO Summit in Madrid, 29 June 2022, https://www.nato.int/strategic-concept/.

35. North Atlantic Treaty Organization, *Vilnius Summit Communiqué*, adopted by Heads of State and Government at the NATO Summit in Vilnius, 11 July 2023, https://www.nato.int/cps/en/natohq/official_texts_217320.htm.

36. Andrew Eversden, "US Army Secretary: 5 Lessons from the Ukraine Conflict," *Breaking Defense*, 1 June 2022, https://breakingdefense.com/2022/06/us-army-secretary-5-lessons-from-the-ukraine-conflict/.

37. Anthony Cordesman, *NATO Force Planning: Rethinking the Defense Industrial Base* (Washington, DC: Center for Strategic and International Studies, July 2022), 1.

38. William Russell, *Defense Industrial Base: DOD Should Take Actions to Strengthen Its Risk Mitigation Approach* (Washington, DC: U.S. Government Accountability Office, July 2022), 27.

39. Alex Vershinin, "The Return of Industrial Warfare," Royal United Services Institute, 17 June 2022, https://www.rusi.org/explore-our-research/publications/commentary/return-industrial-warfare.

40. Phillip Harding, *The British Shell Shortage of the First World War* (Stroud, U.K.: Fonthill, 2015); A. J. A. Morris, *Reporting the First World War: Charles Repington, the Times and the Great War, 1914–1918* (Cambridge: Cambridge University Press), 173–90. The Russians also experienced a shell shortage between 1914 and 1917. Norman Stone, "Organising and Economy for War: The Russian Shell Shortage 1914–1917," in *War, Economy and the Military Mind*, ed. Geoffrey Best and Andrew Wheatcroft (Totowa, NJ: Rowman and Littlefield, 1976), 108–19.

41. Matthew Mpoke Bigg and Steven Erianger, "With Battles Looming, Ukraine's Allies Meet to Plan Arms Supply," *New York Times*, 14 February 2023; Reuters, "Britain Places New BAE Order for Battlefield Munitions," 11 July 2023, https://www.reuters.com/business/aerospace-defense/bae-systems-gets-uk-order-boost-output-battlefield-munitions-ft-2023-07-10/; Natalia Drozdiak, Jonas Ekblom, and Alexander Michael Pearson, "Europe Can't Supply Ukraine with Weapons Fast Enough, Here's Why," Bloomberg, 10 July 2023, https://www.bloomberg.com/news/features/2023-07-09/europe-can-t-supply-ukraine-with-weapons-fast-enough-against-russia?in_source=embedded-checkout-banner.

42. The Economist, "The West Is Struggling to Forge a New Arsenal of Democracy," 19 February 2023, https://www.economist.com/briefing/2023/02/19/the-west-is-struggling-to-forge-a-new-arsenal-of-democracy.

43. Seth Jones, "America's Looming Munitions Crisis," *Foreign Affairs*, 31 March 2023, https://www.foreignaffairs.com/united-states/americas-looming-munitions-crisis.

44. Mick Ryan, "What the Albanese Government Can Learn from Ukraine," *Sydney Morning Herald*, 24 May 2022, https://www.smh.com.au/national/what-the-albanese-government-can-learn-from-ukraine-20220524-p5anxm.html.

45. Steve Holland and Andrea Shalal, "Putin Misled by 'Yes Men' in Military Afraid to Tell Him the Truth, White House and EU Officials Say," Reuters, 31 March 2022, https://www.reuters.com/world/putin-advisers-too-afraid-tell-him-truth-ukraine-us-official-2022-03-30/.

46. Avril Haines, "Fireside Chat with DNI Haines at the Reagan National Defense Forum," 12 December 2022, https://www.dni.gov/index.php/newsroom/news-articles/news-articles-2022/item/2346-fireside-chat-with-dni-haines-at-the-reagan-national-defense-forum.

47. Williamson Murray, MacGregor Knox, and Alvin Bernstein, *The Making of Strategy: Rulers, States and War* (New York: Cambridge University Press, 1994), 19.

48. Margaret MacMillan, "If You Want Peace, Study War," *Persuasion*, 11 January 2021, https://www.persuasion.community/p/if-you-want-peace-study-war-533; Thomas Lindsay, "Have Universities Seen the End of War?," *Real Clear Policy*, 14 May 2014, https://www.realclearpolicy.com/blog/2014/05/15/have_universities_seen_the_end_of_war_944.html.

49. Mick Ryan, *War Transformed: The Future of Twenty-First-Century Great Power Competition and Conflict* (Annapolis: USNI Press, 2022), 165.

CHAPTER 8. LEARNING IS HUMAN

The term "learning is human" is taken from my December 2022 Substack article, which notes that "learning is ultimately a human process." Mick Ryan, "Learning from the War in Ukraine," *Futura Doctrina*, Substack, 19 December 2022, https://mickryan.substack.com/p/learning-from-the-war-in-ukraine.

1. Andrew Harding, "Ukraine War: Russian Threat Growing, Front Line Troops Fear," BBC News, 1 February 2023, https://www.bbc.com/news/world-europe-64455123.

2. Ellie Cook, "Russia's Elite 'Storm-Z' Units Now Effectively 'Penal Battalions'—UK," *Newsweek*, 24 October 2023, https://www.newsweek.com/russia-storm-z-penal-battalions-ukraine-1837234.

3. Karolina Hird et al., "Russian Offensive Campaign Assessment, 30 October 2023," Institute for the Study of War, 30 October 2023, https://www.understandingwar.org/backgrounder/russian-offensive-campaign-assessment-october-30-2023; Jon Jackson, "Russian Soldier Describes Moscow's Use of 'Meat Assault' Tactic," *Newsweek*, 30 October 2023, https://www.newsweek.com/russian-soldier-describes-moscows-use-meat-assault-tactic-1839375#:~:text=Throughout%20the%20war%20that%20Russian,large%20numbers%20of%20those%20regarded.

4. Mick Ryan, "How Ukraine Is Winning in the Adaptation Battle against Russia," *Engelsberg Ideas*, 24 August 2022, https://engelsbergideas.com/essays/how-ukraine-is-winning-in-the-adaptation-battle-against-russia/.

5. Michael Howard, "The Use and Abuse of Military History," *Royal United Service Institute Journal* 107, no. 625 (1962): 4–8.

6. Charles Darwin, *On the Origin of Species: By Means of Natural Selection or the Preservation of Favored Races in the Struggle for Life* (1859; repr., New York: Random House, 1998), 636–37.

7. D. Buss et al., "Adaptations, Exaptions and Spandrels," *American Psychologist*, May 1998, 534.

8. Grant Hammond, *The Mind of War: John Boyd and American Security* (Washington, DC: Smithsonian Institution Press, 2001), 35.

9. Aimée Fox, *Learning to Fight: Military Innovation and Change in the British Army, 1914–1918* (Cambridge: Cambridge University Press, 2017); and Williamson Murray, *Military Innovation in the Interwar Period* (Cambridge: Cambridge University Press, 1998).

10. Eliot Cohen and John Gooch, *Military Misfortunes: The Anatomy of Failure in War* (New York: Vintage Books, 1990).

11. Mick Ryan, "Implementing an Adaptive Approach in Non-Kinetic Counter-insurgency Operations," *Australian Army Journal* 4, no. 3 (2007): 125–40.

12. Ryan, "How Ukraine Is Winning in the Adaptation Battle against Russia."

13. Dima Adamsky, *The Culture of Military Innovation: The Impact of Cultural Factors on the Revolution in Military Affairs in Russia, the U.S., and Israel* (Stanford, CA: Stanford Security Studies, 2010), 141–42.

14. Fox, *Learning to Fight*, 53.

15. Mykhaylo Zabrodskyi et al., "Preliminary Lessons in Conventional Warfighting from Russia's Invasion of Ukraine: February–July 2022," Royal United Services Institute, 30 November 2022, 51, https://rusi.org/explore-our-research/publications/special-resources/preliminary-lessons-conventional-warfighting russias-invasion-ukraine-february-july-2022.

16. Michael Horowitz and Shira Pindyck, "What Is a Military Innovation and Why It Matters," *Journal of Strategic Studies* 46, no. 1 (2023): 97–98.

17. Allan Millett and Williamson Murray, *Military Effectiveness*, vol. 1: *The First World War* (Cambridge: Cambridge University Press, 2010), 2.

18. Risa Brooks and Elizabeth Stanley, eds., *Creating Military Power* (Stanford, CA: Stanford University Press, 2007), 9.

19. David Barno and Nora Bensahel, *Adaptation under Fire: How Militaries Change in Wartime* (New York: Oxford University Press, 2020), 61–63.

20. Barno and Bensahel, 70–71.

21. Williamson Murray, *Military Adaptation in War: With Fear of Change* (Cambridge: Cambridge University Press, 2011), 310.

22. Murray, 310.

23. Meir Finkel, *On Flexibility: Recovery from Technological and Doctrinal Surprise on the Battlefield* (Stanford, CA: Stanford University Press, 2007), 2, 231.

24. Kendrick Kuo, "Dangerous Changes: When Military Innovation Harms Combat Effectiveness," *International Security* 47, no. 2 (Fall 2022): 86.

25. Kuo, 48.

26. *The Economist*, "Why Have Russia's Armed Forces Been So Ineffective in Ukraine?," Graphic Detail, 15 May 2023, https://www.economist.com/graphic-detail/2023/05/15/why-have-russias-armed-forces-been-so-ineffective-in-ukraine.

27. Riley Bailey and Kateryna Stepanenko, "Russian Offensive Campaign Assessment, April 30, 2023," Institute for the Study of War, 30 April 2023, https://www.understandingwar.org/backgrounder/russian-offensive-campaign-assessment-april-30-2023.

28. *What We Need to Learn: Lessons from Twenty Years of Afghanistan Reconstruction* (Washington, DC: Special Inspector for Afghanistan Reconstruction, August 2021), 52–53.

29. John Sopko, "Afghanistan Reconstruction: Lessons from the Long War," *Prism* 8, no. 2 (2019): 37.

30. Robert Scales, "Return to Gettysburg: The Fifth Epochal Shift in the Course of War," *War on the Rocks*, 1 October 2018, https://warontherocks.com/2018/10/return-to-gettysburg-the-fifth-epochal-shift-in-the-course-of-war/.

31. T. X. Hammes, "Game-Changers: Implications of the Russo-Ukraine War for the Future of Ground Warfare," Atlantic Council, 3 April 2023, 13, https://www.atlanticcouncil.org/in-depth-research-reports/issue-brief/gamechangers-implications-of-the-russo-ukraine-war-for-the-future-of-ground-warfare/.

32. Caitlin Kenney, "U.S. Army Delays Doctrine Release to Incorporate Lessons from Ukraine," *Defense One*, 2 June 2022, https://www.defenseone.com/policy/2022/06/us-army-delays-doctrine-release-incorporate-lessons-ukraine/367715/.

33. Ryan, "How Ukraine Is Winning in the Adaptation Battle against Russia."

34. Toshi Yoshihara, *Chinese Lessons from the Pacific War: Implications for PLA Warfighting* (Washington, DC: Center for Strategic and Budgetary Assessments, 2023), i–ii.

35. David Sacks, "What Is China Learning from Russia's War in Ukraine?," *Foreign Affairs*, 16 May 2022, https://www.foreignaffairs.com/articles/china/2022-05-16/what-china-learning-russias-war-ukraine.

36. During my April 2023 visit to Taiwan, the issue of lessons from Ukraine was raised in every discussion with government officials and think tank personnel.

37. Associated Press, "Envoy Says Taiwan Learns from Ukraine War," Voice of America, 21 January 2023.

38. Ben Blanchard, "Taiwan Sees China Taking Lessons from Russia's Ukraine Invasion," Reuters, 24 February 2023, https://www.reuters.com/world/asia-pacific/taiwan-sees-china-taking-lessons-russias-ukraine-invasion-2023-02-24/.

39. Drew Thompson, "Hope on the Horizon: Taiwan's Radical New Defense Concept," *War on the Rocks*, 2 October 2018, https://warontherocks.com/2018/10/hope-on-the-horizon-taiwans-radical-new-defense-concept/; Christopher Ford, *Defending Taiwan: Defense and Deterrence* (Fairfax, VA: National Institute Press, February 2022), 1–4.

40. Nathalie Tocci, "Taiwan Has Learned a Lot from the War in Ukraine—It's Time Europe Caught Up," *Politico Europe*, 20 December 2022, https://www.politico.eu/article/taiwan-lesson-war-ukraine-russia-china-europe-catch-up/; Ben Blanchard, "Analysis: Taiwan Studies Ukraine War for Own Battle Strategy with China," Reuters, 9 March 2023, https://www.reuters.com/business/aerospace-defense/taiwan-studies-ukraine-war-own-battle-strategy-with-china-2022-03-09/.

41. Fan Wang, "Taiwan Extends Mandatory Military Service to One Year," BBC News, 27 December 2022, https://www.bbc.com/news/world-asia-64100577; Derek Grossman, "Ukraine War Is Motivating Taiwan to Better Secure Its Own Future," *RAND Blog*, 13 May 2022, https://www.rand.org/blog/2022/05/ukraine-war-is-motivating-taiwan-to-better-secure-its.html; Kira Rudik, "Taiwan Supports Ukraine and Studies Country's Response to Russian Invasion," Atlantic Council, 15 March 2023, https://www.atlanticcouncil.org/blogs/ukrainealert/taiwan-supports-ukraine-and-studies-countrys-response-to-russian-invasion/.

CHAPTER 9. THE POWER VERTICAL

1. Mark Galeotti, *Putin's Wars: From Chechnya to Ukraine* (Oxford: Bloomsbury, 2022), 69.

2. Graham Turbiville, *Mafia in Uniform: The Criminalization of the Russian Armed Forces* (Fort Leavenworth, KS: Foreign Military Studies Office, 1995), 1.

3. Radio Free Europe / Radio Liberty, "Russia: Defense Minister Outlines Military Reforms," 9 June 1997, https://www.rferl.org/a/1085366.html.

4. Sergey Rogov, *The Evolution of Military Reform in Russia, 2001* (Alexandria: I Corporation, 2001), 14–16.

5. Matthew Bouldin, "The Ivanov Doctrine and Military Reform: Reasserting Stability in Russia," *Journal of Slavic Studies* 17, no. 4 (2004): 619–41.

6. Galeotti, *Putin's Wars*, 112.

7. Michael Kofman, "The Russian Military: A Force in Transition," in Alexander Golts and Michael Kofman, *Russia's Military: Assessment, Strategy, and Threat* (Washington, DC: Center of Global Interests, 2016), 3–8.

8. Olga Oliker, *Russia's Chechen Wars, 1994–2000: Lessons from Urban Combat* (Santa Monica, CA: RAND Corporation, 2001), ix.

9. Timothy Thomas, "The Battle of Grozny: Deadly Classroom for Urban Combat," *Parameters* 29, no. 2 (Summer 1999): 88.

10. Mark Galeotti, *Russia's Wars in Chechnya 1994–2009* (Oxford, U.K.: Osprey, 2014), vii.

11. Mike Eckel, "Two Decades On, Smoldering Questions about the Russian President's Vault to Power," Radio Free Europe, 17 August 2019, https://www.rferl

.org/a/putin-russia-president-1999-chechnya-apartment-bombings/30097551 .html; Rajan Menon and Graham E. Fuller, "Russia's Ruinous Chechen War," *Foreign Affairs* 79, no. 2 (March/April 2000): 32–44.

12. Oliker, *Russia's Chechen Wars, 1994–2000*, xi–xiii.

13. C. Vendil Pallin and F. Westerlund, "Russia's War in Georgia: Lessons and Consequences," *Small Wars and Insurgencies* 20, no. 2 (2009): 410.

14. Pallin and Westerlund, 415.

15. Michael Kofman, "Russian Performance in the Russo-Georgian War Revisited," *War on the Rocks*, 4 September 2018, https://warontherocks.com/2018/09 /russian-performance-in-the-russo-georgian-war-revisited/.

16. Michael Kofman et al., *Lessons from Russia's Operations in Crimea and Eastern Ukraine* (Santa Monica, CA: RAND Corporation, 2017), 20–30.

17. Serhii Plokhy, *The Russo-Ukrainian War* (London: Penguin Books, 2023), 116–17.

18. Lawrence Freedman, "Ukraine and the Art of Limited War," *Survival* 56, no. 6 (2014): 27.

19. Anna Borshchevskaya, "The Russian Way of War in Syria: Threat Perception and Approaches to Counterterrorism," in *Russia's War in Syria: Assessing Russian Military Capabilities and Lessons Learned*, ed. Robert Hamilton, Chris Miller, and Aaron Stein (Philadelphia: Foreign Policy Research Institute, 2020), 15.

20. Hamilton, Miller, and Stein, *Russia's War in Syria*, 128–29.

21. Patrick Kingsley and Ronen Bergman, "Russia Shrinks Forces in Syria, a Factor in Israeli Strategy There," *New York Times*, 19 October 2022, https://www .nytimes.com/2022/10/19/world/middleeast/russia-syria-israel-ukraine.html.

22. Michael Kofman, "An Evaluation of Moscow's Military Strategy and Operational Performance," in Hamilton, Miller, and Stein, *Russia's War in Syria*, 36.

23. Kingsley and Bergman, "Russia Shrinks Forces in Syria."

24. Dima Adamsky, "Russian Campaign in Syria—Change and Continuity in Strategic Culture," *Journal of Strategic Studies* 43, no. 1 (2020): 104–25.

25. Adamsky, 117.

26. Aleksei Ramm, *The Russian Army: Organization and Modernization* (Alexandria: TICNA Corporation, 2001), 45–47.

27. Timothy Thomas, *Russian Combat Capabilities for 2020: Three Developments to Track* (McLean, VA: MITRE Corporation, 2019), 2.

28. Norman Dixon, *On the Psychology of Military Incompetence* (New York: Basic Books, 1976); David Johnson, *Fast Tanks and Heavy Bombers: Innovation in the U.S. Army, 1917–1945* (Ithaca, NY: Cornell University Press, 2003); Dima Adamsky, *The Culture of Military Innovation: The Impact of Cultural Factors on the Revolution in Military Affairs in Russia, the U.S., and Israel* (Stanford,

CA: Stanford Security Studies, 2010); and Frank Hoffman, *Mars Adapting: Military Change during War* (Annapolis: Naval Institute Press, 2021).

29. Meir Finkel, *On Flexibility: Recovery from Technological and Doctrinal Surprise on the Battlefield* (Stanford, CA: Stanford University Press, 2007), 225.

30. Margarita Konaev and Owen J. Daniels, "Agile Ukraine, Lumbering Russia: The Promise and Limits of Military Adaptation," *Foreign Affairs*, 28 March 2023, https://www.foreignaffairs.com/ukraine/russia-ukraine-war-lumbering-agile.

31. Gregory Feifer, *The Great Gamble: The Soviet War in Afghanistan* (New York: HarperCollins, 2009), 119.

32. Michael Kofman et al., *Russian Approaches to Competition* (Washington, DC: Center for Naval Analyses, 2021).

33. Kofman et al., 58.

34. Kofman et al., 61.

35. Daniel Treisman, "Putin Unbound," *Foreign Affairs* 101, no. 3 (May/June 2022): 50–52.

36. Greg Myre, "In Rare Public Speech, the CIA Director Spoke about the Spy Agency's Role in Ukraine," NPR, 14 April 2023, https://www.npr.org/2022/04/14/1092904511/in-rare-public-speech-the-cia-director-spoke-about-the-spy-agencys-role-in-ukrai.

37. Boris Bondarev, "The Sources of Russian Misconduct," *Foreign Affairs* 101, no. 6 (November/December 2022): 38.

38. Andriy Zagorodnyuk, "Ukrainian Victory Shatters Russia's Reputation as a Military Superpower," Atlantic Council, 13 September 2022, https://www.atlanticcouncil.org/blogs/ukrainealert/ukrainian-victory-shatters-russias-reputation-as-a-military-superpower/.

39. Evan Gershkovich et al., "Putin, Isolated and Distrustful, Leans on Handful of Hard-Line Advisers," *Wall Street Journal*, 23 December 2022, https://www.wsj.com/articles/putin-russia-ukraine-war-advisers-11671815184.

40. Bondarev, "The Sources of Russian Misconduct," 39.

41. Adamsky, *The Culture of Military Innovation*, 50.

42. Owen Matthews, *Overreach: The Inside Story of Putin and Russia's War against Ukraine* (London: Mudlark, 2022), 212–13.

43. John Hackett, *The Profession of Arms* (London: Sidgwick and Jackson, 1983), 158.

44. Galeotti, *Putin's Wars*, 158.

45. Michael Kofman and Rob Lee, "Not Built for Purpose: The Russian Military's Fated Force Design," *War on the Rocks*, 2 June 2022, https://warontherocks.com/2022/06/not-built-for-purpose-the-russian-militarys-ill-fated-force-design/.

46. Kofman and Lee.

47. Adamsky, *The Culture of Military Innovation*, 50.

48. Adamsky, "Russian Campaign in Syria," 109–11.

49. Mykhaylo Zabrodskyi et al., "Preliminary Lessons in Conventional Warfighting from Russia's Invasion of Ukraine: February–July 2022," Royal United Services Institute, 30 November 2022, 46, https://rusi.org/explore-our-research /publications/special-resources/preliminary-lessons-conventional-warfighting -russias-invasion-ukraine-february-july-2022.

50. Feifer, *The Great Gamble*, 180.

51. Nathan Hodge, "In Russia's Military, a Culture of Brutality Runs Deep," CNN, 4 April 2022, https://edition.cnn.com/2022/04/04/europe/russia-military-culture -brutality-intl/index.html.

52. Diederik Lohman, *The Wrongs of Passage: Inhuman and Degrading Treatment of New Recruits in the Russian Armed Forces* (New York: Human Rights Watch, 2004), 2.

53. Steven Myers, "Hazing Trial Bares Dark Side of Russia's Military," *New York Times*, 13 August 2006, https://www.nytimes.com/2006/08/13/world/europe /13hazing.html.

54. Zagorodnyuk, "Ukrainian Victory Shatters Russia's Reputation as a Military Superpower."

55. Zabrodskyi et al., "Preliminary Lessons in Conventional Warfighting," 49.

56. Zabrodskyi et al., 51.

57. Zabrodskyi et al., 44.

CHAPTER 10. DYSFUNCTIONAL WARFARE

1. Rob Johnson, "Dysfunctional Warfare: The Russian Invasion of Ukraine," *Parameters* 52, no. 2 (2022): 19.

2. Williamson Murray, *Military Adaptation in War: With Fear of Change* (Cambridge: Cambridge University Press, 2011), 318.

3. Barry Posen, "Russia's Rebound," *Foreign Affairs*, 4 January 2023, https://www .foreignaffairs.com/ukraine/russia-rebound-moscow-recovered-military -setbacks.

4. As Paul Kennedy notes, "A large proportion of the Warsaw Pact total [manpower] consists of Category III units and Red Army reserve units." Paul Kennedy, *The Rise and Fall of the Great Powers: Economic Change and Military Conflict from 1500 to 2000* (New York: Random House, 1987), 508–9.

5. Ioannis-Dionysios Salavrakos, "Russian versus Soviet Military Mobilization in World Wars I and II: A Reassessment," *Saudi Journal of Humanities and Social Sciences* 2, no. 2 (February 2017): 155–68.

6. Ellen Jones, "Social Change and Civil-Military Relations," in *Soldiers and the Soviet State: Civil-Military Relations from Brezhnev to Gorbachev*, ed. Timothy

Colton and Thane Gustafson (Princeton, NJ: Princeton University Press, 2014), 239–40.

7. Lester Grau and Charles Bartles, *The Russian Way of War: Force Structure, Tactics and Modernisation of Russian Ground Forces* (Fort Leavenworth, KS: Foreign Military Studies Office, 2017), 3.

8. Sam Cranny-Evans, "Understanding Russia's Mobilisation," Royal United Services Institute, 28 September 2022, https://rusi.org/explore-our-research/publications/commentary/understanding-russias-mobilisation; Grau and Bartles, *The Russian Way of War*, 15.

9. Chuck Bartles, "Russia's BARS Reserve System Takes Shape," *OE Watch*, Foreign Military Studies Office, 1 April 2022, https://community.apan.org/wg/tradoc-g2/fmso/m/oe-watch-articles-2-singular-format/415158.

10. Vladimir Putin, "Address by the President of the Russian Federation," President of Russia, 21 September 2022, http://en.kremlin.ru/events/president/news/69390; Merlyn Thomas, "Ukraine War: Putin Orders Partial Mobilisation after Facing Setbacks," BBC News, 21 September 2022, https://www.bbc.com/news/world-europe-62984985.

11. Mark Cancian, "What Does Russia's 'Partial Mobilization' Mean?," Center for Strategic and International Studies, 26 September 2022, https://www.csis.org/analysis/what-does-russias-partial-mobilization-mean.

12. Reuters, "After Weeks of Chaos, Russia Says Partial Mobilisation Is Complete," 1 November 2022, https://www.reuters.com/world/europe/russia-completes-partial-mobilisation-defence-ministry-2022-10-31/.

13. Todd Prince, "No Game Changer: Russian Mobilization May Slow, Not Stop, Ukrainian Offensive," Radio Free Europe / Radio Liberty, 22 September 2022, https://www.rferl.org/a/russia-mobilization-ukraine-offensive-analysis/32046211.html; Zoya Sheftalovich, "Putin Claims 'Partial Mobilization' to End in 2 Weeks, with 222,000 Reservists Called Up So Far," *Politico Europe*, 14 October 2022, https://www.politico.eu/article/putin-claims-partial-mobilization-to-end-in-2-weeks-russia-ukraine-war/.

14. Kateryna Stepanenko et al., "Russian Offensive Campaign Assessment," Institute for the Study of War, 13 April 2023, https://www.understandingwar.org/sites/default/files/Russian%20Offensive%20Campaign%20Assessment%2C%20April%2013%2C%202023%20PDF.pdf.

15. Emmanuel Grynszpan, "Russia's Mobilized Soldiers Speak Out: 'We Were Thrown on to the Frontline with No Support,'" *Le Monde*, 10 November 2022, https://www.lemonde.fr/en/international/article/2022/11/10/russia-s-mobilized-soldiers-speak-we-were-thrown-onto-the-frontline-with-no-support_6003764_4.html.

16. Julia Shapero, "Russia Lays Out Plans to Boost Size of Military to 1.5 Million," *The Hill*, 17 January 2023, https://thehill.com/policy/international/3816314 -russia-lays-out-plans-to-boost-size-of-military-to-1-5-million/; Brendan Cole, "Russia Plans Military Expansion as Putin Looks to Turn Tide on War—ISW," *Newsweek*, 18 January 2023, https://www.newsweek.com/putin -russia-ukraine-isw-expansion-war-tide-1774606.

17. Dara Massicot, "Russian Military Operations in Ukraine in 2022 and the Year Ahead," testimony presented before the U.S. Senate Committee on Armed Services on 28 February 2023, https://www.rand.org/content/dam/rand/pubs /testimonies/CTA2600/CTA2646-1/RAND_CTA2646-1.pdf.

18. Dara Massicot, "The Russian Military's Looming Personnel Crises of Retention and Veteran Mental Health," *RAND Blog*, 1 June 2023, https://www.rand.org /pubs/commentary/2023/06/the-russian-militarys-looming-personnel-crises -of-retention.html.

19. Jack Detsch and Amy Mackinnon, "Russia's New Top Commander in Ukraine Is 'Willing to Sell His Soul,'" *Foreign Policy*, 12 April 2022, https://foreignpolicy .com/2022/04/12/russia-new-top-commander-dvornikov-ukraine/.

20. Lawrence Freedman quoted in Chauncey Devega, "Putin's Massive Mistake: Lawrence Freedman on Ukraine and the Lessons of History," *Salon*, 21 November 2022, https://www.salon.com/2022/11/21/putins-massive-mistake-lawrence freedman-on-ukraine-and-the-lessons-of-history/.

21. Liam Jones, "Russians Demand Putin's Commanders Be Punished over Losses in New Year's Eve Attack," *The Independent*, 3 January 2023, https://www .independent.co.uk/news/world/europe/russia-ukraine-makiivka-donetsk -putin-b2255092.html.

22. British Ministry of Defence, *UK Joint Operations Doctrine*, JDP 01 (Swindon: Development, Concepts and Doctrine Centre, 2014), 39.

23. B. A. Friedman, *On Operations: Operational Art and Military Disciplines* (Annapolis: Naval Institute Press, 2021), 5.

24. Allan Millett and Williamson Murray, *Military Effectiveness*, vol. 1: *The First World War* (Cambridge: Cambridge University Press, 2010), 12.

25. Vladimir Putin, "Address by the President of the Russian Federation," President of Russia, 24 February 2022, http://en.kremlin.ru/events/president/news/67843.

26. As a 2022 RUSI study notes, "Russia planned to invade Ukraine over a 10-day period and thereafter occupy the country to enable annexation by August 2022." Mykhaylo Zabrodskyi et al., "Preliminary Lessons in Conventional Warfighting from Russia's Invasion of Ukraine: February–July 2022," Royal United Services Institute, 30 November 2022, 11, https://rusi.org/explore-our-research /publications/special-resources/preliminary-lessons-conventional-warfighting -russias-invasion-ukraine-february-july-2022.

27. Seth Jones, "Russia's Ill-Fated Invasion of Ukraine: Lessons in Modern Warfare," Center for Strategic and International Studies, 1 June 2022, 2, https://www.csis.org/analysis/russias-ill-fated-invasion-ukraine-lessons-modern-warfare.

28. Mick Ryan, "How Ukraine Is Winning in the Adaptation Battle against Russia," *Engelsberg Ideas*, 24 August 2022, https://engelsbergideas.com/essays/how-ukraine-is-winning-in-the-adaptation-battle-against-russia/.

29. Maria Murru and Oleksandr Stashevskyi, "Russia Taking 'Operational Pause' in Ukraine, Analysts Say," AP News, 8 July 2022, https://apnews.com/article/russia-ukraine-government-and-politics-22a6a809761fd4a6404750a9b5b2fbd1.

30. Ironically, the focus on artillery-led operations also drove counter-adaptation activity in the Ukrainian armed forces. Not only did the Russian artillery onslaught result in additional foreign donations of artillery and munitions; it also forced the Ukrainians to develop networked digital systems for faster and more efficient use of artillery. And it drove wider use of UAVs for artillery spotting, more dispersed, faster-moving tactics, and the better use of electronic warfare jamming to degrade Russian artillery radio networks, and the application of more precision weapons by the Ukrainians instead of the more traditional massed use of artillery. This would have a payoff down the track for Ukraine as both sides began to have challenges accessing sufficient artillery ammunition.

31. Joe Inwood, "Ukraine War: What Severodonetsk's Fall Means for the Conflict," BBC News, 26 June 2022, https://www.bbc.com/news/world-europe-61945914.

32. Inwood.

33. Seth Jones, Alexander Palmer, and Joseph S. Bermudez Jr., *Ukraine's Offensive Operations: Shifting the Offense-Defense Balance* (Washington, DC: Center for Strategic and International Studies, 2023), 1.

34. Mick Ryan, "Breach and Breakthrough," *Futura Doctrina*, Substack, 20 July 2023, https://mickryan.substack.com/p/breach-and-breakthrough.

35. Ryan, "Breach and Breakthrough."

36. Grau and Bartles, *The Russian Way of War*, 60–102.

37. Michael Kofman and Rob Lee, "Ukraine Struggles to Scale Offensive Operations," *War on the Rocks* podcast, 20 July 2023, https://warontherocks.com/2023/07/ukraine-struggles-to-scale-offensive-combat-operations/.

38. Brad Martin, "Will Logistics Be Russia's Undoing in Ukraine?," *The Hill*, 10 February 2023, https://thehill.com/opinion/international/3852532-will-logistics-be-russias-undoing-in-ukraine/.

39. BBC News, "Ukraine: Why Has Russia's 64km Convoy near Kyiv Stopped Moving?," BBC News, 3 March 2022, https://www.bbc.com/news/world-europe-60596629.

40. In the Russian armed forces, logistics is referred to as Military Technical Support, but they generally have very similar functions to their Western counterparts: e.g.,

they provide weapons, fuel, food, and clothing; repair and recover equipment; and organize the transport of military items. Grau and Bartles, *The Russian Way of War*, 322.

41. Dimitri N. Filippovych, "The Logistics System of the Soviet and Warsaw Pact Armed Forces in the 1950s and 1960s," in *Blueprints for Battle: Planning for War in Central Europe, 1948–1968*, ed. Jan Hoffenaar and Dieter Krüger (Lexington: University Press of Kentucky, 2012), 109.

42. Per Skoglund, Tore Listou, and Thomas Ekström, "Russian Logistics in the Ukrainian War: Can Operational Failures Be Attributed to Logistics?," *Scandinavian Journal of Military Studies* 5, no. 1 (2022): 100–110.

43. Filippovych, "The Logistics System of the Soviet and Warsaw Pact Armed Forces in the 1950s and 1960s," 115.

44. Alex Vershinin, "Feeding the Bear: A Closer Look at Russian Military Logistics and the Fait Accompli," *War on the Rocks*, 23 November 2021, https://warontherocks.com/2021/11/feeding-the-bear-a-closer-look-at-russian-army-logistics/.

45. Grau and Bartles, *The Russian Way of War*, 324.

46. Fredrik Westerlund and Susanne Oxenstierna, eds., *Russian Military Capability in a Ten-Year Perspective—2019* (Stockholm: Swedish Ministry of Defence, 2019), 26.

47. Vershinin, "Feeding the Bear."

48. Michael Kofman and Rob Lee have written: "As a tiered-readiness force, Russian ground formations (including the airborne and naval infantry) were staffed somewhere between 70 to 90 percent. Consequently, a 3,500 sized brigade might only have 2,500 men at peacetime. When accounting for 30 percent conscripts likely to be in the unit, this meant that no more than 1,700 would be considered deployable. . . . The Russian military especially lacks sufficient light infantry forces for many of the situations it has faced in Ukraine." Michael Kofman and Rob Lee, "Not Built for Purpose: The Russian Military's Fated Force Design," *War on the Rocks*, 2 June 2022, https://warontherocks.com/2022/06/not-built-for-purpose-the-russian-militarys-ill-fated-force-design/.

49. Skoglund, Listou, and Ekström, "Russian Logistics in the Ukrainian War," 107.

50. Writing in the lead-up to the war, Alex Vershinin offered a prescient assessment on Russian capabilities: "The Russian army will be hard-pressed to conduct a ground offensive of more than 90 miles beyond the borders of the former Soviet Union without a logistics pause. It . . . means that Russia is more likely to seize small parts of enemy territory under its logistically sustainable range of 90 miles rather than a major invasion as part of a fait accompli strategy. The Russian government has built armed forces highly capable of fighting on home soil or near its frontier and striking deep with long-range fires. However, they

are not capable of a sustained ground offensive far beyond Russian railroads without a major logistical halt or a massive mobilization of reserves." Alex Vershinin, "Feeding the Bear: A Closer Look at Russian Military Logistics and the Fait Accompli," *War on the Rocks*, 23 November 2021. https://warontherocks.com/2021/11/feeding-the-bear-a-closer-look-at-russian-army-logistics/.

51. Jack Watling and Nick Reynolds, "Meatgrinder: Russian Tactics in the Second Year of Its Invasion of Ukraine," Royal United Services Institute, 19 May 2023, 11–14, https://rusi.org/explore-our-research/publications/special-resources/meatgrinder-russian-tactics-second-year-its-invasion-ukraine.

52. Staff writer, "Russian Military Forces Dazzle after a Decade of Reform," *The Economist*, 2 November 2020.

CHAPTER II. NOT IDIOTS

Note: Ukrainian General Zaluzhnyi was quoted in a December 2022 article, when discussing the Russians, as saying, "They are not idiots." *The Economist*, "Ukraine's Top Soldier Runs a Different Kind of Army from Russia's," 15 December 2022.

1. B. A. Friedman, *On Tactics: A Theory of Victory in Battle* (Annapolis: Naval Institute Press, 2017), 16–17.

2. Friedman, 22.

3. Mick Ryan, *War Transformed: The Future of Twenty-First-Century Great Power Competition and Conflict* (Annapolis: Naval Institute Press, 2022), 148–49.

4. Mick Ryan, "How Ukraine Is Winning in the Adaptation Battle against Russia," *Engelsberg Ideas*, 24 August 2022, https://engelsbergideas.com/essays/how-ukraine-is-winning-in-the-adaptation-battle-against-russia/.

5. William Sayers, "The Severskii Donets River Crossing Operation," *Mystics and Statistics*, Dupuy Institute, 9 June 2022, http://www.dupuyinstitute.org/blog/2022/06/09/the-severskii-donets-river-crossing-operation/.

6. Ryan, "How Ukraine Is Winning in the Adaptation Battle against Russia."

7. Interview with Defence Minister Reznikov by Dmytro Komarov, Year. Off-screen. Minister. Special project of Dmytro Komarov, part 2, 12 May 2023, https://www.youtube.com/watch?v=Kmpy9B7CCH8.

8. Frederick Kagan, "Russian Offensive Campaign Assessment," Institute for the Study of War, 13 November 2022, https://www.understandingwar.org/backgrounder/russian-offensive-campaign-assessment-november-13.

9. Sergio Miller, "Russia's Withdrawal from Kherson," *Wavell Room*, 6 January 2023, https://wavellroom.com/2023/01/06/russias-withdrawal-from-kherson/.

10. Zoya Sheftalovich, "From Jail Cell to Frontline: Russia Turns to Convicts to Help Flailing War Effort," *Politico Europe*, 13 October 2022, https://www.politico.eu/article/ukraine-russia-war-from-jail-cell-to-frontline-moscow-turns-to-convicts-to-help-flailing-war-effort/.

11. *The Economist*, "Russia's Army Is Learning on the Battlefield," 21 May 2023, https://www.economist.com/europe/2023/05/21/russias-army-is-learning-on-the-battlefield

12. Olivia Yanchik, "Human Wave Tactics Are Demoralizing the Russian Army in Ukraine," Atlantic Council, 8 April 2023, https://www.atlanticcouncil.org/blogs/ukrainealert/human-wave-tactics-are-demoralizing-the-russian-army-in-ukraine/.

13. Allan Millett and Williamson Murray, *Military Effectiveness*, vol. 1: *The First World War* (Cambridge: Cambridge University Press, 2010), 51, 101; Trevor Dupuy, *The Evolution of Weapons and Warfare* (New York: Da Capo, 1984), 225–29.

14. John Terraine, *White Heat: The New Warfare, 1914–1918* (London: Book Club Associates, 1982), 286.

15. Bruce Gudmundsson, *Stormtroop Tactics: Innovation in the German Army, 1914–1918* (Westport, CT: Praeger, 1989), 178.

16. Mike Eckel, "What Happened in Vuhledar? A Battle Points to Major Russian Military Problems," Radio Free Europe / Radio Liberty, 17 February 2023, https://www.rferl.org/a/ukraine-russia-battle-vuhledar/32276547.html; Andrew Kramer, "In an Epic Battle of Tanks, Russia Was Routed, Repeating Earlier Mistakes," *New York Times*, 1 March 2023, https://www.nytimes.com/2023/03/01/world/europe/ukraine-russia-tanks.html.

17. Jack Watling and Nick Reynolds, "Meatgrinder: Russian Tactics in the Second Year of Its Invasion of Ukraine," Royal United Services Institute, 19 May 2023, 15–16, https://rusi.org/explore-our-research/publications/special-resources/meatgrinder-russian-tactics-second-year-its-invasion-ukraine.

18. Mykhaylo Zabrodskyi et al., "Preliminary Lessons in Conventional Warfighting from Russia's Invasion of Ukraine: February–July 2022," Royal United Services Institute, 30 November 2022, 38, https://rusi.org/explore-our-research/publications/special-resources/preliminary-lessons-conventional-warfighting-russias-invasion-ukraine-february-july-2022.

19. Thomas Gibbons-Neff, Julian E. Barnes, and Natalia Yermak, "Russia, Learning From Costly Mistakes, Shifts Battlefield Tactics," *New York Times*, 17 June 2023, https://www.nytimes.com/2023/06/17/world/europe/russia-ukraine-war-tactics.html.

20. Samuel Bendett and Jeffrey Edmonds, *Russia's Use of Uncrewed Systems in Ukraine* (Washington, DC: Center for Naval Analyses, 2023), 1.

21. Elisabeth Gosselin-Malo, "Loitering Munitions in Ukraine: Not Game-Changing, but Headache-Inducing," *Defence Technology Magazine*, 26

May 2022, https://www.shephardmedia.com/news/uv-online/loitering
-munitions-in-ukraine-not-game-changing-but-headache-inducing/.

22. Tim Fish, "Loitering with Intent," *Asian Military Review*, 26 December 2022, https://www.asianmilitaryreview.com/2022/12/loitering-with-intent/.

23. Lauren Kahn, "Can Iranian Drones Turn Russia's Fortunes in the Ukraine War?," *Council on Foreign Relations*, 26 October 2022, https://www.cfr.org/in -brief/can-iranian-drones-turn-russias-fortunes-ukraine-war.

24. Jeffrey A. Edmonds and Samuel Bendett, *Russia's Use of Uncrewed Systems in Ukraine* (Washington, DC: Center for Naval Analyses, May 2023), 20–22, 31–34.

25. Samuel Bendett, "Bureaucrat's Gambit: Why Is Dmitry Rogozin Sending Russian Uncrewed Ground Vehicles to Ukraine—and Does It Matter?," Modern War Institute, 10 February 2023, https://mwi.usma.edu/bureaucrats-gambit-why-is -dmitry-rogozin-sending-russian-uncrewed-ground-vehicles-to-ukraine-and -does-it-matter/.

26. The video of the use of the remotely operated, explosive-packed tank can be found at Calibre Obscura (@CalibreObscura), "#Ukraine The Russian Army sent a T-54/55 VBIED filled with 6 tonnes of TNT at AFU lines near Marinka, Donetsk Oblast," Twitter, 1:16 p.m., 18 June 2023, https://twitter.com /CalibreObscura/status/1670510694838546436?s=20.

27. This has included the FGM-148 Javelin, the Saab Bofors Dynamics NLAW, the MILAN lightweight antivehicle missile, the U.S. M72 Light Anti-Vehicle Weapon (and its Soviet copy, the RPG-18), Instala C-90 antitank weapons, Panzerfaust 3 antitank weapons, the disposable AT-4 antitank launcher, the Carl Gustav recoilless rifle, French fifth-generation Akeron MP networked antitank weapons, the RPG-75.

28. Thomas Newdick, "Russia's Increasingly Bizarre 'Artisanal' Armor Looks More Mad Max than Major Power," *War Zone*, 6 April 2022, https://www.thedrive.com /the-war-zone/45108/russias-increasingly-bizarre-artisanal-armor-looks-more -mad-max-than-major-power.

29. Umair Mirza, *Encyclopedia of German Tanks of World War Two: A Complete Illustrated Directory of German Battle Tanks, Armoured Cars, Self-Propelled Guns and Semi-Tracked Vehicles* (London: Arms and Armour, 2000), 96–99; Alex Chadwick, "Soldiers Fabricating Armor for Own Vehicles in Iraq," NPR, 9 December 2004. https://www.npr.org/2004/12/09/4210814/soldiers-fabricating -armor-for-own-vehicles-in-iraq; Joel Rayburn and Frank Sobchak, eds., *The U.S. Army in the Iraq War*, vol. 1 (Carlisle, PA: Strategic Studies Institute and U.S. Army War College Press, 2019); *Slat Armour*, GlobalSecurity.org, accessed 15 April 2022, https://www.globalsecurity.org/military/intro/armor-slat.htm;

Sergyi Way, "Bar Armour," Army Guide, 29 January 2013, http://www.army-guide.com/eng/article/article_2597.html.

30. Martha Raddatz and Mike Cerre, "Soldiers Must Rely on 'Hillbilly Armor' for Protection," ABC News, 8 December 2004, https://abcnews.go.com/WNT/story?id=312959&page=1.

31. By the end of 2023, both Russian and Ukrainian armored vehicles were using various designs for these cages. Additionally, the towed and self-propelled artillery on both sides were using protective cages.

32. Howard Altman, "Ukraine Situation Report: Russia Adding 'Cope Cages' to TOS-1A," *The Warzone*, 10 April 2023, https://www.thedrive.com/the-war-zone/ukraine-situation-report-russia-adding-cope-cages-to-tos-1a; Robert Tollast, "How Javelin Missiles Penetrate Russian Tank Cage Armor," *N World*, 15 April 2023, https://www.thenationalnews.com/world/2022/04/07/how-javelin-missiles-penetrate-russian-tank-cage-armour/; "Russian Tanks in Ukraine Are Sprouting Cages," *The Economist*, 19 March 2022, https://www.economist.com/science-and-technology/russian-tanks-in-ukraine-are-sprouting-cages/21808191; EurAsian Times Desk, "Russia Pounds Ukrainian Positions with TOS-1 'Solntsepyok' Flamethrowers That Were Seen Installed with Cage Armor," *EurAsian Times*, 14 April 2023, https://eurasiantimes.com/russia-pounds-ukrainian-positions-with-tos-1-solntsepyok-flamethrowers/; "The Best Defence Is a Good Offense," *The Economist*, 2 April 2022, 72–73.

33. Thomas Harding, "Captured Modern Russian Tank Allows West to Unlock Defence Systems," *N World*, 7 October 2022, https://www.thenationalnews.com/world/europe/2022/10/07/captured-modern-russian-tank-allows-west-to-unlock-defence-systems/.

34. Watling and Reynolds, "Meatgrinder."

35. Milford Beagle, Jason Slider, and Matthew Arrol, "The Graveyard of Command Posts: What Chornobaivka Should Teach Us about Command and Control in Large-Scale Combat Operations," *Military Review*, May–June 2023, 11.

36. Watling and Reynolds, "Meatgrinder," 24.

37. Justin Bronk, Nick Reynolds, and Jack Watling, "The Russian Air War and Ukrainian Requirements for Air Defence," Royal United Services Institute, 7 November 2022, 9–10, https://rusi.org/explore-our-research/publications/special-resources/russian-air-war-and-ukrainian-requirements-air-defence.

38. Justin Bronk, "The Mysterious Case of the Missing Russian Air Force," *Royal United Service Institute*, 28 February 2022, https://rusi.org/explore-our-research/publications/commentary/mysterious-case-missing-russian-air-force.

39. Robert Dalsjö, Michael Jonsson, and Johan Norberg, "A Brutal Examination: Russian Military Capability in Light of the Ukraine War," *Survival* 64, no. 3 (2022): 7–28.

40. Phillips Payson O'Brien and Edward Stringer, "The Overlooked Reason Russia's Invasion Is Floundering," *The Atlantic*, 10 May 2022, https://www.theatlantic .com/ideas/archive/2022/05/russian-military-air-force-failure-ukraine/629803/.

41. Bronk, Reynolds, and Watling, *The Russian Air War and Ukrainian Requirements for Air Defence*, 1.

42. U.K. Ministry of Defence, *Defence Intelligence Update on Ukraine 22 May 2023*, https://twitter.com/DefenceHQ/status/1660524606682198017?s=20.

43. R. B. Stratton, *The Development of Soviet Air Defense Doctrine and Practice* (Dunn Loring, VA: Historical Evaluation and Research Organization, 1981), 147.

44. John Lepingwell, "Soviet Strategic Air Defense and the Stealth Challenge," *International Security* 14, no. 2 (Fall 1989): 64.

45. Watling and Reynolds, "Meatgrinder," 20.

46. Watling and Reynolds, 20.

47. "UAV Interception System Was Shown at Army-2016 Forum," *Russian Aviation*, 13 September 2016. https://www.ruaviation.com/news/2016/9/13/6857/?h.

48. Adam Lowther and Mahube Siddiki, "Combat Drones in Ukraine," *Air and Space Operations Review* 1, no. 4 (Winter 2022): 12–13.

49. Lowther and Siddiki, 12–13.

50. Philip Butterworth-Hayes, "Russia and Ukraine Rapidly Accelerate C-UAS Capabilities in Face of New Drone Threats," *Unmanned Airspace*, 5 March 2023, https://www.unmannedairspace.info/counter-uas-systems-and-policies /russia-and-ukraine-rapidly-accelerate-c-uas-capabilities-in-face-of-new-drone -threats/; "Russia's Latest Anti-drone System Passes Testing—Tech Firm," *TASS*, 17 March 2023, https://tass.com/defense/1589877.

51. Alex Marquardt, Natasha Bertrand, and Zachary Cohen, "Russia's Jamming of US-Provided Rocket Systems Complicates Ukraine's War Effort," CNN, 6 May 2023, https://edition.cnn.com/2023/05/05/politics/russia-jamming -himars-rockets-ukraine/index.html#:~:text=Russia%20has%20been%20 thwarting%20US,on%20the%20matter%20told%20CNN; Shashnk Joshi, "The Latest in the Battle of Jamming with Electronic Beams," *The Economist*, 3 July 2023, https://www.economist.com/special-report/2023/07/03/the -latest-in-the-battle-of-jamming-with-electronic-beams.

52. Marc Champion, "Russia Is Adapting Arms and Tactics ahead of Ukraine Offensive," *Japan Times*, 19 May 2023, https://www.japantimes.co.jp/news/2023/05/19 /world/russia-tactics-ahead-ukraine-offensive/.

53. John Jessup, "The Soviet Armed Forces in the Great Patriotic War, 1941–5," in *Military Effectiveness*, vol. 3: *The Second World War*, ed. Allan Millett and Williamson Murray (Cambridge: Cambridge University Press, 2010), 273.

CHAPTER 12. UKRAINIAN POST-2014 REFORMS

1. Michael Howard, "The Use and Abuse of Military History," *RUSI Journal* 138, no. 1 (1993): 29.

2. Williamson Murray, *Military Adaptation in War: With Fear of Change* (Cambridge: Cambridge University Press, 2011), 1.

3. Andrew Krepinevich, *The Military-Technical Revolution: A Preliminary Assessment* (Washington, DC: Center for Strategic and Budgetary Assessments, 2002), 3–7.

4. Barry Watts and Williamson Murray, "Military Innovation in Peacetime," in *Military Innovation in the Interwar Period*, ed. Williamson Murray and Allan Millett (Cambridge: Cambridge University Press, 1998), 414.

5. Murray, *Military Adaptation in War*, 5.

6. Watts and Murray, "Military Innovation in Peacetime," 415.

7. The former Soviet Black Sea Fleet was also split between Russia, Ukraine, and Georgia. International Institute for Strategic Studies, *The Military Balance 1992–1993* (London: International Institute for Strategic Studies, 1992), 86–87.

8. Ukraine's decision to surrender the nuclear weapons and delivery vehicles it possessed, in 1994, was controversial domestically at the time and has remained controversial since, particularly in the wake of the 2014 and 2022 Russian invasions. Polina Sinovets, ed., *Ukraine's Nuclear History: A Non-Proliferation Perspective* (Odesa: Odessa I. I. Mechnikov National University, 2022), vi.

9. "Memorandum on Security Assurances in Connection with Ukraine's Accession to the Treaty on the Non-Proliferation of Nuclear Weapons," United Nations, 5 December 1994, https://treaties.un.org/Pages/showDetails .aspx?objid=0800000280401fbb.

10. Mariana Budjeryn and Matthew Bunn, *Budapest Memorandum at 25: Between Past and Future* (Cambridge, MA: Belfer School for Science and International Affairs, 2020), 1.

11. Denys Kiryukhin, "The Ukrainian Military: From Degradation to Renewal," Foreign Policy Research Institute, 17 August 2018, https://www.fpri.org /article/2018/08/the-ukrainian-military-from-degradation-to-renewal/.

12. Muzhenko is quoted in Valeriy Akimenko, "Ukraine's Toughest Fight: The Challenge of Military Reform," *Carnegie Endowment for International Peace*, 22 February 2018, https://carnegieendowment.org/2018/02/22 /ukraine-s-toughest-fight-challenge-of-military-reform-pub-75609.

13. Canadian Government, Operation Unifier, https://www.canada.ca/en /department-national-defence/services/operations/military-operations/current- operations/operation-unifier.html.

14. Olga Oliker et al., *Security Sector Reform in Ukraine* (Santa Monica, CA: RAND Corporation, 2016), ix–xv.

15. Andrew Bowen, *Ukrainian Armed Forces*, Congressional Research Service, 26 January 2022, https://crsreports.congress.gov/product/pdf/IF/IF11862.

16. The 2020 National Security Strategy is available, in Ukrainian, at https://www .president.gov.ua/documents/3922020-3503.

17. Ihor Kabanenko, "Ukraine's New National Security Strategy: A Wide Scope with Foggy Implementation Mechanisms," *Eurasia Daily Monitor*, Jamestown Foundation, 24 September 2020, https://jamestown.org/program/ukraines -new-national-security-strategy-a-wide-scope-with-foggy-implementation -mechanisms/.

18. Public information on the State Program for Development of the Armed Forces is available at http://www.mil.gov.ua/content/oboron_plans/2017-07-31 _National-program-2020_en.pdf.

19. Natalia Spinu, *Ukraine Cybersecurity: Governance Assessment* (Geneva: Geneva Centre for Security Sector Governance, 2020), 7–11.

20. Brad Smith, "Defending Ukraine: Early Lessons from the Cyber War," Microsoft, 22 June 2022, 5, https://query.prod.cms.rt.microsoft.com/cms/api/am/binary /RE50KOK.

21. Nicolò Fasola and Alyssa J. Wood, "Reforming Ukraine's Security Sector," *Survival* 63, no. 2 (2021): 47–48.

22. International Institute for Strategic Studies, *The Military Balance 2015* (London: International Institute for Strategic Studies, 2015), 173.

23. Ministry of Defence of Ukraine, *White Book 2021: Defence Policy of Ukraine* (Kyiv: Ministry of Defence, 2022), 27.

24. In 2016, the Ukrainian military held nearly nine hundred exercises, including those with international participation. For comparison, in 2009, zero full-scale multinational military exercises in the territory of Ukraine were conducted due to lack of funding. Kiryukhin, "The Ukrainian Military."

25. Oleksii Chaharnyi, "Zelenskyy Increases Number of Armed Forces, Signs Laws on National Resistance," *Kyiv Post*, 29 July 2021, https://www.kyivpost.com /ukraine-politics/zelensky-increases-the-number-of-the-armed-forces-signs -laws-on-national-resistance.html.

26. Maciej Zaniewicz, "Ukraine's New Military Security Strategy," *Bulletin*, Polish Institute of International Affairs, 5 May 2021, 1.

27. Zaniewicz, 1.

28. Ministry of Defence of Ukraine, *White Book 2021*, 28.

29. Hanna Shelest, "Defend. Resist. Repeat: Ukraine's Lessons for European Defence," *Policy Brief*, European Council on Foreign Relations, November 2022, 2, https://ecfr.eu/wp-content/uploads/2022/11/Defend.-Resist.-Repeat -Ukraines-lessons-for-European-defence.pdf.

30. Shelest.

31. James Lewis, *Cyber War and Ukraine* (Washington, DC: Center for Strategic and International Studies, 2022), 7–8; Grace Mueller et al., *Cyber Operations during the Russo-Ukrainian War: From Strange Patterns to Alternative Futures* (Washington, DC: Center for Strategic and International Studies, July 2023).

CHAPTER 13. THE ASYMMETRIC HORIZON

1. Volodymyr Horbulin, *How to Beat Russia in the War of the Future* (Kyiv: Bright Books, 2021), 63–64.
2. Allan Millett and Williamson Murray, *Military Effectiveness*, vol. 1: *The First World War* (Cambridge: Cambridge University Press, 2010), 7.
3. Eliot Cohen, *The Big Stick: The Limits of Soft Power and the Necessity of Military Force* (New York: Basic Books, 2016), 226.
4. Stephen Biddle, "Explaining Military Outcomes," in *Creating Military Power: The Sources of Military Effectiveness*, ed. Risa Brooks and Elizabeth Stanley (Stanford, CA: Stanford University Press, 2007), 207.
5. Jack Detsh, "How Ukraine Learned to Fight," *Foreign Policy*, 1 March 2023, https://foreignpolicy.com/2023/03/01/how-ukraine-learned-to-fight/.
6. Margarita Konaev and Owen Daniels, "Agile Ukraine, Lumbering Russia: The Promise and Limits of Military Adaptation," *Foreign Affairs*, 28 March 2023, https://www.foreignaffairs.com/ukraine/russia-ukraine-war-lumbering-agile.
7. Christina Arabia, Andrew Bowen, and Cory Welt, *U.S. Security Assistance to Ukraine* (Washington, DC: Congressional Research Service, 27 February 2023), 1.
8. White House, "Joint Statement on the U.S.-Ukraine Strategic Partnership," 1 September 2021, https://www.whitehouse.gov/briefing-room/statements-releases/2021/09/01/joint-statement-on-the-u-s-ukraine-strategic-partnership/.
9. At the beginning of the Russian invasion in February 2022, the Ukrainian armed forces possessed over 800 main battle tanks, over 1,100 infantry fighting vehicles, and 620 armored personnel carriers. International Institute for Strategic Studies, *The Military Balance 2021* (London: International Institute for Strategic Studies, 2021), 209–11.
10. International Institute for Strategic Studies, *The Military Balance 2021*, 168.
11. Jahara Matisek, Will Reno, and Sam Rosenberg, "The Good, the Bad and the Ugly: Assessing a Year of Military Aid to Ukraine," Royal United Services Institute, 22 February 2023, https://www.rusi.org/explore-our-research/publications/commentary/good-bad-and-ugly-assessing-year-military-aid-ukraine; Richard Thomas, "Operation Interflex: Ukrainian Recruits Prepare for War," *Army Technology*, 11 November 2022, https://www.army-technology.com/features/operation-interflex-ukrainian-recruits-prepare-for-war/.

12. Claire Mills, "Military Assistance to Ukraine since the Russian Invasion," Research Briefing, U.K. House of Commons Library, May 2023, 21–23.

13. Todd Lopez, "DOD Official Says Training for Ukrainians Is Ongoing," *DoD News*, U.S. Department of Defense, 30 March 2023, https://www.defense .gov/News/News-Stories/Article/Article/3347269/dod-official-says-training -for-ukrainians-is-ongoing/; Associated Press, "Expanded U.S. Training for Ukraine Forces Begins in Germany," NPR, 16 January 2023, https://www .npr.org/2023/01/16/1149372572/expanded-us-training-for-ukraine-forces -begins-in-germany; Todd Lopez, "U.S. Plans Combined Arms Training for Ukrainian Soldiers," *DoD News*, U.S. Department of Defense, 15 December 2022, https://www.defense.gov/News/News-Stories/Article/Article/3248075 /us-plans-combined-arms-training-for-ukrainian-soldiers/.

14. Detsh, "How Ukraine Learned to Fight."

15. "Interview with General Valerii Zaluzhnyi by Dmytro Komarov. Off-screen. General. Special project of Dmytro Komarov. Part Three," YouTube, 12 May 2023, https://www.youtube.com/watch?v=TadXxP_26V8.

16. North Atlantic Treaty Organization, *Relations with Ukraine*, 28 July 2023, https://www.nato.int/cps/en/natohq/topics_37750.htm.

17. This was listed as the highest strategic priority by President Zelenskyy during my meeting with him in Kyiv in September 2022.

18. Michael Marrow, "In Ukraine Fight, Integrated Air Defense Has Made Many Aircraft 'Worthless': U.S. Air Force General," *Breaking Defense*, 7 March 2023, https://breakingdefense.com/2023/03/in-ukraine-fight-integrated-air-defense -has-made-many-aircraft-worthless-us-air-force-general/.

19. International Institute for Strategic Studies, *The Military Balance 2021*, 209.

20. North Atlantic Treaty Organization, "Relations with Ukraine," 25 May 2023, https://www.nato.int/cps/en/natohq/topics_37750.htm.

21. Justin Bronk, Nick Reynolds, and Jack Watling, "The Russian Air War and Ukrainian Requirements for Air Defence," Royal United Services Institute, 7 November 2022, 7, https://rusi.org/explore-our-research/publications/special -resources/russian-air-war-and-ukrainian-requirements-air-defence.

22. Bronk, Reynolds, and Watling, 13.

23. Bronk, Reynolds, and Watling, 13.

24. A full description of the capabilities of the Iranian-made drones used by Russia since 2022 is at Uzi Rubin, "Russia's Iranian-Made UAVs: A Technical Profile," Royal United Services Institute, 13 January 2023, https://rusi.org/explore-our-research /publications/commentary/russias-iranian-made-uavs-technical-profile.

25. Isabelle Khurshudyan, "Ukraine Improvises with Aging Air Defenses to Counter Russian Missiles," *Washington Post*, 20 October 2022, https://www .washingtonpost.com/world/2022/10/20/air-defenses-ukraine-missiles-russia/.

26. Volodymyr Zelenskyy, "It Is Necessary to Intensify Common Efforts to Create an Air Shield for Ukraine," speech by President Volodymyr Zelenskyy at the video conference of the leaders of the Group of Seven and Ukraine, 11 October 2022, https://www.president.gov.ua/en/news/neobhidno -zbilshiti-spilni-zusillya-shob-stvoriti-povitryani-78417; Zoya Sheftalovich, "Kyiv Calls for Air Defenses as Putin Brings His Syria Tactics to Ukraine," *Politico Europe*, 10 October 2022, https://www.politico.eu/article /kyiv-calls-for-air-defenses-as-putin-brings-his-syria-tactics-to-ukraine/.

27. Ian Williams, "Russia Doubles Down on Its Failed Air Campaign," Center for Strategic and International Studies, 13 October 2022, https://www.csis.org /analysis/russia-doubles-down-its-failed-air-campaign.

28. Ian Cameron, "Lessons from Ukraine's Current Air Defense Deficit," American Security Project, 30 November 2022, https://www.americansecurityproject.org /lessons-from-ukraines-current-air-defense-deficit/.

29. Michael Peck, "Ukrainians with Cellphones and Machine Guns Are Forcing Russia to Change How It Launches Its Drone Attacks," *Business Insider*, 8 May 2023, https://www.businessinsider.com/ukraine-air-defenses-force -russia-to-change-drones-attack-methods-2023-5; Dan Sabbagh, "Ukrainians Use Phone App to Spot Deadly Russian Drone Attacks," *The Guardian*, 29 October 2022, https://www.theguardian.com/world/2022/oct/29/ukraine -phone-app-russia-drone-attacks-eppo.

30. Ian Williams, *Putin's Missile War: Russia's Strike Campaign in Ukraine* (Washington, DC: Center for Strategic and International Studies, May 2023), 21.

31. Alex Horton et al., "These Are the Western Air Defense Systems Protecting Ukraine," *Washington Post*, 19 May 2023, https://www.washingtonpost.com/world /2023/05/19/ukraine-air-defense-systems-patriot/.

32. Joseph Trevithick, "Ukrainian Teams Hunt Russian Drones with Laser Rifles, Gun Trucks, Apps," *The Warzone*, 8 December 2022, https://www .thedrive.com/the-war-zone/ukrainian-teams-hunt-russian-drones-with -laser-rifles-gun-trucks-apps.

33. Sam Skove, "US Sending Experimental Anti-drone Weapons to Ukraine," *DefenseOne*, 4 April 2023, https://www.defenseone.com/defense-systems/2023 /04/us-sending-experimental-anti-drone-weapons-ukraine/384801/.

34. "Ukraine's Buk SAM Will Receive RIM-7 Sea Sparrow Missiles, Which Solves the Missile Shortage Problem," *Defense Express*, 6 January 2023, https://en.defence -ua.com/weapon_and_tech/ukraines_buk_sam_will_receive_rim_7_sea_ sparrow_missiles_which_solves_missile_shortage_problem-5354.html; Thomas Newdick and Tyler Rogoway, "Sea Sparrow RIM-7 Surface-to-Air Missiles Are Headed to Ukraine," *The Warzone*, 6 January 2023, https://www.thedrive

.com/the-war-zone/sea-sparrow-rim-7-surface-to-air-missiles-are-headed-to
-ukraine.

35. David Rising and Hanna Arhirova, "Western Weapons, Experience Harden Ukrainian Air Defenses against Russian Onslaught," Associated Press, 11 May 2023, https://apnews.com/article/ukraine-russia-war-air-defenses-3f0a918c617 534251e53da4a93121c42.

36. See these posts by the Official Ukrainian Ministry of Defense: Defense of Ukraine (@DefenceU), Twitter, 3:28 a.m., 29 May 2023, https://twitter.com /DefenceU/status/1663115102680236034?s=20; 5:35 a.m., 29 May 2023, https:// twitter.com/DefenceU/status/1663147104959713280?s=20; 1:37 a.m., 28 May 2023, https://twitter.com/DefenceU/status/1662724764727926784?s=20.

37. Reznikov was replaced as Ukrainian defense minister in September 2023 by Rustem Umerov.

38. The Neptune is a Ukrainian-developed anti-ship missile that is likely to have been responsible for the sinking of the *Moskva* in 2022. Jon Guttman, "The Neptune Anti-ship Missile: The Weapon That May Have Sunk the Russian Flagship *Moskva*," *Military Times*, 13 May 2022, https://www.militarytimes com/off-duty/gearscout/2022/05/12/the-neptune-anti-ship-missile-the-weapon -that-may-have-sunk-the-russian-flagship-moskva/.

39. Mick Ryan, "HIMARS Permit Ukrainians to Fight How They Know Best—a Strategy of Corrosion," *Engelsberg Ideas*, 21 July 2022, https://engelsbergideas .com/notebook/himars-permit-ukrainians-to-fight-how-they-know-best-a -strategy-of-corrosion/.

40. Sanya Mansoor, "Why U.S. HIMARS Rockets Are Becoming Increasingly Decisive for Ukraine," *Time*, 4 January 2023, https://time.com/6244479/himars -rockets-ukraine-russia/.

41. Ryan, "HIMARS Permit Ukrainians to Fight How They Know Best."

42. Ryan, "HIMARS Permit Ukrainians to Fight How They Know Best."

43. Ellen Mitchell, "14 Russian Helicopters Likely Destroyed by US-Provided ATACMS Missiles in Ukraine: UK Intel," *The Hill*, 20 October 2023, https://thehill.com /policy/defense/4267375-russian-helicopters-lost-to-us-atacms-missiles -ukraine/.

44. Ryan, "HIMARS Permit Ukrainians to Fight How They Know Best."

45. Adam Lowther and Mahube Siddiki, "Combat Drones in Ukraine," *Air and Space Operations Review* 1, no. 4 (Winter 2022): 6–7.

46. Veronika Melkozerova, "Drone Attack Hits Russia's Engels Airbase for Second Time in a Month," *Politico Europe*, 26 December 2022, https:// www.politico.eu/article/russia-ukraine-war-vladimir-putin-drone-attack -hits-russias-engels-airbase-for-second-time-in-a-month/; Paul McLeary

and Erin Banco, "Ukraine Used Home-Modified Drones to Strike Russian Bases," *Politico*, 7 December 2022, https://www.politico.com/news/2022/12/07 /ukraine-used-home-modified-drones-to-strike-russian-bases-00072936.

47. James Gregory, "UK Confirms Supply of Storm Shadow Long-Range Missiles in Ukraine," BBC News, 11 May 2023, https://www.bbc.com/news/world -europe-65558070.

48. Dan Carney, "Technical Overview of the Storm Shadow Cruise Missile for Ukraine," *Design News*, 12 May 2023, https://www.designnews.com/industry /technical-overview-storm-shadow-cruise-missile-ukraine.

49. Max Hunder, "Inside Ukraine's Scramble for 'Game-Changer' Drone Fleet," Reuters, 24 March 2023, https://www.reuters.com/world/europe/inside -ukraines-scramble-game-changer-drone-fleet-2023-03-24/.

50. Hunder, "Inside Ukraine's Scramble for 'Game-Changer' Drone Fleet"; *The Economist*, "Ukraine Is Betting on Drones to Strike Deep into Russia," 20 March 2023, https://www.economist.com/europe/2023/03/20/ukraine-is-betting -on-drones-to-strike-deep-into-russia; Nate Ostiller, "Ukraine's Secret 'Black Box' Project Revealed to Be Long-Range Attack Drone," *Kyiv Independent*, 16 November 2023, https://kyivindependent.com/ukrainian-intelligences-secret -black-box-project-revealed-to-be-long-range-attack-drone/.

51. Tayfun Ozberk, "Analysis: Ukraine Strikes with Kamikaze USVs—Russian Bases Are Not Safe Anymore," *Naval News*, 30 October 2022, https://www.navalnews .com/naval-news/2022/10/analysis-ukraine-strikes-with-kamikaze-usvs -russian-bases-are-not-safe-anymore/; Stefan Korshak, "Ukrainian Kamikaze Drones Attack Russian Black Sea Fleet Base, Warship Possibly Damaged," *Kyiv Post*, 25 April 2023, https://www.kyivpost.com/post/16251; Sebastien Roblin, Videos Reveal Drone Kamikaze Boat Assault on Russia's Black Sea Fleet," *Forbes*, 29 October 2022, https://www.forbes.com /sites/sebastienroblin/2022/10/29/videos-reveal-drone-kamikaze-boat -assault-on-russias-black-sea-fleet/?sh=1412bbab1e54; Howard Altman, "Russia Claims Ukrainian Drone Boats Attacked Its Navy Ship Off Turkey," *War Zone*, 24 May 2023, https://www.thedrive.com/the-war-zone /russia-claims-ukrainian-drone-boats-attacked-its-navy-ship-off-turkey.

52. Josh Pennington et al., "Ukraine Claims Responsibility for New Attack on Key Crimea Bridge," CNN, 17 July 2023, https://edition.cnn.com/2023/07/16/europe /russia-crimea-bridge-intl-hnk/index.html.

53. H. I. Sutton, "Ukraine's Maritime Drones (USV): What You Need to Know," *Covert Shores*, 11 November 2022, http://www.hisutton.com/Ukraine-Maritime -Drones.html.

54. H. I. Sutton, "Russia Faces New Threat: Ukraine's 'Toloka' Underwater Maritime Drone," *Covert Shores*, 26 April 2023, http://www.hisutton.com/New-Ukraine -Underwater-Maritime-Drone.html.

55. Alius Noreika, "Ukrainian Toloka TLK-150: Looks like a Missile, Acts like One, but Swims Underwater," *Technology.org*, 15 May 2023, https://www.technology .org/2023/05/15/toloka-tlk-150-underwater-missile/.

56. Mick Ryan, "Why HIMARS May Shift the Battlefield Balance in Ukraine," *Sydney Morning Herald*, 12 July 2022, https://www.smh.com.au/world/europe /why-himars-may-shift-the-battlefield-balance-in-ukraine-20220712-p5b0x0 .html.

CHAPTER 14. THE LAST FULL MEASURE

1. Dan Lamothe, Alex Horton, and Karoun Demirjian, "Ukraine's Military Adapts Tactics after Enduring Russia's Initial Invasion," *Washington Post*, 5 March 2022, https://www.washingtonpost.com/national-security/2022/03/05 /ukraine-military-strategy/; Jon Guttman, "Javelin Missile: Made by the U.S., Wielded by Ukraine, Feared by Russia," *Military Times*, 13 May 2022, https:// www.militarytimes.com/off-duty/gearscout/2022/05/12/javelin-missile-made -by-the-us-wielded-by-ukraine-feared-by-russia/; Mark Cancian, "Will the United States Run Out of Javelins before Russia Runs Out of Tanks?," Center for Strategic and International Studies, 12 April 2022, https://www.csis.org /analysis/will-united-states-run-out-javelins-russia-runs-out-tanks.

2. Harrison Kass, "'One Shot One Kill' NLAW Missiles May Have Killed Hundreds of Russian Tanks in Ukraine," *Business Insider,* 11 July 2022, https://www .businessinsider.com/ukraine-nlaw-missiles-may-have-killed-hundreds-of -russian-tanks-2022-7; John Ismay, "Ukraine Is Wrecking Russian Tanks with a Gift from Britain," *New York Times*, 18 March 2022, https://www.nytimes .com/2022/03/18/us/ukraine-antitank-missiles-russia.html.

3. Ben Hall, "Military Briefing: Ukraine's Battlefield Agility Pays Off," *Financial Times*, 26 May 2022, https://www.ft.com/content/9618df65-3551-4d52 -ad79-494db908d53b.

4. Meir Finkel, *On Flexibility: Recovery from Technological and Doctrinal Surprise on the Battlefield* (Stanford, CA: Stanford University Press, 2007), 150.

5. Lawrence Whetten and Michael Johnson, "Military Lessons of the Yom Kippur War," *World Today* 3, no. 30 (1 March 1974): 107.

6. Franz-Stefan Gady, "Ukraine's Army Must Shed Its Soviet Legacy, Says a Military Expert," *The Economist*, 17 March 2023, https://www.economist .com/by-invitation/2023/03/17/ukraines-army-must-shed-its-soviet-legacy -says-a-military-expert.

7. Sam Skove, "Some Ukrainian Troops Are Still Using Soviet Methods, despite U.S. Training," *Defense One*, 7 April 2023, https://www.defenseone.com /threats/2023/04/some-ukrainian-troops-are-still-using-soviet-methods-despite -us-training/384967/.

8. Erik Kramer and Paul Schneider, "What the Ukrainian Armed Forces Need to Do to Win," *War on the Rocks*, 2 June 2023, https://warontherocks.com/2023/06 /what-the-ukrainian-armed-forces-need-to-do-to-win/.

9. Serhii Plokhy, *The Russo-Ukrainian War* (London: Penguin Books, 2023), 231–36.

10. This description of the "expanding torrent" was used by Basil Liddell Hart in his lecture to the Royal United Service Institution on 3 November 1920. Full transcript was published as B. H. Liddell Hart, "The Man in the Dark Theory of Infantry Tactics and the 'Expanding Torrent' System of Attack," *Journal of the Royal United Service Institution* 66, no. 461 (February 1921): 1–22.

11. Jason Beaubien, "Ukraine's Offensive in Kharkiv Was Hard and Bitter, Say Soldiers Who Did the Fighting," NPR, 29 September 2022, https://www.npr .org/2022/09/29/1125278321/ukraine-offensive-russia-borshchova-kharkiv -oblast; Jason Beaubien, "Ukrainian Soldiers' View on Counteroffensive Could Inform Efforts to Dislodge Russia," *All Things Considered*, NPR, 28 September 2022, https://www.npr.org/2022/09/28/1125747340/ukrainian -soldiers-view-on-counteroffensive-could-inform-efforts-to-dislodge-rus; Aaron Santelises, "The Ukrainian Kharkiv Counter-Offensive and Informa- tion Operations," *The Cove*, 2 November 2022, https://cove.army.gov.au/article /ukrainian-kharkiv-counter-offensive-and-information-operations.

12. Frank Ledwidge, "Kharkiv Offensive Has Shown the West That Ukraine Can Win," *The Conversation*, 13 September 2022, https://theconversation.com /kharkiv-offensive-has-shown-the-west-that-ukraine-can-win-190501; Illia Ponomarenko, "With Successful Kharkiv Operation, Ukraine Turns the War in Its Favor," *Kyiv Independent*, 13 September 2022, https://kyivindependent.com/with -successful-kharkiv-operation-ukraine-turns-the-war-in-its-favor/; Kateryna Stepanenko et al., "Russian Offensive Campaign Assessment, September 10," Institute for the Study of War, 10 September 2022, https://www.understanding war.org/backgrounder/russian-offensive-campaign-assessment-september-10.

13. Isabelle Khurshudyan et al., "Inside the Ukrainian Counteroffensive That Shocked Putin and Reshaped the War," *Washington Post*, 29 December 2022, https://www.washingtonpost.com/world/2022/12/29/ukraine-offensive -kharkiv-kherson-donetsk/; "A Stunning Counter-offensive by Ukraine's Armed Forces," *The Economist*, 15 September 2022, https://www.economist.com /europe/2022/09/15/a-stunning-counter-offensive-by-ukraines-armed-forces; David Hambling, "How Ukraine's Lightning Counter-offensive Overwhelmed

Russian Forces with Humvees," *Forbes*, 15 September 2022, https://www.forbes .com/sites/davidhambling/2022/09/15/how-ukraines-lightning-counter -offensive-overwhelmed-russian-forces/?sh=625dbf4b7309.

14. Khurshudyan et al., "Inside the Ukrainian Counteroffensive That Shocked Putin and Reshaped the War."

15. Plokhy, *Russo-Ukrainian War*, 236–42.

16. The exact number of brigades has not been released by the Ukrainian armed forces. However, open-source mapping and geospatial intelligence indicate the figure of six to eight maneuver brigades were used in this operation. Source: MilitaryLand.com, Kharkiv Front April 20–November 12, 2022, https://militaryland .net/maps/russian-invasion/kherson-front/.

17. The number of brigades has not been confirmed by the Ukrainian armed forces. Open-source mapping and geospatial intelligence indicate the figure of twelve to fourteen maneuver brigades were used in this operation. Source: MilitaryLand.com, Kherson Front, April 20–September 23, 2022.

18. Alexandra Chinchilla and Jahara Matisek, "Ukraine's Hidden Advantage: How European Trainers Have Transformed Kyiv's Army and Changed the War," *Foreign Affairs*, 11 May 2023, https://www.foreignaffairs.com/ukraine /russia-war-ukraines-hidden-advantage.

19. Stefan Korshak, "High-Tech Ukraine Assault Brigade Armed by Sweden Nearing Readiness," *Kyiv Post*, 19 May 2023, https://www.kyivpost.com/post/17266.

20. Todd Lopez, "U.S. Plans Combined Arms Training for Ukrainian Soldiers," press release, U.S. Department of Defense, 15 December 2022, https://www .defense.gov/News/News-Stories/Article/Article/3248075/us-plans-combined -arms-training-for-ukrainian-soldiers/; Meghann Myers, "Ukrainian Battalion Completes First Combined-Arms Training in Germany," *Army Times*, 18 February 2023, https://www.armytimes.com/news/your-army/2023/02/17 /ukrainian-battalion-completes-first-combined-arms-training-in-germany/.

21. Korshak, "High-Tech Ukraine Assault Brigade Armed by Sweden Nearing Readiness."

22. Interview with General Valerii Zaluzhnyi by Dmytro Komarov. Off-screen. General. Special Project of Dmytro Komarov. Part Three," YouTube, 12 May 2023, https://www.youtube.com/watch?v=TadXxP_26V8.

23. Glen Grant, "2023—A Time and Chance for Military Change in Ukraine," Maidan, 20 February 2023, https://maidan.org.ua/en/2023/02/glen-grant-2023-a -time-and-chance-for-military-change-in-ukraine/#Conclusion.

24. Valeriy Zaluzhnyi and Mykhailo Zabrodskyi, "Prospects for Running a Military Campaign in 2023: Ukraine's Perspective," *UkrInform*, 7 September 2022, https:// www.ukrinform.net/rubric-ato/3566404-prospects-for-running-a-military

-campaign-in-2023-ukraines-perspective.html?fbclid=IwAR31RCvVxcCRDR _Ci8-CrKsrDSenSlBp8-lFoklOWFgjNkTyivcLkM7zk.

25. Michael Kofman and Rob Lee, "Ukraine Struggles to Scale Offensive Operations," *War on the Rocks* podcast, 20 July 2023, https://warontherocks.com/2023/07 /ukraine-struggles-to-scale-offensive-combat-operations/; conversation between the author and Michael Kofman on initial observations of the Ukrainian 2023 offensive, 21 July 2023; Franz-Stefan Gady, observations on visit to Ukraine, Twitter, 18 July 2023, https://twitter.com/HoansSolo/status/1681240456754077697.

26. Yalda Hakim, "Ukraine War: Zelensky Admits Slow Progress but Says Offensive Is Not a Movie," BBC News, 21 June 2023, https://www.bbc.com/news/world -europe-65971790#.

27. Peter Singer, *Wired for War: The Robotics Revolution and Conflict in the Twenty-First Century* (New York: Penguin Books, 2009), 429–30.

28. "How Ukrainians Modify Civilian Drones for Military Use," *The Economist*, 8 May 2023, https://www.economist.com/science-and-technology/2023/05/08 /how-ukrainians-modify-civilian-drones-for-military-use#.

29. Joe Tidy, "Ukraine Rapidly Expanding Its 'Army of Drones' for Front Line," BBC, 26 April 2023, https://www.bbc.com/news/technology-65389215.

30. A report by RUSI in 2023 found that Ukrainian UAV losses were about ten thousand per month. Jack Watling and Nick Reynolds, "Meatgrinder: Russian Tactics in the Second Year of Its Invasion of Ukraine," Royal United Services Institute, 19 May 2023, iii, https://rusi.org/explore-our-research/publications/special-resources meatgrinder-russian-tactics-second-year-its-invasion-ukraine.

31. T. X. Hammes, "Game-Changers: Implications of the Russo-Ukraine War for the Future of Ground Warfare," Atlantic Council, 3 April 2023, 9–10, https:// www.atlanticcouncil.org/in-depth-research-reports/issue-brief/gamechangers -implications-of-the-russo-ukraine-war-for-the-future-of-ground-warfare/.

32. Mykhaylo Zabrodskyi et al., "Preliminary Lessons in Conventional Warfighting from Russia's Invasion of Ukraine: February–July 2022," Royal United Services Institute, 30 November 2022, 38, https://rusi.org/explore-our-research /publications/special-resources/preliminary-lessons-conventional-warfighting -russias-invasion-ukraine-february-july-2022.

33. Dan Peleschuk, "Ukraine Sets Up Drone Assault Units," Reuters, 27 January 2023, https://www.reuters.com/world/europe/ukraine-sets-up-drone-assault -units-2023-01-27/; News Desk, "Ukraine to Form 'First in the World' Attack Drone Units," *Kyiv Independent*, 27 January 2023, https://kyivindependent .com/general-staff-ukraine-to-form-first-in-the-world-attack-drone-units/.

34. David Brennan, "Ukraine Readies 10,000 Drone Pilots ahead of Counteroffensive: Official," *Newsweek*, 5 May 2023, https://www.newsweek.com

/ukraine-10000-drone-pilots-ahead-counteroffensive-mykhailo-fedorov
-1798579; "Ukraine Is Betting on Drones to Strike Deep into Russia," *The Economist*, 20 March 2023, https://www-economist-com.ezproxy.library.uq.edu.au
/europe/2023/03/20/ukraine-is-betting-on-drones-to-strike-deep-into-russia.

35. The decree can be found at https://www.kmu.gov.ua/news/rozvytok-vyrob
    nytstva-ukrainskykh-bpla-uriad-pidtrymav-vidpovidnu-postanovu?ref
    =kyivindependent.com.

36. News Desk, "Ukrainian Government Facilitates Mass Drone Production," *Kyiv Independent*, 24 March 2023, https://kyivindependent.com
    /ukrainian-government-facilitates-mass-drone-production/.

37. Jason Sherman, "Drone-on-Drone Combat in Ukraine Marks a New Era of Aerial Warfare," *Scientific American*, 3 April 2023, https://www.scientificamerican.com
    article/drone-on-drone-combat-in-ukraine-marks-a-new-era-of-aerial-warfare/.

38. For an example of a Ukrainian drone capturing Russian drones, see the video at the @CasualArtyFan Twitter feed: "Here's something you don't see every day. A Ukrainian drone capturing and then towing 2 Russian drones underneath. Looks like tractors have taken to the sky in the effort to capture as much Russian equipment as possible," Twitter, 2:16 p.m., 9 June 2023, https://twitter.com
    /CasualArtyFan/status/1667264406164590611?s=20.

39. Dan Gettinger, "One Way Attack: How Loitering Munitions Are Shaping Conflicts," *Bulletin of Atomic Scientists*, 5 June 2023, https://thebulletin.org/2023/06
    /one-way-attack-how-loitering-munitions-are-shaping-conflicts/.

40. Kelsey Atherton, "Loitering Munitions Preview the Autonomous Future of Warfare," Brookings Institution, 4 August 2021, https://www.brookings.edu
    /techstream/loitering-munitions-preview-the-autonomous-future-of-warfare/.

41. Dan Gettinger, "One Way Attack Drones: Loitering Munitions of Past and Present," press release, *Vertical Flight Society*, 4 May 2023, https://vtol.org/news
    /press-release-vfs-publishes-study-on-one-way-attack-drones.

42. U.S. Department of Defense, "Fact Sheet on U.S. Security Assistance for Ukraine," press release, 14 April 2022, https://www.defense.gov/News/Releases
    /Release/Article/3000166/fact-sheet-on-us-security-assistance-for-ukraine/.
    Details of the Switchblade 600 can be found at https://www.avinc.com/lms
    /switchblade-600.

43. "How Racing Drones Are Used as Improvised Missiles in Ukraine," *The Economist*, 24 March 2023, https://www.economist.com/the-economist-explains/2023/03/24
    /how-racing-drones-are-used-as-improvised-missiles-in-ukraine; Annika Burgess, "Why Ukraine's Kamikaze Racing Drones Are Causing a Buzz on and off the Battlefield," ABC Australia, 1 April 2023, https://www.abc.net.au/news/2023-04
    -01/fpv-racing-drone-kamikaze-attacks-ukraine-russia-war/102155702; Matthew

Gault, "Ukraine Is Now Strapping RPGs to Racing Drones to Bomb Invading Russians," *Vice*, 3 February 2023, https://www.vice.com/en/article/n7zxp8/ukraine-is-now-strapping-rpgs-to-racing-drones-to-bomb-invading-russians.

44. Watling and Reynolds, "Meatgrinder," iii.

45. Oleksandr Stashevskyi and Frank Bajak, "Deadly Secret: Electronic Warfare Shapes Russia-Ukraine War," Associated Press, 4 June 2022, https://apnews.com/article/russia-ukraine-kyiv-technology-90d760f01105b9aaf1886427dbfba917; Alia Shoaib, "Ukraine's Drones Are Becoming Increasingly Ineffective as Russia Ramps Up Its Electronic Warfare and Air Defenses," *Business Insider*, 3 July 2022, https://www.businessinsider.com/drones-russia-ukraine-war-electronic-warfare-2022-7; Mick Ryan, "How Ukraine Is Winning in the Adaptation Battle against Russia," *Engelsberg Ideas*, 24 August 2022, https://engelsbergideas.com/essays/how-ukraine-is-winning-in-the-adaptation-battle-against-russia/.

46. Ryan, "How Ukraine Is Winning in the Adaptation Battle against Russia."

47. Mick Ryan, "Winning the Adaptation Battle," *Futura Doctrina*, Substack, 12 December 2022, https://mickryan.substack.com/p/winning-the-adaptation-battle.

48. Singer, *Wired for War*, 428.

49. Isabelle Khurshudyan, Mary Ilyushina, and Kostiantyn Khudov, "Russia and Ukraine Are Fighting the First Full-Scale Drone War," *Washington Post*, 2 December 2022, https://www.washingtonpost.com/world/2022/12/02/drones-russia-ukraine-air-war/.

50. Benjamin Jensen, Christopher Whyte, and Scott Cuomo, *Information in War: Military Innovation, Battle Networks, and the Future of Artificial Intelligence* (Washington, DC: Georgetown University Press, 2022), 102, 110–14.

51. Dan Lafontaine, "Army Set to Modernize Blue Force Tracking Network," U.S. Army, 13 July 2018, https://www.army.mil/article/199916/army_set_to_modernize_blue_force_tracking_network.

52. Lara Jakes, "For Western Weapons, the Ukraine War Is a Beta Test," *New York Times*, 15 November 2022; Kateryna Kistol, "Digital Weapons of War: Applications and Software That Help Ukraine to Win," *War.Ukraine.Ua*, 13 December 2022, https://war.ukraine.ua/articles/digital-weapons-of-war-applications-and-software-that-help-ukraine-to-win/.

53. Hammes, "Game-Changers"; Toby Sterling and Stephanie van den Berg, "Ukraine War Shows Urgency of Military AI, Palantir CEO Says," Reuters, 16 February 2023, https://www.reuters.com/technology/ukrainewar-shows-urgency-military-ai-palantir-ceo-says-2023-02-15/.

54. Sam Bendett, "Roles and Implications of AI in the Russian-Ukrainian Conflict," *Russia Matters*, Belfer Center for Science and International Affairs,

Harvard University, 20 July 2023, https://www.russiamatters.org/analysis /roles-and-implications-ai-russian-ukrainian-conflict.

55. Robin Fontes and Jorrit Kamminga, "Ukraine a Living Lab for AI Warfare," *National Defense*, 24 March 2023, https://www.nationaldefensemagazine.org /articles/2023/3/24/ukraine-a-living-lab-for-ai-warfare.

56. Mark Bruno, "Uber for Artillery—What Is Ukraine's GIS Arta System?," *The Moloch*, https://themoloch.com/conflict/uber-for-artillery-what-is-ukraines -gis-arta-system/.

57. Seth G. Jones, Riley McCabe, and Alexander Palmer, *Ukrainian Innovation in a War of Attrition* (Washington, DC: Center for Strategic and International Studies, February 2023), 8–9; David Axe, "There's a Good Reason the Russian Air Force Is Faltering. Ukrainian Air-Defense Crews Have Better Apps," *Forbes*, 18 October 2022, https://www.forbes.com/sites/davidaxe/2022/10/18 /theres-a-good-reason-the-russian-air-force-is-faltering-ukrainian-air-defense -crews-have-better-apps/?sh=36e555ca7960.

58. Kistol, "Digital Weapons of War."

59. David Barno and Nora Bensahel, *Adaptation under Fire: How Militaries Change in Wartime* (Oxford: Oxford University Press, 2020), 246.

60. See the discussion on the "adoption capacity theory" throughout Michael Horowitz, *The Diffusion of Military Power* (Princeton, NJ: Princeton University Press, 2010).

61. Hammes, "Game-Changers," 16.

CHAPTER 15. RACE TO THE SWIFT

1. Don Starry, foreword to Richard Simpkin, *Race to the Swift: Thoughts on Twenty-First Century Warfare* (Delhi: Lancer, 1997), vii.

2. Frank Hoffman, *Mars Adapting: Military Change during War* (Annapolis: Naval Institute Press, 2021), 1.

3. Michael Howard, "The Use and Abuse of Military History," *RUSI Journal* 138, no. 1 (1993): 29.

4. Allan Millett and Williamson Murray, *Military Effectiveness*, vol. 1: *The First World War* (Cambridge: Cambridge University Press, 2010), 2.

5. Risa Brooks and Elizabeth Stanley, eds., *Creating Military Power* (Stanford, CA: Stanford University Press, 2007), 9.

6. Veronika Melkozerova, "Russia May Have Lost an Entire Elite Brigade Near a Donetsk Coal-Mining Town," *Politico Europe*, 12 February 2023, https:// www.politico.eu/article/russia-may-have-lost-an-entire-elite-brigade-near -a-coal-mining-town-in-donbas-ukraine-says/; Karolina Hird et al., "Russian Campaign Assessment," Institute for the Study of War, 10 February 2023,

https://www.understandingwar.org/backgrounder/russian-offensive-campaign
-assessment-february-10-2023.

7. Yalda Hakim, "Ukraine War: Zelensky Admits Slow Progress but Says Offensive Is Not a Movie," BBC News, 21 June 2023, https://www.bbc.com/news/world -europe-65971790#; Michael Kofman and Rob Lee, "Ukraine Struggles to Scale Offensive Operations," *War on the Rocks* podcast, 20 July 2023, https:// warontherocks.com/2023/07/ukraine-struggles-to-scale-offensive-combat -operations/.

8. Mykhaylo Zabrodskyi et al., "Preliminary Lessons in Conventional Warfighting from Russia's Invasion of Ukraine: February–July 2022," Royal United Services Institute, 30 November 2022, 45, https://rusi.org/explore-our-research /publications/special-resources/preliminary-lessons-conventional-warfighting -russias-invasion-ukraine-february-july-2022.

9. Shashank Bengali, "Russia Is Struggling to Replenish Missile Stocks, Ukraine Says," *New York Times*, 4 January 2023, https://www.nytimes.com/live/2023/01/04/ world/russia-ukraine-news.

10. Mike Pietrucha, "Amateur Hour Part II: Failing the Air Campaign," *War on the Rocks*, 11 August 2022, https://warontherocks.com/2022/08/amateur-hour -part-ii-failing-the-air-campaign/.

11. Maximilian Bremer and Kelly Grieco, "In Denial about Denial: Why Ukraine's Air Success Should Worry the West," *War on the Rocks*, 15 June 2022, https:// warontherocks.com/2022/06/in-denial-about-denial-why-ukraines-air-success -should-worry-the-west/?__s=xxxxxxx.

12. Trevor Dupuy, *The Evolution of Weapons and Warfare* (New York: Da Capo, 1984), 172.

13. Patrick O'Neill, "Russia Hacked an American Satellite Company One Hour before the Ukraine Invasion," *MIT Technology Review*, 10 May 2022, https:// www.technologyreview.com/2022/05/10/1051973/russia-hack-viasat-satellite -ukraine-invasion/; Kevin Poireault, "Five Takeaways from the Russian Cyber-Attack on Viasat's Satellites," *InfoSecurity*, 9 May 2023, https://www.infosecurity -magazine.com/news/takeaways-russian-cyberattack/.

14. Raphael Satter, "Satellite Outage Caused 'Huge Loss in Communications' at War's Outset—Ukrainian Official," Reuters, 16 March 2022, https://www .reuters.com/world/satellite-outage-caused-huge-loss-communications-wars -outset-ukrainian-official-2022-03-15/.

15. Christopher Miller, Mark Scott, and Bryan Bender, "UkraineX: How Elon Musk's Space Satellites Changed the War on the Ground," *Politico Europe*, 8 June 2022, https://www.politico.eu/article/elon-musk-ukraine-starlink/.

16. Jeffrey Dastin, "Data Company Palantir to Help Ukraine Prosecute Alleged Russian War Crimes," Reuters, 23 April 2023, https://www.reuters.com/world/europe/data-company-palantir-help-ukraine-prosecute-alleged-russian-war-crimes-2023-04-22/.

17. Lizette Chapman, "Palantir Signs On for Reconstruction Work in War-Torn Ukraine," Bloomberg, 25 May 2023, https://www.bloomberg.com/news/articles/2023-05-25/palantir-signs-on-for-reconstruction-work-in-war-torn-ukraine#xj4y7vzkg.

18. These shortfalls in training were also observed in Erik Kramer and Paul Schneider, "What the Ukrainian Armed Forces Need to Do to Win," *War on the Rocks*, 2 June 2023, https://warontherocks.com/2023/06/what-the-ukrainian-armed-forces-need-to-do-to-win/.

19. Andrew Marshall, "Some Thoughts on Military Revolutions—Second Version," Memorandum for the Record, Office of Net Assessment, U.S. Department of Defense, 23 August 1993.

20. Paul Scharre, *Four Battlegrounds: Power in the Age of Artificial Intelligence* (New York: W. W. Norton, 2023), 302.

21. Michael Horowitz, *The Diffusion of Military Power* (Princeton, NJ: Princeton University Press, 2010).

22. Martin van Creveld, *Technology and War: From 2000 BC to the Present* (London: Brasseys, 1991), 85; Bernard Brodie and Fawn Brodie, *From Crossbow to H-Bomb: The Evolution of the Weapons and Tactics of Warfare* (Bloomington: Indiana University Press, 1973), 55; Max Boot, *War Made New: Technology, Warfare, and the Course of History, 1500 to Today* (New York: Gotham Books, 2006), 59.

23. Hew Strachan, *The First World War* (New York: Penguin Books, 2013), 47.

24. The development of aircraft carrier and submarine warfare is explored in Williamson Murray, *Military Innovation in the Interwar Period* (Cambridge: Cambridge University Press, 1998).

25. Dupuy, *The Evolution of Weapons and Warfare*, 303.

26. Mark Cancian and Tom Karako, "Patriot to Ukraine: What Does It Mean?," Center for Strategic and International Studies, 16 December 2022, https://www.csis.org/analysis/patriot-ukraine-what-does-it-mean.

27. Geoff LaMear, "Sending Patriot Missile Systems to Ukraine Is an Expensive Blunder," *Military.com*, 21 January 2023, https://www.military.com/daily-news/opinions/2023/01/21/sending-patriot-missile-systems-ukraine-expensive-blunder.html.

28. Eric Tegler, "The $1.1 Billion Patriot Missile Battery the U.S. Is Sending to Ukraine Is Symbolic but Not a Gamechanger," *Forbes*, 23 December 2022, https://www

.forbes.com/sites/erictegler/2022/12/23/the-11-billion-patriot-missile-battery-the
-us-is-sending-to-ukraine-is-symbolic-but-not-a-gamechanger/?sh=ac3f1b196f8f.

29. Oren Liebermann, "First on CNN: Ukrainians to Start Training on Patriot Missiles in U.S. as Soon as Next Week," CNN, 11 January 2023, https://edition.cnn
.com/2023/01/10/politics/ukrainians-patriot-missiles-fort-sill/index.html; Lara
Seligman, "'Absolutely a Quick Study': Ukrainians Master Patriot System Faster
than Expected," *Politico*, 21 March 2023, https://www.politico.com/news/2023/03/21
/ukrainian-soliders-patriot-missile-training-oklahoma-00088166.

30. Samya Kullab, "Ukraine Thwarts Russia's 'Exceptional' Missile Assault on
Kyiv," *PBS Newshour*, 16 May 2023, https://www.pbs.org/newshour/world
/russia-launches-exceptional-air-assault-on-kyiv.

31. The Fire Information Resource Management System (FIRMS) provides data on
fires globally. As such, it can be used to indicate where heavy fighting might be
taking place. https://firms.modaps.eosdis.nasa.gov/map/#d:24hrs;@0.0,0.0,3z.

32. Milford Beagle, Jason Slider, and Matthew Arrol, "The Graveyard of Command
Posts: What Chornobaivka Should Teach Us about Command and Control in
Large-Scale Combat Operations," *Military Review*, May–June 2023, 10–15.

33. Boot, *War Made New*, 7.

34. Max Boot, "Russia Is Fighting by the Book. The Problem Is, It's the Wrong
Book," *Washington Post,* 2 November 2022, https://www.washingtonpost.com
/opinions/2022/11/02/max-boot-russia-military-doctrine-ukraine/.

35. Valery Zaluzhnyi, quoted in Simon Shuster and Vera Bergengruen, "Inside the
Ukrainian Counterstrike That Turned the Tide of the War," *Time*, 26 September
2022, https://time.com/6216213/ukraine-military-valeriy-zaluzhny/.

36. Williamson Murray, *Military Adaptation in War: With Fear of Change* (Cambridge: Cambridge University Press, 2011), 320–27.

CONCLUSION

1. Shashank Joshi, "A New Era of High-Tech War Has Begun," *The Economist*, 6
July 2023.

2. Radio Free Europe, "Echoes of World War I Highlighted in Mud, Shattered Trees
of Ukraine," 2 December 2022, https://www.rferl.org/a/ukraine-mud-world
-war-1-russia-invasion/32157465.html.

3. Anatol Lieven, "Ukraine's War Is like World War I, Not World War II,"
Foreign Policy, 27 October 2022, https://foreignpolicy.com/2022/10/27
/ukraines-war-is-like-world-war-i-not-world-war-ii/.

4. Margaret MacMillan, "How Wars Don't End: Ukraine, Russia, and the Lessons
of World War I," *Foreign Affairs* 102, no. 4 (July/August 2023): 55.

5. MacMillan, "How Wars Don't End," 56.

6. Norman Angell, *The Great Illusion: A Study of the Relation of Military Power to National Advantage* (New York: G. P. Putnam's Sons, 1913), x.

7. Colin Gray, *Strategy and Defence Planning: Meeting the Challenge of Uncertainty* (Oxford: Oxford University Press, 2014), 94.

8. I explored the variety of surprises in this war (so far) in detail in Mick Ryan, "Prigozhin Crosses the Rubicon: Surprise Is an Enduring Feature of War," *Futura Doctrina*, Substack, 24 June 2023, https://mickryan.substack.com/p /prigozhin-crosses-the-rubicon.

9. Liam Collins, Michael Kofman, and John Spencer, "The Battle of Hostomel Airport: A Key Moment in Russia's Defeat in Kyiv," *War on the Rocks*, 10 August 2023, https://warontherocks.com/2023/08/the-battle-of-hostomel-airport -a-key-moment-in-russias-defeat-in-kyiv/.

10. Alex Vershinin, "The Return of Industrial Warfare," Royal United Services Institute, 17 June 2022, https://rusi.org/explore-our-research/publications /commentary/return-industrial-warfare.

11. Mick Ryan, "Six Months after Putin's Invasion, What Has This War Taught the West?," *Sydney Morning Herald*, 24 August 2022, https://www.smh.com .au/world/europe/six-months-after-putin-s-invasion-what-has-this-war-taught -the-west-20220823-p5bc35.html.

12. Ryan, "Six Months after Putin's Invasion."

13. Richard Overy, *Why the Allies Won* (New York: W. W. Norton, 1995); Arthur Herman's *Freedom's Forge: How American Business Produced Victory in World War II* (New York: Random House, 2012); Paul Kennedy, *Engineers of Victory: The Problem Solvers Who Turned the Tide in the Second World War* (New York: Random House, 2013).

14. Seth Jones, *Empty Bins in a Wartime Environment: The Challenge to the U.S. Defense Industrial Base* (Washington, DC: Center for Strategic and International Studies, January 2023); Cynthia Cook, *Reviving the Arsenal of Democracy: Steps for Surging Defense Industrial Capacity* (Washington, DC: Center for Strategic and International Studies, March 2023); Peter Layton, "National Mobilisation during War: Past Insights, Future Possibilities," Occasional Paper, National Security College, Canberra, August 2020, https://nsc.crawford.anu .edu.au/sites/default/files/publication/nsc_crawford_anu_edu_au/2020-08 /nsc_national_mobilisation_op_2020_digital.pdf; Layton, "Mobilizing Defence in the 'Fourth Industrial Revolution,'" *The Interpreter*, 27 March 2019, https:// www.lowyinstitute.org/the-interpreter/mobilising-defence-fourth-industrial -revolution; Layton et al., *How to Mobilise Australia* (Canberra: Australian National University, July 2020), https://sdsc.bellschool.anu.edu.au/sites/default /files/publications/attachments/2020-07/cog_52_how_to_mobilise_australia

.pdf; Joanne Nicholson et al., *Defence Mobilisation Planning Comparative Study: An Examination of Overseas Planning* (Santa Monica, CA: RAND Corporation, 2021); U.S. Department of Defense, *Securing Defense-Critical Supply Chains: An Action Plan Developed in Response to President Biden's Executive Order 14017* (Washington, DC: Office of the Secretary of Defense, February 2022).

15. Both the House Armed Service Committee and Senate Armed Service Committee of the U.S. Congress have held recent hearings on this topic. See https://www.congress.gov/event/112th-congress/house-event/LC3176/text?s=1&r=75; and https://armedservices.house.gov/hearings/full-committee-hearing-state -defense-industrial-base. The Congressional Research Service has also written briefs on this topic: https://crsreports.congress.gov/product/pdf/IF/IF10548.

16. One of the foremost experts on the challenges of military adaptation, Williamson Murray, notes in his 2011 book *Military Adaptation in War* that "one of the foremost attributes of military effectiveness must lie in the ability of armies, navies or air forces to recognize and adapt to the actual conditions of combat, as well as to the new tactical, operational and strategic, not to mention political, challenges that war inevitably throws up." Williamson Murray, *Military Adaptation in War: With Fear of Change* (Cambridge: Cambridge University Press, 2011), 1.

17. Philipp Blom, *The Vertigo Years: Change and Culture in the West, 1900–1914* (London: Phoenix Books, 2009), 2–3.

18. Heather Mongilio, "A Brief Summary of the Battle of the Black Sea," *United States Naval Institute News*, 15 November 2023, https://news.usni.org /2023/11/15/a-brief-summary-of-the-battle-of-the-black-sea.

19. Andrew Marshall, "Some Thoughts on Military Revolutions—Second Version," Memorandum for the Record, 23 August 1993, U.S. Department of Defense.

20. David Alberts et al., *Network Centric Warfare: Developing and Leveraging Information Superiority*, 2nd ed. (Washington, DC: DoD C4ISR Cooperative Research Program, 1999), 1.

21. U.S. National Aeronautics and Space Administration (NASA) Fire Information and Resource Management System (FIRMS), https://firms.modaps.eosdis.nasa .gov/map/#d:24hrs;@28.5,0.0,3z.

22. Mark Trevelyan, "'Targeted' Russian Ex-submarine Commander Shot Dead on Morning Run," *Australian Financial Review*, 12 July 2023, https://www.afr.com /policy/foreign-affairs/targeted-russian-ex-submarine-commander-shot-dead -on-morning-run-20230712-p5dnlb; Mariya Knight et al., "Russian Commander Killed while Jogging May Have Been Tracked on Strava App," CNN, 11 July 2023, https://edition.cnn.com/2023/07/11/europe/russian-submarine-commander -killed-krasnador-intl/index.html.

23. Author's interviews with Ukrainian service personnel conducted in Ukraine.

24. Jennifer Shore, "Don't Underestimate Ukraine's Volunteer Hackers," *Foreign Policy*, 11 April 2022, https://foreignpolicy.com/2022/04/11/russia-cyberwarfare-us-ukraine-volunteer-hackers-it-army/.

25. Shane Huntley, "Fog of War: How the Ukraine Conflict Transformed the Cyber Threat Landscape," Google, 16 February 20 23, https://blog.google/threat-analysis-group/fog-of-war-how-the-ukraine-conflict-transformed-the-cyber-threat-landscape/.

26. Isabelle Khurshudyan, Mary Ilyushina, and Kostiantyn Khudov, "Russia and Ukraine Are Fighting the First Full-Scale Drone War," *Washington Post*, 2 December 2022, https://www.washingtonpost.com/world/2022/12/02/drones-russia-ukraine-air-war/.

27. Amy Zegart, "Open Secrets: Ukraine and the Next Intelligence Revolution," *Foreign Affairs* 102, no. 1 (January/February 2023), 70.

28. Alexander Lovelace, *The Media Offensive: How the Press and Public Opinion Shaped Allied Strategy during World War II* (Lawrence: University Press of Kansas, 2022), 15.

29. Jessica Brandt, "Pre-empting Putin: Washington's Campaign of Intelligence Disclosures Is Complicating Moscow's Plans for Ukraine," Brookings Institution, 18 February 2022, https://www.brookings.edu/articles/preempting-putin-washingtons-campaign-of-intelligence-disclosures-is-complicating-moscows-plans-for-ukraine/.

30. Joshua Askew, "Why Does So Much of the Global South Support Russia, Not Ukraine?," Euronews, 31 March 2023, https://www.euronews.com/my-europe/2023/03/29/why-does-so-much-of-the-global-south-support-russia-not-ukraine; Francis Ghiles, *Global South Does Not Buy Western Stance on Ukraine* (Barcelona: Barcelona Centre for International Affairs, 2022); Hans Kundnani, "The War in Ukraine, Democracy, and the Global South: We Have a Problem," International Centre for Defence and Security, 23 May 2023, https://icds.ee/en/the-war-in-ukraine-democracy-and-the-global-south-we-have-a-problem/.

31. Ian Hill, "Russia's Invasion of Ukraine Is Spurring a Transition of Global Order," *The Interpreter*, 22 May 2023, https://www.lowyinstitute.org/the-interpreter/russia-s-invasion-ukraine-spurring-transition-global-order.

32. Sebastien Roblin, "Pilot Explains How Ukraine's Crowdfunded 'Army of Drones' Saves Lives," *Forbes*, 2 May 2023, https://www.forbes.com/sites/sebastienroblin/2023/05/02/interview-pilot-explains-how-ukraines-crowdfunded-army-of-drones-saves-lives/?sh=3739aa3d596c; James Marson, "Crowdfunded Technology Gives Ukraine an Edge on Front Lines," *Wall Street Journal*, 10 January 2023, https://www.wsj.com/articles/crowdfunded-technology-gives-ukraine-an-edge-on-front-lines-11673362520.

33. Dan Taylor, "Ukraine Gets CASEVAC Unmanned Ground Vehicles from Milrem Robotics," *Military Embedded Systems*, 6 September 2022, https://military embedded.com/unmanned/payloads/ukraine-to-get-casevac-unmanned -ground-vehicles-from-milrem-robotics; Samuel Bendett, "Bureaucrat's Gambit: Why Is Dmitry Rogozin Sending Russian Uncrewed Ground Vehicles to Ukraine—and Does It Matter?," Modern War Institute, 10 February 2023, https://mwi.usma.edu/bureaucrats-gambit-why-is-dmitry-rogozin-sending -russian-uncrewed-ground-vehicles-to-ukraine-and-does-it-matter/; Samuel Bendett and Jeffrey Edmonds, *Russia's Use of Uncrewed Systemsw in Ukraine* (Washington, DC: Center for Naval Analyses, 2023).

34. Ryan, "Six Months after Putin's Invasion."

SELECTED BIBLIOGRAPHY

In addition to the traditional resources (e.g., books, reports, and articles) listed below, researching the war in Ukraine has necessitated extensive use of different podcasts and social media, including X (formerly Twitter), Facebook, and Telegram. Some of these resources provide daily updates about different elements of the war, including analysis and mapping products.

The key podcasts I have used in researching this book include the following:

In Moscow's Shadows, https://inmoscowsshadows.wordpress.com/in-moscows-shadows-podcast/

The Russia Contingency, https://warontherocks.com/premium/therussia contingency/page/2/

War on the Rocks, https://warontherocks.com

The key social media resources I have employed in researching this book include the following:

Institute for the Study of War (daily updates), https://twitter.com/TheStudyofWar

Military Land, https://twitter.com/Militarylandnet

Tatarigami_UA, https://twitter.com/Tatarigami_UA

U.K. Ministry of Defence daily update, https://twitter.com/DefenceHQ

Ukrainian Ministry of Defense:

Facebook (daily operational updates): https://www.facebook.com/GeneralStaff.ua/

Telegram: https://t.me/ministry_of_defense_ua

X (Twitter): https://twitter.com/DefenceU

War Mapper: https://twitter.com/War_Mapper
War Monitor: https://twitter.com/WarMonitor3
War Translated: https://twitter.com/wartranslated

▓ ▓ ▓

Adamsky, Dima. "The Art of Net Assessment and Uncovering Foreign Military Innovations: Learning from Andrew W. Marshall's Legacy." *Journal of Strategic Studies* 43, no. 5 (2020): 611–44.

———. "Cross-Domain Coercion: The Current Russian Art of Strategy." Proliferation Papers 54. Institut Français des Relations Internationales, Paris, 2015.

———. *The Culture of Military Innovation: The Impact of Cultural Factors on the Revolution in Military Affairs in Russia, the U.S., and Israel.* Stanford, CA: Stanford Security Studies, 2010.

———. "Russian Campaign in Syria—Change and Continuity in Strategic Culture." *Journal of Strategic Studies* 43, no. 1 (2020): 104–25.

Allin, Dana. "Ukraine: The Shock of Recognition." *Survival* 2, vol. 64 (2022): 201–8.

Altman, Howard. "Ukraine Situation Report: Russia Adding 'Cope Cages' to TOS-1A." *The Warzone*, 10 April 2023. https://www.thedrive.com/the-war-zone/ukraine-situation-report-russia-adding-cope-cages-to-tos-1a.

———. "Ukraine Situation Report: This May Be Russia's First Kamikaze Drone Boat Attack." *The Warzone*, 10 February 2023. https://www.thedrive.com/the-war-zone/ukraine-situation-report-this-maybe-russias-first-kamikaze-drone-boat-attack.

Angell, Norman. *The Great Illusion: A Study of the Relation of Military Power to National Advantage.* New York: G. P. Putnam's Sons, 1913.

Arabia, Christina, Andrew Bowen, and Cory Welt. *U.S. Security Assistance to Ukraine.* Washington, DC: Congressional Research Service, 27 February 2023.

Arbatov, Alexei. "The Transformation of Russian Military Doctrine: Lessons Learned from Kosovo and Chechnya." Marshall Center Papers No. 2. Marshall Center, Garmisch, Germany, 2000.

Archick, Kristin. *Russia's War against Ukraine: European Union Responses and U.S.-EU Relations.* Washington, DC: Congressional Research Service, 6 February 2023.

Australian Army. *Adaptive Campaigning.* Canberra: Australian Army, 2006.

———. *LWD1: The Fundamentals of Land Power.* Canberra: Australian Army, 2017.

Babbage, Ross. *Stealing a March: Chinese Hybrid Warfare in the Indo-Pacific*, vol. 1. Washington, DC: Center for Strategic and Budgetary Assessments, 2019.

———. *Winning without Fighting: Chinese and Russian Political Warfare Campaigns and How the West Can Prevail*, vol. 1. Washington, DC: Center for Strategic and Budgetary Assessments, 2019.

Baldor, Lolita. "Ukraine Uses US-Provided Long-Range ATACMS Missiles against Russian Forces for the First Time." *AP News*, 18 October 2023. https://apnews.com/article/atacms-ukraine-longrange-missiles-5fd95f32449d14da22b82d57d6ccab22.

Barabba, Vincent, and Ian Mitroff. *Business Strategies for a Messy World: Tools for Systemic Problem-Solving*. New York: Palgrave Macmillan, 2014.

Barno, David, and Nora Bensahel. *Adaptation under Fire: How Militaries Change in Wartime*. New York: Oxford University Press, 2020.

———. "The Other Big Lessons the US Army Should Learn from Ukraine." *War on the Rocks*, 27 June 2022. https://warontherocks.com/2022/06/the-other-big-lessons-that-the-us-army-should-learn-from-ukraine/.

Barrios, Ricardo. *China-Russia Relations*. Washington, DC: Congressional Research Service, 24 February 2023.

Baxter, William. *Soviet Airland Battle Tactics*. Vovato, CA: Presidio, 1986.

Beagle, Milford, Jason Slider, and Matthew Arrol. "The Graveyard of Command Posts: What Chornobaivka Should Teach Us about Command and Control in Large-Scale Combat Operations." *Military Review*, May–June 2023, 10–15.

Becker, Torbjörn, Beatrice Weder di Mauro, Tymofiy Mylovanov, Kenneth Rogoff, Simon Johnson, Sergei Guriev, Yuriy Gorodnichenko, and Barry Eichengreen. *A Blueprint for the Reconstruction of Ukraine*. London: Centre for Economic Policy Research, 2022.

Belton, Catherine. *Putin's People: How the KGB Took Back Russia and Then Took On the West*. New York: Farrar, Straus and Giroux, 2022.

Bendett, Samuel. "Bureaucrat's Gambit: Why Is Dmitry Rogozin Sending Russian Uncrewed Ground Vehicles to Ukraine—and Does It Matter?" Modern War Institute, 10 February 2023. https://mwi.usma.edu/bureaucrats-gambit-why-is-dmitry-rogozin-sending-russian-uncrewed-ground-vehicles-to-ukraine-and-does-it-matter/.

———. "Roles and Implications of AI in the Russian-Ukrainian Conflict." *Russia Matters*, Harvard Kennedy School: Belfer Center for Science and International Affairs, 20 July 2023. https://www.russiamatters.org/analysis/roles-and-implications-ai-russian-ukrainian-conflict.

Bendett, Samuel, and Jeffrey Edmonds. *Russia's Use of Uncrewed Systems in Ukraine*. Washington, DC: Center for Naval Analyses, 2023.

Best, Geoffrey, and Andrew Wheatcroft, eds. *War, Economy and the Military Mind*. Totowa, NJ: Rowman and Littlefield, 1976.

Betliy, Oleksandra. "Ukraine Needs a Financial Lifeline, Too." Carnegie Endowment for International Peace, 5 December 2022. https://carnegieendowment.org/2022/12/05/ukraine-needs-financial-lifeline-too-pub-88569.

Biddle, Stephen. *Military Power: Explaining Victory and Defeat in Modern Battle*. Princeton, NJ: Princeton University Press, 2006.

———. "Ukraine and the Future of Offensive Maneuver." *War on the Rocks*, 22 November 2022. https://warontherocks.com/2022/11/ukraine-and-the-future-of-offensive-maneuver/.

Biddle, Stephen, and Stephen Long. "Democracy and Military Effectiveness: A Deeper Look." *Journal of Conflict Resolution* 48, no. 4 (August 2004): 525–46.

Biden, Joseph. "What America Will and Will Not Do in Ukraine." *New York Times*, 31 May 2022. https://www.nytimes.com/2022/05/31/opinion/biden-ukraine -strategy.html.

Binnendijk, Hans, and Richard Kugler. "Adapting Forces to a New Era: Ten Trans- forming Concepts." *Defense Horizons* 5. Washington, DC: National Defense University Press, November 2001. https://ndupress.ndu.edu/Publications/ Article/1215538/adapting-forces-toa-new-era-ten-transforming-concepts/.

Blainey, Geoffrey. *The Causes of War*. New York: Free Press, 1973.

Blanchard, Ben. "Analysis: Taiwan Studies Ukraine War for Own Battle Strategy with China." Reuters, 9 March 2023. https://www.reuters.com /business/aerospace-defense/taiwan-studies-ukraine-war-own-battle-strategy -with-china-2022-03-09/.

———. "Taiwan Sees China Taking Lessons from Russia's Ukraine Invasion." Reuters, 24 February 2023. https://www.reuters.com/world/asia-pacific /taiwan-sees-china-taking-lessons-russias-ukraine-invasion-2023-02-24/.

Blanken, Leo, Hy Rothstein, and Jason Lepore, eds. *Assessing War: The Challenge of Measuring Success and Failure*. Washington, DC: Georgetown University Press, 2015.

Bloch, Jean. *The Future of War in Its Technical, Economic and Political Relations*. Boston: Ginn and Company, 1899.

Bobbitt, Philip. *The Shield of Achilles: War, Peace, and the Course of History*. London: Penguin Books, 2002.

Bonadonna, Reed. *Soldiers and Civilization: How the Profession of Arms Thought and Fought the Modern World into Existence*. Annapolis: Naval Institute Press, 2017.

Bondarev, Boris. "The Sources of Russian Misconduct." *Foreign Affairs* 101, no. 6 (November/December 2022): 36–55.

Boot, Max. "Russia Is Fighting by the Book. The Problem Is, It's the Wrong Book." *Washington Post*, 2 November 2022. https://www.washingtonpost.com /opinions/2022/11/02/max-boot-russia-military-doctrine-ukraine/.

———. *War Made New: Technology, Warfare, and the Course of History, 1500 to Today*. New York: Gotham Books, 2006.

Boston, Scott, Michael Johnson, Nathan Beauchamp-Mustafaga, and Yvonne K. Crane. *Assessing the Conventional Force Imbalance in Europe: Implications for Countering Russian Local Superiority*. Santa Monica, CA: RAND Corporation, 2018.

Bouldin, Matthew. "The Ivanov Doctrine and Military Reform: Reasserting Stability in Russia." *Journal of Slavic Studies* 17, no. 4 (2004): 619–41.

Bourke, Joanna. *An Intimate History of Killing: Face-to-Face Killing in Twentieth-Century Warfare*. London: Granta Books, 1999.

Bowen, Andrew. *Ukrainian Armed Forces*. Washington, DC: Congressional Research Service, June 2021.

Boyd, John. "Destruction and Creation." Unpublished paper, 3 September 1976.

———. "Patterns of Conflict: Warp XII." Unpublished briefing. Quantico, VA: Alfred Gray Research Center Archives, March 1978.

Brands, Hal, ed. *The New Makers of Modern Strategy: From the Ancient World to the Digital Age*. Princeton, NJ: Princeton University Press, 2023.

———. *What Good Is Grand Strategy?* Ithaca, NY: Cornell University Press, 2014.

Braumoeller, Bear. *Only the Dead: The Persistence of War in the Modern Age*. New York: Oxford University Press, 2019.

Breen, Bob. *A Short History of the Adaptive Army Initiative 2007–2010*. Canberra: Australian Army, 2014.

Brodie, Bernard, *Strategy in the Missile Age*. Princeton, NJ: Princeton University Press, 1959.

Brodie, Bernard, and Fawn Brodie. *From Crossbow to H-Bomb: The Evolution of the Weapons and Tactics of Warfare*. Bloomington: Indiana University Press, 1973.

Bronk, Justin. "The Mysterious Case of the Missing Russian Air Force." Royal United Service Institute, 28 February 2022. https://rusi.org/explore-our-research /publications/commentary/mysterious-case-missing-russian-air-force.

———. "Ukraine Needs Air Defense Assistance to Protect Hard Won Victories on the Ground." *War on the Rocks*, 16 November 2022. https://warontherocks .com/2022/11/ukraine-needs-air-defense-assistance-to-protect-hard-won -victories-on-the-ground/.

Bronk, Justin, Nick Reynolds, and Jack Watling. "The Russian Air War and Ukrainian Requirements for Air Defence." Royal United Services Institute, 7 November 2022. https://rusi.org/explore-our-research/publications/special-resources /russian-air-war-and-ukrainian-requirements-air-defence.

Brooks, Risa, and Elizabeth Stanley, eds. *Creating Military Power: The Sources of Military Effectiveness*. Stanford, CA: Stanford University Press, 2007.

Brown, Ian. *A New Conception of War*. Quantico, VA: Marine Corps University Press, 2018.

Budjeryn, Mariana, and Matthew Bunn, *Budapest Memorandum at 25: Between Past and Future*. Cambridge: Belfer School for Science and International Affairs, 2020.

Burgess, Matt. "Ukraine's Volunteer 'IT Army' Is Hacking in Uncharted Territory." *Wired*, 27 February 2022. https://www.wired.co.uk/article/ukraine-it-army -russia-war-cyberattacks-ddos.

Burke, Anthony. "Jus Ad Bellum (Just War Theory)." In *Key Concepts in Military Ethics*, edited by Deane-Peter Baker, 107–11. Sydney: Sydney University Press, 2015.

Cannadine, David, ed. *Blood, Toil, Tears and Sweat: The Speeches of Winston Churchill*. Boston: Houghton Mifflin, 1990.

Chad, Serena. *A Revolution in Military Adaptation: The US Army in the Iraq War*. Washington, DC: Georgetown University Press, 2011.

Chaharnyi, Oleksii. "Zelensky Increases Number of Armed Forces, Signs Laws on National Resistance." *Kyiv Post*, 29 July 2021. https://www.kyivpost.com /ukraine-politics/zelensky-increases-the-number-of-the-armed-forces-signs -laws-on-national-resistance.html.

Charap, Samuel, Dara Massicot, Miranda Priebe, Alyssa Demus, Clint Reach, Mark Stalczynski, Eugeniu Han, and Lynn E. Davis. *Russian Grand Strategy: Rhetoric and Reality*. Santa Monica, CA: RAND Corporation, 2021.

Chase, Michael, Jeffrey Engstrom, Tai Ming Cheung, Kristen Gunness, Scott W. Harold, Susan Puska, and Samuel K. Berkowitz. *China's Incomplete Military Transformation: Assessing the Weaknesses of the People's Liberation Army (PLA)*. Santa Monica, CA: RAND Corporation, 2015.

Chatzky, Andrew, and James McBride. "China's Massive Belt and Road Initiative." Council on Foreign Relations Backgrounder, 28 January 2020. https://www.cfr .org/backgrounder/chinas-massive-belt-and-road-initiative.

Cheung, Tai Ming, ed. *Forging China's Military Might: A New Framework for Assessing Innovation*. Baltimore: Johns Hopkins University Press, 2014.

Clark, Brian, Daniel Patt, and Harrison Schramm. *Mosaic Warfare*. Washington, DC: Center for Strategic and Budgetary Assessments, 2020.

Clarke, Michael, Adam Henschke, Matthew Sussex, and Tim Legrand, eds. *The Palgrave Handbook of National Security*. Cham, Switzerland: Palgrave Macmillan, 2022.

Coats, Daniel R. *Statement for the Record: Worldwide Threat Assessment of the U.S. Intelligence Community*. Washington, DC: Office of the Director of National Intelligence, January 2019.

Cohen, Eliot. *The Big Stick: The Limits of Soft Power and the Necessity of Military Force*. New York: Basic Books, 2016.

———. "Putin's Regime Faces the Fate of His Kerch Strait Bridge." *The Atlantic*, 10 October 2022. https://www.theatlantic.com/ideas/archive/2022/10/putins -regime-faces-the-fate-of-his-kerch-bridge/671693/.

———. *Supreme Command: Soldiers, Statesmen, and Leadership in Wartime*. New York: Free Press, 2002.

Cohen, Eliot, and John Gooch. *Military Misfortunes: The Anatomy of Failure in War*. New York: Vintage Books, 1990.

Cole, Brendan. "Russia Plans Military Expansion as Putin Looks to Turn Tide on War—ISW," *Newsweek*, 18 January 2023. https://www.newsweek.com/ putin-russia-ukraine-isw-expansion-war-tide-1774606.

Collins, Liam, Michael Kofman, and John Spencer. "The Battle of Hostomel Airport: A Key Moment in Russia's Defeat in Kyiv." *War on the Rocks*, 10 August 2023. https://warontherocks.com/2023/08/the-battle-of-hostomel-airport-a-key-moment-in-russias-defeat-in-kyiv/.

Colton, Timothy, and Thane Gustafson, eds. *Soldiers and the Soviet State: Civil-Military Relations from Brezhnev to Gorbachev.* Princeton, NJ: Princeton University Press, 2014.

Cook, Cynthia. *Reviving the Arsenal of Democracy: Steps for Surging Defense Industrial Capacity.* Washington, DC: Center for Strategic and International Studies, March 2023.

Cook, Ellie. "Russia's Elite 'Storm-Z' Units Now Effectively 'Penal Battalions'—UK." *Newsweek*, 24 October 2023. https://www.newsweek.com/russia-storm-z-penal-battalions-ukraine-1837234.

Cooper, Helene, Eric Schmitt, and Thomas Gibbons-Neff. "Soaring Death Toll Gives Grim Insight into Russian Tactics." *New York Times*, 2 February 2023. https://www.nytimes.com/2023/02/02/us/politics/ukraine-russia-casualties.html.

Cooper, Julian. "Russia's Updated National Security Strategy." NATO Defence College, 19 July 2021. https://www.ndc.nato.int/research/research.php?icode=704.

Cordesman, Anthony. *NATO Force Planning: Rethinking the Defense Industrial Base.* Washington, DC: Center for Strategic and International Studies, July 2022.

———. *U.S. Competition with China and Russia: The Crisis-Driven Need to Change U.S. Strategy.* Washington, DC: Center for Strategic and International Studies, May 2020.

Cranny-Evans, Sam. "Understanding Russia's Mobilisation." *Commentary,* Royal United Services Institution, 28 September 2022. https://rusi.org/explore-our-research/publications/commentary/understanding-russias-mobilisation.

Dahm, Michael. "Chinese Debates on the Military Utility of Artificial Intelligence." *War on the Rocks*, 5 June 2020. https://warontherocks.com/2020/06/chinese-debates-on-the-military-utility-of-artificial-intelligence/.

Dalsjö, Robert, Michael Jonsson, and Johan Norberg. "A Brutal Examination: Russian Military Capability in Light of the Ukraine War." *Survival* 64, no. 3 (2022): 7–28.

Dempsey, Martin. *No Time for Spectators: The Lessons That Mattered Most from West Point to the West Wing.* Arlington, VA: Missionday, 2020.

Detsch, Jack. "Russia's New Top Commander in Ukraine Is 'Willing to Sell His Soul.'" *Foreign Policy*, 12 April 2022. https://foreignpolicy.com/2022/04/12/russia-new-top-commander-dvornikov-ukraine/.

Devega, Chauncey. "Putin's Massive Mistake: Lawrence Freedman on Ukraine and the Lessons of History." *Salon*, 21 November 2022. https://www.salon.com/2022/11/21/putins-massive-mistake-lawrence-freedman-on-ukraine-and-the-lessons-of-history/.

Diesen, Glenn. *Russia's Geoeconomic Strategy for Greater Eurasia*. New York: Routledge, 2018.

Dixon, Norman. *On the Psychology of Military Incompetence*. New York: Basic Books, 1976.

Doris, Andrew, and Thomas Graham. "What Putin Fights For." *Survival* 64, no. 4 (2022): 75–88.

Doughty, Ralph, Linton Wells, and Theodore Hailes, eds. *Innovative Learning: A Key to National Security*. Fort Leavenworth, KS: Army University Press, 2015.

Douhet, Giulio. *The Command of the Air*. Translated by Dino Ferrari. Washington, DC: Office of Air Force History, 1983.

Dowling, Jonathan, and Gerard Milburn. "Quantum Technology: The Second Quantum Revolution." *Royal Society* 361 (2003): 1655–74.

Dupuy, Trevor. *The Evolution of Weapons and Warfare*. New York: Da Capo Press, 1984.

———. *Understanding War: History and Theory of Combat*. New York: Paragon House, 1987.

Eisenhower, Dwight. *Crusade in Europe*. New York: Doubleday and Company, 1948.

Engstrom, Jeffrey. *Systems Confrontation and System Destruction Warfare*. Santa Monica, CA: RAND Corporation, 2018.

Eversden, Andrew. "US Army Secretary: 5 Lessons from the Ukraine Conflict." *Breaking Defense*, 1 June 2022. https://breakingdefense.com/2022/06 us-army-secretary-5-lessons-from-the-ukraine-conflict/.

Fasola, Nicolò, and Alyssa J. Wood. "Reforming Ukraine's Security Sector." *Survival* 63, no. 2 (2021): 41–54.

Fedor, Julie, Markku Kangaspuro, Jussi Lassila, and Tatiana Zhurzhenko, eds. *War and Memory in Russia, Ukraine and Belarus*. Cham, Switzerland: Palgrave Macmillan, 2017.

Feifer, Gregory. *The Great Gamble: The Soviet War in Afghanistan*. New York: HarperCollins, 2009.

Ferguson, Kirstin. *Head and Heart: The Art of Modern Leadership*. Melbourne: Viking, 2023

Finkel, Meir. *Military Agility: Ensuring Rapid and Effective Transition from Peace to War*. Lexington: University of Kentucky Press, 2020.

———. *On Flexibility: Recovery from Technological and Doctrinal Surprise on the Battlefield*. Stanford: Stanford University Press, 2007.

Finney, Nathan, ed. *On Strategy: A Primer*. Fort Leavenworth, KS: Army University Press, 2020.

Fontes, Robin, and Jorrit Kamminga. "Ukraine a Living Lab for AI Warfare." *National Defense*, 24 March 2023. https://www.nationaldefensemagazine.org /articles/2023/3/24/ukraine-a-living-lab-for-ai-warfare.

Ford, Christopher. *Defending Taiwan: Defense and Deterrence.* Fairfax, VA: National Institute Press, February 2022.

Foster, Richard, Andre Beaufre, and Wynfred Joshua, eds. *Strategy for the West: American-Allied Relations in Transition.* London: Macdonald and Company, 1974.

Fox, Aimée. *Learning to Fight: Military Innovation and Change in the British Army, 1914–1918.* Cambridge: Cambridge University Press, 2017.

Fox, Amos, and Andrew Rossow. "Making Sense of Russian Hybrid Warfare: A Brief Assessment of the Russo-Ukrainian War." Land Warfare Paper 112. Association of the U.S. Army, Arlington, VA, 2017.

Freedman, Lawrence. "Beyond Surprise Attack." *Parameters* 47, no. 2 (Summer 2017): 7.

———. *Command: The Politics of Military Operations from Korea to Ukraine.* London: Penguin Random House UK, 2022.

———. *The Future of War: A History.* New York: Public Affairs Press, 2017.

———. "The Meaning of Strategy, Part 1." *Texas National Security Review* 1, no. 1 (November 2017): 90–105. https://tnsr.org/2017/11/meaning-strategy-part-origin-story/.

———. "The Problem with Donbas." *Comment Is Freed*, 31 March 2022. https://samf.substack.com/p/the-problem-with-the-donbas?utm_source=twitter&s=r.

———. "A Reckless Gamble." *Comment Is Freed*, 25 February 2022. https://samf.substack.com/p/a-reckless-gamble.

———. *Strategy: A History.* Oxford: Oxford University Press, 2013.

———. "Ukraine and the Art of Limited War." *Survival* 56, no. 6 (2014): 7–38.

———. *Ukraine and the Art of Strategy.* Oxford: Oxford University Press, 2019.

Fridman, Ofer. *Strategiya: The Foundations of the Russian Art of Strategy.* London: Hurst and Company, 2021.

Friedman, B. A. *On Operations: Operational Art and Military Disciplines.* Annapolis: Naval Institute Press, 2021.

———. *On Tactics: A Theory of Victory in Battle.* Annapolis: Naval Institute Press, 2017.

Friedrich, Julia, and Theresa Lutkefend. *The Long Shadow of Donbas: Reintegrating Veterans and Fostering Social Cohesion.* Berlin: Global Public Policy Institute, 2021.

Fry, Douglas, ed. *War, Peace, and Human Nature: The Convergence of Evolutionary and Cultural Views.* Oxford: Oxford University Press, 2013.

Fuller, J. F. C. *The Foundations of the Science of War.* London: Hutchinson and Co., 1926.

Gaddis, John. *The Cold War.* London: Penguin Books, 2005.

———. *On Grand Strategy.* London: Penguin Books, 2019.

Gady, Franz-Stefan, and Michael Kofman. "Ukraine's Strategy of Attrition." *Survival* 65, no. 2 (2023): 7–22.

Galeotti, Mark. "The Mythical 'Gerasimov Doctrine' and the Language of Threat." *Critical Studies on Security* 7, no. 2 (2019): 157–61.

———. *Russia's Wars in Chechnya, 1994–2009*. Oxford, U.K.: Osprey, 2014.

Ganster, Ronja, Jacob Kirkegaard, Thomas Kleine-Brockhoff, and Bruce Stokes. *Designing Ukraine's Recovery in the Spirit of the Marshall Plan: Principles, Architecture, Financing, Accountability: Recommendations for Donor Countries.* Washington, DC: German Marshall Fund of the United States, September 2022.

Gartner, Scott. *Strategic Assessment in War*. New Haven, CT: Yale University Press, 1997.

Gat, Azar. *Military Thought in the Nineteenth Century*. New York: Oxford University Press, 1992.

———. *War in Human Civilization*. Oxford: Oxford University Press, 2006.

Gavrilov, Viktor. "Soviet Union Military Planning, 1948–1968." In *Blueprints for Battle: Planning for War in Central Europe, 1948–1968*, 121–30. Lexington: University Press of Kentucky, 2012.

Gfoeller, Emmanuel. "Gap Warfare: The Case for a Shift in America's Strategic Mindset." *Real Clear Defense*, 28 May 2020. https://www.realcleardefense.com /articles/2020/05/28/gap_warfare_the_case_for_a_shift_in_americas_strategic _mindset_115325.html.

Glenshaw, Paul. "Secret Casualties of the Cold War." *Air and Space Magazine*, December 2017. https://www.airspacemag.com/history-of-flight/secret -casualties-of-the-cold-war-180967122/.

Golts, Alexander, and Michael Kofman. *Russia's Military: Assessment, Strategy, and Threat*. Washington, DC: Center of Global Interests, 2016.

Gould-Davies, Nigel. "Putin's Strategic Failure." *Survival* 64, no. 2 (2022): 7–16.

Government of China. *China's National Defense in the New Era*. Beijing: Government of China, July 2019.

———. *Thirteenth Five-Year Science and Technology Military-Civil Fusion Development Special Plan*. Beijing: Government of China, September 2017. http://www .aisixiang.com/data/106161.html.

Government of Japan. *Defence of Japan 2017*. Tokyo: Government of Japan, 2017.

———. *Defence of Japan 2018*. Tokyo: Government of Japan, 2018.

Government of the United Kingdom. *The Integrated Operating Concept 2025*. London: Ministry of Defence, 30 September 2020.

Grant, Glen. "2023—a Time and Chance for Military Change in Ukraine." *Maidan Website*, 20 February 2023. https://maidan.org.ua/en/2023/02/ glen-grant-2023-a-time-and-chance-for-military-change-in-ukraine/.

Grau, Lester, trans. and ed. *The Bear Went over the Mountain: Soviet Combat Tactics in Afghanistan*. Washington, DC: National Defense University Press, 1996.

Grau, Lester, and Charles Bartles. *The Russian Way of War: Force Structure, Tactics and Modernisation of Russian Ground Forces*. Fort Leavenworth, KS: Foreign Military Studies Office, 2016.

Gray, Colin. "Comparative Strategic Culture." *Parameters* 14, no. 4 (Winter 1984): 26–33.

———. *The Future of Strategy*. Cambridge: Polity, 2015.

———. *Modern Strategy*. Oxford: Oxford University Press, 1999.

———. *Strategy and Defence Planning: Meeting the Challenge of Uncertainty*. Oxford: Oxford University Press, 2014.

———. "War—Continuity in Change and Change in Continuity." *Parameters* 40, no. 2 (Summer 2010): 5–13.

———. *War, Peace, and Victory: Strategy and Statecraft for the Next Century*. New York: Simon and Schuster, 1990.

Gretskiy, Igor. *Russia's Propaganda War: Russia's War in Ukraine Series No. 9*. Tallinn, Estonia: International Centre for Defence and Security, August 2022.

Grisogono, Anne-Marie. "The Implications of Complex Adaptive Systems Theory for C2." Paper for the Command and Control Research and Technology Symposium, Cambridge, U.K., 26–28 September 2006.

———. "Success and Failure in Adaptation." Paper for the Sixth International Conference on Complex Systems, Boston, 25–30 June 2006.

Grossman, Derek. "Ukraine War Is Motivating Taiwan to Better Secure Its Own Future." *RAND Blog*, 13 May 2022. https://www.rand.org/blog/2022/05/ukraine-war-is-motivating-taiwan-to-better-secure-its.html.

Grynszpan, Emmanuel. "Russia's Mobilized Soldiers Speak Out: 'We Were Thrown on to the Frontline with No Support.'" *Le Monde*, 10 November 2022. https://www.lemonde.fr/en/international/article/2022/11/10/russia-s-mobilized-soldiers-speak-we-were-thrown-onto-the-frontline-with-no-support_6003764_4.html.

Gudmundsson, Bruce. *Stormtroop Tactics: Innovation in the German Army, 1914–1918*. Westport, CT: Praeger, 1989.

Hackett, John. *The Profession of Arms*. London: Sidgwick and Jackson, 1983.

Hammes, T. X. "Cheap Technology Will Challenge U.S. Tactical Dominance." *Joint Force Quarterly* 81 (2016). 76–85.

———. "The Future of Warfare: Small, Many, Smart vs Few and Exquisite?" *War on the Rocks*, 16 July 2014. https://warontherocks.com/2014/07/the-future-of-warfare-small-many-smart-vs-few-exquisite/.

———. "Game-Changers: Implications of the Russo-Ukraine War for the Future of Ground Warfare." Atlantic Council, 3 April 2023. https://www.atlanticcouncil.org/in-depth-research-reports/issue-brief/gamechangers-implications-of-the-russo-ukraine-war-for-the-future-of-ground-warfare/.

Hammond, Grant. *The Mind of War: John Boyd and American Security.* Washington, DC: Smithsonian Institution Press, 2001.

Hanson, Victor Davis. *The Father of Us All: War and History, Ancient and Modern.* New York: Bloomsbury, 2010.

———. *The Western Way of War: Infantry Battle in Classical Greece.* Berkeley: University of California Press, 2009.

———. "Why Technology Favors Tyranny." *The Atlantic,* October 2018, 64–70.

Harding, Andrew. "Ukraine War: Russian Threat Growing, Front Line Troops Fear." *BBC News,* 1 February 2023. https://www.bbc.com/news/world-europe-64455123.

Harding, Emily. "Scenario Analysis on a Ukrainian Insurgency." Washington, DC: Center for Strategic and International Studies, February 2022.

Harding, Phillip. *The British Shell Shortage of the First World War.* Stroud, U.K.: Fonthill, 2015.

Harris, Shane, Karen DeYoung, Isabelle Khurshudyan, Ashley Parker, and Liz Sly. "Road to War: U.S. Struggled to Convince Allies, and Zelensky, of Risk of Invasion." *Washington Post,* 16 August 2022. https://www.washingtonpost.com/national-security/interactive/2022/ukraine-road-to-war/?itid=sf_world_ukraine-russia_russia-gamble_p002_f001.

———. "Russia Planning Massive Military Offensive against Ukraine Involving 175,000 Troops, U.S. Intelligence Warns." *Washington Post,* 3 December 2021. https://www.washingtonpost.com/national-security/russia-ukraine-invasion/2021/12/03/98a3760e-546b-11ec-8769-2f4ecdf7a2ad_story.html.

Harrison, Mark. "Resource Mobilization for World War II: The USA, UK, USSR, and Germany, 1939–1945." *Economic History Review* 41, no. 2 (1988): 171–92.

Heginbotham, Eric, Michael Nixon, Forrest E. Morgan, Jacob L. Heim, Jeff Hagen, Sheng Li, Jeffrey Engstrom, Martin C. Libicki, Paul DeLuca, and David A. Shlapak. *The U.S.-China Military Scorecard: Forces, Geography, and the Evolving Balance of Power 1996–2017.* Santa Monica, CA: RAND Corporation, 2015.

Herman, Arthur. *Freedom's Forge: How American Business Produced Victory in World War II.* New York: Random House, 2012.

Heuser, Beatrice. *The Evolution of Strategy: Thinking War from Antiquity to the Present.* Cambridge: Cambridge University Press, 2010.

———. "Victory, Peace and Justice: The Neglected Trinity." *Joint Forces Quarterly,* no. 69 (Second Quarter 2013): 11.

———. *War: A Genealogy of Western Ideas and Practices.* Oxford: Oxford University Press, 2022.

Higham, Robin, and Frederick Kagan, eds. *The Military History of the Soviet Union.* New York: Palgrave, 2022.

Hill, Fiona, and Angela Stent. "The World Putin Wants." *Foreign Affairs* 101, no. 5 (September/October 2022): 108–22.

Hird, Karolina, Riley Bailey, Grace Mappes, George Barros, Layne Philipson, Nicole Wolkov, and Mason Clark. "Russian Campaign Assessment, 10 February 2023." Institute for the Study of War, 10 February 2023. https://www.understandingwar .org/backgrounder/russian-offensive-campaign-assessment-february-10-2023.

Hoehn, Andrew, Andrew Parasiliti, Sonni Efron, and Steven Strongin. *Discontinuities and Distractions: Rethinking Security for the Year 2040*. Santa Monica, CA: RAND Corporation, 2018.

Hoffenaar, Jan, and Dieter Krüger, eds. *Blueprints for Battle: Planning for War in Central Europe, 1948–1968*. Lexington: University Press of Kentucky, 2012.

Hoffman, Frank G. "American Defense Priorities after Ukraine." *War on the Rocks*, 2 January 2023. https://warontherocks.com/2023/01 /american-defense-priorities-after-ukraine/.

———. *Conflict in the 21st Century: The Rise of Hybrid Wars*. Washington, DC: Potomac Institute for Policy Studies, December 2007.

———. "Examining Complex Forms of Conflict: Gray Zone and Hybrid Challenges." *Prism* 7, no. 4 (November 2018): 30–47.

———. "Healthy Skepticism about the Future of Disruptive Technology and Modern War." *Geopoliticus* (Foreign Policy Research Institute blog), 4 January 2019. https://www.fpri.org/article/2019/01/healthy-skepticism-about-the-future-of -disruptive-technology-and-modern-war/https://www.fpri.org/article/2019/01 /healthy-skepticism-about-the-future-of-disruptive-technology-and-modern -war/.

———. *Mars Adapting: Military Change during War*. Annapolis: Naval Institute Press, 2021.

———. "The Missing Element in Crafting National Strategy: A Theory of Success." *Joint Forces Quarterly* 97 (March 2020): 55–64.

———. "Will War's Nature Change in the Seventh Military Revolution?" *Parameters* 47, no. 4 (Winter 2017–18): 23, 31.

Hoffman, Samantha, and Matthew Knight. *China's Messaging on the Ukraine Conflict*. Canberra: Australian Strategic Policy Institute, May 2022.

Holmes, James, and Toshi Yoshihara. *Red Star over the Pacific: China's Rise and the Challenge to U.S. Maritime Strategy*. 2nd ed. Annapolis: Naval Institute Press, 2018.

Horbulin, Volodymyr. *How to Beat Russia in the War of the Future*. Kyiv: Bright Books, 2021.

Horowitz, Michael. *The Diffusion of Military Power*. Princeton, NJ: Princeton University Press, 2010.

Horowitz, Michael, and Shira Pindyck. "What Is a Military Innovation and Why It Matters." *Journal of Strategic Studies* 46, no. 1 (2023): 97–98.

Horowitz, Michael, and Stephen Rosen. "Evolution or Revolution?" *Journal of Strategic Studies* 28, no. 3 (2005): 437–48.

Howard, Glen E. *Russia's Military Strategy and Doctrine*. Washington, DC: Jamestown Foundation, 2018.

Howard, Michael. *The Causes of War*. 2nd ed. Cambridge, MA: Harvard University Press, 1983.

———. *The Franco-Prussian War*. 2nd ed. New York: Routledge, 2001.

———. "Military Science in an Age of Peace." *RUSI Journal* 119, no. 1 (March 1974): 3–11.

———. "The Use and Abuse of Military History." *RUSI Journal* 138, no. 1 (1993): 26–30.

Hunder, Max. "Inside Ukraine's Scramble for 'Gamechanger' Drone Fleet." Reuters, 24 March 2023. https://www.reuters.com/world/europe /inside-ukraines-scramble-game-changer-drone-fleet-2023-03-24/.

Husain, Amir, ed. *Hyperwar: Conflict and Competition in the AI Century*. Austin: Spark Cognition Press, 2018.

Ikle, Fred. *Every War Must End*. New York: Columbia University Press, 1971.

International Institute for Strategic Studies. *The Military Balance 1992–1993*. London: International Institute for Strategic Studies, 1992.

———. *The Military Balance 2020*. London: International Institute for Strategic Studies, 2020. https://www.iiss.org/publications/the-military-balance /military-balance-2020-book.

Inwood, Joe. "Ukraine War: What Severodonetsk's Fall Means for the Conflict." BBC News, 26 June 2022. https://www.bbc.com/news/world-europe-61945914.

Ioanes, Ellen. "China Steals U.S. Designs for New Weapons, and It's Getting Away with the Greatest Property Theft in Human History." *Business Insider*, 25 September 2019. https://www.businessinsider.com.au/esper-warning-china -intellectual-property-theft-greatest-in-history-2019-9?r=US&IR=T.

Jackson, Jon. "Russian Soldier Describes Moscow's Use of 'Meat Assault' Tactic." *Newsweek*, 30 October 2023. https://www.newsweek.com/russian-soldier -describes-moscows-use-meat-assault-tactic-1839375#:~:text=Throughout%20 the%20war%20that%20Russian,large%20numbers%20of%20those%20regarded.

Janowitz, Morris. *The Professional Soldier: A Social and Political Portrait*. New York: Free Press, 1964.

Jee, Charlotte. "The First U.S. Trial of CRISPR Gene Editing in Cancer Patients Suggests the Technique Is Safe." *MIT Tech Review*, 7 February 2020. https:// www.technologyreview.com/f/615157/the-first-us-trial-of-crispr-gene-editing -in-cancer-patients-suggests-the-technique-is-safe/.

Jensen, Benjamin, and John Paschkewitz. "Mosaic Warfare: Small and Scalable Are Beautiful." *War on the Rocks*, 23 December 2019. https://warontherocks .com/2019/12/mosaic-warfare-small-and-scalable-are-beautiful/.

Jensen, Benjamin, Christopher Whyte, and Scott Cuomo. *Information in War: Military Innovation, Battle Networks, and the Future of Artificial Intelligence.* Georgetown: Georgetown University Press, 2022.

Johnson, David. *Fast Tanks and Heavy Bombers: Innovation in the U.S. Army, 1917–1945.* Ithaca, NY: Cornell University Press, 2003.

Johnson, Rob. "Dysfunctional Warfare: The Russian Invasion of Ukraine." *Parameters* 52, no. 2 (2022): 5–20.

Johnson, Rob, Martijn Kitzen, and Tim Sweijs. *The Conduct of War in the 21st Century: Kinetic, Connected and Synthetic.* London: Routledge, 2021.

Joint Chiefs of Staff. *DOD Dictionary of Military and Associated Terms.* Washington, DC: Department of Defense, November 2021.

Jomini, Antoine. *The Art of War.* London: Greenhill Books, 1996.

Jones, Bruce. "The New Geopolitics." Brookings Institution, 28 November 2017. https://www.brookings.edu/blog/order-from-chaos/2017/11/28/the-new-geopolitics/.

———. "This Will Be Hard (and Could Get Worse)." In *Lessons from Ukraine,* Brookings Institution, 24 February 2023. https://www.brookings.edu/essay/lessons-from-ukraine/.

Jones, Seth. *Empty Bins in a Wartime Environment: The Challenge to the U.S. Defense Industrial Base.* Washington, DC: Center for Strategic and International Studies, January 2023.

———. *Russia's Ill-Fated Invasion of Ukraine: Lessons in Modern Warfare.* Washington, DC: Center for Strategic and International Studies, June 2022.

Jones, Seth, Riley McCabe, and Alexander Palmer. *Ukrainian Innovation in a War of Attrition.* Washington, DC: Center for Strategic and International Studies, February 2023.

Jones, Seth, Alexander Palmer, and Joseph S. Bermudez Jr. *Ukraine's Offensive Operations: Shifting the Offense-Defense Balance.* Washington, DC: Center for Strategic and International Studies, 2023.

Jonsson, Oscar. *The Russian Understanding of War: Blurring the Lines between War and Peace.* Washington, DC: Georgetown University Press, 2019.

Juurvee, Ivo. "Civil Defence in Ukraine: Preliminary Lessons from the First Months of War." Tallinn, Estonia: International Centre for Defence and Security, November 2022.

Kabanenko, Ihor. "Ukraine's New National Security Strategy: A Wide Scope with Foggy Implementation Mechanisms." *Eurasia Daily Monitor,* Jamestown Foundation, 24 September 2020. https://jamestown.org/program/ukraines-new-national-security-strategy-a-wide-scope-with-foggy-implementation-mechanisms/.

Kagan, Frederick. *Russian Offensive Campaign Assessment, November 13.* Institute for the Study of War, 13 November 2022. https://www.understandingwar.org/backgrounder/russian-offensive-campaign-assessment-november-13.

Kagan, Robert. "The Twilight of the Liberal World Order." Brookings Institution, 24 January 2017. https://www.brookings.edu/research/the-twilight-of-the-liberal-world-order/.

Kahn, Lauren. "Can Iranian Drones Turn Russia's Fortunes in the Ukraine War?" Council on Foreign Relations, 26 October 2022. https://www.cfr.org/in-brief/can-iranian-drones-turn-russias-fortunes-ukraine-war.

Kallenborn, Zachery. "Autonomous Drone Swarms as WMD." Modern War Institute, 28 May 2020. https://mwi.usma.edu/swarms-mass-destruction-case-declaring-armed-fully-autonomous-drone-swarms-wmd/.

Kanet, Roger, ed. *Routledge Handbook of Russian Security*. New York: Routledge, 2019.

Kavanagh, Jennifer. "The Ukraine War Shows How the Nature of Power Is Changing." Carnegie Endowment for International Peace, 16 June 2022. https://carnegieendowment.org/2022/06/16/ukraine-war-shows-how-nature-of-power-is-changing-pub-87339.

Keegan, John. *A History of Warfare*. New York: Alfred A. Knopf, 1993.

Kennedy, Paul. *Engineers of Victory: The Problem Solvers Who Turned the Tide in the Second World War*. New York: Random House, 2013.

———. *The Rise and Fall of the Great Powers: Economic Change and Military Conflict from 1500 to 2000*. New York: Random House, 1987.

Kenney, Caitlin. "US Army Delays Doctrine Release to Incorporate Lessons from Ukraine." Defense One, 2 June 2022. https://www.defenseone.com/policy/2022/06/us-army-delays-doctrine-release-incorporate-lessons-ukraine/367715/.

Kim, Patricia. "The Limits of the No-Limits Partnership." *Foreign Affairs* 102, no. 2 (March/April 2023): 94–105.

Kingsley, Patrick, and Ronen Bergman. "Russia Shrinks Forces in Syria, a Factor in Israeli Strategy There." *New York Times*, 19 October 2022. https://www.nytimes.com/2022/10/19/world/middleeast/russia-syria-israel-ukraine.html.

Kirby, Paul. "Ukraine War: EU Set to Miss Target of a Million Shell Rounds." BBC News, 14 November 2023. https://www.bbc.com/news/world-europe-67413025.

Kiryukhin, Denys. "The Ukrainian Military: From Degradation to Renewal." Foreign Policy Research Institute, 17 August 2018. https://www.fpri.org/article/2018/08/the-ukrainian-military-from-degradation-to-renewal/.

Knight, Will. "Ukraine's Quest for Homegrown AI Drones to Take On Russia." *Wired*, 13 April 2023. https://www.wired.com/story/fast-forward-ukraines-quest-for-homegrown-ai-drones-to-take-on-russia/.

Knox, MacGregor, and Williamson Murray, eds. *The Dynamics of Military Revolution, 1300–2050*. Cambridge: Cambridge University Press, 2001.

Kofman, Michael. "The Moscow School of Hard Knocks: Key Pillars of Russian Strategy." *War on the Rocks*, 21 November 2019. https://warontherocks.com/2019/11/the-moscow-school-of-hard-knocks-key-pillars-of-russian-strategy-2/.

———. "Russian Performance in the Russo-Georgian War Revisited." *War on the Rocks*, 4 September 2018. https://warontherocks.com/2018/09/russian-performance-in-the-russo-georgian-war-revisited/.

———. "The Russo-Ukrainian War Ten Months In: Taking Stock." *Riddle*, 28 December 2022. https://ridl.io/wp-content//uploads/pdf/15887/the-russo-ukrainian-war-ten-months-intaking-stock.pdf.

Kofman, Michael, Anya Fink, Dmitry Gorenburg, Mary Chesnut, Jeffrey Edmonds, and Julian Waller. *Russian Military Strategy: Core Tenets and Operational Concepts*. Arlington: Center for Naval Analysis, October 2021.

Kofman, Michael, Dmitry Gorenburg, Mary Chesnut, Paul Saunders, Kasey Stricklin, and Julian Waller. *Russian Approaches to Competition*. Washington, DC: Center for Naval Analyses, 2021.

Kofman, Michael, and Rob Lee. "Not Built for Purpose: The Russian Military's Fated Force Design." *War on the Rocks*, 2 June 2022. https://warontherocks.com/2022/06/not-built-for-purpose-the-russian-militarys-ill-fated-force-design/.

Kofman, Michael, Katya Migacheva, Brian Nichiporuk, Andrew Radin, Olesya Tkacheva, and Jenny Oberholtzer. *Lessons from Russia's Operation Crimea and Eastern Ukraine*. Santa Monica, CA: RAND Corporation, 2017.

Kolbert, Elizabeth. "Peace in Our Time: Steven Pinker's History of Violence." *New Yorker*, 26 September 2011. https://www.newyorker.com/magazine/2011/10/03/peace-in-our-time-elizabeth-kolbert.

Konaev, Margarita, and Owen J. Daniels. "Agile Ukraine, Lumbering Russia: The Promise and Limits of Military Adaptation." *Foreign Affairs*, 28 March 2023. https://www.foreignaffairs.com/ukraine/russia-ukraine-war-lumbering-agile.

Kramer, Erik, and Paul Schneider, "What the Ukrainian Armed Forces Need to Do to Win." *War on the Rocks*, 2 June 2023. https://warontherocks.com/2023/06/what-the-ukrainian-armed-forces-need-to-do-to-win/.

Krepinevich, Andrew. *The Military-Technical Revolution: A Preliminary Assessment*. Washington, DC: Center for Strategic and Budgetary Assessments, 2002.

Kreps, Sarah. *Taxing Wars: The American Way of War Finance*. Oxford: Oxford University Press, 2018.

Kuo, Kendrick. "Dangerous Changes: When Military Innovation Harms Combat Effectiveness." *International Security* 47, no. 2 (Fall 2022): 48–87.

Kuzio, Taras. "Why Russia Invaded Ukraine." *Horizons. Journal of International Relations and Sustainable Development*, no. 21 (Summer 2022): 40–51.

Latimer, Jon. *Deception in War*. London: John Murray, 2001.

Layton, Peter, Zach Lambert, Nathan K. Finney, and Chris Barrie. "How to Mobilise Australia." Centre of Gravity Paper, Australian National University, Canberra, July 2020.

Leonhard, Robert. *Fighting by Minutes: Time and the Art of War*. Westport, CT: Praeger, 1994. Reprint (Kindle), KC Publishing, 2017.

Levine, Michael. "The Limits of Victory: Evaluating the Employment of Military Power." *Prism* 10, no. 1 (2022): 57–71.

Liang, Qiao, and Xiangsui Wang. *Unrestricted Warfare*. Beijing: PLA Literature and Arts Publishing, February 1999.

Liddell Hart, B. H. "The Objective in War." *Naval War College Review* 5, no. 4 (December 1952): 1–30.

Lohman, Diederik. *The Wrongs of Passage: Inhuman and Degrading Treatment of New Recruits in the Russian Armed Forces*. New York: Human Rights Watch, 2004.

Lovelace, Alexander. *The Media Offensive: How the Press and Public Opinion Shaped Allied Strategy during World War II*. Lawrence: University Press of Kansas, 2022.

Luttwak, Edward. *The Grand Strategy of the Soviet Union*. New York: St. Martin's, 1983.

———. *Strategy: The Logic of War and Peace*. Cambridge, MA: Belknap Press of Harvard University Press, 2001.

Luxmoore, Matthew. "A Year into War, Ukraine Faces Challenges Mobilizing Troops." *Wall Street Journal*, 23 March 2023. https://www.wsj.com/articles/a-year-into-war-ukraine-faces-challenges-mobilizing-troops-64dcdc49.

Lynn, John. *Battle: A History of Combat and Culture*. New York: Westview, 2003.

MacMillan, Margaret. "How Wars Don't End: Ukraine, Russia, and the Lessons of World War I." *Foreign Affairs* 102, no. 4 (July/August 2023): 52–65.

———. "Leadership at War: How Putin and Zelensky Have Defined the Ukrainian Conflict." *Foreign Affairs*, 29 March 2022. https://www.foreignaffairs.com/articles/ukraine/2022-03-29/leadership-war.

———. *War: How Conflict Shaped Us*. New York: Random House, 2020.

———. "Which Past Is Prologue? Heeding the Right Warnings from History." *Foreign Affairs* 99, no. 5 (September/October 2020): 12–22.

Mahnken, Thomas, ed. *Competitive Strategies for the 21st Century: Theory, History, and Practice*. Stanford, CA: Stanford University Press, 2012.

———. *Technology and the American Way of War since 1945*. New York: Columbia University Press, 2008.

Mahnken, Thomas, Ross Babbage, and Toshi Yoshihara. *Countering Comprehensive Coercion: Strategies against Authoritarian Political Warfare*. Washington, DC: Center for Defense and Strategic Studies, May 2018.

Mankoff, Jeffrey. *Russia's War in Ukraine: Identity, History and Conflict*. Washington, DC: Center for Strategic and International Studies, April 2022.

Mansoor, Peter, and Williamson Murray, eds. *The Culture of Military Organizations*. Cambridge: Cambridge University Press, 2019.

Mansoor, Sanya. "Why U.S. HIMARS Rockets Are Becoming Increasingly Decisive for Ukraine." *Time*, 5 January 2023. https://time.com/6244479/himars-rockets-ukraine-russia/.

Marshall, Andrew. "Competitive Strategies: History and Background." Unpublished paper. U.S. Department of Defense, 3 March 1988.

———. "Some Thoughts on Military Revolutions (Second Version)." Memorandum for the Record. U.S. Department of Defense, 23 August 1993.

Martin, Brad. "Will Logistics Be Russia's Undoing in Ukraine?" *The Hill*, 10 February 2023. https://thehill.com/opinion/international/3852532-will-logistics -be-russias-undoing-in-ukraine/.

Massicot, Dara. "Anticipating a New Russian Military Doctrine in 2020: What It Might Contain and Why It Matters." *War on the Rocks*, 9 September 2019. https:// warontherocks.com/2019/09/anticipating-a-new-russian-military-doctrine-in -2020-what-it-might-contain-and-why-it-matters/.

———. "Russian Military Operations in Ukraine in 2022 and the Year Ahead." Testimony presented before the U.S. Senate Committee on Armed Services on 28 February 2023. https://www.rand.org/content/dam/rand/pubs/testimonies /CTA2600/CTA2646-1/RAND_CTA2646-1.pdf.

———. "The Russian Military's Looming Personnel Crises of Retention and Veteran Mental Health." *RAND Blog*, 1 June 2023. https://www.rand.org/pubs /commentary/2023/06/the-russian-militarys-looming-personnel-crises-of -retention.html.

———. "What Russia Got Wrong." *Foreign Affairs*, March/April 2023, 78–93.

———. "Why Vladimir Putin Is Likely to Be Disappointed." *New York Times*, 17 October 2022. https://www.nytimes.com/2022/10/17/opinion/russia-ukraine -military-putin.html?smid=tw-nytopinion&smtyp=cur.

Matloff, Maurice. *Strategic Planning for Coalition Warfare, 1943–1944.* Washington, DC: Center of Military History, U.S. Army, 1953.

Matthews, Owen. *Overreach: The Inside Story of Putin's War against Ukraine.* London: Mudlark, 2022.

Mazarr, Michael, Jonathan S. Blake, Abigail Casey, Tim McDonald, Stephanie Pezard, and Michael Spirtas. *Understanding the Emerging Era of International Competition: Theoretical and Historical Perspectives.* Santa Monica, CA: RAND Corporation, 2018.

McCullough, Amy. "Goldfein's Multi-domain Vision." *Air Force Magazine*, 29 August 2018. https://www.airforcemag.com/article/goldfeins-multi-domain-vision/.

McDermott, Roger. "Gerasimov Unveils Russia's Strategy of Limited Actions." *Eurasia Daily Monitor*, 6 March 2019. https://jamestown.org/program/gerasimov -unveils-russias-strategy-of-limited-actions/.

McFate, Sean. *The New Rules of War: Victory in the Age of Durable Disorder.* New York: William Morrow, 2019.

McGrath, Rita. "Transient Advantage." *Harvard Business Review*, June 2013. https:// hbr.org/2013/06/transient-advantage.

Melkozerova, Veronika. "Russia May Have Lost an Entire Elite Brigade Near a Donetsk Coalmining Town." *Politico Europe*, 12 February 2023. https://www .politico.eu/article/russia-may-have-lost-an-entire-elite-brigade-near-a-coal mining-town-in-donbas-ukraine-says/.

Menon, Rajan, and Graham E. Fuller. "Russia's Ruinous Chechen War." *Foreign Affairs* 79, no. 2 (March/April 2000): 32–44.

Miller, Greg, and Catherine Belton. "Russia's Spies Misread Ukraine and Misled Kremlin as War Loomed." *Washington Post*, 19 August 2022. https://www.wash ingtonpost.com/world/interactive/2022/russia-fsb-intelligence-ukraine-war/.

Miller, Sergio. "Anatomy of a Russian Army Village Assault." *Wavell Room*, 1 February 2023. https://wavellroom.com/2023/02/01/anatomy-of-a-russian -army-village-assault/.

———. "The Battle for Bakhmut—Wagner Trench Warfare Tactics." *Wavell Room*, 15 December 2022. https://wavellroom.com/2022/12/15/the-battle-for-bakhmut/.

———. "Russia's Withdrawal from Kherson." *Wavell Room*, 6 January 2023. https:// wavellroom.com/2023/01/06/russias-withdrawal-from-kherson/.

Millett, Allan, and Williamson Murray. "Lessons of War." *National Interest* 14 (Winter 1988): 83–95.

———, eds. *Military Effectiveness*, vol. 1: *The First World War*. Cambridge: Cambridge University Press, 2010.

Ministry of Defence of Ukraine. *White Book 2021: Defence Policy of Ukraine*. Kyiv: Ministry of Defence, 2022.

Mirza, Umair. *Encyclopedia of German Tanks of World War Two: A Complete Illus-trated Directory of German Battle Tanks, Armoured Cars, Self-Propelled Guns and Semi-Tracked Vehicles*. London: Arms and Armour, 2000.

Mitchell, Ellen. "14 Russian Helicopters Likely Destroyed by US-Provided ATACMS Missiles in Ukraine: UK Intel." *The Hill*, 20 October 2023. https://thehill.com /policy/defense/4267375-russian-helicopters-lost-to-us-atacms-missiles-ukraine/.

Monaghan, Andrew. "How Russia Has Upgraded Its Military Strategy by Drawing Deep on History." *Engelsberg Ideas*, 21 February 2022. https://engelsbergideas .com/notebook/how-russia-has-upgraded-its-military-strategy-by-drawing -deep-on-history/.

———. "Putin's Russia: Shaping a 'Grand Strategy'?" *International Affairs* 89, no. 5 (September 2013): 1221–36.

———. *Russian Grand Strategy in the Era of Global Power Competition*. Manchester: Manchester University Press, 2022.

Mongilio, Heather. "A Brief Summary of the Battle of the Black Sea." *United States Naval Institute News*, 15 November 2023. https://news.usni org/2023/11/15/a-brief-summary-of-the-battle-of-the-black-sea.

Montgomery, Bernard. *The Path to Leadership*. London: Collins, 1961.

Morris, Ian. *War: What Is It Good For? The Role of Conflict in Civilization from Primates to Robots*. London: Profile Books, 2014.

Mueller, Grace Benjamin Jensen, Brandon Valeriano, Ryan Maness, and Jose Macias. *Cyber Operations during the Russo-Ukrainian War: From Strange Patterns to Alternative Futures*. Washington, DC: Center for Strategic and International Studies, July 2023.

Mueller, John. "War Has Almost Ceased to Exist." *Political Science Quarterly* 124, no. 2 (Summer 2009): 297–321.

Mueller, Robert. *Report on the Investigation into Russian Interference in the 2016 Presidential Election*. Vol. 1. Washington, DC: Department of Justice, March 2019.

Murray, Williamson. *Military Adaptation in War: With Fear of Change*. Cambridge: Cambridge University Press, 2011.

———. *Military Innovation in the Interwar Period*. Cambridge: Cambridge University Press, 1998.

———. *War, Strategy, and Military Effectiveness*. Cambridge: Cambridge University Press, 2011.

Murray, Williamson, MacGregor Knox, and Alvin Bernstein. *The Making of Strategy: Rulers, States, and War*. New York: Cambridge University Press, 1994.

Muzalevsky, Roman. *Strategic Landscape 2050: Preparing the U.S. Military for New Era Dynamics*. Carlisle, PA: Strategic Studies Institute and U.S. Army War College Press, 2017.

National Intelligence Council. *Global Trends: Paradox of Progress*. Washington, DC: National Intelligence Council, January 2017.

———. *Mapping the Global Future*. Washington, DC: National Intelligence Council, 2004.

Newdick, Thomas. "Russia's Increasingly Bizarre 'Artisanal' Armor Looks More Mad Max than Major Power." *War Zone*, 6 April 2022. https://www.thedrive.com/the-war-zone/45108/russias-increasingly-bizarre-artisanal-armor-looks-more-mad-max-than-major-power.

Nicholson, Joanne, Peter Dortmans, Marigold Black, Marta Kepe, Sarah Grand-Clement, Erik Silfversten, James Black, Theodora Ogden, Livia Dewaele, and Pau Alonso Garcia-Bode. *Defence Mobilisation Planning Comparative Study: An Examination of Overseas Planning*. Santa Monica, CA: RAND Corporation, 2021.

North Atlantic Treaty Organization. *Allied Joint Doctrine, AJP-01*. Brussels: NATO Standardization Office, February 2017.

———. *Comprehensive Assistance Package for Ukraine*. Fact Sheet, July 2016. https://www.nato.int/nato_static_fl2014/assets/pdf/pdf_2016_09/20160920_160920-compreh-ass-package-ukraine-en.pdf.

———. *NATO 2022 Strategic Concept*. Adopted by Heads of State and Government at the NATO Summit in Madrid, 29 June 2022. https://www.nato.int/strategic-concept/.

———. *Relations with Ukraine*. 22 February 2023. https://www.nato.int/cps/en /natolive/topics_37750.htm.

———. *Vilnius Summit Communiqué*. Adopted by Heads of State and Government at the NATO Summit in Vilnius, 11 July 2023. https://www.nato.int/cps/en/natohq /official_texts_217320.htm.

Nouwens, Meia. "China's 2019 Defence White Paper: Report Card on Military Reform." International Institute of Strategic Studies, 26 July 2019. https://www .iiss.org/blogs/analysis/2019/07/china-2019-defence-white-paper.

O'Brien, Phillips Payson, and Edward Stringer. "The Overlooked Reason Russia's Invasion Is Floundering." *The Atlantic*, 10 May 2022. https://www.theatlantic .com/ideas/archive/2022/05/russian-military-air-force-failure-ukraine/629803/.

O'Hanlon, Michael. *The Science of War*. Princeton, NJ: Princeton University Press, 2009.

———. *Technological Change and the Future of Warfare*. Washington, DC: Brookings Institution Press, 2000.

Olden, Brian, Dimitar Radev, Kris Kauffmann, and Dag Detter. *Ukraine: Technical Assistance Report—Public Financial Management Overview*. Washington, DC: International Monetary Fund, February 2016.

Oliker, Olga. *Russia's Chechen Wars 1994–2000: Lessons from Urban Combat*. Santa Monica, CA: RAND Corporation, 2001.

Oliker, Olga, Lynn E. Davis, Keith Crane, Andrew Radin, Celeste Gventer, Susanne Sondergaard, James T. Quinlivan, Stephan B. Seabrook, Jacopo Bellasio, and Bryan Frederick. *Security Sector Reform in Ukraine*. Santa Monica, CA: RAND Corporation, 2016.

Orttung, Robert. "The Consequences of Putin's Centralization of Power," *Demokratizatsiya: The Journal of Post-Soviet Democratization* 30, no. 4 (Fall 2022): 433–40.

Ostiller, Nate. "Ukraine's Secret 'Black Box' Project Revealed to Be Long-Range Attack Drone." *Kyiv Independent*, 16 November 2023. https://kyivindependent .com/ukrainian-intelligences-secret-black-box-project-revealed-to-be-long -range-attack-drone/.

Overholt, William. *China's Crisis of Success*. Cambridge: Cambridge University Press, 2018.

Overy, Richard. *Why the Allies Won*. New York: W. W. Norton, 1995.

Pallin, C. Vendil, and F. Westerlund. "Russia's War in Georgia: Lessons and Consequences." *Small Wars and Insurgencies* 20, no. 2 (2009): 400–424.

Paret, Peter. *The Cognitive Challenge of War: Prussia 1806*. Princeton, NJ: Princeton University Press, 2009.

Paret, Peter, Gordon A. Craig, and Felix Gilbert, eds. *Makers of Modern Strategy from Machiavelli to the Nuclear Age*. Princeton, NJ: Princeton University Press, 1986.

Payne, Kenneth. "Artificial Intelligence: A Revolution in Strategic Affairs?" *Survival* 60, no. 5 (October–November 2018): 7–32.

———. *Strategy, Evolution, and War: From Apes to Artificial Intelligence.* Washington, DC: Georgetown University Press, 2018.

Pearson, Robert. "Four Myths about Russian Grand Strategy." Center for Strategic and International Studies, 22 September 2020. https://www.csis.org/blogs /post-soviet-post/four-myths-about-russian-grand-strategy.

Pickett, George, James Roche, and Barry Watts. "Net Assessment: A Historical Review." In *On Not Confusing Ourselves,* edited by Andrew Marshall, J. J. Martin, and Henry Rowen, 158–85. Boulder, CO: Westview, 1991.

Pinker, Steven. *The Better Angels of Our Nature: Why Violence Has Declined.* New York: Penguin Books, 2011.

Plokhy, Serhii. *The Gates of Europe: A History of Ukraine.* New York: Basic Books, 2017.

———. *The Russo-Ukrainian War.* London: Penguin Books, 2023.

———. *Unmaking Imperial Russia: Mykhailo Hrushevsky and the Writing of Ukrainian History.* Toronto: Toronto University Press, 2005.

Porter, Michael. *Competitive Strategy: Techniques for Analyzing Industries and Competitors.* New York: Free Press, 1980.

Posen, Barry. *A Defense Concept for Ukraine.* Moscow: Carnegie Endowment for International Peace, 1996.

Pothier, Fabrice. "Five Challenges That NATO Must Overcome to Stay Relevant." International Institute for Security Studies, 4 April 2019. https://www.iiss.org /blogs/analysis/2019/04/five-challenges-for-nato.

Prince, Todd. "No Game Changer: Russian Mobilization May Slow, Not Stop, Ukrainian Offensive." *Radio Free Europe Radio Liberty,* 22 September 2022. https:// www.rferl.org/a/russia-mobilization-ukraine-offensive-analysis/32046211.html.

Putin, Vladimir. "Address by the President of the Russian Federation." President of Russia, 21 February 2022. http://en.kremlin.ru/events/president/transcripts/67828.

———. "Address by the President of the Russian Federation." President of Russia, 24 February 2022, http://en.kremlin.ru/events/president/transcripts/67843.

———. "Address by the President of the Russian Federation." President of Russia, 21 September 2022, http://en.kremlin.ru/events/president/news/69390.

———. "New Year Address to the Nation." President of Russia, 31 December 2022. http://en.kremlin.ru/events/president/transcripts/70315.

———. "On the Historical Unity of Russians and Ukrainians." President of Russia, 12 July 2021. http://en.kremlin.ru/events/president/news/66181.

———. Presidential Address to Federal Assembly, 21 February 2023. http://en.kremlin. ru/events/president/news/70565.

Raddatz, Martha, and Mike Cerre. "Soldiers Must Rely on 'Hillbilly Armor' for Protection." ABC News, 8 December 2004. https://abcnews.go.com/WNT/story?id=312959&page=1.

Rand, Lindsay, and Berit Goodge. "Information Overload: The Promise and Risk of Quantum Computing." *Bulletin of the Atomic Scientists*, 14 November 2019. https://thebulletin.org/2019/11/information-overload-the-promise-and-risk-of-quantum-computing/.

Rapp, William. "Civil-Military Relations: The Role of Military Leaders in Strategy Making." *Parameters* 45, no. 3 (Autumn 2015): 13–26.

Rayburn, Joel, and Frank Sobchak, eds. *The US Army in the Iraq War*. Vol. 1. Carlisle, PA: Strategic Studies Institute and U.S. Army War College Press, 2019.

Redecker, Christine, Miriam Leis, Matthijs Leendertse, Yves Punie, Govert Gijsbers, Paul Kirschner, Slavi Stoyanov, and Bert Hoogveld. *The Future of Learning: Preparing for Change*. Luxembourg: Joint Research Centre–Institute for Prospective Technological Studies, 2011.

Reid, Anna. "Putin's War on History." *Foreign Affairs* 101, no. 3 (May/June 2022): 54–63.

Rid, Thomas. *Active Measures: The Secret History of Disinformation and Political Warfare*. New York: Farrar, Straus, and Giroux, 2020.

Roberts, Brad. "On Theories of Victory, Red and Blue." Livermore Papers on Global Security No. 7. Livermore, CA: Lawrence Livermore National Laboratory Center for Global Security Research, June 2020.

Rogov, Sergey. *The Evolution of Military Reform in Russia, 2001*. Alexandria: CNA Corporation, 2001.

Rosen, Stephen. *Winning the Next War: Innovation and the Modern Military*. Ithaca, NY: Cornell University Press, 1991.

Royal College of Defence Studies. *Getting Strategy Right (Enough)*. London: Ministry of Defence, 2017.

Rudik, Kira. "Taiwan Supports Ukraine and Studies Country's Response to Russian Invasion." Atlantic Council, 15 March 2023. https://www.atlanticcouncil.org/blogs/ukrainealert/taiwan-supports-ukraine-and-studies-countrys-response-to-russian-invasion/.

Rumelt, Richard. *Good Strategy, Bad Strategy: The Difference and Why It Matters*. London: Profile Books, 2011.

Russian Federation. *National Security Strategy*. Moscow: Ministry of Foreign Affairs, December 2015.

———. *On the National Security Strategy of the Russian Federation*. Moscow: Ministry of Foreign Affairs, July 2021.

Russian General Staff. *The Soviet-Afghan War: How a Superpower Fought and Lost*. Translated by Lester Grau and Michal Gress. Lawrence: University Press of Kansas, 2002.

Ryan, Michael. "An Australian Intellectual Edge for Conflict and Competition in the 21st Century." Centre of Gravity Paper 48, Australian National University, Canberra, March 2019.

——. "How Ukraine Can Win a Long War: The West Needs a Strategy for After the Counteroffensive." *Foreign Affairs*, 30 August 2023. https://www.foreignaffairs.com/ukraine/win-long-war-strategy-counteroffensive.

——. *Human Machine Teaming for Future Ground Forces*. Washington, DC: Center for Strategic and Budgetary Assessments, 2018.

——. "The Ingenious Strategy That Could Win the War for Ukraine." *Sydney Morning Herald*, 17 May 2022. https://www.smh.com.au/world/europe/the-ingenious-strategy-that-could-win-the-war-for-ukraine-20220517-p5alz4.html.

——. "The Intellectual Edge: A Competitive Advantage for Future War and Strategic Competition." *Joint Force Quarterly* 96 (First Quarter 2020): 6–11.

——. "Pathway to Victory: The Ukrainian Strategy of Corrosion." *Australian Journal of Defence and Strategic Studies* 5, no. 1 (July 2023): 87–96.

——. "Putin Has Mastered the Art of Atrocity, but It Won't Win Him This War." *Sydney Morning Herald*, 11 October 2022. https://www.smh.com.au/world/europe/putin-has-mastered-the-art-of-atrocity-but-it-wont-win-him-this-war-20221010-p5bop6.html.

——. "Ukraine Can Win This War—on These Five Conditions." *Sydney Morning Herald*, 19 August 2022. https://www.smh.com.au/world/europe/ukraine-can-win-this-war-on-these-five-conditions-20220817-p5bajr.html.

——. "Vladimir Putin's Plan A in Ukraine Failed, but His Revised Theory of Victory Is Coming into View." Australian Broadcasting Corporation, 12 July 2022. https://www.abc.net.au/news/2022-07-12/russia-ukraine-putins-revised-theory-of-victory/101227820.

——. *War Transformed: The Future of 21st Century Great Power Competition and Conflict*. Annapolis: Naval Institute Press, 2022.

Sanger, David, and Jim Tankersley. "U.S. Warns Russia of 'Catastrophic Consequences' if It Uses Nuclear Weapons." *New York Times,* 25 September 2022. https://www.nytimes.com/2022/09/25/us/politics/us-russia-nuclear.html.

Scales, Robert H., Jr. *Future Warfare Anthology*. Carlisle, PA: U.S. Army War College, 2000.

——. "Return to Gettysburg: The Fifth Epochal Shift in the Course of War." *War on the Rocks*, 1 October 2018. https://warontherocks.com/2018/10/return-to-gettysburg-the-fifth-epochal-shift-in-the-course-of-war/.

——. *Yellow Smoke: The Future of Land Warfare for America's Military*. Oxford, U.K.: Rowman and Littlefield, 2003.

Scharre, Paul. *Army of None: Autonomous Weapons and the Future of War*. New York: W. W. Norton, 2019.

———. *Four Battlegrounds: Power in the Age of Artificial Intelligence.* New York: W. W. Norton, 2023.

Scheck, Justin, and Thomas Gibbons-Neff. "Stolen Valor: The U.S. Volunteers in Ukraine Who Lie, Waste and Bicker." *New York Times,* 25 March 2023. https://www.nytimes.com/2023/03/25/world/europe/volunteers-us-ukraine-lies.html.

Schelling, Thomas. *Arms and Influence.* New Haven, CT: Yale University Press, 1966.

Schollars, Todd. "German Wonder Weapons: Degraded Production and Effectiveness." *Air Force Journal of Logistics* 27, no. 3 (Fall 2003): 60–75.

Schwartz, Peter. *The Art of the Long View.* New York: Bantam Doubleday Dell, 1991.

Seely, Robert. "Defining Contemporary Russian Warfare." *RUSI Journal* 162, no. 1 (2017): 50–59.

Serafin, Tatiana. "Ukraine's President Zelensky Takes the Russia-Ukraine War Viral." *Orbis* 66, no. 4 (Fall 2022): 460–76.

Setear, John, Carl H. Builder, Melinda D. Baccus, and E. Wayne Madewell. *The Army in a Changing World: The Role of Organizational Vision.* Santa Monica, CA: RAND Corporation, 1990.

Sheftalovich, Zoya. "From Jail Cell to Frontline: Russia Turns to Convicts to Help Flailing War Effort." *Politico Europe,* 13 October 2022. https://www.politico.eu/article/ukraine-russia-war-from-jailcell-to-frontline-moscow-turns-to-convicts-to-help-flailing-war-effort/.

———. "Kyiv Calls for Air Defenses as Putin Brings His Syria Tactics to Ukraine." *Politico Europe,* 10 October 2022. https://www.politico.eu/article/kyiv-calls-for-air-defenses-as-putin-brings-his-syria-tactics-to-ukraine/.

———. "Putin Claims 'Partial Mobilization' to End in 2 Weeks, with 222,000 Reservists Called Up So Far." *Politico Europe,* 14 October 2022. https://www.politico.eu/article/putin-claims-partial-mobilization-to-end-in-2-weeks-russia-ukraine-war/.

———. "Ukraine Counteroffensive: Kyiv Claims Gains in Bakhmut." *Politico Europe,* 8 June 2023. https://www.politico.eu/article/ukraine-claims-gains-bakhmut-amid-reports-counteroffensive-russia-hanna-maliar/.

Shelest, Hanna. "Defend. Resist. Repeat: Ukraine's Lessons for European Defence." Policy Brief, European Council on Foreign Relations, November 2022. https://ecfr.eu/wp-content/uploads/2022/11/Defend.-Resist.-Repeat-Ukraines-lessons-for-European-defence.pdf.

Sherr, James, and Igor Gretskiy. *Why Russia Went to War: A Three-Dimensional Perspective.* Tallinn, Estonia: International Centre for Defence and Security, January 2023.

Shirk, Susan. *Fragile Superpower: How China's Internal Politics Could Derail Its Peaceful Rise.* Oxford: Oxford University Press, 2007.

Simpkin, Richard. *Race to the Swift: Thoughts on Twenty-First-Century Warfare.* Delhi: Lancer, 1997.

Singer, Peter. "What Is China Learning from the Ukraine War?" *Defense One*, 3 April 2022. https://www.defenseone.com/ideas/2022/04/what-lessons-china-taking -ukraine-war/363915/.

———. *Wired for War: The Robotics Revolution and Conflict in the Twenty-First Century*. New York: Penguin Books, 2009.

Singer, Peter, and Emerson Brooking. *Like War: The Weaponization of Social Media*. New York: Houghton Mifflin Harcourt, 2018.

Sinovets, Polina, ed. *Ukraine's Nuclear History: A Non-proliferation Perspective*. Odessa: Odessa I. I. Mechnikov National University, 2022.

Skoglund, Per, Tore Listou, and Thomas Ekström. "Russian Logistics in the Ukrainian War: Can Operational Failures Be Attributed to Logistics?" *Scandinavian Journal of Military Studies* 5, no. 1 (2022): 99–110.

Snegovaya, Maria. *Putin's Information Warfare in Ukraine: Soviet Origins of Hybrid Warfare*. Russia Report 1. Washington, DC: Institute for the Study of War, September 2015.

Snyder, Jack. *The Soviet Strategic Culture: Implications for Limited Nuclear Operations*. Santa Monica, CA: RAND Corporation, 1977.

Snyder, Timothy. *Bloodlands: Europe between Hitler and Stalin*. New York: Basic Books, 2010.

———. "How to Talk about the War?" *Thinking About*, 6 March 2022. https://snyder .substack.com/p/how-to-talk-about-the-war.

———. *The Road to Unfreedom*. New York: Tim Duggan Books, 2018.

Soldatov, Andrei, and Irina Borogan. "Putin's Warriors: How the Kremlin Has Co-opted Its Critics and Militarized the Home Front." *Foreign Affairs*, 6 December 2022. https://www.foreignaffairs.com/russian-federation/putin-warriors.

Sopko, John. "Afghanistan Reconstruction: Lessons from the Long War." *Prism* 8, no. 2 (2019): 26–39.

Speier, Richard, George Nacouzi, Carrie Lee, and Richard M. Moor. *Hypersonic Missile Nonproliferation: Hindering the Spread of a New Class of Weapons*. Santa Monica, CA: RAND Corporation, 2017.

Spinu, Natalia. *Ukraine Cyber Security: Governance Assessment*. Geneva: Geneva Centre for Security Sector Governance, 2020.

Starry, Don. "To Change an Army." *Military Review*, March 1983, 20–27.

Stepanenko, Kateryna, Karolina Hird, Riley Bailey, Madison Williams, Layne Philipson, George Barros, and Frederick W. Kagan. *Russian Offensive Campaign Assessment, 17 January 2023*. Institute for the Study of War, 17 January 2023. https://understandingwar.org/backgrounder/russian-offensive -campaign-assessment-january-17-2023.

Stewart, Phil. "U.S. Studying India Anti-satellite Weapons Test, Warns of Space Debris." *Reuters*, 28 March 2019. https://www.reuters.com/article/us-india-satellite

-usa/u-s-studying-india-anti-satellite-weapons-test-warns-of-space-debris
-idUSKCN1R825Z/.

Stoicescu, Kalev. *The Kremlin's Aims and Objectives*. Tallinn: International Centre for Defence and Security, May 2022.

Stoker, Donald, and Craig Whiteside. "Blurred Lines: Gray-Zone Conflict and Hybrid War—Two Failures of American Strategic Thinking." *Naval War College Review* 73, no. 1 (2020): 13–48.

Stone, David. *War Summits: The Meetings That Shaped World War II and the Postwar World*. Washington, DC: Potomac Books, 2005.

Stott, Alexander. "The Weakening Logistics Chain of the Russo-Ukrainian War: An Unfolding Case Study." *The Cove*, 3 March 2022. https://cove.army.gov.au /article/weakening-logistics-chain-russo-ukrainian-war.

Strachan, Hew. "The Changing Character of War." Lecture at the Graduate Institute of International Relations, Geneva, 9 November 2006.

———. *Clausewitz's "On War": A Biography*. New York: Grove, 2007.

———. *The Direction of War: Contemporary Strategy in Historical Perspective*, Cambridge: Cambridge University Press, 2013.

———. *The First World War*. New York: Penguin Books, 2013.

Strassler, Robert, ed. *The Landmark Thucydides: A Comprehensive Guide to the Peloponnesian War*. Translated by Richard Crawley. New York: Free Press, 1998.

Sun, Tzu. *The Art of War*. Translated by Ralph Sawyer. Boulder, CO: Westview, 1994.

Sweeney, John. *Killer in the Kremlin: The Explosive Account of Putin's Reign of Terror*. London: Penguin Random House, 2022.

Tallis, Benjamin. *To Ukraine with Love: Essays on Russia's War and Europe's Future*. Self-published, December 2022.

Terraine, John. *White Heat: The New Warfare 1914–1918*. London: Book Club Associates, 1982.

Tharoor, Ishan. "Putin Makes His Imperial Pretensions Clear." *Washington Post*, 13 June 2022. https://www.washingtonpost.com/world/2022/06/13/putin-imperia l-russia-empire-ukraine/.

Thomas, Timothy. "The Battle of Grozny: Deadly Classroom for Urban Combat." *Parameters* 29, no. 2 (Summer 1999): 87–102.

———. *Russian Combat Capabilities for 2020: Three Developments to Track*. McLean, VA: MITRE Corporation, 2019.

Thompson, Drew. "Hope on the Horizon: Taiwan's Radical New Defense Concept." *War on the Rocks*, 2 October 2018. https://warontherocks.com/2018/10/hope -on-the-horizon-taiwans-radical-new-defense-concept/.

Thorne, Christopher. *Allies of a Kind: The United States, Britain and the War against Japan, 1941–1945*. Oxford: Oxford University Press, 1978.

Ti, Ronald. *Russian Military Logistics*. Tallinn: International Centre for Defence and Security, June 2022.

Tocci, Nathalie. "Taiwan Has Learned a Lot from the War in Ukraine—It's Time Europe Caught Up." *Politico Europe*, 20 December 2022. https://www.politico .eu/article/taiwan-lesson-war-ukraine-russia-china-europe-catch-up/.

Toler, Aric. "Ukrainian Hackers Leak Russian Interior Ministry Docs with Evidence of Russian Invasion." *Global Voices*, 13 December 2014. https:// globalvoices.org/2014/12/13/ukrainian-hackers-leak-russian-interior-ministry -docs-with-evidence-of-russian-invasion/.

Treisman, Daniel. "Putin Unbound." *Foreign Affairs* 101, no. 3 (May/June 2022): 40–53.

United Kingdom, Ministry of Defence. *Defence in a Competitive Age*. London: U.K. Ministry of Defence, March 2021.

———. *Global Strategic Trends: The Future Starts Today*. 6th ed. Swindon: Defence Concepts and Doctrine Centre, 2018.

———. *Information Advantage*. Joint Concept Note 2/18. Swindon: Defence Concepts and Doctrine Centre, 2018.

———. "Operation Interflex: UK Training of Ukrainian Recruits." Joint-forces. com, 10 November 2023. https://www.joint-forces.com/uk-operations /68782-operation-interflex-uk-training-of-ukrainian-recruits.

———. *UK Defence Doctrine*. Swindon: Defence Concepts and Doctrine Centre, November 2014.

U.S. Army. *Army Doctrine Publication 3-90: Offense and Defense*. Washington, DC: Headquarters Department of the Army, July 2019.

———. *Establishing a Lessons Learned Program*. Notebook 11–33. Fort Leavenworth, KS: Center for Army Lessons Learned, 2011.

———. *The Operational Environment and the Changing Character of Warfare*. Fort Eustis, VA: Department of the Army, October 2019.

U.S. Army Training and Doctrine Command. *The U.S. Army in Multidomain Operations 2028*. Fort Eustis, VA: Department of the Army, December 2018.

U.S. Department of Defense. *Doctrine for the Armed Forces of the United States*. Washington, DC: Joint Chiefs of Staff, 2017.

———. *The Joint Force in a Contested and Disordered World*. Washington, DC: Joint Chiefs of Staff, July 2016.

———. *Joint Operations*. Washington, DC: U.S. Department of Defense, January 2017.

———. *Securing Defense-Critical Supply Chains. An Action Plan Developed in Response to President Biden's Executive Order 14017*. Washington, DC: Office of the Secretary of Defense, February 2022.

———. *Summary of the 2018 National Defense Strategy of the United States of America*. Washington, DC: U.S. Department of Defense, 2018.

———. *Sustaining U.S. Global Leadership: Priorities for 21st-Century Defense*. Washington, DC: U.S. Department of Defense, 2012.

U.S. Government. *Interim National Security Strategic Guidance.* Washington, DC: White House, 2021.

———. *US National Security Strategy.* Washington, DC: White House, October 2022.

U.S. Marine Corps. *Competing.* Washington, DC: Headquarters U.S. Marine Corps, December 2020.

———. *A Concept for Distributed Operations.* Washington, DC: Headquarters U.S. Marine Corps, April 2005.

———. *Force Design 2030.* Washington, DC: Headquarters U.S. Marine Corps, March 2020.

U.S. Office of the Director of National Intelligence. *Annual Threat Assessment of the U.S. Intelligence Community.* Washington, DC: Office of the Director of National Intelligence, April 2021.

Van Crevald, Martin. *Command in War.* Cambridge, MA: Harvard University Press, 1985.

———. *Fighting Power: German and U.S. Army Performance, 1939–1945.* London: Praeger, 1982.

———. *Supplying War: Logistics from Wallenstein to Patton.* Cambridge: Cambridge University Press, 1977.

van Pelt, Michel. *Rocketing into the Future: The History and Technology of Rocket Planes.* Chichester, U.K.: Praxis, 2012.

Vershinin, Alex. "Feeding the Bear: A Closer Look at Russian Military Logistics and the Fait Accompli." *War on the Rocks,* 23 November 2021. https://warontherocks.com/2021/11/feeding-the-bear-a-closer-look-at-russian-army-logistics/.

———. "The Return of Industrial Warfare." Royal United Services Institute, 17 June 2022. https://www.rusi.org/explore-our-research/publications/commentary/return-industrial-warfare.

Von Clausewitz, Carl. *On War.* Translated by Michael Howard and Peter Paret. Princeton, NJ: Princeton University Press, 1976.

Vosoughi, Soroush, Deb Roy, and Sinan Aral. "The Spread of True and False News Online." *Science* 359 (2018): 1146–51.

Watling, Jack. *The Arms of the Future: Technology and Close Combat in the Twenty-First Century.* London: Bloomsbury, 2023.

———. "The Ukraine War Has Found the Machinery of Western Governments Wanting." Royal United Services Institute, 8 August 2023. https://rusi.org/explore-our-research/publications/commentary/ukraine-war-has-found-machinery-western-governments-wanting.

Watling, Jack, Oleksandr V. Danylyuk, and Nick Reynolds. "Preliminary Lessons from Russia's Unconventional Operations during the Russo-Ukrainian War, February 2022–February 2023." Royal United Services Institute, 29 March

2023. https://rusi.org/explore-our-research/publications/special-resources/preliminary-lessons-russias-unconventional-operations-during-russo-ukrainian-war-february-2022.

Watling, Jack, and Nick Reynolds. "Meatgrinder: Russian Tactics in the Second Year of Its Invasion of Ukraine." Royal United Services Institute, 19 May 2023. https://rusi.org/explore-our-research/publications/special-resources/meatgrinder-russian-tactics-second-year-its-invasion-ukraine.

Weick, Karl, and Kathleen Sutcliffe. *Managing the Unexpected: Assuring High Performance in an Age of Complexity.* San Francisco: Jossey-Bass, 2001.

Welfrens, Paul. *Russia's Invasion of Ukraine: Economic Challenges, Embargo Issues, and a New Global Economic Order.* Cham, Switzerland: Palgrave Macmillan, 2022.

Westerlund, Fredrik, and Susanne Oxenstierna, eds. *Russian Military Capability in a Ten-Year Perspective—2019.* Stockholm: Swedish Ministry of Defence, 2019.

Wilde, Gavin. *Cyber Operations in Ukraine: Russia's Unmet Expectations.* Washington, DC: Carnegie Endowment for International Peace, December 2022.

Williams, Ian. *Putin's Missile War: Russia's Strike Campaign in Ukraine.* Washington, DC: Center for Strategic and International Studies, May 2023.

Wohlstetter, Roberta. *Pearl Harbor: Warning and Decision.* Stanford, CA: Stanford University Press, 1962.

Wylie, J. C. *Military Strategy: A General Theory of Power Control.* Annapolis: Naval Institute Press, 1989.

Xi Jinping. "Report at the 19th National Congress of the Communist Party of China." *Xinhua,* 18 October 2017. http://www.xinhuanet.com/english/special/2017-11/03/c_136725942.htm.

Xu, C. "Intelligent War: Where Is the Change?" *Military Forum,* 21 January 2020. http://www.81.cn/jfjbmap/content/2020-01/21/content_252681.htm.

Yekelchyk, Serhy. *The Conflict in Ukraine: What Everyone Needs to Know.* Oxford: Oxford University Press, 2015.

Yoshihara, Toshi. *Chinese Lessons from the Pacific War: Implications for PLA Warfighting.* Washington, DC: Center for Strategic and Budgetary Assessments, 2023.

Zabrodskyi, Mykhaylo, Jack Watling, Oleksandr V. Danylyuk, and Nick Reynolds. "Preliminary Lessons in Conventional Warfighting from Russia's Invasion of Ukraine: February–July 2022." Royal United Services Institute, 30 November 2022. https://rusi.org/explore-our-research/publications/special-resources/preliminary-lessons-conventional-warfighting-russias-invasion-ukraine-february-july-2022.

Zagorodnyuk, Andriy. "Ukrainian Victory Shatters Russia's Reputation as a Military Superpower." Atlantic Council, 13 September 2022. https://www

.atlanticcouncil.org/blogs/ukrainealert/ukrainian-victory-shatters-russias
-reputation-as-a-military-superpower/.

Zaluzhnyi, Valeriy, and Mykhailo Zabrodskyi. "Prospects for Running a Military
Campaign in 2023: Ukraine's Perspective." *UkrInform*, 7 September 2022. https://
www.ukrinform.net/rubric-ato/3566404-prospects-for-running-a-military
-campaign-in-2023-ukraines-perspective.html?fbclid=IwAR31RCvVxcCRDR
_Ci8-CrKsrDSenSlBp8-lFoklOWFgjNkTyivcLkM7zk.

Zegart, Amy. "Open Secrets: Ukraine and the Next Intelligence Revolution." *Foreign
Affairs* 102, no. 1 (January/February 2023): 54–70.

Zelenskyy, Volodymyr. "Address by the President of Ukraine." Kyiv, 24 February 2022.
https://www.president.gov.ua/en/news/zvernennya-prezidenta-ukrayini-73137.

———. *A Message from Ukraine: Speeches 2019–2022*. London: Hutchieson Heinemann, 2022.

———. "New Year Greetings of President of Ukraine Volodymyr Zelenskyy."
Kyiv, 31 December 2022. https://www.president.gov.ua/en/news/novorichne
-privitannya-prezidenta-ukrayini-volodimira-zelens-80197.

———. "Speech by the President of Ukraine at the 58th Munich Security Conference." Munich, 19 February 2022. https://www.president.gov.ua/en/news
/vistup-prezidenta-ukrayini-na-58-j-myunhenskij-konferenciyi-72997.

———. "Speech by the President with the Annual Message to the Verkhovna Rada of
Ukraine on the Internal and External Situation of Ukraine." Kyiv, 28 December 2022.
https://www.president.gov.ua/en/news/zvernennya-prezidenta-ukrayini-73137.

———. "Ukraine Has Always Been a Leader in Peacemaking Efforts; If Russia Wants to End This War, Let It Prove It with Actions." Speech at the G20
Summit, Kyiv, 15 November 2022. https://www.president.gov.ua/en/news
/ukrayina-zavzhdi-bula-liderom-mirotvorchih-zusil-yaksho-rosi-79141.

———. "We Stand, We Fight, and We Will Win. Because We Are United.
Ukraine, America, and the Entire Free World." Address in a joint meeting of
the U.S. Congress, 22 December 2022. https://www.president.gov.ua/en/news
/mi-stoyimo-boremos-i-vigrayemo-bo-mi-razom-ukrayina-amerika-80017.

■ INDEX

◼◼◼ ABOUT THE AUTHOR

MICK RYAN is a retired major general in the Australian Army and a distinguished graduate of the Johns Hopkins University School of Advanced International Studies, as well as the U.S. Marine Corps Command and Staff College and School of Advanced Warfare. He has commanded at the platoon, squadron, regiment, task force, and brigade levels and is a passionate advocate of professional education and lifelong learning. Ryan has also led strategic planning organizations in the Australian Army as well as several reform programs in the past decade. He is a Fellow at the Center for Strategic and International Studies and the Lowy Institute. He is the author of *War Transformed: The Future of Twenty-First-Century Great Power Competition and Conflict* (Naval Institute Press, 2022).